AGING AND IDENTITY

AGING AND IDENTITY

A Humanities Perspective

Edited by
Sara Munson Deats and
Lagretta Tallent Lenker

Westport, Connecticut
London

Library of Congress Cataloging-in-Publication Data

Aging and identity : a humanities perspective / edited by Sara Munson
    Deats and Lagretta Tallent Lenker.
        p.   cm.
    Includes bibliographical references and index.
    ISBN 0-275-96479-5 (alk. paper)
    1. Aged in popular culture.   2. Old age in literature.   3. Aged in
art.   4. Aged in mass media.   5. Aging in literature.   6. Aging in
art.   I. Deats, Sara Munson.   II. Lenker, Lagretta Tallent.
HQ1061.A444   1999
305.26—dc21   98-41089

British Library Cataloguing in Publication Data is available.

Library of Congress Catalog Card Number: 98-41089
ISBN: 0-275-96479-5

First published in 1999

Praeger Publishers, 88 Post Road West, Westport, CT 06881
An imprint of Greenwood Publishing Group, Inc.
www.praeger.com

Printed in the United States of America

The paper used in this book complies with the
Permanent Paper Standard issued by the National
Information Standards Organization (Z39.48–1984).

10 9 8 7 6 5 4 3 2

We dedicate this book with admiration to
LEE LEAVENGOOD.
She teaches us by her example and enriches
us with her energy, creativity, and
ceaseless dedication
to the art and purpose of living.

Age cannot wither her, nor custom stale
Her infinite variety.
William Shakespeare

Contents

Acknowledgments   xi

Introduction   1
Sara Munson Deats and Lagretta Tallent Lenker

PART I THE AGING MALE IN LITERATURE

1 The Dialectic of Aging in Shakespeare's *King Lear*
   and *The Tempest*   23
   Sara Munson Deats

2 Shakespeare Teaching Geriatrics: Lear and Prospero
   as Case Studies in Aged Heterogeneity   33
   Kirk Combe and Kenneth Schmader

3 Why? versus Why Not?: Potentialities of Aging
   in Shaw's *Back to Methuselah*   47
   Lagretta Tallent Lenker

4 Hemingway's Aging Heroes and the Concept of *Phronesis*   61
   Phillip Sipiora

5 Bertrand Russell in His Nineties: Aging and the
   Problem of Biography   77
   William T. Ross

PART II THE AGING FEMALE IN LITERATURE

6 Work, Contentment, and Identity in Aging Women
   in Literature   89
   Rosalie Murphy Baum

7 Old Maids and Old Mansions: The Barren Sisters of
   Hawthorne, Dickens, and Faulkner   103
   Maryhelen C. Harmon

8 The Aging Artist: The Sad but Instructive Case of
   Virginia Woolf   115
   Joanne Trautmann Banks

PART III AGING IN THE COMMUNITY

9 The Sacred Ghost: The Role of the Elder(ly) in
   Native American Literature   129
   David Erben

10 Aging and the African-American Community:
   The Case of Ernest J. Gaines   139
   Charles J. Heglar and Annye L. Refoe

11 Aging and the Continental Community: Good Counsel
   in the Writings of Two Mature European Princesses,
   Marguerite de Navarre and Madame Palatine   149
   Christine McCall Probes

12 Aging and Academe: Caricature or Character   161
   Helen Popovich and Deborah Noonan

13 Aging and the Public Schools: Visits of Charity—
   The Young Look at the Old   169
   Ralph M. Cline

PART IV AGING IN THE FINE AND POPULAR ARTS

14 Aging and Contemporary Art   183
   Linnea S. Dietrich

15 The Return Home: Affirmations and Transformations
   of Identity in Horton Foote's *The Trip to Bountiful*   191
   Carol J. Jablonski

16 Animated Gerontophobia: Ageism, Sexism, and
   the Disney Villainess   201
   Merry G. Perry

17 8½ and Me: The Thirty-Two-Year Difference   213
   Norman N. Holland

   Notes   229

   Bibliography   231

   Index   247

   About the Editors and Contributors   255

Acknowledgments

The editors gratefully acknowledge the support of the University of South Florida School of Continuing Education and the Institute on Aging for the conference that led to the creation of this volume. Richard Taylor and Donna Cohen, directors of these agencies, deserve special thanks. Larry Polivka, Director of the Florida Policy Exchange Center on Aging, provided early support and continual encouragement for both the conference and this publication.

This project would not have been possible without the patience, dedication, and superb technical support of Merry Perry. Her creativity, intelligence, and professionalism permeate every page of this volume.

Finally, we thank Gordon Deats and Mark Lenker for their love and patience during the completion of this and many other time-consuming projects.

Introduction

Sara Munson Deats and Lagretta Tallent Lenker

Matthew Arnold once stated that literature enshrines the best that has been said and thought in the world. This study affirms the more comprehensive view that not only literature but the humanities as a whole transmit multiple reflections on human life that have shaped our social mores for good or ill. Moreover, this study asserts that the humanities continue to bear a vital relationship to situations experienced by individuals in almost any given culture. On the one hand, literature, the arts, and the media mirror the conventional mores and attitudes of their own social milieu, even as history records these mores and attitudes. However, since all societies contain multiple clashing ideologies, these aesthetic forms may also reflect the concepts of a residual culture or anticipate the tenets of an emerging one, often establishing a dialectical tension between these competing discourses. In addition, the way in which individuals view the world is largely determined by the language they use to describe the phenomenon that they experience as reality and by the images (in literature, painting, sculpture, the performing arts, and, perhaps most of all, the media) through which they depict this phenomenon. We suggest, therefore, that these cultural forms construct as well as encode the conventional perceptions of individuals in a given society; they intervene in history even as they reflect history. It follows, therefore, that literature, the arts, and the media not only mirror society's conventions, but also create them.

The chapters in this volume examine both the ways in which the humanities have contributed to the construction of stereotypic images of aging in our society and the ways in which the humanities can be employed to deconstruct these images. The contributors to this volume believe that in

striving to become more receptive to individual diversity and to offer alternatives to society's limiting stereotypes of the elderly, we can benefit not only
from studying positive examples of aging presented in literature, the arts, and
the media, but also from questioning the conventional negative conceptions
of aging so often inscribed in these aesthetic forms. Through this process, we
may become aware that many of the stereotypes portrayed in these artistic
forums as natural and universal are actually socially constructed artifacts.
Moreover, by studying the ways in which the images of aging are constructed
in these artistic media, we can become more cognizant of the ways in which
our conceptions of aging are constructed in society. Thus, literature, the arts,
and the media can provide both negative and positive examples of the recep-
tivity we seek to acquire in viewing the aging process; and by opening up our
doors of perception — reading, listening, and looking with awareness — we can
learn to deconstruct the negative stereotypes of aging that we encounter, while
also seeking positive exempla as templates for reconstructing ourselves and
our society (Lenker and Polivka 1996, 3–4).

   Not only the attitudes of the general public but also the theories of philosophers, psychologists, and various clinicians have throughout history been informed — perhaps even determined — by the insights of the humanities, particularly
of literary artists. Freud, an avid reader and critic of Shakespeare, was obviously
influenced by that keen observer and recorder of human behavior, and although
psychoanalytic critics frequently use Freud's theories to illumine Shakespeare's
playtexts, awareness of Shakespeare's insights into human motivation and
responses can also help us to understand the genesis of many of Freud's theories. A number of prestigious contemporary theorists, including thanatologist
Edwin Shneidman, psychologist Leonard Shengold, and feminist theorist
Elaine Showalter, have noted the reciprocal relationship between literature
and psychology. Shneidman (1989) employs Captain Ahab in *Moby Dick* as a
prototypic case history for studying the suicidal personality; Shengold (1989)
focuses on the lives and works of Anton Chekov, Charles Dickens, Rudyard
Kipling, and George Orwell in his analysis of child abuse; Showalter (1985a)
details the way in which Shakespeare's depiction of Ophelia has played a
pivotal role in the construction of conventional ideas of female insanity (Deats
and Lenker 1989, 206–207). More directly related to our study, psychologist
Erik Erikson (1979) finds in the interior journey of Dr. Borg in Ingmar
Bergman's film *Wild Strawberries* an exemplum of his own theories of the
human life cycle, and literary critic Margaret Morganroth Gullette (1993)
demonstrates how a group of "midlife decline" novels, written by male authors during the early years of the twentieth century, helped to forge the link
between male creative decline and aging that is conventionally accepted even
today. The work of these five theorists validates the premise that not only does
art imitate life, but life, returning the compliment, frequently imitates art.

   Underlying much of the commentary cited is the assumption that art, particularly literature, mirrors reality, and that by studying great art, scientists, as

well as literary critics, can gain insights into human nature. However, postmodern criticism has effectively interrogated this mimetic association between art and life, the word and the world. Yet even if we reject the view that art mirrors nature, we may agree that art certainly inscribes the ideologies of a given culture and that one of the primary goals of criticism is to make visible these ideologies. It follows, therefore, that studying the way in which stereotypes of any kind—gender, race, class, or age—are constructed within a work of art can help us to learn about—and to challenge—the construction of stereotypes within our own society.

Gerontologists have already begun to interrogate the primarily negative stereotypes of aging that have dominated both cultural and scientific forums for centuries. Challenging the traditional portrait of old age as a time of infirmity and senility, contemporary gerontologists are evolving what Harry R. Moody (1988) calls a "dialectical gerontology," an "approach to the study of human aging that acknowledges the contradictory features of old age and tries to locate these contradictions within a developmental or historical framework"(p. 28–29). As part of this dialectical methodology, Moody calls for a complementarity between the humanities and the sciences, between meaning and causes, between hermeneutics and empiricism, in order to achieve the emancipatory goals of the new "critical gerontology."

Acknowledging the contradictory aspects of the aging process, many gerontologists insist that the ineluctable deterioration traditionally associated with age has been exaggerated. Gerontologist Bernice Neugarten observes, "Fully half of all people now 75 to 84 are free of health problems that require special care or curb their activities. . . . Even in the very oldest group, those above 85, more than one-third report no limitation due to age" ("Older" 1988, 76). More optimistic than most practitioners, gerontologists John Rowe and Robert Kahn (1987) go so far as to state flatly, "In many data sets that show substantial average decline with age, we can find older persons with minimal physiologic loss, or *none at all*, when compared to the average of their younger counterparts" (p. 143–144, emphasis added). Moreover, although most gerontologists may be less optimistic than Rowe and Kahn, many would agree that although some physiological debility generally accompanies the aging process, loss is only half of the picture, because aging can also bring growth, expansion, even emancipation. Betty Friedan (1993, 71–103) posits a Janus-faced portrait of age: On the one hand, this portrait presents the weak face of deterioration and decline traditionally depicted by the medical profession—the face we all shun and fear; on the other hand, this portrait presents the strong face of maturation and liberation drawn by contemporary gerontologists—the face also worn by many vitally aging individuals. Most important of all, gerontologists are beginning to stress the heterogeneity of the aging process, which has too often been submerged beneath society's reductive stereotypes. To quote gerontologist George Maddox, "The more you study the actual behavior and health of older people, the more you see that aging is a social and not just a biological phenomenon. These terrible things you see happening to some people in age are not the inevitable ticking of the biological clock. Age is not a time bomb. Even the new emphasis on age as a crisis, the midlife crises, etc. is misleading. When you come to one of these life crises or transitions that are supposed to be so traumatic, the people who cope, grow" (Friedan 1993, 117).

But is this acceptance of heterogeneity, this acknowledgment of a strong as well as a weak face of age, only wishful thinking, a fairy tale designed to protect us from our dark fears of senescence? Friedan (1993) marshals a plethora of reassuring clinical evidence to support a resounding "No!" According to Friedan, the most recent scientific research has discovered "some *positive* changes in certain mental abilities, as well as muscular, sexual, and immune processes, that can compensate for age-related" deterioration (p. 68). Friedan's assertion finds persuasive support in the research of psychologist Marion Perlmutter (1988), who insists that "our society has inappropriately focused on decline when describing age change in late life" (p. 247). Perlmutter argues that though from a biological perspective aging may be connected with decline, from a psychological point of view, this link is both unnecessary and inaccurate. Indeed, the eminent gerontologist submits that "it is probably unnecessary, or even inappropriate, to assume distinct phenomena of development and aging," since "age change is multidirectional and multicausal" (p. 249). While recognizing the diversity of the aging process, Perlmutter does, however, acknowledge recurrent trends or patterns (although these may be culturally constructed rather than biologically determined). Studies cited by Perlmutter suggest that although some cognitive abilities may decline with age, others, such as vocabulary, remain stable over time, whereas still others, such as expertise in one's profession or occupation, may actually improve with age. Thus, although from a physical perspective aging may mean deterioration, from a psychological vantage point it may offer compensatory benefits (pp. 254–256).

Gerontologists also posit emotional growth as a component of creative aging. New research cited by Friedan (1993, 85) indicates that individuals over sixty-five who do not decline seem to become more harmoniously "integrated in their various characteristics as they grow older. They also become increasingly individual" and progressively different from their age peers who do decline (p. 85).

One aspect of this personality integration — what sociologist David Gutmann (1977, 312) refers to as "sex-role cross over" — seems to occur in the years after parenthood. According to Gutmann's cross-cultural studies, in many societies sexual polarization becomes established during parenthood in response to the presumed needs of the child for certain kinds of emotional and physical security. Thus, each sex surrenders to the other the attributes that might interfere with the special mode of security that societies have traditionally constructed for each sex. As Gutmann explains,

Male providers of physical security give up the dependency needs that would interfere with their courage and endurance; these they live out through identification
with their wives and children. By the same token, women, the providers of emotional security, give up the aggression that could alienate their male providers or that
could damage a vulnerable and needful child. Each sex lives out, through the other,
those aspects of their nature that could interfere with adequate performance in the
parental role, and that could therefore be lethal to their children. (p.312)

Gutmann (1977, 312; 1987) goes on to suggest that later in life, in many
different cultures, men feel free to reclaim their passive, nurturing, contemplative qualities (attributes traditionally gendered "feminine" and repressed
by men during parenthood), whereas women feel free to discover their assertive, commanding, or adventurous traits (attributes traditionally gendered
"masculine" and repressed by women during parenting). According to
Gutmann's hypothesis, therefore, one of the great benefits of aging is the
freedom to reclaim the buried aspects of the self.

Gutmann's conclusions are supported by two popular recent examinations
of the aging process, Terri Apter's *Secret Paths* and Gail Sheehy's *New Passages*. Apter (1995) typifies women in "mid-life" (forties and fifties) as follows:
"Women in fact do not lose power as they age. Instead they gain it. They gain
it through self-confidence and through self-knowledge. They gain it by their
new directness and their refusal to repeat past patterns of compromise" (p.
76). Apter goes even further than Gutmann in insisting, "Older women become more assertive and more content" (p. 77). Moreover, she avers that
"the balance of power shifts between men and women over the life span" (p.
77). In her sampling of eighty "midlife" women from many different social
strata and occupational circles, she found that "older women feel relatively
less dependent on their partners, and older men become relatively more dependent on theirs" (p. 77). A number of contemporary novels narrate the
association of female aging with emancipation and expansion. Indeed, the
motif is so prevalent in contemporary fiction that Barbara Frey Waxman (1990,
2) has identified it as a separate genre, what she calls the *Refungsroman*, or
novel of ripening. Sheehy (1995) affirms this conclusion, proposing that when
individuals reach their fifties, rigid role divisions dissolve and men and women
become more alike, taking on the characteristics of their gender opposite (p.
318–319). All of these researchers—Gutmann, Friedan, Apter, and Sheehy—
conclude that in their post-midlife years women and men achieve the freedom to develop their entire personalities, aspects of which have been repressed
by society's rigid—and, we would add, deleterious—gender polarization. Thus,
according to these theorists, the liberation and integration of former suppressed
facets of the self seem to be keys to vital old age.

Certain external circumstances also appear to foster a flourishing old age.
Friedan (1993, 87) notes that much research done in the last ten years in

nursing homes and retirement communities reveals that autonomy, the extent to which one is able to make one's own decisions, strongly affects both performance and well-being in aging. Other theorists, such as gerontologists Harry Moody (1992) and George J. Agich (1993), also stress autonomy as a necessary ingredient of affirmative aging, both within and outside of long-term care. In her discussion of dynamic seniors, Sheehy (1995, 357–368) expands the concept of independence to include the courage to take risks and an openness to change as crucial aspects of a vital, even of a zestful old age.

Friedan (1993) identifies a final quality that gerontologists have found integral to creative aging. She observes that frequently a fulfilled old age requires a shift in priorities—a voluntary relinquishment of the sex–power race and an orientation around human relations. Simone de Beauvoir (1972), in her landmark book *The Coming of Age*, anticipates many of the findings of contemporary gerontology when she insists on the necessity of human relatedness to a meaningful life at any age: "One's life has value so long as one attributes value to the life of others, by means of love, friendship, indignation, compassion" (p. 803). Charles J. Fahey and Martha Holstein (1993) support this view, arguing persuasively for the necessity of community involvement (be that "community" the family, the church, or the larger society) as an aspect of positive aging. Friedan (1993, 90–91) further refers to a number of studies showing that *connectedness*, as well as autonomy, has a direct effect on mortality, concluding that both of these attributes are critical to a vital, fulfilling old age. The research of gerontologist Cecelia Hurwick (Sheehy 1995) validates Friedan's conclusions. In a longitudinal study of women in their seventies, eighties, and nineties who had remained active and creative well into old age, Hurwick describes these zestful seniors as follows: "They had mastered the art of 'letting go' of their egos gracefully so they could concentrate their attention on a few fine-tuned priorities. They continued to live in their homes but involved themselves in community or worldly projects that they found of consuming interest. Close contact with nature was important to them, as was maintaining a multigenerational network of friends. And as they grew older they found themselves concerned more with feeding the soul than the ego" (p. 144).

A number of feminist psychologists, among them Jean Baker Miller, Dorothy Dinnerstein, Nancy Chodorow, and Carol Gilligan, speculate that in our Western society women are conditioned to foster relationships and men to develop autonomy. The gerontological discoveries adduced so far suggest that the melding of these seemingly contradictory (but actually complementary) qualities provides one of the secrets of creative aging.

Traditionally, old age has been associated with the attainment of wisdom; however, citing the work of Margaret Clark, James E. Birren, and Erik and Joan Erikson, Friedan (1993, 119–122) argues for a new professional emphasis on the wisdom acquired through aging as a significant feature of the paradigm shift occurring in contemporary gerontology. Erik Erikson's (1982, 61–

65; 1979) influential theory that wisdom frequently emerges in the last (or eighth) stage of life has been a catalyst to a renewed interest in the age-old association of wisdom with old age. Erikson develops his theory of the human life cycle around a Hegelian model in which the successful resolution of each life-stage crisis involves the synthesis of two dialectical qualities; thus, affirmative aging includes a balance between the thesis, Integrity (a sense of life's wholeness and coherence), and the antithesis, Despair (a sense of life's meaninglessness or stagnation), which produces the synthesis, Wisdom (an informed and detached attitude toward life when confronting death). This wisdom also represents the culmination of all the syntheses achieved in the successful resolution of previous life crises: Hope, Will, Purpose, Competence, Fidelity, Love, and Care. More empirical than Erikson, Birren (1985) further characterizes wisdom as including the following very desirable traits: reflectiveness ("meaning that the individual acts less impulsively and is more concerned with the review of relevant information" [p. 34]), mastery over emotional responses, forbearance, a wealth of experience, a familiarity with cultural backgrounds and an understanding of what decisions are acceptable, and a capacity for divergent thinking. The focus of Birren, Clark, and the Eriksons has been expanded by Paul B. Baltes, Jacqui Smith, Ursula M. Staudinger, and Doris Sowarka (1990) of the Max Planck Institute for Human Development and Education in Berlin. Baltes and his colleagues define wisdom as "an expert knowledge system in the domain of fundamental life pragmatics (life planning, life management, and life review)." Wisdom is also associated with "exceptional insight into human development and life matters," and "exceptionally good judgment, advice and commentary about difficult life problems" (p. 68, 74–75). Although the research of Baltes and his colleagues is still ongoing, the data accumulated so far has led to the hypothesis that although not all older persons will be wise, among wise persons there will be a disproportionate number of elderly individuals. For a useful survey of the literature on aging and wisdom, we refer the reader to Ronald J. Manheimer's "Wisdom and Method"(1992).

Heterogeneity, diversity, balance of contraries, wisdom — these then are the characteristics of old age identified by contemporary gerontologists, traits very different from those depicted in traditional stereotypes of aging.

To return to Moody's "dialectical gerontology," we suggest that the chapters in this collection, concentrating as they do on the treatment of aging in literature, the fine arts, and the popular media, demonstrate this dialectic through their exploration of artistic works that inscribe both the strong and weak faces of age — and multiple different combinations of empowerment and vulnerability on the spectrum between these polarities. Gerontologists Melanie Angiollilo and Charles F. Longino, Jr. (1996) warn against limiting the diversity of the aging experience to a dualistic positive–negative model, and thus reinscribing the stereotypes that one may wish to explode. Despite the conventional association of aging with physical, mental, and emotional decline, many of these chapters discover surprisingly positive images of aging in the artistic works examined. Moreover, these positive portraits often exhibit the melding of "feminine" and "masculine" qualities identified by Gutmann, as well as the linking of autonomy and relatedness stressed by Fahey and Holstein, Friedan, and Hurwick, and the acquisition of wisdom emphasized by Baltes and his colleagues, and by Birren, Clark, and the Eriksons. Conversely, other chapters uncover the predictable negative face of infirmity and deterioration that has traditionally dominated our Western cultural perspective. However, the majority of these chapters encounter in the analyzed works the dialectical tension between positive and negative aspects of the aging process already discussed. The very multiplicity of the portraits of aging presented in these artistic works reinforces the stress on heterogeneity characteristic of contemporary gerontology.

We insist, therefore, that because of their traditional focus on the multiplicity of experience, the humanities, and particularly literary criticism, may offer valuable techniques not only for realizing the interdisciplinary interaction advocated by Moody, but also for examining the Janus-face of age limned by other contemporary gerontologists. Gerontologist Thomas R. Cole (1992a) supports this conviction, lamenting that some necessary ingredient seems to be missing from a purely scientific and professional approach to gerontology, a lack he believes can be supplied by the humanities. As Cole points out, even though postmodern theory has interrogated the validity of language as an avenue to truth, the humanities still possess a language, however contested, to talk about moral and spiritual concerns, the very concerns that Cole believes should be addressed by gerontology. Moreover, because the humanities emphasize "description, interpretation, explanation, and appreciation of the variety, uniqueness, complexity, originality, and unpredictability of human beings striving to live and know themselves," Cole sees these disciplines as offering a valuable lens through which to view the phenomenon of aging (p. xi, xiii). The chapters in this volume seek to capture the variety, uniqueness, complexity, originality, and unpredictability of the aging individual as this heterogeneity has been inscribed in the literature, art, and popular culture of many different societies. We hope through this process to contribute to the development of the critical gerontology espoused by Moody and Cole.

Although even the most ardent devotee of the humanities would hesitate to suggest that reading great literature or viewing great art necessarily makes one a better person, we submit that the art that endures (whether it be literature, painting, sculpture, or film), because it offers multiple perspectives of experience and because it evokes empathy, tends to encourage tolerance, open-mindedness, and compassion, values vital to the study of aging. Moreover, we believe that if these values are to become more fully incorporated into our society, the humanities must leave their academic ivory tower and sally forth into the marketplace to speak out and be heard. This is precisely what the chapters in this collection are attempting to achieve.

DEFINITIONS

Perhaps we should heed the dictum of Socrates and pause to define our terms, particularly the key terms of this study, which are some of the most emotionally charged and ambiguous words in our language: "aging," "elder," "old," and "old age." From birth to death we all age, and from womb to tomb our chronological progress is obsessively and meticulously recorded: on our driver's licenses, on our passports, in the newspapers (if we are unfortunate enough to be celebrities), on the end papers of our books, and at our birthday parties. Moreover, a number of the privileges, benefits, and detriments of our society are linked to chronological age: voting, smoking, drinking, driving, being drafted, retiring. However, despite the centrality of "age" to our social agendas, "aging," "old," and their synonyms and euphemisms remain highly relative and fluid terms. Although we all age, this term does not acquire its derogatory connotations until we become a certain age, and that age differs with our life stage. The term "old" is similarly slippery. To the very young, all adults are "old." To the flower children of the 1960s, anyone over thirty was "old" and thus not to be trusted. As Kathleen Woodward (1991) observes, recounting an anecdote concerning ninety-five-year-old Amelia Freud who considered one hundred years to be "old," "People often label as 'old' only those who are older than they are" (p. 6). Official identifications of aging show a similar mobility, and citizens of the United States are variably certified as "senior" at fifty (for membership in AARP), sixty-two (for purposes of airline and entertainment discounts), and sixty-five (for social security benefits).

Historically, our Western culture has tended to focus on aging almost exclusively in terms of physical deterioration, but, as noted, gerontologists are becoming increasingly aware of the many spectrums of age: chronological age (the numerical total of years lived), biological age (the strength, health, vigor, and elasticity of the body, which frequently bear little relationship to chronological age), social age (the culturally constructed, often prescriptive behaviors arbitrarily linked to a chronological numeral), and individual age (our own self-image, which is often at variance with all the other markers of age). Researchers like James E. Birren, George L. Maddox, James Wiley, and Kathleen Woodward observe that traditional markers of age are not always in synchrony, since there may be wide disparities between biological, chronological, psychological, and social age, and a single individual may decline physically in the later years while growing psychologically. While Woodward (1991, 6) discusses the relativity of the terms "age" and "youth," Maddox and Wiley (1976) categorize the diverse processes of senescence differently, dividing them into biological age, psychological age, and social age, and insisting that "these components do not correlate in a precise way, and this fact must be taken into account in research on aging" (p. 28). Birren (1985, 30–31) adopts the categories of Maddox and Wiley and, like his colleagues, argues for the relativity of these emotionally charged words. Affirming the variability and relativity of such terms as "aging" and "old," Moody (1993) explains, "We are seeing an erosion of the cultural boundaries that separate youth, adulthood, and old age, and we have entered a period in which norms for age-appropriate behavior are in flux." According to Moody, therefore, "Today old age as a period of life is becoming less determinate, less role-governed, and other life stages are moving in that direction as well" (p. xx, xix). Thus, as Birren, Maddox, Moody, Wiley, and Woodward show, the meanings of terms like "youth" and "age" are being dissolved today, as are other established boundaries in our society, such as sex, gender, sexuality, and race.

But this dissolving of boundaries, culturally desirable as it is, poses a linguistic problem for the theorist in aging studies. For if the conventional meanings of the terms "aging," "elder," and "old" have eroded, how can one use these terms with any precision? Yet how can one write an essay on aging without adopting the lexicon of one's society? In answer to this dilemma, we will follow the practice of Jacques Derrida (1976)—who argues for the fluidity and indecidibility of all language—employing these terms for purposes of communication while implicitly placing them under erasure for purposes of interrogation. Gayatri Chakravorty Spivak (1976) explains Derrida's practice of placing a term "*sous rature*," or "under erasure": "This is to write a word, cross it out, and then print both word and deletion. (Since the word is inaccurate, it is crossed out. Since it is necessary [for communication], it remains legible)" (p. xiv). Therefore, although throughout this study we apply to these imprecise, perhaps inaccurate words their conventional denotations, we ask the reader to imagine that each time these necessary but virtually meaningless terms—"aging," "elder," "old," and "old age"—are employed, we are placing them under erasure in Derridean fashion.

HISTORY

This collection is the culmination of many years of studying and writing about the reciprocal relationship between the humanities and social issues, and behind this volume lies a decade of directing conferences and editing books on this subject, including conferences on "Literature and Youth Suicide," "Literature and Spouse Abuse," and "Gender and Academe," all of which developed into published collections of essays.[1] On October 1994, we officially joined the dialogue on aging through the presentation of an interdisciplinary conference, "Aging and Identity: A Humanities Perspective," sponsored by eight University of South Florida departments and featuring scholars in gerontology and the humanities from both USF and across the country. These scholars gathered together to study the ubiquitous aging process and to consider some of the more promising discoveries of current research that challenge the biomedical model of aging as a process of disease and decline. Playing to a standing-room-only crowd of teachers, social workers, writers,

clinicians, and others interested in aging issues, these scholars explored attitudes toward aging depicted in the writings and art of various cultures and
historical periods, and through these analyses attempted to provide alternatives to our late-twentieth-century fixation on youth. Using an interdisciplinary methodology, the participants focused on a reexamination of what aging
has traditionally meant and what it can mean. Several speakers reminded the
audience that although the science of gerontology is relatively new, our fascination with age is not. Throughout history, writers, artists, and other humanists have concentrated on the aging process and the pleasures and perils of
the last stages of life, and these scholars demonstrated how examining these
efforts can result in a reevaluation of the myths and stereotypes of aging and
to a deconstruction of ingrained theories that equate the last half of life with
boredom, loneliness, and misery. A total of sixteen presenters investigated
various strategies for maintaining one's identity and dignity in old age and
some ways that the humanities can contribute to this laudable goal. Betty
Friedan capped the conference with a talk about her latest book, *The Fountain of Age*.

   If the hallmark of a successful conference is the discussion generated among
the audience, both during the meeting and afterwards, "Aging and Identity"
was an unqualified success. Audience evaluations praised the speakers and
their subject matter as "thought provoking," "rich in cultural diversity," and
"a good mix of genres (film, novels, paintings, etc.)." The crux of the discussion occurred, however, when several clinical workers queried the panel of
scholars about how the humanities can aid their day-to-day work with the
poor, ill, and often despondent elderly. Larry Polivka, conference moderator
and Director of the Florida Policy Exchange Center on Aging, responded
that the humanities can help older people to understand the narratives of
their own lives and can also assist gerontologists and others who work with
the elderly in their efforts to preserve their clients' dignity, identity, and self-
worth. (Lenker and Polivka 1996, 6). To achieve the goals enunciated by Polivka
and also to promote the paradigm shift currently revolutionizing gerontology, we have collected these presentations, with a few additional invited essays, into the present volume.

CONTENT

   During the past decade, the study of aging from a humanities perspective
has flourished, with a particular focus on literature as a well-stocked laboratory for gerontological research. These studies can be roughly divided into
the following categories.

   Category 1 comprises the anthologies of literary works (poems, short stories,
dramas, etc.) treating the subject of aging that have proliferated during the past
two decades. These anthologies are of great value to humanistic gerontologists
(or gerontological humanists) as sources for the examination of aging.[2]

Category 2 contains the numerous theoretical treatises published during the last two decades that address the potential partnership between the humanities (primarily, but not exclusively, literature) and gerontology. First, these theoretical essays consider both the potential benefits and the potential hazards of this proposed collaboration, while overwhelmingly concluding that the advantages outweigh the detriments and that this reciprocal relationship can help both disciplines more fully to understand the phenomenon of aging. Second, these essays frequently employ the strategies of the humanities, particularly those of literary criticism and often those of postmodern criticism, to interrogate, probe, and comprehend the construction of aging in our society and in those of other times and places. Our study attempts to both expand and exemplify this critique by applying the techniques of this "critical gerontology" to an analysis of the treatment of aging in literary, artistic, and popular culture forums.[3]

Category 3 is composed of essays investigating the relationship between chronological age and literary or artistic style, between the psychology of aging and the psychology of creativity. Some of the chapters in this volume adopt this focus, exploring the dynamic between aging and creativity as revealed in the maxims of the "mature" Princess of Navarre, in the novels of the middle-aged Virginia Woolf, and in the writings of the nonagenarian Bertrand Russell.[4]

Category 4 incorporates the many essays and books analyzing the image of aging in the humanities, with particular reference to literature. For an excellent overview of critical analyses of the treatment of aging in literature see Anne M. Wyatt-Brown (1992), "Literary Gerontology Comes of Age." This category contains by far the richest and most diverse body of material, far too vast a corpus to survey at this time. We will, therefore, limit our discussion to a few approaches that we judge most valuable to the study of aging. Some very useful cross-cultural studies compare the treatment of aging in the literature, and less often in the plastic arts, of different cultures. Some provocative interdisciplinary studies employ the concepts of Freud, Lacan, or, less often, object-relations theorists to view the representation of aging in literature through a psychoanalytical lens. Still other commentators have discovered entire new subgenres of literature devoted to the representation of aging: the *Volledungsroman*, or novel of "concluding," the *Refungsroman*, or novel of "ripening," and the midlife progress novel. However, the vast majority of these studies adapt the "image of women" approach so popular in feminist literary criticism to an examination of the "image of aging" in literature.[5] The majority of chapters in this collection also adopt this popular approach, while enlarging this critique to include not only literature but also the fine and popular arts. In this endeavor, the essayists often employ a strategy similar to Elaine Showalter's (1985b) "feminist critique," while modifying these tactics to explode the stereotypes of aging rather than those of gender and to expose the biases of a gerontophobic rather than a misogynistic society.

Category 5 looks to other branches of the humanities beside literature and the arts—history, philosophy, and religion—to deepen our understanding of the meaning of the aging experience.

This collection participates in this rich and complex debate, involving itself in at least three of these five interpretive strategies while seeking to expand the dialogue to include a fuller treatment of age-related studies of the fine arts and popular culture as well as of literature. Moreover, far more deliberately than most published studies, this volume seeks to exemplify through specific analyses the theories of the new critical gerontology.

The texts analyzed in this volume cover a broad spectrum of media (literature, fine art, cinema, television), literary genres (poetry, drama, the novel, the short story, the essay, biography), time periods (early modern to postmodern), and ethnicities (British, French, Italian, Anglo-American, African American, Native American). The inclusion of multiple time periods reflects our assumption that the human angst over aging is as old as history, though as current as today's advice column. The inclusion of multiple media substantiates our belief that the concern with this human reality transcends artistic medium and genre as well as time period. However, the inclusion of multiple ethnic groups demonstrates the degree to which aging is viewed differently by different cultures in different eras, thereby validating our conviction that attitudes toward aging are largely social constructs. Indeed, the belief in the cultural interpretation—if not necessarily the biological process—of aging as a social construct provides a nexus uniting the chapters in this collection.

This volume is divided into four parts. The first part, "The Aging Male in Literature," includes five essays examining portraits of the aging patriarch in the texts of three highly influential, canonical male writers: Shakespeare, Shaw, and Hemingway. The final essay explores the biographical construction of another eminent aging writer, Bertrand Russell.

In her chapter, "The Dialectic of Aging in Shakespeare's *King Lear* and *The Tempest*," Sara Munson Deats posits that long before gerontologists discovered the dialectic of aging, Shakespeare was exploring this tension. She argues that Lear, in particular, combines the face of senescent decline traditionally drawn by pessimistic practitioners in the medical profession with the face of growth and liberation depicted by contemporary gerontologists. Prospero, on the other hand, at least by the opening of *The Tempest*, has learned the lessons taught by experience and has emerged as a figure empowered by age. Yet despite these obvious differences, both characters, according to Deats, anticipate to a remarkable degree the two faces of age identified by Friedan and many contemporary gerontologists in their deconstruction of the age mystique.

Kirk Combe and Kenneth Schmader, in their chapter, "Shakespeare Teaching Geriatrics: Lear and Prospero as Case Studies in Aged Heterogeneity," like Deats, focus on the two faces of age as represented by Shakespeare, but whereas Deats interprets both Lear and Prospero as embodying to different degrees both the positive and negative aspects of aging, Combe and Schmader view these two elder monarchs as diametrically opposed portraits of aged individuals, with Lear exemplifying the frail elder and Prospero the well elder. Using the principles of geriatric assessment, including a comparison with similar examples from the Duke Geriatric Evaluation and Treatment (GET) Clinic, Combe and Schmader appraise these two characters as case histories representing positive and negative aspects of aging. The authors conclude that compared to present-day clinical case histories, Shakespeare provides a rich and very different narrative of aging individuals that may prove useful in teaching geriatrics and gerontology. The first two chapters in this volume thus exemplify the collaboration between the humanities and gerontology advocated by critical gerontology by presenting two studies that employ the methodologies of literary criticism and medical case history respectively to analyze the same author and the same texts.

Lagretta Tallent Lenker's chapter, "Why? versus Why Not?: Potentialities of Aging in Shaw's *Back to Methuselah*," examines the double visage of aging as depicted in the work of another influential English playwright, George Bernard Shaw. As Lenker notes, *Heartbreak House* proffers both the positive and negative aspects of aging in the octogenarian Captain Shotover, while *Caesar and Cleopatra* presents an exemplar of affirmative aging in its eponymous superman. Lenker's work concentrates, however, on the potentialities of aging as dramatized in Shaw's magnum opus on aging, *Back to Methuselah*, concluding that Shaw's extravaganza anticipates the discoveries of humanistic gerontology in several ways: in its stress on the social constructiveness of traditional concepts of aging, in its advocacy of a multidisciplinary approach to the study of aging, and in its realization that society must totally change its attitudes toward aging if human potential is to be achieved. Lenker concludes that Shaw provides a revolutionary vision of the potentialities of aging that has rarely been equaled.

Almost as optimistic, however, is Phillip Sipiora's analysis of the treatment of age in the works of another highly esteemed male writer, Ernest Hemingway. Sipiora's chapter, "Hemingway's Aging Heroes and the Concept of *Phronesis*," investigates the portrayal of elderly male characters in Hemingway's texts, ranging from the short story, "A Clean Well-Lighted Place," to the novels *The Sun Also Rises* and *A Farewell to Arms* to the novella *The Old Man and the Sea*. Drawing upon the theories of Erik Erikson and other researchers into the association of wisdom and aging, Sipiora discovers that the elderly "code-holders" in these texts, whether they be protagonists or relatively minor figures, share a quality that Hemingway consistently links with fulfilled aging, the quality of *phronesis* or practical judgment. Sipiora concludes that the *phronesis* shared by Hemingway's "beloved gerontes" becomes an index of the respect that the author feels for the elderly, who through experience and suffering have acquired practical wisdom.

The chapter by William T. Ross, "Bertrand Russell in His Nineties: Aging and the Problem of Biography," shifts to less-traveled terrain, leaving the construction of aging in fictional texts to explore the fashioning of aging in biography, in this case, the fabrication of the nonagenarian Bertrand Russell. Ross argues that although the actions and writings of the ninety-plus-year-old author and political activist certainly indicate a man of exceptional mental vigor, his biographers, influenced perhaps by stereotypic notions of aging, tend to represent Russell in his nineties as senile. Ross further points out that in his vocal political commitment Russell failed to conform to accepted patterns of "growth" that depict the elderly as serene and disengaged, and this may be the reason that Russell was accused of mental insufficiency despite a public record of competency. Ross's essay thus provides a sobering caveat concerning the power of stereotypes to control not only the way we decipher literary characters but also the way we interpret the actions of living human beings.

Women have traditionally been defined by their social roles — wives, mothers, spinsters, professional women — and part II evaluates the way in which some of these roles have been portrayed in the treatment of "The Aging Female in Literature." In her essay entitled "Work, Contentment, and Identity in Aging Women in Literature," Rosalie Murphy Baum analyzes the relationship between age, gender, and occupation in twentieth-century fiction. In her brief survey of the fiction of this century, Baum identifies an unexpected disparity between the portraits of aging men and women. Aging male protagonists often find their happiness, even their identities, at risk, and their later years associated with decline and deterioration. Conversely, the aging women in twentieth-century fiction — written by women — frequently live lives of contentment and accomplishment and continue to develop and realize their identities in their later years, especially those engaged in some kind of satisfying work (whether this be teaching English, writing fiction, translating Horace, working in a laundry, quilting, or even gambling). Baum examines this surprisingly optimistic depiction of the aging "working" woman through her analysis of seven female characters: Katherine Mansfield's Miss Brill, James Joyce's Maria, Eudora Welty's Edna Earle Ponder and her unnamed woman in "The Purple Hat," Dorothy Canfield Fisher's Aunt Mehetabel, Alice Walker's Andrea Clement White, and May Sarton's Pickthorn. Like so many of contributors to this volume, Baum discovers that these writers have anticipated many of the tenets of contemporary humanistic gerontology.

If Baum finds in twentieth-century fiction by women a new awareness that the last stages of life can be as rich and full as the earlier ones, Maryhelen C. Harmon, in her chapter, "Old Maids and Old Mansions: The Barren Sisters of Hawthorne, Dickens, and Faulkner," exposes the extremely negative image of elderly women, especially the "never-married woman," in the texts of three male literary giants. Harmon considers four fictional avatars of the legendary abandoned virgins in the folk-tale of the avenging willies: Hepzibah Pyncheon in Nathaniel Hawthorne's *The House of the Seven Gables* and Edith in his "The White Old Maid"; Miss Havisham in Charles Dickens's *Great Expectations*; and Emily Grierson in William Faulkner's "A Rose for Emily." According to Harmon, scrutiny of these fictional "old maids" reveals four barren sisters imprisoned not only in their crumbling mansions, but also in the cultural imperatives of their age. She further concludes that, at least in their treatments of aging spinsters, the three male creators of these devastating fictional portraits, like their old maids, remain incarcerated within the restricting stereotypes of their own societies.

The final chapter in this part, "The Aging Artist: The Sad but Instructive Case of Virginia Woolf" by Joanne Trautmann Banks, considers the link between aging and creativity in both the life and works of one of the greatest female novelists of the twentieth century. Banks observes that although Woolf was certainly one of this century's most imaginative thinkers, this innovative artist provides no positive role models for aging, either in her life or in her art, primarily because she could not reimagine herself as an older woman. Possible reasons for this surprising failure are that Woolf (1) had no family role models for aging, (2) needed creative interaction with friends to feel "real," (3) practiced a philosophy that hindered the achievement of Eriksonian integrity, and (4) found in her fifties that she could no longer move smoothly between the world as it is and the world as she envisioned it. Banks suggests that Woolf's failure to cope successfully with aging offers lessons for all of us who love literature and life.

Part III, "Aging in the Community," changes direction to examine the aging process from the perspectives of social groups and institutions. The first three chapters in this section investigate the diverse attitudes toward aging revealed in the literature of three different ethnic groups: Native American, African American, and Continental. The final two chapters relate the image of aging to two dominant cultural institutions: the academic community and our public schools.

In the first of these chapters, "The Sacred Ghost: The Role of the Elder(ly) in Native American Literature," David Erben discusses the honorific status of the aged in Native American culture. According to Erben, the tribe, the repository of meaning and value, endures through time and appeals to the past for authority, and the source for this reverence for the past is respect for elders. Erben demonstrates this dynamic by analyzing works by Leslie Marmon Silko in which Native American characters confront the clash between the dominant ideology and their own Native American culture. These characters achieve a resolution of this conflict through the wise guidance of their elders. In comparing the respected role of the elderly in Native American literature to the often comic or pathetic depiction of the aged in Anglo-American fiction, Erben again illustrates the two faces of age.

The second chapter in this part considers the literature of another marginalized group existing within the majority culture: the African-American community. In "Aging and the African-American Community: The Case of Ernest J. Gaines," Charles J. Heglar and Annye L. Refoe note that mainstream culture tends to stereotype the elderly as sedentary, set in their ways, and physically or emotionally inactive. Conversely, they argue, African-American literature offers a wealth of alternative views that demonstrate the emancipatory possibilities of late life. Realizing the impracticality of attempting a survey of the rich and various literary contributions of the African-American culture within the scope of a single essay, Heglar and Refoe focus on Ernest J. Gaines as the author who most successfully epitomizes the tendency among African-American authors to situate the elderly center stage in their fiction. According to Gaines, the aged in African-American fiction do not simply exist, they "survive with dignity," a resilience that they pass on to the next generation. Heglar and Refoe demonstrate the symbiotic relationship between the younger and older generations as it informs three novels by Gaines: *The Autobiography of Miss Jane Pittman, A Lesson Before Dying,* and *A Gathering of Old Men.*

Given the limitations of space, Christine McCall Probes also does not attempt a comprehensive survey of the multifaceted treatment of aging in French literature. Rather, her chapter, "Aging and the Continental Community: Good Counsel in the Writings of Two Mature European Princesses, Marguerite de Navarre and Madame Palatine," centers on the strong face of age as embodied in the writings and lives of two "mature" Early Modern European princesses. Probes posits that although a positive view of aging may be found in all of the literary genres of Early Modern France, nowhere is it so striking as in the *Heptaméron* of Marguerite de Navarre and the *Lettres françaises* of Madame Palatine. Moreover, the reader of these two literary texts may receive a "double" encouragement, since each work serves as an example of late-life creativity as well as a celebration of the wisdom of age. Probes thus sees the lives and literary creations of these two princesses as exemplifying the equation of wisdom and aging stressed by so many contemporary psychologists and gerontologists.

Helen Popovich and Deborah Noonan, in their examination of the image of the aging academic in literature, "Aging and Academe: Caricature or Character," find heterogeneity, rather than uniformity. Their survey does, of course, discover many caricatures of the stereotypic aging professor: on the one hand, a monster of egotism; on the other, an absentminded buffoon doting on trivia. This egocentric, often ridiculous monster appears over and over in the literature of many different cultures: Roger Chillingworth in Nathaniel Hawthorne's *The Scarlet Letter,* Serebrykov in Anton Chekhov's *Uncle Vanya,* Father Dolan in James Joyce's *A Portrait of the Artist as a Young Man,* Mr. Ramsey in Virginia Woolf's *To the Lighthouse,* and Old Spenser in J. D. Salinger's *The Catcher in the Rye,* to mention but a few. However, Popovich and Noonan also uncover a number of surprisingly three-dimensional portraits of elder academics, such as James Hilton's Mr. Chips, Frances Gray Patton's Miss

Dove, Willa Cather's Godfrey St. Peter, and John William's William Stoner, characters who exemplify the integrity, dignity, and wisdom associated with positive aging by humanistic gerontologists. Like so many of the writers in this volume, Popovich and Noonan find multifaceted, even contradictory portraits of the elderly in the literature they analyze.

If the old have been warehoused, and young people's interaction with them dramatically reduced—as so many social critics complain—where then does young America interact with old America? Ralph M. Cline provides an answer: in the venerable American Literature class required of all high school juniors. In his chapter, "Aging and the Public Schools: Visits of Charity—The Young Look at the Old," Cline surveys the literature included in the vast majority of American literature textbooks (selections read in this course are remarkably consistent throughout the nation), highlighting short stories centrally concerned with the interaction between the young and the old. As a high school instructor, Cline frequently teaches these short stories to high school juniors in American Literature classes. In his essay, Cline first analyzes the depiction of aging in four of these short stories—Eudora Welty's "A Visit of Charity" and "A Worn Path," Katherine Anne Porter's "The Jilting of Granny Weatherall," and Nathaniel Hawthorne's "Dr. Heidegger's Experiment"—and then describes the reaction of his students to the images of the aged limned in these works. Cline's conclusions are both surprising and encouraging: He discovers that the portrayals of aging in these stories and the high school students' reactions to these portraits are as varied as the case histories of aging identified by contemporary gerontologists.

Not only literature, but the visual arts—painting, sculpture, and film—have been and continue to be a powerful influence, forming and informing society's conception of "reality." Part IV of this volume, "Aging in the Fine and Popular Arts," concentrates on the power of these cultural forms both to mirror and to shape society's perceptions of the aging process. Although acknowledging that visual art can popularize negative images of elders, the first chapter in this section demonstrates how art can also contribute positive images of aging people which, in turn, build positive attitudes and encourage achievement. However, most social commentators would concur that the most puissant force shaping the attitudes of our society today are the visual and auditory images emerging from our television and cinema screens. The last three chapters in this volume consider the attitude toward aging as presented through the eye of the camera in a number of different films.

The first chapter in this part attempts to address the question, "What is the place of creativity, of identity, of meaning, in the second half of life?" In "Aging and Contemporary Art," Linnea S. Dietrich explores late-life creativity in both male and female contemporary artists. Moreover, defying traditional interpretations of the "late style," Dietrich finds in the art of these creative elders not a rejection but a celebration of the body. Western art has conventionally inscribed negative stereotypes of aging that decry the aging body and exalt the youthful form, conveying the idea that old age must abandon the flesh for the spirit. However, Dietrich has discovered a cadre of significant contemporary artists, still productive in their later years, whose work demonstrates their makers' vitality by affirming the body, sexuality, and gender.

The second chapter analyzes the 1985 screen version of Horton Foote's play, *The Trip to Bountiful*. According to Carol J. Jablonski, in her chapter, "The Return Home: Affirmations of Aging and Transformations of Identity in Horton Foote's *The Trip to Bountiful*," this film uses the vehicle of a "return-to-home narrative" to explore the task of maintaining identity in late life, following the developmental trajectory suggested by Erik Erikson and many humanistic gerontologists. In its portrayal of an elderly woman's efforts to escape the apartment of her son and daughter-in-law and return to her childhood home, *The Trip to Bountiful* challenges culturally inscribed notions of what it means to be old and infirm. In this richly paradoxical film, the ostensibly frail elder ultimately emerges as the well elder, the dependent becomes the guide, and all preconceptions of aging are shattered as the oxymoronic face of age is again revealed.

The third chapter in this part puts one of our most venerated cultural icons under the critical microscope. Walt Disney's films have long been a powerful force in raising the consciousness of our society. From their inception, these films made humans more aware of the rights and value of other species by graphically depicting humanity's inhumanity from the perspective of its animal victims. More recently, Disney's films have grappled with some of society's other significant issues and exploded some of its most treasured stereotypes, sympathetically portraying the bookworm beauty (*Beauty and the Beast*), the Native American and the powerful woman leader (*Pocahontas*), and both the physically handicapped and the ethnic outcast (*The Hunchback of Notre Dame*). However, as Merry G. Perry vividly demonstrates in her chapter, "Animated Gerontophobia: Ageism, Sexism, and the Disney Villainess," in terms of the depiction of the elderly female, Disney's films have been unable to transcend the prejudices of the society that produced them. Employing the ideas of Simone de Beauvoir and Betty Friedan, Perry exposes the ageism and sexism implicit in Disney's rendering of the aging villainess in six popular films—*Snow White, Cinderella, Sleeping Beauty, The Little Mermaid, 101 Dalmatians*, and *The Rescuers*—and considers the insidious influence of such prejudicial inscriptions on the development of our youth.

The final chapter in this collection, "8½ and Me: The Thirty-Two-Year Difference," conflates a number of different methodologies. In this chapter, Norman N. Holland analyzes the attitude toward aging presented in a cinematic text written and directed by an older director and evaluated by himself, first as a young man and then thirty-two years later as an older one. He thus simultaneously explores the attitude toward aging revealed in the film and the changing perspectives wrought by age on the critic's evaluation of the film. By considering the text itself, the author/director, and the spectator/critic, Holland achieves a kind of total criticism of the relationship between aging and creativity.

CONCLUSION

On his seventy-fifth birthday, actor Maurice Chevalier was asked how he felt at that advanced age. The Gaelic boulevardier jauntily replied, "Not so bad when you consider the alternative." While we may appreciate Chevalier's playful wit, many of us may also feel strongly that the later years of life should be more than merely an evasion of dying. Indeed, the chapters in this volume seek to demonstrate that the older years—the years after the fiftieth, sixtieth, seventieth, eightieth, and ninetieth birthdays—can include as fulsome a variety of experiences as do the childhood years before the tenth birthday, the adolescent years before the twentieth birthday, the young adult years before the thirtieth birthday, or any other of the decades of life. We fervently hope that these essays will help readers to recognize the multiplicity of identities and opportunities that can be possible even until the final year of life.

Although we must be careful not to minimize the real hardships and sufferings that poverty, decaying health, and loss of loved ones bring to many aging individuals, we must also be aware of the alternative scenario often played out on this stage of life. In this alternate script, many seniors find the final years every bit as satisfying as Robert Browning suggested when he wrote, "Grow old along with me!/ the best is yet to be." Or, to cite F. Scott-Maxwell, a more recent commentator on the meaning of aging, "The late clarities will be put down to our credit I feel sure. . . . The last years may matter most" (Moody 1993, xxxix).

PART I

THE AGING MALE
IN LITERATURE

The Dialectic of Aging in Shakespeare's
King Lear and *The Tempest*

Sara Munson Deats

Shakespeare's King Lear and Prospero dramatize many of the problems confronting almost everyone fortunate enough to survive to "a ripe old age": the problem of allowing their children the freedom to live their own lives, the problem of coping with retirement, and the problem of accepting change and finding it a challenge and an opportunity rather than a threat. In his wise examination of these prickly issues, Shakespeare anticipates many of the tenets of contemporary gerontology as summarized by Betty Friedan (1993) in her provocative book, *The Fountain of Age.*

In the Introduction to this book, Lagretta Lenker and I examine the Janus-faced portrait of age posited by Friedan (1993) and the group of contemporary practitioners and theorists whom she terms "the underground gerontologists." One aspect of this double portrait is the weakened face of senescent decline traditionally drawn by pessimistic practitioners of medicine; the other aspect is the strong, vital face of growth and liberation depicted by contemporary gerontologists. Friedan cites an abundance of reassuring scientific research to support her image of the strong face of age. This research, focusing particularly on emotional growth and personality integration as characteristic of creative aging, demonstrates that positive psychological and even physiological changes can compensate for age-related declines (p. 68–96). Friedan finds ballast for her thesis in the research of sociologist David Gutmann(1977, 312; 1987, 2–7). According to Gutmann, one primary aspect of this age-related integration, what he calls "sex-role crossover," occurs in the years after parenthood is over. Gutmann's transcultural studies provide evidence that later in life—in many different societies—men develop their passive, nurturing, contemplative qualities (attributes traditionally gendered "feminine"), whereas women discover their assertive, commanding, or adventurous traits (attributes traditionally gendered "masculine"). He hypothesizes that earlier in life, women and men are forced to suppress these facets of their personalities in order to play the polarized roles of the passive nurturer and aggressive hunter–fighter in which they have been cast by society; only after parenting is over can they feel free to claim and develop these buried aspects of their selves. Thus, by expanding what Carl Jung termed their "contra-sexual" traits, older people have the latitude to become more androgynous than their younger counter-parts. Gutmann concludes that this integration of the personality may be one of the primary rewards of vital aging.

Recent scientific research has discovered other attributes characteristic of vitally aging individuals. These include, on the one hand, the maintenance of one's autonomy and the courage to take risks; on the other hand, they incorporate the rejection of the dominance game and the embracing of rela-tionships. Researchers describe the most creative seniors as individuals who achieve unfettered self-confidence and autonomy while basking in the warmth of close relationships (Friedan 1993, 87–92; Apter 1995, 76–77; Sheehy 1995, 318–319, 414).

Another group of theorists, inspired by the pioneering studies of Erik Erikson (1982, 58–65; 1979), have revived the traditional association of old age with wisdom. As discussed in the Introduction, Erikson develops his influential theory of the human life cycle around a Hegelian model in which the suc-cessful resolution of the central crisis of each life stage involves a synthesis of two dialectical qualities. In treating old age, the eighth and final life stage, Erikson posits a tension between the thesis Integrity (an awareness of life's wholeness and coherence) and the antithesis Despair (a horror at life's frag-mentation and meaninglessness) which, in positive aging, merges into the synthesis Wisdom ("a kind of informed and detached concern with life in the face of death itself").[1]

Contemporary research thus suggests that vitally aging individuals seem to synthesize contradictions: "feminine" and "masculine" traits, growth and de-cline, strength and weakness, integrity and despair. Friedan (1993) summa-rizes the contradictions inherent in her double-visaged portrait of old age, explaining that "in speaking to many gerontologists personally, attending their lectures and seminars," she found "ample additional evidence of the view of age as pure pathology." Yet she also discovered "glimmers of another approach: the study of age as a state of becoming and being, not merely as ending" (p. 72). Or, to impose my own theatrical metaphor on Friedan's conclusions, she found some practitioners who regarded aging as the prelude to the final cur-tain, while others affirmed that aging should be seen as the opening of a new act, not the dénouement of life's play.

But what, the reader may ask, does all of this have to do with William Shakespeare? In this chapter, I seek to demonstrate that long before contemporary gerontologists discovered the dialectic of aging, Shakespeare, that most innovative and influential of literary artists, was exploring this dialectic. Moreover, the Janus-faced portrait that he frequently limns, particularly of the aging male, anticipates to a remarkable degree the two faces of age identified by Friedan in her deconstruction of the mystique of age.

King Lear dramatizes the tragic story of an aged monarch who plans to abdicate and divide his kingdom among his three daughters. Although he has already decided to give the most opulent portion to his youngest and favorite daughter Cordelia, he stages a "love contest," a kind of grand retirement party, complete with hyperbolic platitudes and all the trimmings, everything except the traditional gold watch. As part of this retirement party, he requires his three daughters to compete for land with vows of love. When Cordelia refuses to play the demeaning role assigned to her, Lear throws a tantrum and banishes her. The Earl of Kent, one of Lear's most devoted retainers, supports Cordelia's courage and candor, and he too is banished by the choleric King. Thus the imperious old King exiles the two people who love him most and becomes vulnerable to manipulation by self-seeking family members and subjects. The rest of the play details Lear's abuse at the hands of his two remaining daughters, Goneril and Regan, his flight into the storm accompanied only by his Fool and two disguised friends, his education through suffering, and his reconciliation with his beloved Cordelia. However, the crusty old King learns too late, and having already unleashed the forces that will destroy him, loses Cordelia and dies of a broken heart.

Initially, the play appears to reenact all the most dreaded aspects of the aging mystique, presenting Lear's senescence as a descent into senility, debility, and loss. At the beginning of the play Lear has unquestioningly accepted society's deleterious stereotype of old age as second childhood. Although still vigorous and commanding, Lear has decided to retire and spend his final days in the "kind nursery" of his daughter Cordelia's love; he thus talks of crawling toward death before he has even begun to stumble. Most contemporary audiences would probably agree that the octogenarian King should be allowed to retire if he so desires. His daughter Regan certainly thinks so, as well. In Act 2, in response to Lear's laments, "I gave you all," Regan snaps, "And in good time you gave it" (2.4.252; all Shakespeare quotations taken from Bevington 1997). However, using Lear's Fool as a choral figure, the play makes it clear that, at least from an early modern perspective, King Lear, as God's viceroy on earth, does not have the prerogative simply to retire at will. The King's wise Fool ridicules Lear's double mistake—his decision not only to abdicate but also to divide his kingdom between his daughters, thus relinquishing his authority as both a ruler and a father: "When thou clovest thy crown i'th'middle and gav'st away both parts, thou bor'st thine ass on thy back o'er the dirt. Thou hadst little wit in thy bald crown when thou gav'st thy golden one away." (1.4.157–161)

Nevertheless, although Lear's decision to divide his kingdom and abdicate from the throne would doubtlessly have been viewed as egregiously irresponsible by a Jacobean audience, I agree with Laurel Porter (1984, 60) that the play focuses not so much on the permissibility of Lear's retirement as on his attitude toward it, an issue also relevant to contemporary audiences. Like so many individuals today, Lear wishes to retire and yet not retire. Unable to give up the dominance game, unwilling to accept aging and retirement as new stages in life's cycles, Lear yearns to be coddled in the nursery of Cordelia's care while still throwing his weight around, retaining "The name and all th' addition to a king" (1.1.136), including an old-boy retinue of one hundred knights. Of course, this desire to retain authority while relinquishing responsibility, however impractical, is a very human wish, one frequently exhibited by individuals, particularly men, who have retired from important leadership positions. Having gladly surrendered onerous responsibility, they have a difficult time letting go of power, and often harass their wives and children in their efforts to establish lost authority.

Under such circumstances, retirement can be a difficult experience for everyone involved. My mother-in-law, frazzled after dealing with a retired CEO who tried to establish himself as chairman of the groaning board, frequently complained that she married her husband for better or worse, but not for lunch. Most of us have seen this scenario enacted, if not in our own families at least in the households of our friends. A wife who has spent years overseeing the household suddenly finds her domain invaded by an idle administrator searching for a project through which to demonstrate his trained powers of taking charge. The beleaguered wife must cook meals with a husband who wants to be plant manager in the kitchen. When she goes to the neighborhood grocery store, the vice-president in charge of quality control wishes to offer his services. She puts dirty clothes in the washer and gets directions from her live-in corporate efficiency expert. And perhaps most exasperating of all, the wife is expected to serve as an around-the-clock audience for a former executive accustomed to expounding his views to a phalanx of rapt subordinates. As more and more women begin to break through the glass ceiling and assume more prestigious and responsible positions, husbands of retired female executives may begin to share the frustrations that so many wives experience today.

We never know for certain whether or not these tendencies exacerbate problems between Lear and Goneril when the retired King goes to live with his daughter, but the imperious old monarch certainly epitomizes these proclivities. In regard to retirement, as well as in learning to share the love of his daughters with their husbands, Lear is unable to accept the view, widely endorsed by most gerontologists and psychologists, that different stages in people's physical and psychological development frequently require different activities and responses.

Goneril and Regan, Lear's two ungrateful daughters, like their father, embody traditional attitudes toward aging, associating it exclusively with both mental and physical decline. Both daughters interpret Lear's rashness and irresponsibility as the "infirmity of his age" (1.1.296). Moreover, they treat their parent like a child, berating him, "I pray you, Father, being weak, seem so" (2.4.202), a negative concept of old age similar to that presented by Lear earlier in the same scene when he whines to Regan, "Dear daughter, I confess that I am old;/Age is unnecessary [old people are useless]" (2.4.154–155). Lear's two daughters also wish to deprive their father of his followers and thus of his autonomy while they "look after him"; thus, they strip him of his familiar support group and reduce him to a state of total dependency. Ultimately, both sisters seek to marginalize and control their elderly father. Following an all too familiar clinical pattern, Lear first becomes disoriented, then angry, then depressed, and finally goes mad.

However, throughout the action and dialogue, the play offers a contradictory concept of old age. Early in the play, the sage Fool comments on the traditional association of wisdom with aging: "Thou shouldst not have been old til thou hadst been wise" (1.5.43–44). Later, having survived the turbulence of the physical storm while still suffering the turmoil of the psychological tempest, the mad Lear recognizes, "They flattered me like a dog and told me I had white hairs in my beard ere the black ones were there" (4.6.96–98). Lear here associates having white hair with being wise; thus, to be told that one is old (has white hair) is seen as a form of flattery predicated on the equation of old age with wisdom.

Paradoxically, as this quotation exemplifies, Lear's progress into madness is accompanied by a journey into self-awareness. Socrates once stated that "the unexamined life is not worth living," and this appears to be the life that the imperious Lear has lived for the eighty years preceding his disastrous decision to divide his kingdom and retire. Indeed, initially all of Lear's actions affirm Regan's acerbic observation that the King "hath ever but slenderly known himself" (1.1.296–297). Yet after his banishment of Cordelia and Kent and his alienation from his eldest daughter Goneril, schooled by his tutor the Fool in adversity's classroom, the old man, perhaps for the first time in his life, begins to interrogate his own actions, and his probing question, "Who is it that can tell me who I am?" (1.4.227) starts Lear on his painful quest for self-knowledge. Shocked by the ingratitude of Goneril, Lear recognizes and admits his injustice, acknowledging that he has been a fool in his treatment of Cordelia (1.4.265–270; 1.5.24). Enraged at Goneril's disrespect, Lear leaves his daughter's house and goes to meet Regan at Gloucester's castle. Here, rejected by Regan as well as Goneril, on the verge of madness from the cruel treatment of his daughters, Lear, in authentic tragic fashion, starts to ask insoluble questions. Earlier he had queried, "Who am I?" Now, in his speech, "O, reason not the need!" he asks, in effect, "What do individuals need in order to be human?" (2.4.266–272). Finally, stripped of kingdom, daughters, retainers, even the roof over his head, and cast out into the raging storm, Lear, again probably for the first time in his life, shows genuine concern for another human being. Cold and shivering amid the towering tempest, the

King forgets himself and succors his faithful Fool; transcending his own misery, he empathizes with all the cold, hungry, homeless outcasts of society,
realizing that when he had reigned in glory and power, he had been callously
indifferent to the suffering of his subjects:

> Poor naked wretches, wheresoe'er you are,
> That bide the pelting of this pitiless storm,
> How shall your houseless heads and unfed sides,
> Your looped and windowed raggedness, defend you
> From seasons such as these? O, I have ta'en
> Too little care of this! Take physic, pomp;
> Expose thyself to feel what wretches feel,
> That thou mayst shake the superflux to them
> And show the heavens more just. (3.4.28–36)

In this difficult passage, Lear exhorts the rich to cure themselves of their
egotism and complacency ("take physic, pomp") by experiencing the suffering of the cold, hungry wretches of the world, concluding that if the "haves"
could learn to empathize with the "have nots," they would be moved to share
their excess with those who have nothing ("shake the superflex to them"),
thereby establishing the justice on earth that the gods have failed to enact
("show the heavens more just"). In the storm, therefore, Lear gains a Utopian
vision of a world in which each is provided according to need, where there is
superfluity for none and sufficiency for all. However, the burden of the vision
is too great to bear and he goes mad.

And then, in the last act of the play, something wonderful happens. Reunited with his beloved daughter Cordelia and encircled and succored by
her love, Lear reclaims his powers (even as Gutmann [1987], so many years
later, asserts that the elderly tend to do). But the power he displays is very
different from the authority he so valorized at the beginning of the play. The
man who ever but slenderly knew himself receives a dazzling self-awareness:
The wrathful bully learns patience; the dictatorial tyrant learns responsibility; and the authoritarian patriarch learns to accept, even cherish, the feminine within himself. I agree with Coppelia Kahn (1986) that Lear's odyssey is
essentially a search for the benevolent mother whom he ultimately discovers
in the persona of his loving daughter Cordelia. However, I would modify
Kahn's thesis to argue that Lear discovers the long-sought-for mother in the
storm, before his reunion with Cordelia, and that he initially finds this nurturing parent not in Cordelia but within himself. Janet Adelman (1992) further develops Kahn's thesis, arguing that "Lear's confrontation with his
daughters . . . repeatedly leads him back to the mother ostensibly occluded
by the play." Moreover, she insists that "in recognizing his daughters as part
of himself, he will be led to recognizing not only his terrifying dependence
on female forces outside of himself but also an equally terrifying femaleness
within himself—a femaleness that he will come to call 'mother'" (p. 104).

But whereas Adelman finds Lear's discovery of the feminine aspect of his nature terrifying, I find it—however frightening initially—to be ultimately invigorating and transforming. Carolyn Asp (1986), adopting a Freudian methodology rather than the object-relations approach of Kahn and Adelman, also sees Lear's journey as a search for the benevolent mother. Like the vital seniors identified by Friedan, Gutmann, Apter, and Sheehy, Lear learns to integrate his "feminine" and "masculine" qualities, seeking both relatedness and autonomy, balancing empathy with strength.

Moreover, like the creative seniors described by contemporary gerontologists, Lear's value system changes as he matures. After traveling through natural and psychological storms and achieving the halcyon haven of Cordelia's love, Lear has totally lost interest in the power race. Authority becomes, for him, "A dog's obeyed in office" (4.6.158–159); political struggles are reduced to, "Who loses and who wins; who's in; who's out" (5.3.15); relatedness replaces power as the goal of life. At the age of "fourscore and upward" (4.7.62), King Lear is totally transformed; contrary to conventional wisdom, the old dog does indeed learn new tricks, smashing all stereotypes of aging. Susan Snyder (1982, 451–459) interprets the tragedy of Lear as the drama of an old man coming to terms with death, arguing that Lear's career from initial denial to anger to bargaining to depression to ultimate acceptance parallels the course of many dying patients observed by thanotologist Elizabeth Kubler-Ross. Although I find many aspects of Snyder's argument very persuasive, I interpret Lear's reconciliation with Cordelia and his celebration of their life together, even in prison, more affirmatively than does Snyder, seeing the play as the drama of an old man coming to terms not so much with death as with life. However, I also acknowledge that Lear never totally matures, since he never learns to love Cordelia enough to give her up. Ultimately, Lear's growth and expansion is not a success story, since he learns too late to accept—even embrace—aging. First, he is captured and imprisoned, thereby losing his autonomy. Shortly afterward, his deepest personal relationship is severed by the death of his beloved Cordelia, the one person who connects him with humanity. Thus, despite his stunning self-actualization, he cannot survive this last fatal wound and dies of a broken heart.

The appropriate interpretation of Lear's enlightenment and death, and the degree of optimism or pessimism evoked by these events, have been much debated by commentators of the play. The responses of critics range from O. J. Campbell's (1948) Christian interpretation of the tragedy as a "sublime morality play" celebrating humanity's quest for eternal, enduring values ("The Salvation of Lear") to J. Stampfer's (1960) absurdist reading of the play as a rejection of all essential values, even the validity of penance, in an ironic and perhaps even "imbecile" universe ("The Catharsis of King Lear"). I favor the via media reading of such commentators as Arthur Sewell (1951: "Tragedy and the Kingdom of Ends") and Maynard Mack (1965: King Lear in Our Time), who interpret the play as an affirmation of the human values of community and relatedness within a problematic universe. Richard C. Fallis (1989) also offers a particularly sensitive reading of the play: "King Lear, then, is a mythic statement of the pain of education, especially in old age. Lear must learn that children can turn on parents for no apparent reason, that plain speech means more than praise, that madness is only a step beyond wisdom (or perhaps a step on the way to it), and that even purification by suffering may not be enough to sustain one's self in a world where deprivation is the norm" (p. 38).

For a genuine celebration of aging, one must wait for Shakespeare's last play, *The Tempest*. According to scholarly consensus, Shakespeare wrote *King Lear* in 1606 at the age of forty-two. Approximately five years later, at forty-seven, he reprised the tragic story of Lear in the triumphant saga of Prospero. *The Tempest* dramatizes the adventures of the Duke of Milan, who, enthralled with the study of magic, neglects his state responsibilities, is deposed by his ungrateful brother, and with his infant daughter Miranda is set adrift on the rough seas. However, Prospero and his daughter do not perish; instead, they find a providential haven on an island peopled only by spirits. Through his most potent magic Prospero establishes absolute rule over the creatures of the island, including the blithe spirit Ariel and the beast/man Caliban. As the play opens, the magus has conjured a mighty tempest which wafts the ships of his usurping brother and the brother's allies from the course of their journey and deposits them on Prospero's enchanted island. Here the traitors are subjected to ordeals and torments before being granted clemency by the injured magician. (Significantly, some of the malefactors repent, some do not, but all are guardedly forgiven.) After forgiving his enemies, Prospero arranges his daughter's marriage to Ferdinand, the son of his former foe, the King of Naples. He then relinquishes his magic power, breaking his staff and drowning his book, and the play ends as he makes plans to return to Milan and resume his dukedom.

Striking similarities link the two irascible, negligent rulers, Lear and Prospero. Although the text never specifies his age, Prospero, like Lear, is clearly elderly, as he himself affirms in his lines to Ferdinand, "Sir, I am vexed./ Bear with my weakness. My old brain is troubled./ Be not disturbed with my infirmity" (4.1.158–160). Because of these lines and other clues in the play, and despite his daughter's youth, Prospero is always presented as venerable and often played with a white beard. (Unaccountably, both *King Lear* and *The Tempest* unrealistically give their aged patriarchs very young daughters; Miranda is fourteen, Cordelia probably not much older.) The trajectory of both rulers is very similar and both experience a kind of enlightenment through suffering. Originally, Lear and Prospero are both irresponsible and gullible: Lear abdicates his obligations as king and divides his kingdom between his children, exiling his dutiful daughter Cordelia while believing the hollow flattery of Goneril and Regan; Prospero neglects his kingly duties to practice magic and, duped by his treacherous brother Antonio, delegates more and more authority to an unworthy subaltern; Prospero later trusts the bestial Caliban, lodging him within his own cell and treating him like a surrogate son. In addition, both protagonists are betrayed by those whom they trusted, and are banished by an ungrateful family member into a hostile natural environment: Goneril and Regan cruelly abuse their father and drive him into the storm; Antonio usurps the dukedom of his brother and casts him adrift on the sea; later Prospero is again betrayed when his surrogate son Caliban tries to rape his daughter Miranda. However, in the midst of their sufferings, both banished rulers are sustained by their love for a young daughter. After experiencing treachery from those whom they favored, both Lear and Prospero overreact, becoming increasingly choleric: Lear rages in the storm, cursing his ungrateful daughters; Prospero chastises Caliban with sadistic severity and subjects his enemies to cruel torments. Ultimately, both Lear and Prospero learn not only to acknowledge responsibility for their actions but also to express their repressed femininity: Lear, tutored by the Fool in the hard lesson of self-knowledge through suffering, learns empathy; Prospero, schooled by Ariel, eschews vengeance and forgives his enemies, recognizing that "The rarer action is/ In virtue than in vengeance" (5.1.27–28). At the end of the play, Prospero even accepts the beast/man Caliban as his own responsibility: "This thing of darkness I/ Acknowledge mine" (5.1.278–279). In his earlier years as Duke of Milan before the action of the play begins, Prospero was apparently too lenient and gullible; during most of the action of the play he appears too strict and severe. At the end of the play, like the creative elders discussed by Gutmann, Prospero, like Lear, achieves a balance between traits traditionally gendered "feminine" (nurturance, forgiveness) and those gendered "masculine"(autonomy, domination). Finally, Prospero, like Lear, experiences a shift in priorities: Realizing the danger of unlimited power in the hands of a fallible human being, he rejects the absolute puissance that he asserts on the island in favor of responsible governing in Milan, while melding autonomy with relatedness and caring.

However, salient differences also distinguish Shakespeare's final drama of empowerment from his earlier tragedy of defeat. Prospero learns the lessons taught by age before it is too late and thus transforms a potential tragedy into a bittersweet comedy. Whereas Lear is rendered vulnerable by age, Prospero is empowered through his magic; unlike Lear who rants helplessly at the storm, Prospero bends the tempestuous forces of nature to his commands. Yet ultimately Prospero willingly surrenders his omnipotent power; revising the trajectory of Lear, he gives up absolute authority to assume responsibility. He resigns from his role as omnipotent magus to take on a new endeavor; retirement thus becomes for him not a finale but a new beginning. Moreover, by retiring from isolation on a sequestered island to active participation in social governance, Prospero reverses the progression espoused by "disengagement" theorists, who view withdrawal from social activities and duties as an important aspect of "normal" old age (Cumming and Henry 1961). Lastly, unlike Lear, who is never willing to relinquish his authority over his beloved daughter Cordelia, Prospero plans Miranda's marriage and encourages her independence, loving her enough to let her go. Prospero thus provides one of the most positive images of seniority in all of literature, epitomizing the vital, creative aging documented by contemporary gerontologists.

By demonstrating two such different concepts of aging—vulnerability versus power, incapacity versus empowerment—Shakespeare anticipates the discoveries of contemporary gerontologists by stressing the heterogeneity of aging, suggesting that society's association of senescence with ineluctable impairment is a social construct, not a biological inevitability. This is a view frequently expressed by "underground gerontologists," like George Maddox, who insist, "When you've seen one older person, you haven't seen them all. Older people do not become more alike by becoming old. In many areas, they become more varied" (Friedan 1993, 117). Moreover, Erikson's (1982) identification of the final stage in the life cycle as a dialectic between integrity and despair, which in creative elders culminates in wisdom, could serve as a gloss on both Lear and Prospero. In *King Lear*, throughout the third and fourth acts, the octogenarian King wrestles with his newfound integrity and his concomitant despair. After his reunion with Cordelia, these antitheses merge into the wisdom of the last act. However, tragically, Lear learns too late the wisdom taught by age, and the eve of his maturation becomes the day of his death. On his magical island, Prospero also battles between integrity and despair, although the conflict has been almost resolved before the play begins and we primarily witness the less perilous combat between integrity and anger. Finally, schooled by Ariel, even as Lear is tutored by the Fool, Prospero achieves a triumphant wisdom.

However, the dénouement of *The Tempest* evokes pathos as well as triumph. There is regret as well as satisfaction in the irrevocable abdication of power; there is sadness as well as joy in the surrender of a beloved daughter to her future mate; there is sorrow in the awareness that all lives, even successful ones, must someday end, as Prospero reminds us: "And thence retire me to my Milan, where/ Every third thought shall be my grave" (5.1.314–315). Thus, even the triumphant aging of Prospero, like all senescence, is shadowed by the penumbra of mortality.

Nevertheless, despite the poignancy of its last act, the dominant impression of *The Tempest*—at least in my reading—remains celebration rather than sadness. I like to think that the evolution from the tragic, vulnerable Lear to the empowered Prospero reflects Shakespeare's own acceptance of aging as he approached the landmark birthday of fifty, not very old today, but considering the life expectancy at Shakespeare's time probably equivalent to around seventy-five in our own society. Many scholars interpret Prospero's valediction to magic as Shakespeare's own farewell to the stage, his own retirement speech, particularly since *The Tempest* is generally accepted as Shakespeare's last play. If the character of Prospero can be seen as the mouthpiece for Shakespeare, then the final lines of Prospero offer an instructive inspiration. As he embraces the beginning of his retirement, Prospero closes the play with the words "set me free." This, I believe, epitomizes the strong face of age.

CHAPTER 2

Shakespeare Teaching Geriatrics: Lear and Prospero as Case Studies in Aged Heterogeneity

Kirk Combe and Kenneth Schmader

> Sir, I am vexed.
> Bear with my weakness. My old brain is troubled.
> Be not disturbed with my infirmity.
> (Prospero *The Tempest* 4.1.158–160)

> I am a very foolish fond old man,
> Fourscore and upward, not an hour more nor less;
> And, to deal plainly,
> I fear I am not in my perfect mind.
> (Lear *King Lear* 4.7.61–64)

During this century, a number of critical studies of aging in Shakespeare have been undertaken. The great majority of these predate 1980; most are from the 1940s. The older pieces in particular conjecture about Shakespeare's outlook on aging and how those attitudes are manifest in various characters in the plays (Draper 1946; Miles 1940; Cox 1942; Chew 1948; Sims 1943). All of these studies focus on Shakespeare's use of Elizabethan views of old age (Gilbert 1967; Coffman 1934; Smith 1976; Smith 1978), which normally take some form of an "Ages of Man" schema (Covey 1989). Moreover, most of these authors pursue the task of reading Shakespeare's plays biographically: they try to discern (invent) what Shakespeare himself felt about the aging process. More recent scholarship has applied current thinking—both in the field of literary theory and of gerontology—to the treatment of aging in Shakespeare. For example, Carolyn Asp (1986) takes a Freudian approach to *King Lear*; Laurel Porter (1984) reads that same play as essentially a crisis of retirement; and Herbert S. Donow (1992) examines both age-appropriate behavior and ageism in Shakespeare, particularly in the case of Falstaff, while also exploring generational continuity, exploitative elders, and gerontophobia in *Lear* (Donow 1994). Old age in Shakespeare has even become the subject of dissertations (Coggin 1982). However, none of these studies combine the findings of gerontological research and the assessment techniques of geriatrics with the literary study of Shakespeare.

With an increased understanding of gerontology and geriatrics (Gold and Schmader 1993), today we are better equipped than ever to understand Shakespeare's elderly characters. Specifically, one of the most important principles to emerge from gerontological research is that of "aged heterogeneity." The principle of aged heterogeneity maintains that the elderly are more diverse than younger persons in physical, psychological, social, and functional characteristics. Such variability in the elderly has been demonstrated in gerontological studies of social support, financial resources, emotional health, cognitive function, and physiology; moreover, it has been the subject of recent essays (Rowe and Kahn 1987; Maddox 1987, 1991). The clinical manifestation of aged heterogeneity is the wide spectrum of health and disease found in the elderly. Geriatric health-care workers see patients of similar chronological age that possess few, if any, problems compared to those with multiple co-morbidities, multiple medications, cognitive impairment, depression, social isolation, and functional disability. We believe Shakespeare's plays exhibit this spectrum of aging at work, enough so that important elderly characters in his plays are treated in genuinely different ways. In particular, an appreciation for the heterogeneity of the elderly reveals itself best in the plays *King Lear* and *The Tempest*. In those works, Shakespeare stages diametrically opposed views of aged individuals and the aging process in the characters of Lear and Prospero. Prospero ages well, while Lear dwindles into a frail elder.

Our project, then, appraises these two Shakespearean characters from a current gerontological perspective and with the most recent geriatric evaluative procedures. We will present a case study of a well elder from the Duke University Medical Center Geriatric Evaluation and Treatment Clinic and then evaluate Prospero as an example of aging well. After a case presentation of a frail elder from the Duke GET Clinic, we will assess Lear as an example of unsuccessful aging. These case studies of Prospero and Lear entail a profile of the subject's social health, psychological health, and functional status. Following the case studies is a discussion of why we think an amalgamation of literary and medical investigation yields insights valuable to the understanding of aging. We must emphasize at the outset of this chapter, however, the precise character and function of our interdisciplinary study. We are not primarily interested in adding interpretive finesse to either text by Shakespeare—although we believe that literary study is enhanced by learning about life, in this case the aging process. Neither do we pretend that characters from a play are actual patients for clinical study and treatment; such a notion risks making trivial both the process of diagnosis and the real medical problems of elderly people. Rather, we propose that clinical work in geriatrics as well as the study of gerontology itself can be significantly enhanced by reading the literature of aging, and especially by reading these two plays by Shakespeare. As Martha Holstein (1994) has written, the study of literature "has not been integrated into gerontological research and education" (p. 822). In both gerontological research and clinical geriatrics, literary works dealing with the phenomenon of aging are, at best, marginalized. In this chapter, we intend to demonstrate not only that Shakespeare's plays might serve as valuable training material for students of geriatrics and gerontology, but that the plays themselves have something to teach us about the process of aging and, more importantly, about the narrative of aging. Since postmodern theory maintains that as humans we are inherently creatures of language—even creatures trapped by our language—it is reasonable to assume that our knowledge of and attitude toward the elderly will depend a great deal upon how we talk about them.

CASE STUDIES

Case 1: The Well Elder

The patient is an eighty-year-old male who came to the Duke Geriatric Evaluation and Treatment Clinic at the urging of his daughter for a general geriatric assessment. Other than occasional back pain while climbing a ladder, the patient had no specific complaints. He denied problems with fatigue, eating, sleeping, memory, thinking, and mood. He was completely independent in all his basic and instrumental activities of daily living (ADLs). His main reason for coming to the clinic was to maintain his excellent health and independence. Past medical history was significant only for dilatation of a benign esophageal stricture. He took no medication. He had graduated from college, first worked in the family business (a large manufacturing company), and later owned a custom kitchen business. He was widowed six years ago and retired to a university community to be close to his daughter. He spent his time on construction activities, such as building a roof for the carport, installing electric wiring in a new outbuilding, and working on a vegetable garden. The physical examination was essentially normal, as was his complete blood count, blood chemistries, and thyroid profile. The focus of the intervention in the clinic was preventive care.

Prospero as Shakespeare's Well Elder

The most obvious themes of *The Tempest* are political ones. Prospero, as the rightful Duke of Milan, recovers his position and power usurped twelve years earlier by his brother Antonio in league with Alonso, the scheming King of Naples. Equally, Prospero has usurped the remote island of his exile from its first owner, the monstrous Caliban. During the play, rebellion fills the air.

Antonio convinces Sebastian, brother of the King of Naples, to murder Alonso and assume his throne. Caliban plots with the drunkards Stefano and Trinculo to kill Prospero and rule the island themselves. Due to the potency of Prospero's magic, neither plot comes to fruition. Prospero controls the actions of every character in the play in order to enact his return to authority. Yet amid the political debates of Shakespeare's drama exists a telling account of aging as well. Prospero is dominated by two equally urgent motivations: his need to avenge himself politically *and* his need to prepare himself for later life, particularly with regard to situating his daughter Miranda in an advantageous marriage with Ferdinand, the Prince of Naples. Therefore, in *The Tempest*, not only does Prospero seek to regain his dukedom, but we also see him engaged in the process of designing his inevitable disengagement from life due to aging and, finally, death (Kerrigan 1986, 178–179).

The key to Prospero's retirement is his success at arranging a new and appropriate environment for himself and Miranda. He achieves this objective with spectacular results. While father and daughter begin the play occupying an austere cell on a deserted island in the middle of the Mediterranean Sea, he will end his days in a palace of a thriving European city with relationships and finances sufficient for his needs, and she will be the Queen of Naples. As Prospero says to Alonso at play's end,

> And in the morn
> I'll bring you to your ship, and so to Naples,
> Where I have hope to see the nuptial
> Of these our dear-beloved solemnized;
> And thence retire me to my Milan, where
> Every third thought shall be my grave. (5.1.310–315)

In his loving and undemanding relationship with his daughter, Prospero is quite similar to our GET Clinic patient. Not only has he ensured the future of Miranda and established for himself a vital network of social support, but he anticipates and accepts his coming loss of influence and power gracefully. Far from being a source of caregiver stress to those around him, Prospero never distresses those he loves. During the magical masque Prospero stages for the young lovers, Ferdinand exclaims, "Let me live here ever! / So rare a wondered father and a wife / Makes this place Paradise" (4.1.122–124).

Instead of mishandling his considerable powers, Prospero displays great wisdom, both by not relinquishing "this rough magic" (5.1.50) until after his stratagems for retirement are complete and guaranteed, and by not foolishly attempting to retain his power beyond what is reasonable to his situation. As a result, along with his secure social environment, Prospero enjoys the absence of ageist biases against him during the play. All of these actions, as we shall see, place him in marked contrast with Lear.

Prospero owes his excellent social situation to his equally impressive level of psychological health. Also, as in the case of the well elder at the GET

Clinic, he is active mentally, with his reasoning, language skills, and judgment all preserved. His mastery of white magic has come about as a consequence of intense, lifelong study, and his current ability to manipulate his knowledge is no fluke or series of cheap tricks. Rather, Prospero's magic is an apt symbol of human perception and intelligence. However, Prospero's ultimate act of reasoned thinking comes when, at the height of his power over his enemies, he forgives the serious crimes they have committed against him (5.1.25-28). Such discretion strikes one as the act of a vigorous and alert elder applying the accumulated abilities and experiences of a lifetime to the circumstances at hand. Moreover, Prospero's personality and behavior remain stable throughout the play. We have the impression that even with the loss of his dukedom suffered at midlife, during his retirement in Milan Prospero will enjoy ample satisfaction while reviewing his time on earth.

At the same time, however, we must resist the urge to believe that Shakespeare has given us in Prospero a portrait of an unrealistic super-ager. A certain sadness colors his outlook. For example, when Miranda finally sees the crowd of humans her father has brought onto their island—for the most part a pack of usurpers and would-be murderers—she exults, "O wonder! / How many goodly creatures are there here! / How beauteous mankind is! O brave new world / That has such people in 't!" while Prospero retorts ironically to his daughter's enthusiasm, "'Tis new to thee" (5.1.184–187). Prospero seems to realize that no matter how much he provides for his child, certain hard lessons of life will have to be learned on her own. Nonetheless, Prospero's emotional state is one of sadness at life changes, not one of disabling depression. Prospero feels the effects of advancing age, but does not succumb to them.

Similarly, Prospero experiences mild forgetfulness. This occurs in act four, scene one, during the performance of the masque, when Prospero remembers Caliban's rebellion: "I had forgot that foul conspiracy/ Of the beast Caliban and his confederates/ Against my life. The minute of their plot/ Is almost come" (4.1.139–142). His realization brings the magic show to an abrupt end, so much so that Ferdinand comments, "Your father's in some passion/ That works him strongly," to which Miranda replies, "Never till this day/ Saw I him touched with anger so distempered" (4.1.143–145). One might believe that the source of her father's distemper is the coming attempt on his life. Yet given the overwhelming power of Prospero's magic and the manner with which it effortlessly solves every crisis of the play, rendering Caliban's attempted murder harmless, and given the fact that earlier in the play Prospero demonstrated his full appreciation of this subhuman servant's capacity for foul deeds, a better explanation of Prospero's troubled mood seems in order. Is Prospero experiencing memory problems, or perhaps difficulty tracking the complex workings of his own machinations? Is Prospero showing signs of age? After all, one's assassination hardly seems the kind of event likely to slip one's mind. Ariel not only hesitates to remind Prospero of it, but winds up having to bring his master up to speed on the details:

> ARIEL   I thought to have told thee of it, but I feared
>   Lest I might anger thee.
> PROSPERO Say again, where didst thou leave these varlets?
> ARIEL   I told you, sir, they were red-hot with drinking. (4.1.168–171)

At this relatively late point in the play, and at this critical juncture when Prospero begins to draw all of his various strategies to a climax, Shakespeare unmistakably interjects the impasse of aging into Prospero's character. The magician explains his disquiet to Ferdinand thus: "Sir, I am vexed. / Bear with my weakness. My old brain is troubled. / Be not disturbed with my infirmity" (4.1.158–160). Not only is this incident the first sign of difficulty or lack of control on Prospero's part, but it is also the first mention in the play of his being old. By "my weakness" and "my infirmity," Prospero likely—in fact, probably—refers to his age. For the remainder of the play, Prospero continues to be self-conscious about his age and approaching death. If nothing else, this awareness gives his retirement planning a poignant sense of urgency. Yet at the same time Prospero's memory impairment and slowed thinking are not sufficient to interfere with daily living.

Thus, as in our GET Clinic case study of the eighty-year-old man living near his daughter, Prospero enters into his retirement socially and psychologically fit, physically active and healthy, and functionally independent. He betrays no debilitating problems with fatigue, eating, sleeping, memory, thinking, or mood. We can imagine Prospero continuing his love of books and study in retirement, receiving visits at his Milan palace from Miranda and his grandchildren, and maybe even conjuring up a bit of his old magic to rewire a cloister on the manor grounds. If he climbs a ladder during the work, he may complain of back pain; otherwise, nothing but preventive care is indicated.

Case 2: The Frail Elder

An eighty-three-year-old male with a history of hypertension, osteoarthritis, and mild visual and hearing impairment was brought to the Duke GET Clinic by his daughter because of declining functional status and concerns about inadequate care by other family members. The patient was well until two to three years prior to the appointment when he developed a gradual, progressive decline in memory, intellectual performance, and orientation. He became unable to manage his financial affairs, prepare meals, do housework, drive, and recently needed prompting for dressing and bathing. Episodes of nighttime confusion and agitation were common. The daughter was concerned about his safety because of his wandering out of the house at night and the lack of adequate supervision. At times the patient responded to his cognitive decline with some sadness and crying spells, but no melancholia or anhedonia. There were no focal neurological symptoms, history of stroke, or alcohol use. Current medications included hydrochlorothiazide and ibuprofen, although medication compliance was questionable.

The patient was a retired teacher from a well-to-do family with significant financial resources; he was also an esteemed member of the community. He was widowed and had three children. Two children were intermittently living in and out of the patient's house, but they provided no care or psychological support. They had spent considerable amounts of the patient's money, until the other daughter obtained power of attorney and took over her father's financial affairs. Friends in the community would check on the patient regularly, although at times he did not recognize them. The daughter at the appointment lived in a distant city and tried to take care of her father's affairs at long distance, but this situation and conflicts with her siblings had become too stressful. The patient's physical exam was remarkable for mildly elevated blood pressure, poor hygiene, dry scaling skin and hair, and small scattered bruises on his extremities. His neurological exam showed mildly diminished visual and auditory acuity: otherwise, normal cranial nerves were evident, as were normal strength, sensation, reflexes, coordination, gait, and balance. The patient showed an inability to carry out motor commands (apraxia). His mental status examination revealed memory impairment, disorientation, diminished verbal fluency, inability to perform calculations, and impaired writing and spelling. Mini-mental status exam score was 15/30. He was alert, followed commands appropriately, and had full range of affect. After brain imaging and metabolic work-up, the diagnostic impression was dementia, probable Alzheimer's disease. The plan was to move the patient to a supervised living environment to assist with impaired basic and instrumental ADLs and to ensure his safety.

Lear as Shakespeare's Frail Elder

As in *The Tempest*, considerable political debate resonates in *King Lear*. However, unlike the situation in Shakespeare's romance, politics take a back seat to issues of aging in Shakespeare's tragedy. Whereas Prospero astutely negotiates reentry into a public domain to affect security for his old age, Lear blunders his way from public sway to a solitary, private death. Lear's personal catastrophe in the grips of old age forms the main action of the play.

Prospero's ideal retirement planning and tender concern for his daughter differ sharply from Lear's disastrous retirement planning and turbulent emotions directed at his daughters. Wisely, Prospero relinquishes his power after his retirement is assured and prepares Miranda for an independent life. Foolishly, Lear surrenders his power before his retirement is secure and attempts to saddle his children, Cordelia in particular, with the onerous task of tending to a rash old man (Asp 1986, 202). Whereas Prospero goes to great lengths to make sure that Ferdinand is a worthy match for Miranda, Lear, once Cordelia refuses to play his senseless game of flattery, will have nothing to do with his youngest daughter's marriage, even refusing Cordelia her dowry. While Prospero moves from cell to palace, thus arranging an appropriate environment for his retirement, Lear backslides during the play from palace to heath to hovel to prison cell to grave. Along the way he loses his network of family and friends, his financial security, a safe home environment, and any sense of life satisfaction—all things that Prospero regains. Neither does Lear concern himself with smoothly passing on the business of life to the next generation or accepting the loss of influence and power gracefully. Instead, he seeks to continue to enjoy the privilege of power but without the responsibility of power, divesting himself of the burden of rule while maintaining the entitlement of power and status. This scheme includes the retired king's unworkable plan of alternately descending on Goneril's and Regan's households with his retinue of one hundred knights for prolonged and costly stays. By far the most poignant difference between Prospero and Lear, however, is the fact that the former is in complete control of what is going on around him, while the latter abjectly has lost control of the course of his later life.

The most striking feature of the play is how rapidly Lear's social support deteriorates. As in the GET Clinic case study of the frail elder, Lear's increasing isolation results from a tragic combination of cognitive impairment, caregiver stress, and generational conflict. However, these things are difficult to disentangle, making it impossible to determine which came first. The play begins with the king making a series of very bad decisions. Not only does he intend to divide his kingdom in three, but worse still, he pits his three daughters against each other in a contest of love. Henceforth, Lear's judgment becomes only more reckless. He disowns Cordelia when she refuses to be obsequious. He banishes his loyal retainer, Kent, for speaking the truth about Lear's folly in disowning Cordelia. At the close of act one, scene one, the stage is set for Lear's downward social spiral, but we have no very clear notion as to *why* this descent into the horrors of old age is to occur. Filled with terror and pity, we can only watch it happen.

Because of Lear's actions, Cordelia experiences an unparalleled caregiver burden. Expatriated at the beginning of the play, by the end Lear's only loving child has mobilized a French army solely for the purpose of rescuing her father from her sisters. For a brief time she is able to retrieve and care for the ailing Lear, but when her army is defeated by the forces of Goneril and Regan, Cordelia is hung. A magnified version of the conscientious daughter from our clinical illustration of poor aging, Cordelia likewise finds managing both her father's affairs and conflicts with her siblings too arduous at long distance. However, when Cordelia tries to place her father in safe surroundings, she herself is destroyed. Perhaps the most pitiable victim of Lear's poor aging is not himself, but his youngest daughter, "my poor fool" (5.3.311) as he refers to Cordelia. In her role as primary caregiver, Cordelia behaves too virtuously for her own good in this imperfect world. Many primary caregivers today suffer this same dilemma between love and duty toward an elderly relative on one hand, and the unfairness of an impossible burden on the other. Yet even Lear's unloving children undergo strain when dealing with their father. Lear's Fool chides the old king for having "mad'st thy daughters thy mothers" (1.4.169–170).

Of all the actions by Lear, perhaps his scheme to time-share the hospitality of his remaining daughters contributes most to his collapsing network of support. Goneril is the first to feel the onus of providing care for her old father. She complains,

> Every hour
> He flashes into one gross crime or other
> That sets us all at odds. I'll not endure it.
> His knights grow riotous, and himself upbraids us
> On every trifle. (1.3.4–8)

Whether her assertions are well-founded or not—and, given Lear's supercilious attitude early in the play, it seems plausible for him to display such behavior—when Goneril reproaches Lear for his improper conduct and tells him to act his age, Lear explodes in anger, curses his daughter, and swears to reassume his station as king: "Thou shalt find/ That I'll resume the shape which thou dost think/ I have cast off forever" (1.4.306–308). His threat only fuels the fire of Goneril's resentment, not to mention her anxiety to acquire and maintain power. Lear withdraws to Regan's house where, by conspiracy of the daughters, he finds no better welcome and soon is reduced to begging for Regan's indulgence and care. Soon after that he finds himself homeless.

Yet along with caregiver stress, Goneril and Regan are even more notable for gerontophobia directed against Lear. At the end of the play's opening scene, amazed by events initiated by their father, the sisters worriedly confer:

> GONERIL You see how full of changes his age is; the
> observation we have made of it hath not been little.
> He always loved our sister most, and with what poor
> judgment he hath now cast her off appears too grossly.
> REGAN 'Tis the infirmity of his age. Yet he hath ever
> but slenderly known himself.
> GONERIL The best and soundest of his time hath been but rash. Then
> must we look from his age to receive
> not alone the imperfections of long-ingraffed condition, but
> therewithal the unruly waywardness that in
> firm and choleric years bring with them.
> REGAN Such unconstant starts are we like to have from him as this of
> Kent's banishment. (1.1.292–304)

From the point of view of his acquisitive daughters, even though Lear appears always to have been prone to hasty determinations, this magnitude of bad judgment seems suddenly new to him. More seriously, they judge these fresh examples of "unruly waywardness" to be a direct result of his old age—Lear is over eighty—and thus more than the product of the "long-engrafted condition" of his youthful impulsiveness. Goneril and Regan fret that as a choleric personality to begin with, Lear will become intolerable as old age continues. Are they right, or is Lear a victim of ageism? Would they draw the same conclusion about Lear's decisions had he been forty? More to the point, would they have dared conspire against him had he been a younger man? We are faced with a chicken and an egg dilemma here—perhaps Shakespeare's intention. Lear behaves foolishly, motivated by concerns that the playwright seems uninterested in making clear to us. At the same time, Goneril and Regan (and eventually Edmund in his plot against Edgar and Gloucester) readily convince themselves that they are at the mercy of an exploitative elder, and eagerly set about to satisfy their greed. But which came first, Lear's imperious manner or Goneril and Regan's fear of the elderly? Whatever the answer, this opening misintelligence drives the fatal action of the rest of the drama. To protect themselves, the sisters resolve to strip their father as quickly as possible of the power and status he has reserved for himself. Their actions, of course, send Lear deeper into his tailspin. Similar dynamics seem to be at work in the relationship between the eighty-three-year-old man of the Duke case study and the two children who exploit his weakened condition. Shakespeare's tragedy is set into motion, therefore, if not by generational conflict, then by extreme generational misapprehension (Donow 1994, 75–76). In this atmosphere, the lethal elements of rational disorder, caregiver burden, and ageism fester. The collision of frail age with callous or conscientious youth triggers mistrust, rage, and torment.

Along with failing family support, Lear suffers the loss of the larger community as well. As friends concerned for the king's welfare, Kent loses his place at court and Gloucester is brutally blinded by Lear's enemies. Without these powerful retainers, Lear has no chance of preserving his status even as a retired king. Thus Lear's original retirement plan of subdividing his kingdom culminates in debacle. Before he himself expires, probably from sheer physical and emotional exhaustion, he sees all of his children killed and his kingdom rent by factionalism and left leaderless: Lear's privation is overwhelming. Gone is his power, status, money, social network, home, and life. Whereas Prospero regains in his old age all that was taken from him in his youth, all that Lear ever attained in his youth he loses in his old age.

Finally, just as Prospero benefits from his preserved mental health, Lear suffers from numerous psychological difficulties. We have already seen that his reasoning and his judgment are questionable. Similarly, his personality and behavior become increasingly erratic. Emotionally, Lear cannot help but fall into disabling depression and despair over the turn of events he suffers. Perhaps most important, Lear develops significant cognitive impairment that has many of the features of delirium in the elderly (Fogan 1989; Lipowski 1989).

Throughout acts one and two, even though Lear displays poor judgment and becomes increasingly angry, he is neither cognitively impaired nor delusional. Lear develops symptoms of delirium only in act three, scene four, when, during the chaos of the tempestuous night, he encounters Edgar disguised as Tom, a Bedlam beggar in the hovel. At this point, Lear becomes disoriented, unable to attend to conversations and events around him, and irrationally self-absorbed. Despite Kent's telling him flatly that Tom "hath no daughters, sir" (3.4.68), Lear engages in a rambling conversation with the beggar, insisting that, like himself, Tom has been brought to this horrible state by ungrateful daughters. When we see Lear again two scenes later, in the company of his Fool and the madman Edgar/Tom, the old king has become detached from reality. He is disoriented concerning time and place, floats at random amid past events, and appears to hallucinate, uttering such remarks as "The little dogs and all, / Tray, Blanch, and Sweetheart, see, they bark at me," and "Make no noise, make no / noise. Draw the curtains. So, so. We'll go to supper / i' the morning" (3.6.61–62, 82–84). When Gloucester enters asking where he can find the king, Kent replies, "Here, sir, but trouble him not; his wits are gone" (3.6.87). Probably, Lear has been reduced to this state by severe emotional and physical distress: Cordelia seemingly has rejected him; Goneril and Regan have turned him out of doors; before finding the hovel for shelter, he has endured the violence of the storm.

The development of Lear's confusional episode at night suggests "sundowning": nighttime confusion commonly seen in frail elders (Rowe and Kahn 1987; Besdine, Dicks, and Rowe 1990). After sunrise, Lear slowly regains normal cognition. In act four, scene six, we find Lear wandering the early morning fields crowned with weeds and flowers. In his encounter with Edgar and Gloucester, Lear initially seems to spout non sequiturs similar to those he voiced in the hovel the night before. However, it quickly becomes evident that his monologues betray not confusion, but estimable social and existential insight (e.g., "Through tattered clothes small vices do appear; / Robes and furred gowns hide all" [4.6.164–165]. Soon Edgar marvels at Lear's declarations: "o, matter and impertinency mixed, / Reason in madness!" (4.6.174–175). Lear then correctly recognizes Gloucester (who, unlike Edgar and Kent, is not in disguise) and even seems to contemplate revenge (4.6.176–180). Once Lear comes under Cordelia's care, where he sleeps long and is dressed in fresh clothing, his understanding and orientation revive for the remainder of the play: "Where have I been? Where am I? Fair daylight?/ I am mightily abused. I should ev'n die with pity/ To see another thus" (4.7.53–57).

Once more in the daylight and under proper care, Lear immediately recognizes Cordelia and, although shaky, quite logically wonders if somehow he has been brought to safety in France. Not simply recovery, however, Lear's cognizance is in fact better than it was before his episode of delirium. Suddenly, the old king has a clearer picture of *himself* as well:

> I am a very foolish fond old man,
> Fourscore and upward, Not an hour more nor less;
> And, to deal plainly,
> I fear I am not in my perfect mind.
> . . . You must bear with me.
> Pray you now, forget and forgive.
> I am old and foolish. (4.7.61–64, 88–90)

As in our GET Clinic case study of the frail elder, Lear's retirement is marred by mental, emotional, and physical decline, as well as by functional dependence. By play's end, Lear relies entirely on others to maintain his activities of daily living as well as preserve his physical safely.

Discussion

The principle of aged heterogeneity motivates Shakespeare's tragedy of unfortunate aging in *King Lear* and his romance of opportune aging in *The Tempest*. It seems that Shakespeare recognizes and dramatically represents the variability of aging as a basic human fact, and analysis of other elderly characters in his plays, such as Falstaff, Polonius, Shylock, and a host of others, would confirm this supposition. Of course, the concept of individuality among the elderly is not completely new. The sixteenth-century French doctor Andreas Laurentius maintained that old age was not strictly chronological; many people will be old at forty, he remarks, while many others will still seem young at sixty (Smith 1976, 235). Laurentius's treatise on old age was translated into English in 1599, and could thus have influenced current views on aging during the Elizabethan period. Simple observation of differences in well-being among the elderly could also have informed Shakespeare's portraits of old age. Therefore, we should not be surprised if the methods of current geriatric practice yield positive results when applied to his plays. In the end, we must marvel less at Shakespeare's ability to portray the phenomenon of aging in a way that conforms to the discoveries of modern-day scientific analysis, and more at his capability to teach us about the process of aging four hundred years after he wrote. In *The Tempest*, he shows us that it is possible to age well. In *King Lear*, he demonstrates that old age may be fraught with suffering and particularly that the clash of insensitive youth with frail age is deadly. As a playwright, Shakespeare not only understands the complexities of aging and knows how to depict them accurately on stage, he also exhibits his customary artistic mastery when applying that knowledge to achieve breathtaking dramatic effect.

Yet what more can be drawn from these poignant, centuries-old case studies of human aging? As a geriatric clinician or gerontological researcher, why bother to read Shakespeare? One compelling reason is that Shakespeare provides a dramatic framework for the teaching of geriatrics by illuminating the events and lives of aged characters. For example, students of geriatrics and gerontology would be usefully humbled when wrestling with the confounding muddle of Lear's case history. They would be exercised in trying to solve a problem which appears to have no clear solution; they would be made alert and sympathetic to the fundamental obscurity of how each of us ages; they would cultivate a critical habit of investigation that precludes facile assumptions about the elderly. Reading Shakespeare's dramatic depictions of aging, as well as similar literary representations of the aging experience, would serve in these ways as a potent and beneficial educative tool (Holstein 1994, 822). Particularly as a training device for clinical assessment procedures, Shakespeare's plays could act as an eye-opening, sensitizing means to humanize patients for the clinical student. Health-care professionals would learn to read their aged clients not as mere biological systems in decline, but as human individuals undergoing physical, mental, social, and, most important, personalized crisis. *King Lear*, in particular, might act vividly as a heuristic device helping doctors and staff recognize various characteristics of aging in clinical practice (Holstein 1994, 824).

Another reason to study Shakespeare emerges from the realm of semiotics, the study of language as a sign system. Human lives are in essence stories, narratives composed minute by minute. Language not only colors but creates our individual realities (Eagleton 1983, 127–150; Norris 1982, 18–41). The case study, a language-bound life narrative, is essential to geriatric practice as a problem-solving tool and to gerontological inquiry as a window onto normative aging. In this chapter, we have presented two very different types of case studies, each endeavoring to capture, summarize, and explain a human being faced with the vagaries of aging. One kind of narrative contains routine clinical case studies from the Duke Geriatric Evaluation and Treatment (GET) Clinic, somewhat abbreviated for considerations of space, but nonetheless actual examples of a well elder and a frail elder. The other kind of narrative has been Shakespearean drama, specifically two plays in which the aging process figures vitally in the story of the main characters. Our question regarding these two types of narrative accounts of aging is simple. Which account is more useful, more true to life: the clinical study or the Shakespeare play? One might assume that the GET Clinic case studies are more scientific, more "factual"; after all, Shakespeare writes fiction. Yet *are* the medical case studies in fact better attuned to the reality of the human condition as we age? For example, both accounts presented of the frail elder are distressing. However, we submit that the GET Clinic life narrative is even more frightening, and in some ways more tragic, than Shakespeare's *King Lear*. The clinical case study tersely and dispassionately observes the bare circumstances of a human life in decline. In that narrative, a human being subtly becomes deindividualized as "an eighty-three-year-old man," "the patient," "an esteemed member of the community," "widowed and had three children," and finally "probable Alzheimer's disease." His personhood as well as his lived experience are minimized, even marginalized, a phenomenon accomplished with words alone. As a result of this taxonomical approach, treatment of the elderly individual inevitably will tend toward conventionalization. No matter how well intended, labels inherently dehumanize and, in a real sense, victimize those to whom they refer. Labeling may cause us to conveniently neglect to deal with people as complete and complex human beings. Once this branding happens, we no longer see people; instead, we see categories, groupings, even commodities. This process should be sobering, frightening, and pitiable to us all.

Shakespeare's play, on the other hand, forces us to contemplate the individual human inside the "frail elder." *King Lear* explores in detail the psychological and social factors of aging, the political and economic elements of the aging Lear's life, even the unknowable pieces to his private puzzle. Lear exemplifies the sheer mystery of aging. The play urges us to view aging not as a scientific, rational, and quantifiable process but as something vexing, enigmatic, and endlessly intricate. Madness is not a satisfactory explication of the character of Lear. Lear is not insane; he is old. In *King Lear*, we witness the awesome phenomenon of a single aging person. Moreover, in this portrait, Shakespeare directs our attention to matters fundamental to the human experience. Disturbingly and unscientifically, these matters lead not to certainty and convenient categorization with regard to growing old, but to open-ended, unmanageable, even insoluble questions about human aging.

We contend that grappling with rather than ignoring the individuality of aging brings with it a wealth of clinical and research benefits. It teaches us not to dehumanize the aging person as the Other; it encourages us to take into account the whole life, not just the old life; it enables us to admit ambiguity into our assessment of the aging process; and it provides us with a powerful hedge against ageism (Holstein 1994, 822–823, 825–826). Above all, concern with the individuality of aging yields better care for the elderly individual. Of course, no one expects the clinician or researcher to assess and write up the individual ager with the ardor and linguistic sophistication that Shakespeare lavishes on his imaginary characters. Science and medicine demand a high level of regimen and standardization in order to function effectively. Unlike literary critics who can afford to throw up their hands stoically when faced with the semiotic unknowability of dramatic creations, clinicians must often act within an informational abyss in an effort to administer help to the real human beings in need. To some extent, systematic assessment makes those difficult decisions possible. Yet are such life narratives as accurate as they could be? Are aged individuals most effectively treated as types and statistical probabilities? In an era of managed health care when the initiative and innovative spark of the individual practitioner is increasingly monitored and reduced while at the same time patients become ever more objectified, such a functional humanistic application of Shakespeare to medical practice and erudition seems more germane than ever.

CHAPTER 3

Why? versus Why Not?: Potentialities of Aging in Shaw's *Back to Methuselah*

Lagretta Tallent Lenker

I abandon the legend of Don Juan with its erotic associations and go back to the legend of the Garden of Eden. I exploit the external interest of the philosopher's stone which enables men to live forever.

(Shaw 1970a, 5. 339)

For England, the question of what "to do" about an increasingly long-lived population has generated a search for a philosopher's stone of sorts ever since the age of the trade guilds. This issue most often disregarded dreams of immortality and took tangible form in debates about practical assistance for the elderly, what we now know as a pension. As with any discussion of entitlements, contentiousness characterized the debate, and momentum fluctuated between calls for a public- or a private-sector solution to the problems of the aged. Public outcry demanding attention to old-age poverty and isolation escalated in the late Victorian era, and once and future notables such as Sidney Webb, Charles Booth, and Joseph Chamberlain joined the fray (Quadagno 1982, 176–179). Characteristically, Herbert Stead delivered impassioned appeals: "For the worn-out worker, man or woman, who has helped to build the fabric of your national life, demand not charity, but justice. . . . How many homes have been broken up, how many an aged toiler has been cast into the dungeon of the workhouse, how many an aged heart has broken, how many multitudes of hoary heads have gone down with sorrow to the grave, how many have slowly starved to death — for want of the pension that might have been theirs." (Quadagno 1982, 197, 170). In 1893, elder problems warranted a royal commission to consider the institution of a pension. Two years later this commission "reported that the situation of the aged poor was extremely serious, but it could not agree on a single solution" (p. 179). The Victorian belief in thrift and self-reliance underlay much of the resistance to the institution of a pension; most Victorians suspected that character flaws in the individual resulted in destitution in old age (p. 180).

Against this backdrop of consternation about aging and a myriad of other issues, the Fabian Society entered the scene. Founded on the principle that the surest revolution comes by change from within the system, the Fabians attempted to influence public policy on concerns ranging from free trade to women's rights (see *Fabian Essays in Socialism*; Shaw [1889] 1961). Although primarily driven by other matters, prominent Fabians repeatedly acknowledged the problems of an aging population. The Fabian Annie Besant expressed the views of many when she averred, "It should be added that children and workers incapacitated by age or sickness should receive an equal share with the communal employees. As all have been children, are at times sick, and hope to live to old age, all in turn would share the advantage; and it is only just that those who have labored honestly in health and maturity should enjoy the reward of labor in sickness and through old age" ([1889], 1961, 204–205). Finally, thanks to the efforts of many groups, including the Fabians and other concerned individuals, a coalition of the Liberal government and organized labor persuaded Parliament to pass the Old Age Pensions Act in 1909, which paid "5 shillings a week to all British subjects of age 70 whose income did not exceed 26s a year." However, applicants had to prove that they were not lunatics and had not received poor relief since January of 1908. These qualifications provided another source of great tension and were finally removed in 1919 (Quadagno 1982, 188).

Despite the volatility and importance of aging issues, the Fabian essayist and activist Bernard Shaw left the practical issues of daily existence to his colleagues, while asserting the need for philosophical underpinnings for the redistribution of wealth, especially old age pensions (Shaw [1889] 1961, 196). He frequently stated that financial support in old age did not solve the problems of the elderly, even arguing in his characteristically overstated style that a year's traveling in youth was more beneficial than an old age pension (pp. 186–187).

However, political and historical analyses do not constitute the only record of the debate over age-related matters. Always an influence on contemporary social issues, literature also reflected the social tenor of the times on aging issues. Writers such as Charles Dickens and Samuel Butler give us bleak portraits of the cruel existence of the elderly, a fact of life often romanticized through the filter of the Victorian gaze (Quadagno 1982, 1). However, like Dickens and Butler, Shaw was no romantic. Despite his relative reticence in addressing aging issues in his essays, his dramatic treatments of aging are both important and profound and display what Harry R. Moody (1988) terms the "dialectic of aging," dramatizing the pleasures and the perils of later life.

Unsurprisingly, Shaw's fictions reveal more social relevance than the writings of those who sentimentally depict aging and the aged. Shaw also explores alternatives to the "normal" aging process, a notion that places him characteristically ahead of his time. Indeed, sixty-eight years after Shaw wrote *Back to Methuselah*, his magnum opus on aging, the renown gerontologist W. Andrew Achenbaum (1989) averred, "If we are to understand and realize the potential that is associated with the 'third quarter of life,' . . . we must systematically investigate the physical, intellectual, interpersonal, structural, and cultural factors that inhibit and facilitate growth in later years. Literature provides a wonderful laboratory for such gerontological research" (p. xxi). I think Shaw would agree and would be pleased.

Many critical interpretations of these fictional portrayals of the aging process fall into categories established by Anne Wyatt-Brown (1992): "The material published so far in literary gerontology can be divided into the following categories. Briefly, they consist of (1) analyses of literary attitudes toward aging; (2) humanistic approaches to literature and aging; (3) psychoanalytic explorations of literary works and their authors; (4) applications of gerontological theories about autobiography, life review, and midlife transitions; and (5) psychoanalytically informed studies of the creative process" (p. 332). From his own social policy, however, Shaw fashions a sixth category, a futuristic glimpse of what is possible concerning aging. His work evolves into a blend of art and politics that resembles the contemporary critical theory referred to as new historicism/cultural materialism. Shaw, the Fabian, realized that what humanity has created could be modified, even changed (his Fabian pronouncements form much of the Preface to *Back to Methuselah*). Shaw, the artist, was aware of the expressive relationship between drama and social/cultural phenomenon and the generation of energy that both produce (Holroyd 1991, 35). Similarly, the contemporary theorist Edward Said intuits that all texts are "worldly, to some degree they are events, . . . they are . . . a part of the social world, human life, and . . . the historical moments in which they are located and interpreted" (Waxman 1990, 3). Moody's stance is even stronger, insisting that "culture and literary art can be used for various purposes, including . . . social criticism and putting forward alternative images of aging" (Cole et al. 1993, xxxii).

One tenet of new historicist/cultural materialist criticism asks the question, "Does art mirror life or does life mirror art?" In the case of Shaw, the answer is "yes" to both. Shaw's dramas inform and are formed by the social fabric of the late Victorian and early twentieth-century eras, weaving a complicitous critique, a reciprocal arrangement whereby the plays both comment on the times in which Shaw worked and simultaneously shape the discourses and ideologies of those times. From a new historicist perspective, therefore, the dramas of Shaw are active participants in the social, cultural, and even political "marketplaces," not idealized artistic icons that transcend the cultural milieu of their original context. Critics sometimes describe new historicism as a process, not a theory. This process involves considering literary works from the perspective of actual events occurring during the period in which the work was created. For Shaw, those predominant historical events include the seemingly endless debates over old-age pensions, society's proper treatment of the elderly, and the Darwinian/Neo-Darwinian theories of evolution. Accordingly, new historicism helps us to understand that often society's "sacred cows," our universal truths are, in reality, historically specific social constructs, the by-products of men's and women's attempts to cope with their own environments and the institutions of their social milieu. By providing a mechanism for the observation of these institutions over time, new historicism interrogates our most ingrained essentialist notions—even those time-honored shibboleths about the inevitability and negativity of the aging process.

Shaw uses his art in exactly this societal manner. Early in his dramatic career, Shaw states, "But 'for art's sake' alone I would not face the toil of writing a single sentence" (1970d, 2: 527). His hallmark is the discussion play, wherein he utilizes his dramatic skills to examine an idea or social problem. For my purposes, three Shavian works embody the range of Shaw's fascination with aging. *Heartbreak House* proffers both positive and negative aspects of aging in the eighty-year-old Captain Shotover. Confounded by his adult daughters, this patriarch must resort to rum and to a fantastic facade of a ship inside his home to maintain his identity as a master of the sea. Yet Ellie, the young friend of his daughter Hesione, finds in Shotover the "life with a blessing" that she has sought unsuccessfully in younger men. *Heartbreak House* thus presents both the bane and the blessing of aging while suggesting that Shotover's old age is "horrible," not because of his long life but because the creative potential of this life is frustrated by a destructive society. Conversely, Shaw's formula for healthy aging is embodied in his portrait of Caesar. *Caesar and Cleopatra* dramatizes in the male protagonist the closest Shaw ever comes to a perfect synthesis. Smashing and transcending society's stereotypes, Caesar becomes an unassuming, self-deprecating titan who can laugh at himself and his aging humanity while performing feats worthy of a superman. *Back to Methuselah*, however, constitutes Shaw's tour de force on aging. Shaw calls the epic drama his "contribution to the modern Bible" (1970a, 5: 269), subtitling the work "A Metabiological Pentateuch." In his fanciful way, in 1921 Shaw anticipated what humanistic gerontologists expound today, seventy-five years later. In his preface to *Back to Methuselah*, Shaw declares that for certain organisms, "death is neither natural nor inevitable" (5: 268). He posits that, given the varying nature of "man's" lifetime, death at a certain age, usually seventy years, should not be accepted as natural. (Although a dedicated feminist, Shaw lived at a time when the generic masculine term was used to designate the entire human race. I use Shaw's term while putting it in quotes.) He also demonstrates quite graphically that modern "man" does not live enough to reach his potential. These concepts are embedded in Shaw's drama of age.

Shaw himself hails *Back to Methuselah* as an "important and even extraordinary work" and promises that it would "interest biologists, religious leaders, and lovers of the marvelous in fiction as well as lovers of the theatre." He further insists, "It is [my] scientific, religious, and political testament as well as [my] supreme exploit in dramatic literature" (Holroyd 1991, 32). Others have been less impressed. Stanley Hall ([1922] 1972), writing about the aging process in 1922, dismisses Shaw's self-proclaimed masterpiece as "of no practical import to our age or to the aged" and deems Shaw's ancients as "direct antitheses of Nietzsche's supermen" (pp. 143, 144). The reviewer Marie Stopes pronounces *Back to Methuselah* "harmful to the soul of man," while the seldom-charitable T. S. Eliot blasts *Back to Methuselah*—the adjective "lamentable" is the kindest he could muster (Holroyd 1991, 54). So Shaw, following his own formula for humanity's psycho-social organization, becomes the lonely realist—a visionary among scoffing idealists (Shaw 1986, 48–53). Yet the play proved to be first a literary and, despite its vast length, eventually a qualified theatrical success (Holroyd 1991, 53–59).

Nevertheless, critical debate continues. Literary scholars cannot agree on what the play is "about." For instance, Stanley Weintraub (1971, 293–308) interprets *Back to Methuselah* as an antiwar piece, a critique of our immaturities as a species causing "man's" inhumanity to "man." Margery Morgan (1972, 334) proposes religion as the play's predominant theme; Richard Dietrich (1989, 132) refines this thesis, calling *Back to Methuselah* Shaw's "Old Testament"; John Bertolini (1991) finds the theme of death pervading the drama; and Eric Bentley (1957, 53–62) offers philosophy and religion as the focus of the text. Each of these stellar theorists is guided by the contents of both play and preface. Yet because of space constraints I will concentrate on the dramatic work itself, which undoubtedly is grounded in Shaw's Preface.

One unimpeachable theme of Shaw's magnum opus is the "why not" of the Serpent's speech, the premise that our chronological standards of "old age" are sociological not biological constructs and that human life, as we now know it, has not begun to reach its potential. In each of the play's five parts—the 291-page play (excluding preface and postscript) itself mirrors the eternal nature of Shaw's thesis—major scenes dramatize age as a function of societal and/or individual choice not as a biological given.

Appropriately, Shaw's method for presenting his version of the philosopher's stone is blatant fantasy, an accepted dramatic genre. Shaw not only adopts this mode, which Martin Meisel (1984) labels an "extravaganza," for *Back to Methuselah*, but it serves as his primary genre for subsequent plays until his death. Meisel explains, "In these plays, fantasy is frankly embraced, not only for event and setting but often for the kind of irrational proposition rationally pursued that both Aristophanes and Gilbert used as fundamental comic ideas" (p. 381). However, Shaw was not merely amusing himself and his audience; as usual, he employed drama to make his social arguments more palatable and to gain a wider audience for his ideas (Shaw 1970a, 5: 269). Thus, Shaw exploited accepted theatrical techniques, such as anachronism and extrapolation to score his social points (Meisel 1984, 415). Typically, he also embroidered his very serious treatise with humor, often in the form of exaggeration and overstatement (Dietrich 1989, 110). One of the long-lived characters in Part 2 reveals Shaw's strategy: "Like all revolutionary truths, it [the Archbishop's realization of his own longevity] began as a joke" (Shaw 1970a, 5: 460). Shaw's methods of delivering his social messages almost always exemplify the old maxim that "the truest things are often said in jest."

Part 1, entitled "In the Beginning," considers the concept of how our societal sacred cows came into being. Anticipating contemporary social constructionism, Shaw's underlying message purports that whatever "mankind" has invented is not preordained or an essential part of human nature and therefore can be changed. This first episode deals primarily with Adam and Eve's grapplings with significant issues which have remained significant in both Shaw's day and in our own—life, death, love, hate, and fear. Shaw ingeniously introduces these topics in a manner that not only echoes the Genesis theme but also invokes what has become known as the primary patriarchal prerogative—the act of naming. The Serpent, Shaw's intellectual foil to Adam and Eve, names not only species and things but also emotions and events that constitute human life. Together, these three explore the concepts of "birth," "death," "mother," "fear," and "hope" (Shaw 1970a, 5: 345–356). During this conversation, Shaw deftly suggests the possible origins of our most basic instincts and emotions and how these early constructions affect society today.

In order to underscore the relevance of this early scene to the issues of his own time, Shaw also introduces conversations between Adam, Eve, the Serpent, and, later, Cain that not only comment on topical controversies of his own period but also foreshadow debates that still rage in the twentieth century. Adam and Eve discuss fundamental gender issues such as the division of labor (Shaw 1970a, 5: 364, 369) and the importance of each member of a married couple having a life of one's own (5: 343). Cain "invents" the class system because he wishes for other humans to perform labor that he does not care to do himself (5: 367). Anthropological themes further arise when Cain and his father debate the virtues and benefits of agriculture versus those of hunting (5: 365), an issue contested by anthropologists today. Shaw also allows himself the pleasure of insinuating that one of his ubiquitous themes has been important since the beginning of time, the emergence of the hero or superman (5: 365).

These various conversations frame the main subject of the play, the length of humanity's life span. Set in the Garden of Eden, this act dramatizes Adam's and Eve's delights and despairs at the exploration of their brave new world. In keeping with the play's cyclical and evolutionary structure, Shaw suggests that even the first people had ancestors, that the Ancient Lilith had given Adam and Eve life, an existence to which they were not very well suited.

Accordingly, the play calls into question the rationale for Shaw's philosopher's stone—the very antithesis of today's burning fascination with youth—the enigma of age, what Betty Friedan terms the "Fountain of Age" (1993). Adam and Eve discover the paradox of mortal existence, the desire for immortality balanced against the longing to be relieved of that immortality. Because Adam and Eve expect to live forever, the tediousness of their secure existence becomes apparent. Adam complains of having to endure himself, yet Eve understands the need to preserve human existence, to insure that humanity survives (Shaw 1970a, 5: 343, 358).

Soon, these tensions evoke the need for change, and in Part 1 the characters work out basic evolutionary tenants. The Serpent serves as the link between generations, between Lilith and her progeny, Adam and Eve. The Serpent also becomes a combination temptress/raisonneur, who not only raises interesting questions but also, through her ability to invent names and supply historical facts, supplies plausible answers to these questions. (Shaw himself would have loved to play this part!) Through the Serpent, Adam and Eve learn that, using her mighty will, Lilith had discerned how to perpetuate herself:

I remember Lilith, who came before Adam and Eve. . . . She saw death . . . and she knew then that she must find out how to renew herself. . . . She said it must never be again; that the burden of renewing life . . . was too much for one. And when she cast the skin, lo! There was not one new Lilith but two: one like herself, the other like Adam. (Shaw 1970a, 5: 47)

The discovery that eternal life was unbearable, that the tediousness of life without end was overwhelming, led to the search for a solution whereby Adam and Eve could perpetuate life without immortality for themselves. When the Serpent suggests that they can extend themselves by reproducing, she introduces the concept of generations (Shaw 1970a, 5: 352). Consequently, Adam, in a defining moment, arbitrarily sets the life span: "I will live a thousand years; and then I will die and take my rest" (5: 357).

Another key motif soon appears, this time introduced by Eve: "But is it [1000-year life span] long enough for the other things, the great things?" (Shaw 1970a, 5: 377). This conception of the immaturity of those without centuries of experience reverberates throughout the "metabiological pentateuch." Eve experiences another troublesome thought as she realizes that as a result of hers and Adam's will, "Death is gaining on life" (5: 376). This foreboding manifests itself in the actions and philosophies of their son Cain, the first murderer. These dialectics of life versus death, longing for cessation versus necessity for maturation, are explored in Part 1 and continue into Part 2.

This next stage in the cycle takes place in the time in which Shaw was writing and consequently becomes the most topical and the most problematic for audiences from the 1920s to the present. It also contains some of Shaw's most scathing social criticism: a damning critique of war whereby political leaders accomplish nothing but the killing of their own sons (Shaw 1970a, 5: 437); a harsh indictment of contemporary religion, insisting that life is too short to take religion seriously (5: 381), stressing that contemporary religion is pragmatic enough to suit all points of view (5: 400), and blasting the church of England as over-burdened with bishops and dogma (5: 403); and, finally, a spoof of the puritanical, joyless quality of nineteenth-century science (Morgan 1972, 337). Through this social criticism, Shaw once again demonstrates that "idealists," Shaw's term for the "good people," cause all the trouble (Shaw 1986).

In Part 2, Shaw assembles representatives of early twentieth-century England's most respectable "types" to examine the issue of the human lifespan. Shaw's ensemble includes two prominent scientists (the Brothers Barnabas), a clergyman (Rev. Haslam), two aging politicians (Burge and Lubin — romans à clef for Asquith and David Lloyd George), and a "new woman" (Savvy Barnabas, the daughter, who most nearly represents Shaw's point of view). With the possible exception of Savvy, these characters illustrate the theory of the Barnabas Brothers that humanity has devolved since Adam and Eve, and that "Life is too short for men to take it seriously" (Shaw 1970a, 5: 381). In other words, people currently in power are too immature to guide humanity's destiny throughout the ages (5: 415).

According to one character in the play, humanity has continued down this slippery slope, and this resulting rampant immaturity has caused the present sorry state of affairs — war, political and economic turmoil, and the like. As a compromise between Adam's one-thousand-year lifespan and the 1920s average of sixty to seventy years, the Barnabas Brothers suggest an average lifespan of three hundred years, which should give humanity a sufficient maturation period to understand and govern itself with more responsibility and wisdom (Shaw 1970a, 5: 433). This carefully considered but somewhat arbitrary fixing of the lifespan adumbrates Hendricks's and Leedham's 1989 hypothesis that age is at least a partially constructed phenomenon (Bagnell and Soper 1989, 6, 9). In typical Shavian fashion, the cook and parlor maid in the Barnabas household are the only people besides its inventors who take the theory of long life seriously (Shaw 1970a, 5: 387). The ruling gentry refuse to consider that they lack the maturity and wisdom to perform their duties responsibly. This shortsightedness constitutes a Shavian slap at those responsible for the plight of the poor elderly at that time (Quadagno 1982, 171–190).

Shaw invests Part 2 with suggestions that resonate with humanistic gerontologists today. In his fantastic fashion, Shaw proposes that various disciplines contribute to our definition and understanding of advancing age. Holroyd (1991)credits Shaw with this insight concerning creative evolution: "He [Shaw] wanted to erase the distinction between scientists and imaginative artists" (p. 41). I focus specifically on Shaw's crossdisciplinary perception as it illumines his theories about the human life span and the aging process. In the Preface to Back to Methuselah, Shaw (1970a) posits, "If Man now fixes the term of his life at three score and ten years he can fix it at three hundred or three thousand, or even until a sooner-or-later inevitable accident makes an end" (5: 268–269). Shaw develops this idea in Part 2 when the Brothers Barnabas and others and Burge-Lubin explain the link between art and science regarding the life span lies in the stuff of legend. They declare that the story of the Garden of Eden remains the most scientific document about creation that humankind possesses (1970a, 5: 422–423).

Thus, Shaw foreshadows Friedan and others who believe that the purely clinical approach to aging studies leaves much to be desired. As Thomas Cole (1992a) so eloquently states

[My work] approaches aging with a different epistemological stance—one that strives for contextual understanding and interpretation along with explanation and that considers scientific method to be one way of knowing among others. Again, the humanities have become important in late twentieth-century gerontology precisely because conventional scientific and professional gerontology has retreated into a formal, technical rationality that lacks a shared discourse for addressing moral, aesthetic, and spiritual issues or for appreciating their historical and cultural contexts. (pp. xii–xiii)

Cole's late-twentieth-century declaration shares affinity with Shaw's early twentieth-century, perhaps overstated but still telling maxim that "the poem is our real clue to biological science" (Shaw 1970a, 5: 422).

Part 2 also contains Shaw's deceptively simple formula for extending the life span. While the politicians frantically discuss how to bottle and dispense the "stuff" that prolongs human life, the Brothers Barnabas reveal the real secret—convincingly spread the word that "man" can reach a three-hundred-year life span and soon the long lived will be the norm not the exception. (Shaw 1970a, 5: 432)

This theory conforms to Shaw's notions of creative evolution and the Life Force (see Epistle Dedicatory of *Man and Superman* [1970d 2: 493–530] and Preface to *Back to Methuselah* [1970a 5: 256–339]), a thesis that brought Shaw much scorn from notable contemporaries such as T. S. Eliot (1926), who derided the "potent ju-ju of the Life Force" (p. 389). Nevertheless, today's theorists might be more sympathetic. Betty Friedan (1993) queries, "What do we actually experience as we go through the process of growing old? How much of what we see is imposed by our society's views, how much is self-imposed? . . . There are truly fearful realities reflected—and imposed—by that [society's] image. To break through that image, we must first understand why, how, and by whom it is perpetuated. We must also glimpse some new possibilities and new directions, both as individuals and as a society, that belie that image" (p. 31). These profound questions consumed Shaw while writing his own version of the "fountain of age."

Part 3 of *Back to Methuselah* demonstrates that "the thing"—living until three hundred—can actually happen, at least on stage. In this act, Shaw takes great care to show both the glory and the agony of true old age and illustrates the intergenerational conflicts that may result from such disparity in life spans.

However, as Holroyd (1991) posits, in this section of the play Shaw abandons dramatic action for "bureaucratic rearrangements and technological innovations" (p. 48). Nevertheless, despite the play's dramatic stasis, insights into the aging process—present and future—abound. As Part 3 opens, we are told that England in the year 2170 (Shaw 1970a, 5: 456) is awash in "too-old-at-forty" sentiments (5: 442). Workers must retire at forty-three after thirty years of service, despite rumblings to the contrary. Here, through the ruminations of Burge-Lubin, Shaw forecasts one of our taxing contemporary problems, alluding to the problems of forced retirement, with one being "put out to pasture" before one's time (5: 442).

Yet when the existence of long livers (individuals who live to be approximately three hundred years old) is discovered, the Government's chief concern is of an actuarial nature: Someone who has lived to be two hundred eighty-three years old has drawn two hundred-plus years of unwarranted old-age income! (Shaw 1970a, 5: 451–458). Eventually, as more long livers appear, the discussion shifts to Moody's dialectic of aging and Friedan's two faces of age—the paradox between the detriments and the emancipatory possibilities of old age (Moody 1988, 19; Friedan 1993, 71–103). In exchange for wisdom and maturity (Shaw 1970a, 5: 468), the first long livers relinquish family, friends, and companionship. The two hundred and seventy-five-year-old Mrs. Lutestring (the Barnabas's housemaid of Part 2) explains: "Long life is complicated, even terrible; but it is glorious all the same. I would no more change places with an ordinary woman than with a mayfly that lives only a day" (5: 471). The two hundred and eighty-three-year-old archbishop (recognizable as the Reverend William Haslam) relates the long-lived point of view in the intergenerational conflict: he avers that the "shortlived" are immature in nature, consumed with sexual desire and therefore repugnant to the elders (5: 475). Thus, Part 3 serves as a bridge between the dreams about and the accepted actuality of expanded human life. As Hendricks and Leedham note, "Above all, literature can make people aware of living existence by the fact that things can be otherwise." (Bagnell and Soper 1989, 5). Shaw dramatizes this point relatively subtly in Part 3, while in Part 4 his fantastic imagination blazes forth.

In Parts 2 and 3, the long lived and those who dreamed of long life were in the minority and constituted the "other"—the oddities against which "normal" society reacted. Shaw reverses this pattern in Part 4 as the "short lived," in a holiday spirit and under the guise of seeking wisdom, invade the land of the long livers, set in Galway Bay, Ireland, in A.D. 3000. Holroyd (1991) characterizes this "synopsis of the last one thousand years of history with its emphasis on humankind's tragic wars as the 'weakest' part of Shaw's cycle" (pp. 49–50). However, despite exemplifying Shaw's drama of ideas at its most tedious, Part 4 offers crucial insights for our analysis of Shaw's views on aging. The principal vehicle for these ideas is the debate between the short-lived Elderly Gentleman and his long-lived hosts in Ireland. The Elderly Gentleman, or Daddy as his hosts dub him disparagingly, and the species he represents illustrate in this setting what Laurence McCollough (1994) terms "arrested aging," a phenomenon that occurs when one's circumstances, especially the past, "oblige an individual to become old" (p. 185). Daddy, retired as Chairman of the All-British Synthetic Egg and Vegetable Cheese Trust and now president of the Baghdad Historical Society (Shaw 1970a, 5: 496) and vice-president of the Travellers' Club (5: 500), arrives in the land of the long livers to visit a site of historical importance (5: 511), not, as his hosts expect, to have his mind made flexible (5: 496). Yet as a microcosm of the entire play this section juxtaposes opinions toward the aging process in such a way that increasingly "flexible" attitudes toward the subject of aging emerge. First, the long livers diagnose a "deadly disease called discouragement" as the curse of short livers, especially when they interact with their long-lived counterparts (5: 493). One surmises that this caveat against discouragement is a self-reflexive, autobiographical reference, a comment on the isolation and loneliness Shaw felt personally and saw as the affliction of his peers. According to the long livers, great care should be taken to guard against the often-fatal ravages of discouragement. Life should be full and hopeful—a caution that one suspects Shaw is delivering to humanity in general.

In this section, the theme of intergenerationarity appears once again, as Shaw (1970a) dramatizes the difficulties with communication (5: 494, 520) and the lack of mutual appreciation for the diverse perspectives of those at different stages of the life span (5: 494–495). In a passage that equates age with wisdom, Daddy and his traveling party expect to find sagacity and advice about the future from the famous one hundred and seventy-year-old Oracle (5: 532). Yet despite the assertions of the long lived that one can voluntarily add to his or her life span, when Daddy renounces the insincerity of his own race and implores the Oracle to grant him permission to stay with the long livers, his wish, though granted, does not lead to increased wisdom and longevity. Instead, he dies immediately in an apparent acknowledgment by Shaw that recognition of the inadequacy of the short lived is not enough. One must be vigilant against discouragement and be strong enough to survive its ravages. Those with insufficient stamina will not prevail.

In Part 5, Shaw (1970a) projects the human race into the year 31920 and depicts a society that resembles classical Greece (5: 564). Here other intergenerational struggles occur; artificial life and intelligence are introduced and quickly destroyed; and the human life cycle, now much altered, is depicted. Expanding on the classical setting, Shaw peoples this section of the play with near-mythical figures, thereby underscoring the archetypal significance of the aging process. Jennifer McLerran and Patrick McKee (1991) note the particular importance of archetypes and myths in our artistic and literary depiction of aging: "Like other archetypes, the image of the aging man or woman evokes responses in us which we urgently want to express but which elude direct, literal language. Such responses find their proper expression not in literal statement, but indirectly, through the arts of allegory, myth, and symbol" (p. ix). Shaw employs the archetypal "He and She Ancients," the "Newly Born," and the mythical Pygmalion to depict his version of the final stage of the human life span, a concept that even Shaw's descriptive skill perhaps could not sustain without the power of myth and symbol. While the inhabitants of this otherworldly time and place bear some linguistic and behavioral resemblance to characters in the first four sections, human existence has evolved toward Shaw's concept of the essence of life as pure thought. In this world, life renews itself as humans hatch from eggs fully grown into young adulthood and, if they are among the elect, progress into an "ancient," a person of infinite capacity and a true incarnation of the Life Force. Shaw envisions a world where people would rather study mathematics than enjoy worldly pleasures (5: 625). With pure reason as the ultimate destiny of the human race, Shaw effectively elimi-nates, among other things, the ravages of age on the body.

Shaw also employs archetypes as he returns from the future and completes his circular myth. By briefly reintroducing Adam, Eve, Cain, the Serpent, and Lilith, Shaw assesses the results of the evolutionary Life Force. After mixed reviews from the others, Lilith utters the final words of the play and sounds a hopeful note: "I am Lilith: I brought life into the whirlpool of force, and compelled my enemy, Matter, to obey a living soul. But in enslaving Life's enemy I made him Life's master; for that is the end of all slavery; and now I shall see the slave set free and the enemy reconciled, the whirlpool becomes all life and no matter" (Shaw 1970a, 5: 630–631).

This Shavian extravaganza proves relevant to our contemporary discussion of aging in a number of significant ways. First, Shaw understood that society's ideas about aging (like those on many other important social issues) are a product of our imagination. In other words, even given the inevitability of the aging process (whenever it occurs), our concepts of what happens to one at a certain age and how one should act as a result are largely constructed and therefore can be deconstructed. In the late twentieth century, Friedan (1993, 31) champions this thesis. Second, like today's humanistic gerontologists (Harry Moody and Thomas Cole, for example), Shaw (1970a) also intuited that many disciplines have valid insights into the study of the aging process (5: 422). Finally, Shaw realized that society must search beyond providing the practi-cal accommodations for the aged such as pensions and affordable housing if humankind is to reach its potential. He puts his credo concerning the hu-man lifespan in the mouth of the Serpent in Part 1: "You see things; and you say 'Why?' Always 'Why?' I dream of things that never were; and I say 'Why not?'" (5: 345). This ringing exchange exemplifies the sixth category of liter-ary treatments of aging noted earlier, the visionary hypothesis of future possi-bilities concerning aging. This often-appropriated question has helped to propel individuals to greatness. However, the "why not," or the more phantasmagorical element of Shaw's equation, has confounded Shaw's con-temporaries and his critics regarding *Back to Methuselah*.

Nevertheless, when we examine this complex drama through the filter of aging studies, we realize that Shaw's visionary if outlandish ideas render the play a model for the depiction of alternative approaches to the study of the human life span. In this text, Shaw leaves the mundane analysis of old-age pensions and other quotidian concerns to others. Instead, he insists that our aging humanity can only benefit from rigorous questioning of the accepted norms regarding the aging process. If humanity is to reach the potential of the "fountain of age," we must, with Shaw, encourage less emphasis on the "why?" and more on the "why not?"

CHAPTER 4

Hemingway's Aging Heroes and the Concept of *Phronesis*

Phillip Sipiora

In his introduction to *Men at War*, published in 1942, Ernest Hemingway tells the reader, "Learn about the human heart and the human mind in war from this book" (p. xx). One may well paraphrase this sentiment by stating that there is a great deal to learn about aging successfully in Hemingway's fiction. Ernest Hemingway has long been regarded as a writer who takes an active interest in the teaching function of literature, the process of *docere* that the ancient Greeks considered integral to all good literature. Indeed, a significant body of criticism on Hemingway's works has centered around the well-known "Hemingway Code" — a pragmatic and "good faith" mode of existential behavior, of conducting one's life in accordance with a code of proper conduct, of living virtuously and courageously, and of confronting adversity with grace under pressure.

There are many ways of reading Hemingway and his articulation of values, of course, but one neglected area, in my view, has been reading Hemingway as an overtly rhetorical writer, a writer who employs explicit rhetorical strategies as techniques and themes in structuring and sustaining his narrative style. I would like to propose a rhetorical way of reading some of Hemingway's major works in terms of their profiles of aging heroes. More specifically, I plan to explore aging protagonists in works ranging from the short story, "A Clean Well-Lighted Place," to the novella that won a Nobel prize, *The Old Man and the Sea*.

For much of the past seventy years, a significant portion of Hemingway criticism has focused on certain values of his protagonists: courage, grace under pressure, fidelity to political ideals, self-restraint, temperance, and so forth. Yet there is a recurring value associated with a number of Hemingway "heroes" or "codeholders," who may be relatively minor characters, such as the Counts Mippipopolous and Greffi in *The Sun Also Rises* and *A Farewell to Arms*, as well as major protagonists, such as the Old Waiter in "A Clean Well-Lighted Place" and Santiago in *The Old Man and the Sea*. This value to which I refer is the quality of *phronesis*, usually translated as practical judgment or "judicial thinking." The written record of *phronesis* dates back to the ancient Greeks, particularly Isocrates (436–338 B.C.) and Aristotle (384–322), both of whom emphasized this principle in their respective schools. According to Isocrates ([1929] 1968a), the "wise" individual must always be aware that he or she lives in a contingent universe: "People of intelligence . . . ought not to think that they have exact knowledge of what the result will be, but to be minded towards these contingencies as men who exercise their best judgment" (p. 8). Isocrates ([1929] 1968b) considers the ability to act wisely the mark of education, of individuals "who manage well the circumstances which they encounter day by day, and who possess a [sense of] judgment which is accurate in meeting occasions as they arise and rarely misses the expedient course of action" (pp. 30–31). *Phronesis* in the Isocratean tradition becomes a guiding principle for Hemingway's wise men. According to Aristotle, *phronesis* is a fundamental component of effective rhetoric, of an individual making his or her way in the world. In his *Rhetoric* (1967), Aristotle argues that in order for an individual to give the appearance of *ethos*, or personal integrity, he or she must display practical judgment (or "common sense"). Yet *phronesis* is more than intellectual decision making and more than a rhetorical strategy. According to Aristotle, *Phronesis* is integrally coupled with virtue. In the *Nichomachean Ethics* ([1926] 1982), Aristotle's most systematic treatment of ethics, practical wisdom (or prudence), along with moral virtue, determines humankind's proper function.

What *phronesis* always represents is an understanding of the "ways of the world," an acute sensitivity to a critical logic of human existence that can be attained only through extensive experience and suffering. Paul Baltes and his colleagues (1990) define this special kind of wisdom as "an expert knowledge system in the domain of fundamental life pragmatics" (p. 68). One must come to know value by paying a price, and that existential price buys knowledge of the "real world." To age productively and profitably in the world of Hemingway means to purchase an inner peace that consists of an intuitive system of continuous adjustments to the exigencies of daily living. At its deepest level, *phronesis* produces an emotional peacefulness derived from knowing that one has earned an internal compass through productive aging that always points in the right direction. What is striking about the quality of *phronesis* in the works of Hemingway is that it is so commonly associated with mature characters. Indeed, throughout his fiction, Hemingway reveals a deep reverence for the aged who have acquired *phronesis*, Hemingway's respected gerontes. In describing some aging heroes who exemplify this process, I would like to examine four protagonists who illustrate varying expressions of *phronesis*.

A TALE OF TWO WAITERS

Let me first consider one of Hemingway's most powerful short stories, "A Clean Well-Lighted Place." The plot is relatively uncomplicated. An old patron appears in a café late one night shortly before 2:30 in the morning. He is at least eighty years old. There are two waiters in the café, a young waiter and an old waiter. The aged habitue wants to continue drinking, but the young waiter anxiously urges him to surrender the night, so that the waiters can close up the café and the young waiter can go home to his young wife. However, the old customer is drunk and depressed, so he seeks refuge in a lighted café, away from the confusion, terror, and fear of the darkness outside. We are told that he had tried to hang himself a week earlier, but he is clean, doesn't spill his brandy, and usually leaves a generous gratuity (one might say that he observes a universal code of café patronage.) He comes to the café, a clean well-lighted place, in order to escape the pain of living.

The old waiter is aware that the anguish of living requires a system of rituals, intellectual as well as social, acquired over time, to counteract—or at least resist for a little while—the angst of the always-present abyss. The old waiter commiserates with the suffering of the old man, who needs some brandy in a clean well-lighted café in order to hold at bay the demons of the night. The aging soldiers of the night need one another to survive. In the words of Simone de Beauvoir (1972), "One's life has value so long as one attributes value to the life of others, by means of love, friendship, indignation, compassion" (p. 803). The old waiter has learned through a lifetime of experience that one must acquire antidotes to the emptiness that constitutes human experience: dignity, a certain cleanness, order, a little light to shut out the inner and outer darkness, and, most important, a sensitivity to the suffering of others. This sensibility is what constitutes the old waiter's "earned knowledge."

The young waiter does not understand the old man's *Weltanschauung* and confuses material wealth with emotional security: "'Last week he tried to commit suicide,' one waiter said. 'Why?' 'He was in despair.' 'What about?' 'Nothing.' 'How do you know it was nothing?' 'He has plenty of money'" (Hemingway [1938] 1966, 379). The young waiter, who has experienced little and suffered even less, understands nothing of the pain of the night so familiar to the old waiter and the old patron. The neophyte server, in his inexperience, not only overvalues the importance of financial security, but is also insensitive to the old patron's need for antidotes to the demons of the night. The young waiter twice states his wish that the old man were dead: "The old man looked at him. 'Another brandy,' he said. 'You'll be drunk,' the waiter said. The old man looked at him. The waiter went away. 'He'll stay all night,' he said to his colleague. 'I'm sleepy now. I never get to bed before three o'clock. He should have killed himself last week'" (p. 380).

The waiters are clearly counterpoints to one another, revealing the young waiter's lack of practical wisdom and the old waiter's deeper awareness of the complexities of life. As Carlos Baker (1952) suggests, "The old waiter and the young waiter are in opposition: They stand (by knowledge, temperament, experience, and insight) on either side of one of the great fences which exist in the world" (p. 124). The old waiter, a "reality instructor" to his youthful counterpart, understands the existential dread of the old customer and in an argument with the other waiter vigorously defends the old patron's right to drink late and leisurely in a clean well-lighted place: "'Why didn't you let him stay and drink?' the unhurried waiter asked. 'They were putting up the shutters. 'It is not half-past two.' 'I want to go home to bed.' 'What is an hour?' 'More to me than to him.' . . . 'We are of two different kinds,' the older waiter said. He was now dressed to go home. 'It is not only a question of youth and confidence although those things are very beautiful. Each night I am reluctant to close up because there may be some one who needs the café.' (Hemingway [1938] 1966, 381–382). The old waiter comprehends the importance of places of refuge like the café, sanctuaries of retreat, even if they offer but a brief respite from the anxiety of "nothing," of *nada*. As Steven Hoffman (1990) suggests, "In his crucial meditation at the end, the old waiter makes it quite clear that *nada* is not an individual state but one with grave universal implications" (1990, 173). The old waiter recounts to himself the characteristics of a clean, well-lighted café:

Turning off the electric light he continued the conversation with himself. It is the light of course but it is necessary that the place be clean and pleasant. You do not want music. . . . What did he fear? It was not fear or dread. It was a nothing that he knew too well. It was all a nothing and a man was nothing too. It was only that and light was all it needed and a certain cleanness and order. Some lived in it and never felt it but he knew it was all nada y pues nada y nada y pues nada. (Hemingway [1938] 1966, 382–383)

The old waiter does not attempt to "explain" reality to himself or feign an understanding of life's unanswerable questions—an impossibility he realizes very well; on the contrary, he reaffirms strategies of living that hold *nada* at bay. The old waiter knows the dread of *nada*, as Nathan Scott (1974) has suggested: "Now it is blackness beyond a clean, well-lighted place—this 'nothing full of nothing' that betrays 'confidence'; that murders sleep, that makes the having of plenty of money of no consequence at all—it is this blackness, ten times black, that constitutes the basic metaphysical situation in Hemingway's fiction" (p. 214). The old waiter recognizes the necessity of pragmatic defenses against the "abyss," a clean well-lighted café to counteract the "nothing" on the other side. He calls attention to this perspective in his parody of the "Our Father" prayer: "Our nada who art in nada, nada be thy name thy kingdom nada thy will be nada in nada as it is in nada. . . . Hail full of nada, nothing is with thee" (Hemingway [1938] 1966, 383). The old waiter leaves the bar, to "lie in the bed and, finally, with daylight, he would go to sleep. After all, he said to himself, it is probably only insomnia. Many must have it"

(p. 383). In this practical insight, purchased through age and experience, the old waiter recognizes the dark, common terrors of living, which can be resisted only through experiences of containment, like spending a lonely evening in a clean well-lighted café. The old waiter's *phronesis* arms him with dignity and self-respect to thwart the terrors of *nada* that so often appear in Hemingway's fiction, as Jackson Benson (1969) has observed: "A threat to selfhood is the ultimate threat, involving the ultimate horror that the irrational forces of the world can accomplish" (p. 130). The old patron, a doppelgänger to the old waiter, seeks the same refuge.

The young waiter's lack of suffering desensitizes him to the anguish of those who have lived much. He has lived little, learned less, and earned nothing in the currency of *phronesis*. As Baker (1952) characterizes him, "The young waiter would like to go home to bed, and is impatient with the old drinker of brandy. The old waiter, on the other hand, knows very well why the old patron comes often, gets drunk, stays late, and leaves only when he must. For the old waiter, like the old patron, belongs to the great brotherhood" (p. 124). In contrast to the old waiter, the young waiter knows nothing of *nada*: "To him [the young waiter], *nada* can only signify a personal privation. Nothing refers to the absence of those objects capable of providing material satisfaction" (Gabriel 1961, 542). The old waiter and his alter ego, the old patron, understand the fright and horror of *nada* and, together, they share the only defense they have—a bond of camaraderie in the struggle against the terrors of the night. These phronetic *gerontes* share much in common with their counterparts, the calculating counts.

THE TALES OF THE CALCULATING COUNTS

The Sun Also Rises (1926) and *A Farewell to Arms* (1929) are, arguably, Hemingway's two most powerful novels, written at the crest of the 1920s, Hemingway's most productive decade. In these works, Hemingway reveals a carefully honed style and aesthetic sensibility that caught the world's attention and influenced generations of writers to come. These novels illustrate the author's careful attention to detail and character development, particularly his portraiture of sympathetic aging figures. These master narratives depict older characters who have acquired *phronesis* through a lifetime of learning through experience. Their stories might be called "the tales of the calculating counts," Count Mippipopolous and Count Greffi.

In *The Sun Also Rises*, Hemingway's chronicle of the lost generation, Count Mippipopolous is a strategic figure because he represents an idealized, "aged" projection of the narrator, Jake Barnes. According to Earl Rovit (1983), "the novel contains one tutor, Count Mippipopolous" (p. 149). By implication, the young Jake Barnes is the tyro of the novel. The novel chronicles the activities of postwar debauchery in France and Spain, and early sections of the novel focus on the introduction and development of the main characters, principally Jake Barnes and Brett Ashley. Count Mippipopolous is a pivotal figure because he is admired by both Jake and Brett for the values he holds. Late one riotous night, the Count brings Brett to meet Jake at his apartment. In describing Mippipopolous to the just-roused Jake, Brett refers to him as "quite one of us. . . . He's one of us, though. Oh, quite. No doubt. One can always tell" (Hemingway 1926, 32), suggesting strongly that the three of them share values. Brett has only recently met the count, but she is impressed with his money and connections: "Knows hell's own amount about people. Don't know where he got it all. Owns a chain of sweatshops in the States" (p. 32). Moreover, she tells Jake, "I rather liked the count" (p. 33). Brett's description of the Count is uncontested by Jake, who appears to be quite willing to embrace anyone accepted by a fellow code-holder.

The following morning the Count, never one to ignore social decorum, returns to Jake's apartment with Brett to "make things right" with the concierge for the raucous wee-hour visit. The concierge is effusive in her praise of the Count and Brett: "He was very large. Very, very large. She was very nice. Very, very nice" (Hemingway 1926, 52). It is clear that Brett and the Count have ingratiated themselves with Jake's savvy concierge, who previously "had owned a drink-selling concession at the Paris race-courses" (p. 53). The implication is clear: In the proprietary world of the concierge, individuals define themselves by comporting themselves in a socially accepted manner, which means that they know and practice the "values." One strategic value is that of making practical judgments according to the exigencies of the occasion. Brett and the Count behaved badly the night before in rousing the concierge, but they repair the damage with the Count's two hundred francs, and purchase respectability, at least in the eyes of the concierge. Mippipopolous later tells Jake, "I thought we ought to give her a little something for last night" (p. 54).

This small incident illustrates a significant theme in Hemingway's work, which might be called a theory of value exchange. One pays for everything in life, either sooner or later. In some cases the "bill" comes early, in other situations it comes later, but it always comes. This exchange is part of the code: Everything of value in life must be earned. Jake is clearly impressed when he meets the Count for the first time. Mippipopolous, always in observance of formalities, brings Jake some flowers, whether he likes them or not. The Count later returns with some very fine wine, bedazzling Jake with his ability to "live well." The Count informs Brett and Jake that he got the wine from "a friend of mine that's in the business. . . . He's got thousands of acres" (Hemingway 1926, 56). The Count's vintner friend is a baron, we later learn, but Mippipopolous tells the titleless Jake (Brett is "Lady" Ashley) that titles are of little significance: "I assure you sir. . . . It never does a man any good. Most of the time it costs you money" (p. 57). Count Mippipopolous is most interested in living a life from which one comes to "know the values." All else is superficial, including titles.

The avuncular Count is a connoisseur of fine wine, food, women, and cigars and he has come to know the value of each. He remarks to Jake, in typical understatement, "I always like a good meal" (Hemingway 1926, 57). He then impresses Jake with his "American cigar," which he cuts with a "gold cutter he wore on one end of his watch-chain. . . . I like a cigar to really draw," he explains, "Half the cigars you smoke don't draw" (p. 57). The Count then reveals his appreciation for Brett: "You got class all over you. . . . You got the most class of anybody I ever seen. You got it. That's all" (p. 58). Mippipopolous then serves the champagne, but not until it is sufficiently chilled. To serve a wine before its time would breach the Count's code of fine living, particularly because it would be a violation of "good timing," a integral dimension of *phronesis*. (This capacity reveals the Count's understanding of the ancient concept of *kairos*, or that which is "timely," "appropriate," proportionate," "fitting," or "occasional.") He admonishes Brett to drink her wine slowly, taking in its full flavor and aroma rather than hurriedly seeking its intoxicating effects. The Count's value system also extends to the observance of a strict code of propriety in maintaining relationships. He comments to Brett, for example, that he always measures his words in dealing with friends: "I never joke people. Joke people and you make enemies. That's what I always say" (p. 58). It is clear that the Count has pondered the values that he cherishes.

Count Mippipopolous has learned his values from extensive experience and some suffering. He says to Brett, "Yes, my dear, I have been around very much. I have been around a very great deal" (Hemingway 1926, 59). The Count has earned his values, in part, because he is a seasoned veteran of seven wars and four revolutions. He impresses Brett and Jake when he shows them his arrow wounds, received in Abyssinia. Brett interprets the Count's scars as proof that he shares her values, and presumably Jake's too. Brett reacts to the wounds with a sense of shared experience: "I told you he was one of us. Didn't I? . . . I love you, count. You're a darling" (p. 60). The Count responds by summarizing the relationship between his wounds and his values: "'You see, Mr. Barnes, it is because I have lived very much that now I can enjoy everything so well'. . . . 'I know,' said the count. 'That is the secret. You must get to know the values'" (p. 60). The Count then demonstrates his values, taking Brett and Jake to dinner and functioning as their professional escort. After dinner, as Brett and Jake exit a nightclub, Jake turns around for one last look at the Count: "As we went out the door I looked back and there were three girls at his table" (p. 64). Women, too, play an important role in the Count's value system.

Count Mippipopolous is presented as an individual who has learned from living and suffering, and has earned practical wisdom. Some readers, perhaps even most readers in our time, may discount the epicurean nature of his values—"expertise" in selecting wines, food, cigars, and women. Yet one cannot discount the reverence in which he is held by Jake and Brett, precisely because he has matured through a life of conflict. Indeed, as Rovit (1963) has pointed out, "Jake has learned—in part from Count Mippipopolous—that illusions (sure beliefs projected into the future) are the first things one must discard if one wants to learn how to live life" (p. 156). This Count has come to know life's strategic lessons and values and he is an imposing model for the young Jake Barnes. "The Count," according to Rovit, "has found things that he cannot lose" (p. 150). What he has discovered is a way to calculate life based on the principle of *phronesis*, and he shares this pragmatic, value-earned way of life with Count Greffi.

A *Farewell to Arms*, Hemingway's first war novel, deals with the protagonist's military experience in the Italian ambulance corps. The story is a *Bildungsroman*, a novel about the education of a young man. The novel depicts a youthful Frederic Henry, who struggles to learn how to live in an angst-ridden, unforgiving world. Lieutenant Henry has been wounded in the war and has deserted the ambulance service in his private farewell to arms. He and Catherine Barkley, his pregnant lover, reunite in Stresa, a town near the Swiss border. Chapter thirty-five, in which Frederic meets Count Greffi, is an "interlude" chapter; it separates Henry's escape from the Italian army from his daring flight with Catherine to the safety of Switzerland. In his hotel in Stresa, Frederic is told that his old friend, Count Greffi, wants to play billiards with him. The Count is ninety-four years old. In response to Frederic's question about the Count's health, the barman depicts Count Greffi as a man in fine fettle: "He's younger than ever. He drank three champagne cocktails last night before dinner" (Hemingway 1929, 254). We also learn that the Count has recently beaten the barman in billiards. His skill is such that, according to the barman, "There's nobody here for him to play with" (p. 254). Frederic remembers him well as "an old man with white hair and beautiful manners. . . . While we played billiards we drank champagne. I thought it was a splendid custom and he gave me fifteen points in a hundred and beat me" (p. 254). Later, Lieutenant Henry arranges to play billiards with Count Greffi. The game begins and quickly it becomes clear that the Count functions as a "reality instructor" for young Henry. Philip Young describes the Count as "Completely real, once again and at once" (p. 91). The encounter between Frederic and the Count concludes with the Count trouncing Henry in spite of having given the lieutenant a generous handicap of eighteen points. As in so many Hemingway stories, the values that characters hold are often revealed through intimate conversations. The Count agrees to converse in English, not his native language, in deference to his tired young friend. They speak briefly about literature, but the subject quickly turns to a discussion of the count's life and his values:

Count Greffi smiled and turned the glass with his fingers. "I had expected to become very devout as I grow older but somehow I haven't," he said. "It is a great pity." "Would you like to live after death?" I asked and instantly felt a fool to mention death. But he did not mind the word. "It would depend on the life. This life is very pleasant. I would like to live forever," he smiled. "I very nearly have." We were sitting in the deep leather chairs, the champagne in the ice-bucket and our glasses on the table between us. "If you live to be as old as I am you find many things strange." (Hemingway 1929, 261)

Count Greffi manifestly attempts to counsel his young friend about "appearances" and "realities" in the contest of life. Things may not be what they seem to be, implies the Count, and it is only through age, experience, and wisdom that an individual becomes able to distinguish between appearances and realities. Count Greffi does not become more devout as he grows older because he understands devotion to be a human construction. "It is a pity," he says, because life would be more predictable if one could count on eternal verities such as religion. Without an inherited "code of living" under the guise of religion, individuals like Count Mippipopolous and Count Greffi must construct their own codes. Count Greffi tells Frederic that he too will find things "strange" if he lives long enough, which reinforces the Count's perspective that gaps between appearances and realities grow as one acquires experience and wisdom. Subalterns such as Jake Barnes and Frederic Henry pursue aged wise men like the counts because they know that there is much to learn from these phronetic exemplars. These young men passionately seek to acquire the stratagems—rather than the "truths"—by which they too will grow in their abilities to make critical distinctions in life.

Lieutenant Henry is clearly an admirer of Count Greffi, but the Count is concerned that what he says to his young friend may be confused with wisdom in the form of "eternal truths": "'You never seem old.' 'It is the body that is old. Sometimes I am afraid I will break off a finger as one breaks a stick of chalk. And the spirit is no older and not much wiser.' 'You are wise.' 'No, that is the great fallacy; the wisdom of old men. They do not grow wise. They grow careful'" (Hemingway 1929, 261).

Count Greffi's "wisdom" contradicts—and transcends—his denial that he has acquired insight, since his character embodies practical wisdom. He has clearly gained much through his extraordinarily long life, particularly the ability to make prudent judgments. Like Count Mippipopolous, he has come to know "the values"; yet, unlike Count Mippipopolous, Greffi's values center around love, friendship, and a comforting serenity in the knowledge that a full life engages a chain of existential moments without fear. In rejecting sectarian beliefs, Count Greffi accepts human existence as the ultimate transcendental experience, and this understanding is the kind of wisdom—*phronesis*—that Frederic longs to possess.

Frederic soon begins to intuit that the Count represents the process of practical insight rather than the product of accumulated wisdom: "'What do you think of the war really?' I asked. 'I think that it is stupid.' 'Who will win it?' 'Italy.' 'Why?' 'They are a younger nation.' 'Do younger nations always win wars?' 'They are apt to for a time.' 'Then what happens?' 'They become older nations.' 'You said you were not wise.' 'Dear boy, that is not wisdom. That is cynicism.' 'It sounds very wise to me.' 'It's not particularly. I could quote you the examples on the other side'" (Hemingway 1929, 262). This exchange serves to reinforce the tentative and conditional nature of the Count's "knowledge." The Count has lived long enough to know that the merits of a particular course of action may lie more in the framing of the proposition

than in the identification of some abstract, apodictic "reality." Indeed, he is
prepared to offer Frederic counterarguments to his own opinion. The closing
scene between the two men dramatically underscores the Count's emphasis
on the uncertainty of life, which necessarily requires precise yet flexible rules
of living: "Thank you," Frederic says, "And I hope that you will live forever."
"Thank you," the Count responds, "And if you ever become devout pray for
me if I am dead. I am asking several of my friends to do that" (pp. 262–263).
The Count's requests for prayers from his friends ("if" he succumbs) is not
inconsistent with his refusal to pray for himself. Having denied the possibility
of absolute truth, wisdom, and knowledge in his conversation with Frederic,
it would hardly be surprising that he would not categorically deny the possibility of transcendental experience. And yet there is another reason for the
Count's request to Frederic. The Count believes that love is a religious feeling, and the knowledge that Frederic is praying for him affirms the Count's
belief that human relationships are vitally important. The Count has arrived
at this perspective from a long, long life of earned knowledge and judicial
thinking, much like that of Hemingway's most beloved gerontes, Santiago,
the ancient Cuban fisherman.

A TALE OF AN ANCIENT FISHERMAN

The Old Man and the Sea is Hemingway's longest, strongest portrait of a
productive aging experience. The fable begins with a portrait of Santiago in
dire circumstances: "He was an old man who fished alone in a skiff in the
Gulf Stream and he had gone eighty-four days now without taking a fish"
(Hemingway 1952, 9). This introductory trope of hyperbole alerts us to the
fact that we are dealing with no ordinary, "realistic" protagonist; we are in the
realm of archetypal myth and Santiago is the stoic exemplar. Although
Santiago shares much with Hemingway's earlier representations of phronetic
aging, his symbolic role significantly differs from that of the old waiter and
Counts Mippipopolous and Greffi. The ancient fisherman is represented as
a much larger than life ur-protagonist through metaphorical representations
of him as a Christ-like figure. These associations affirm his inner strength in
the face of staggering adversity: his struggle to defeat external and internal
antagonists—the adversarial marlin, the sharks, the elements—and the many
trials that test his mettle. Santiago's tale is one of indefatigable stoicism in the
face of overwhelming odds, his supernatural courage enabled by intellectual
and physical abilities to adapt to changing circumstances, explicit indica-
tions of his prudence. Santiago, like the old waiter and the two counts, has
learned and earned much from a life of painful experiences.

Although there is no single passage that dramatically exemplifies Santiago's
wisdom and courage, every page of this powerful novella chronicling the
three days of his struggle with the natural world reveals his accumulated
phronesis and the critical decisions it allows him to make in the contest of his

life. As Philip Young (1966) characterizes him, "Santiago is a master who sets his lines with more care than his colleagues, but he has no luck any more. It would be better to be lucky, he thinks, but he will be skillfully exact instead; then when luck comes he will be ready for it" (p. 127). Santiago's characterization as prudent and phronetic does not imply that he is always right nor does he know everything; indeed, Santiago acknowledges having made many mistakes in life. Santiago's *phronesis* is exemplified by his flexibility; he consistently demonstrates an ability to act and think according to the exigencies of the particular circumstance in which he finds himself.

One example of Santiago's *phronesis* is his ability to manufacture productive and consoling metaphors that sustain him through incredible adversity. There is great wisdom in these life-sustaining figures of speech, and they are clearly more than "mere" metaphors. For example, Santiago implicitly compares himself to Joe DiMaggio (understood as a popular heroic figure) in his rhetorical question: "Do you believe that the great DiMaggio would stay with a fish as long as I will stay with this one? . . . I am sure he would and more since he is young and strong. Also, his father was a fisherman" (Hemingway 1952, 68). Santiago frequently uses these rhetorical/psychological/metaphorical strategies as phronetic calculations to reinforce his determination. Practical wisdom serves at least two functions in this novella. *Phronesis* is necessary for the activation of a preliminary, "internal" dialectic which, in turn, gives rise to an "intelligence" that expresses itself in words and actions. Moreover, Santiago's interior monologues, which are rife in the narrative, are mechanisms for revealing and discovering *phronesis*.

Before he embarks on his odyssey, we are told that Santiago is unlike the other fishermen. In his conversation with Manolin, his alter ego and tyro, Santiago makes it clear that he is proudly different from the others and has accumulated wisdom, which he categorizes as "tricks": "'I am a strange old man.' 'But are you strong enough now for a truly big fish?' 'I think so. And there are many tricks'" (Hemingway 1952, 14).

Much like the old waiter, Santiago understands the supreme importance of maintaining fictions in order to fight despair, as he jokes with Manolin about nets and food they do not have: "There was no cast net and the boy remembered when they had sold it. But they went through this fiction every day. There was no pot of yellow rice and fish and the boy knew this too" (Hemingway 1952, 16). Early in the novella, the narrator explicitly compares Santiago to other fishermen, pointing out that Santiago has superior knowledge which will serve him well when his luck is good: "He looked down into the water and watched the lines that went straight down into the dark of the water. He kept them straighter than anyone did, so that at each level in the darkness of the stream there would be a bait waiting *exactly* where he wished it to be for any fish that swam there" (p. 32, emphasis added). Santiago is no accidental fisherman; he relies on his superior knowledge and experience in choosing the prudent course of action for each occasion.

As the marlin is hooked and the drama unfolds, Santiago understands precisely what is going on both beneath and on the surface of the sea. "What a fish," he remarks, "He has it sideways in his mouth and he is moving off with it" (Hemingway 1952, 43). Although Santiago hunts with precision, he recognizes the significance of superstition: "Then he will turn and swallow it, he thought. He did not say that because he knew that if you said a good thing it might not happen" (p. 43). This "silence" is yet another example of Santiago's systematic code of behavior. Like the old waiter and the counts, he has learned from a lifetime of knowledge-earning experience that successful living requires appropriate action in certain circumstances. Santiago makes no claim to absolute confidence in knowing that he will rise to meet whatever circumstance confronts him: "What will I do if he decides to go down. I don't know. What'll I do if he sounds and dies. I don't know. But I'll do something. There are plenty of things I can do" (p. 45). "Plenty of things" includes a deep well of responses to the exigencies of living, earned by a lifetime of productive experience and suffering.

Santiago must necessarily be a gerontic hero. A younger protagonist, Manolin for example, would be ineffectual as a representation of a wise man with the accumulated sum of many years of hard-earned living. A younger fisherman would grow impatient struggling with the huge marlin, perhaps attempting reckless action in an attempt to land the fish. Santiago's travail with the marlin lasts a long time, and there are moments when he does not know what to do, although he realizes that he should not do anything that will aid the marlin's efforts to free himself: "I can do nothing with him and he can do nothing with me, he thought. Not as long as he keeps this up. . . . Then he thought, think of it always. Think of what you are doing. You must do nothing stupid" (Hemingway 1952, 47–48). Reminding himself to think is always an important part of Santiago's code, and it sustains him (as it does the old patron and old waiter) to fight off the loneliness that too often accompanies old age: "I wish I had the boy. To help me and to see this. No one should be alone in their old age, he thought. But it is unavoidable. I must remember to eat the tuna before he spoils in order to keep strong. Remember, no matter how little you want to, that you must eat him in the morning" (p. 48). Thus, the prudent activity of interior dialogue triggers the will to govern the body. Santiago continually uses this mechanism of auto-conversation as a means of maintaining himself in his lonely war with the giant marlin, a contest in which one of them must die. The affirmative residue of such strategies of living reinforce the vitality of this *Reifungsroman*.

There are times between the ebb and flow of his death bout with the great marlin that Santiago comes to identify and sympathize with his "brother" of the sea—perhaps a *gerontes* himself—as the fisherman ponders the mind and capability of his adversary: "Then he began to pity the great fish that he had hooked. He is wonderful and strange and who knows how old he is, he thought" (Hemingway 1952, 48). The second morning, as the conflict intensifies, Santiago loses his bait. Always the pragmatist, Santiago again wonders what would have happened if he had Manolin with him: "Aloud he said, I wish I had the boy" (p. 51). Indeed, many times Santiago utters this same wish, which indicates the old man's practicality and humility. He knows from years of experience that it is impossible for one man, however experienced and determined, to bring home such a fish. Yet Santiago will not allow this knowledge to discourage him. On the contrary, he uses his loneliness as a force of self-motivation: "But you haven't got the boy, he thought. You have only yourself and you had better work back to the last line now, in the dark or not in the dark, and cut it away and hook up the two reserve coils. So he did it" (p. 52). Once again, Santiago's interior dialogue shows itself to be part of a systematic code that enables him to attend to the pragmatic activities of his life as well as bolster his fortitude.

The ancient fisherman is alone in his little skiff, but he is not entirely alone. In his mental meandering, Santiago reveals a kind of metaphysical presence, perhaps even bordering on philosophic wisdom, that suggests a pantheistic perspective. He is not only a brother to his adversary, but he is also kin to all of the other creatures of the sea and air: "He looked across the sea and knew how alone he was now. . . . The clouds were building up now for the trade wind and he looked ahead and saw a flight of wild ducks etching themselves against the sky over the water, then blurring, then etching again and he knew no man was ever alone on the sea" (Hemingway 1952, 60–61). Santiago comforts himself in the knowledge that his practical understanding of nature is superior to that of his fishermen competitors: "He thought of how some men feared being out of sight of land in a small boat and knew they were right in the months of sudden bad weather. But now they were in hurricane months and, when there are no hurricanes, the weather of hurricane months is the best of all the year" (p. 61). Later he concludes that he is safe from the natural elements, at least for the present: "There will be bad weather in three or four days, he said. But not tonight or tomorrow" (p. 80). Santiago does not fear nature because his practical wisdom gives him an inner strength that sustains him throughout his darkest hours. The windmills of his mind never cease to turn.

This gerontic hero, like Count Greffi, is not a religious man. However, his lack of faith in a supernatural Being does not prevent him from praying to God for perseverance in his struggle: "I am not religious at all, he said. But I will say ten Our Fathers and ten Hail Marys that I should catch this fish, and I promise to make a pilgrimage to the Virgin of Cobre if I catch him. That is a promise. He commenced to say his prayers mechanically" (Hemingway 1952, 65). This litany of prayers and promises to a deity that does not exist is curious indeed. Later, the old man bargains with God for perseverance: "God help me endure. I'll say a hundred Our Fathers and a hundred Hail Marys. But I cannot say them now. Consider them said. . . . I'll say them later" (p. 87). One cannot say whether God operates on the installment plan or not, but Santiago clearly posits a deity who is flexible in His business transactions.

Yet Santiago's invocations and "deals" surely serve a pragmatic, secular purpose: they bolster his resolve to tenaciously abide in his pursuit of his brother/antagonist. "God" serves as another rhetorical strategy—indeed, as the cosmic metaphor which inspires Santiago to continue his pursuit. The fisherman uses God in the same way he employs other devices to reinforce his will. These gestures are exemplary illustrations of literary auto-persuasion.

The old man battles the giant marlin for nearly two days without sleep, yet neither rival shows any sign of surrender. Santiago worries that the ability to think—his most important weapon—will be diminished unless he rests. This issue is so serious that he resorts to uttering a litany of imperative commands to himself: "You must devise a way so that you sleep a little. . . . If you do not sleep you will become unclear in the head. . . . But remember to sleep. . . . Make yourself do it and devise some simple and sure way about the lines. Now go back and prepare the dolphin" (Hemingway 1952, 77). This passage demonstrates that Santiago's phronetic abilities are not instinctive; they are volitionally intellectual and his will must summon his mind to keep them operational.

In spite of Hemingway's explicit depiction of Santiago's moral and intellectual virtues, the old man does make errors in judgment. After gutting the dolphin fish, he eats it and realizes that he has made two critical errors: "What an excellent fish dolphin is to eat cooked. . . . And what a miserable fish raw. I will never go in a boat again without salt or limes. If I had brains I would have splashed water on the bow all day and drying, it would have made salt. . . . It was a lack of preparation" (Hemingway 1952, 80). The old man also regrets his failure to adjust to his limitations and to changing circumstances: "Why was I not born with two good hands? he thought. Perhaps it was my fault in not training that one properly" (p. 85). Poor judgment and lack of foreplanning are not characteristic of Santiago, but these admissions of error do serve to call attention to his honesty and fallibility. The ancient fisherman may be an archetypal hero, but he is not superhuman.

Like so many Hemingway heroes, Santiago realizes that there is a price to be paid for everything in life. Santiago "earns" his marlin because the great fish must pay for his adversary's expertise. As the marlin begins to run with the line, Santiago remarks, "Make him pay for the line, he thought. Make him pay for it" (Hemingway 1952, 82). Santiago understands all too well that both he and the marlin are subject to the same cosmic laws of exchange: "The line went out and out and out but it was slowing now and he was making the fish earn every inch of it" (p. 83). Santiago's cumulative experience levies a high price for the marlin's struggle to live.

It isn't until the third day that Santiago actually sees the marlin for the first time. The fisherman is stunned at the immense size of his adversary. Santiago looks his "brother" in the eye and exerts himself to "be calm and strong, old man" (Hemingway 1952, 91). The contest between the aged adversaries has always been intensely personal, but now there is a physical closeness to their struggle that intensifies their relationship. Santiago is struck by the marlin's majesty and beauty. Indeed, the old man is so enraptured by his close death-encounter with his alter ego that he does not care who ultimately prevails: "You are killing me, fish, the old man thought. But you have a right to. Never have I seen a greater, or more beautiful, or a calmer or more noble thing than you, brother. Come on and kill me. I do not care who kills who" (p. 92). Greatness, nobility, and beauty, of course, are equally characteristic of the ancient fisherman.

Santiago prevails and after three torturous days the marlin finally succumbs. Fatigued from exhaustion, the old man lashes his prize to the side of the skiff and heads for home on a southwest course. His wisdom and experience chart the course, for which he needs no compass: "He only needed the feel of the trade wind and the drawing of the sail" (Hemingway 1952, 97). Santiago and his alter ego together "sail like brothers," unthreatened until the first shark attacks. The old man's wisdom and experience lead him quickly to conclude that he will lose his brother: "The old man's head was clear and good now and he was full of resolution but he had little hope. It was too good to last" (p. 101). Santiago defends his soul mate, using a small harpoon to fend off the attack. The old man kills the first shark, but not until the marlin has become disfigured (and therefore desecrated). At this moment Santiago utters his well-known words of affirmation: "Man is not made for defeat. . . . A man can be destroyed but not defeated" (p. 103). Other sharks follow the first, as Santiago well knows they will, and he defends what is left of his prize with a handmade harpoon constructed from an oar and a knife. At this juncture the old man realizes that his actions represent a way of life, a life lived well, something far larger than being a fisherman: "But he liked to think about all things that he was involved in and since there was nothing to read and he did not have a radio, he thought much and he kept on thinking about sin. You did not kill the fish only to keep alive and to sell for food, he thought. You killed him for pride and because you are a fisherman" (p. 105). The sharks smell blood and, by midnight of the third day, the great marlin is lost piece by piece, in spite of Santiago's valiant efforts to fight off dozens of sharp-toothed attackers.

Santiago ultimately loses the rest of his great marlin, minus the skeleton, as the predators eat away the conquest of a lifetime, but these adversaries cannot take away the dignity which the ancient fisherman asserts in his heroic struggle. The old man returns home, his pride intact: "He sailed lightly now and he had no thoughts nor any feelings of any kind. He was past everything now and he sailed the skiff to make his home port as well and intelligently as he could" (Hemingway 1952, 119). Upon meeting Manolin after returning home, the old man is spiritually renewed. He immediately begins making plans to return to the sea, to an active life guided by *phronesis*: "We must get a good killing lance and always have it on board. You can make the blade from a spring leaf from an old Ford. We can grind it in Guanabacoa. It should be sharp and not tempered so it will break" (p. 125). In spite of his devastating loss, Santiago continues to live by the principle of prudence. After losing the struggle of his life, he comes home that night to dream of lions and his pride in the life that he has lived, a life of virtue and prudence, inextricably intertwined. Santiago, the quintessential Hemingway superman, sleeps the sleep of the just.

Why are so many of Hemingway's aging heroes supermen? Because each in his own way has purchased wisdom with the currency of productive experiences that have generated stable (yet always evolving) personalities capable of holding off the demons of the night, like those that frighten the old man in "A Clean Well-Lighted Place." In the words of Young (1966), "Hemingway has written about life: a struggle against the impossible odds of unconquerable natural forces in which—given such a fact as that of death—a man can only lose, but which he can dominate in such a way that his loss has dignity, itself the victory" (p. 128). Hemingway's aging heroes may have something to teach their younger counterparts.

CHAPTER 5

Bertrand Russell in His Nineties:
Aging and the Problem of Biography

William T. Ross

In *The Fountain of Age*, Betty Friedan (1993) invents the term "compassion-ate ageism" to describe sympathetic and well-intentioned attitudes toward the elderly that have disastrous effects. All too often, she argues, misplaced compassion for the elderly displaces admiration for vigor, for contributions to society, and ultimately for agency itself. The most painful effect of this age-ism is that finally "the aged come to accept the negative stereotype and to act in accordance with the role of senior citizens" (Levin and Levin 1980, 100). It follows (and Friedan makes this clear) that when seniors do not "act in accor-dance" they become the recipients of discouraging and even punishing be-havior on the part of their younger brethren and, I would add, even on the part of the senior cohort that has already acquiesced in the negative stereo-type. It is interesting to keep Friedan's observations in mind when one ob-serves the later years of Bertrand Russell, who certainly did not accept such stereotypes and lived to be ninety-eight.

In 1937 the then sixty-five-year-old Bertrand Russell predicted that he would live to be ninety and imagined how his obituary might appear in the *Times* of London in 1962. The last two paragraphs are a remarkable display of his pre-science; in the next to last, he correctly predicts World War II and his role in it:

In the Second World War he took no public part, having escaped to a neutral coun-try just before its outbreak. In private conversation he was wont to say that homicidal lunatics were well employed in killing each other, but that sensible men would keep out of their way while they were doing it. Fortunately this outlook, which is reminis-cent of Bentham, has become rare in this age, which recognizes that heroism has a value independent of its utility. True, much of what was once the civilized world lies in ruins; but no right-thinking person can admit that those who died for the right in the great struggle have died in vain. (Russell 1950,174–175)

In the second and concluding paragraph, he predicts his own longevity and the sense of alienation that would accompany those final years:

His life, for all its waywardness, had a certain anachronistic consistency, reminiscent of that of the aristocratic rebels of the early nineteenth century. His principles were curious, but, such as they were, they governed his actions. In private life he showed none of the acerbity which marred his writings, but was a genial conversationalist and not devoid of human sympathy. He had many friends, but had survived almost all of them. Nevertheless, to those who remained he appeared, in extreme old age, full of enjoyment, no doubt owing, in large measure, to his invariable health, for politically, during his last years, he was as isolated as Milton after the Restoration. He was the last survivor of a dead epoch. (1950, 174–175)

The tone of disapproval is, of course, not self-criticism but rather what this aristocratic rebel thought the staid, genteel *Times* would direct his way. And the prophesied "facts" are remarkably prescient. The war came as he thought it would and found him in a then-neutral country—the United States. But between 1937 and 1939, when the enormity of the evil of Hitler's state became evident to him, he altered the pacifist convictions that had sent him to jail during World War I. As to his description of his behavior in his last years, it is almost completely correct. He often felt like the last survivor of a dead epoch because, in fact, he was. His grandfather, Lord John Russell, from whom his title (since 1931 he had been officially Earl Russell) descended, had been a prime minister six years before Queen Victoria began her long reign. John Stuart Mill had been his "godfather" (the quotation marks are necessary since both his parents were agnostics). Moreover, in a sense he was as isolated as Milton in his later years, since he tended throughout his life to be as politically antiestablishment as possible.

But he was wrong on one score; he did not live to be ninety—he lived to be ninety-eight. Moreover, in his nineties his antiestablishment attacks, first on nuclear proliferation and then on the Vietnam War, won him a legion of younger and sometimes renowned followers whose admiration made his last days far different from those of the English epic poet. However, the adulation did not stifle his independence. Two weeks before his death, as his health was finally failing, he dictated a strong statement opposing Israel's aerial attacks on Egypt. Ronald Clark (1976) reproduces part of it in his biography:

The aggression committed by Israel must be condemned, not only because no State has the right to annex foreign territory, but because every expansion is also an experiment to discover how much more aggression the world will tolerate. . . . We are frequently told that we must sympathize with Israel because of the suffering of the Jews in Europe at the hand of the Nazis. I see in this suggestion no reason to perpetuate any suffering. What Israel is doing today cannot be condoned, and to invoke the horrors of the past to justify those of the present is gross hypocrisy. (p. 638)

This harsh criticism of Israel is doubtless still controversial today, but in 1970, as Clark (1976) points out, it was unheard of in the Anglo-American world. However, I do not reproduce it in order to resurrect foreign policy debates. What I would point out is that this critique bears all the marks of an individual totally in control of his faculties: the prose is lucid, the diction unambiguous, and the progression of thought logical and consistent. No one would have any trouble understanding exactly what Russell meant. The passage written by the ninety-eight-year-old Russell, in other words, is just as comprehensible and as stylistically admirable as the one written by the sixty-five-year-old philosopher/author. (And both, we can assume, are much more competent than most discourse authored at any age.)

The question I want to raise is why, if a man could write so well and reveal in that writing such a principled and ordered mind, do sympathetic biographers raise the specter of "aging" and even "senility" over the report of his final years. One must keep in mind that biographers do not simply report facts; they must construct narratives of motive and explanation to make sense of the facts and to explain the behavior of their subject. These narratives can rightly be called fictive because biographers are no more privy to the actual workings of their subject's mind than anyone else. It is not surprising, therefore, that these explanations often fall back on stereotypical expectations for human behavior, often using "aging" as an explanation for actions for no other reason than that they occurred in a certain decade of the subject's life. But "aging" or "growing older" or "diminished faculties" are often more than just explanations of convenience; when they are insisted upon most emphatically, one can be pretty sure that the action so "excused" is one that the biographer does not approve. Ironically, for Russell, that "certain decade" was his tenth. If he had died at eighty, perhaps biographers would have described his seventies in the same terms.

Before looking at what the biographers actually say, let us review—hastily—the accomplishments of that last decade and remind ourselves of what kind of figure Russell had been for a long time before that. Russell is correct in pointing out his "waywardness" (if by this he means straying from accepted norms of behavior) and his "curious" principles. In short, he was always a rebel. Married four times (divorced three) and decidedly promiscuous, he was an outspoken agnostic, an advocate of what we would call free love and birth control when both were absolutely scandalous, a pacifist in the midst of his country's war fever, an advocate of radical educational experimentation for children, and, somewhat unpredictably, a foe of the Soviet Union when most of his intellectual cohorts were decidedly enamored with it. In other words, the attribution of "rebel" holds for his entire life. Moreover, as surely will become evident, Russell would certainly have agreed with Pifer (1986) that automatically conferring "veteranship" or passive status on an over-sixty-five like himself was "patronizing, demeaning, even insulting, and certainly unwanted" (p. 402).

In addition to making a monumental contribution to modern philosophical thinking, Russell was also a prolific author on a host of topics in the behavioral, social, and political sciences. From age eighty-eight until he died ten years later, he published six books, including three volumes of his autobiography, led a campaign against nuclear armaments in Britain that resulted in his going to prison for a week (he served his time in a prison hospital), engaged in a well-publicized exchange of letters with President Kennedy and Premier Khrushchev during the Cuban Missile crisis, protested against the Vietnam War and set up a very controversial international War Crimes tribunal to "try" those considered perpetrators of that war, and, in general, through his actions, public statements, and occasional journalistic pieces managed to get himself far more noticed than at any other period of a rather public life.

Indeed, although almost all these activities were extremely controversial, they are not the sort of activities normally associated with senility. Yet his most recent biographer, Caroline Moorehead (1993), lets the charge of senility go unanswered in one extremely problematic paragraph about Russell in the early 1960s:

Nothing, however, was to inflame him more than the war in Vietnam, which he saw not as an isolated campaign but as an inevitable consequence of America's policies of global intervention. Though his revulsion against the war was shared by many, it provoked outbursts of such vitriol on his part that even his most ardent British admirers were perplexed. There was something about this vituperation—and particularly the unsubtle language in which it was expressed—so different from the voice of reason which had first captivated them, that led many to ask whether Russell was not becoming senile. They mourned the earlier eloquence, not just for its pleasing use of the English language but for its effectiveness. (p. 521)

The next paragraph of Moorehead's (1993) biography veers off into the background of the war, avoiding the issue of Russell's senility. Yet the whole paragraph, which describes the consequences of this alleged senility, is misleading. It is true that Russell's positions and rhetoric distressed a lot of admirers, but Russell had been disappointing admirers throughout his life. He disappointed some of his fellow faculty at Trinity College, Cambridge, during World War I, with his opposition to that war. (In fact, they voted him out of the college.) He disappointed many of his friends—including H. G. Wells— in the early 1920s, by writing a book extremely critical of the Soviet Union. He disappointed a lot of pacifist friends during the 1930s by first writing a book arguing for pacifist resistance to Britain's getting involved in a European war and then announcing publicly that he had changed his mind. All but one of these examples comes from before he turned sixty, the age at which one can usually start being accused of senility. As for "ardent" admirers, anyone who remembers the antiwar mood of the time and the inflamed rhetoric that grew out of it can be forgiven for suspecting that Russell acquired far more ardent supporters than he lost, especially when his War Crimes Tribunal generated massive international publicity. In fact, the vociferousness of some of the attacks coupled with the biographers' attitude recalls Friedan's (1993) notion of the active elderly being punished for not being quiescent, or, as Gutmann (1977, 8) says, proves that we are not comfortable with the elderly unless we deny their potencies.

Moreover, it is fair to describe much of Russell's prose as "eloquent," but suffice it to say that there are several earlier "eloquences." The style of "A Poor Man's Worship" is not the style of A History of Western Philosophy, for example. And despite Russell's logical and stylistic gifts, his output was often so hurried that he had slipped into unpleasing and certainly unsubtle sentences before. It is, in fact, the biographer's logic that is unsubtle. That "they" mourned does not mean that there was any empirical basis for that mourning, and the biographer should so note. But the biographer is half seduced herself by the explanatory power of "senility" and therefore lets it slip by—or perhaps "slip by" is not the best phrase. "Vitriol," "vituperation," and "unsubtle," after all, are her phrases and mark her participation in the condemnation of Russell's verbal behavior. A reference to senility is obviously an easy way for her to clear her subject of any conscious fault for what she sees as shortcomings in his discourse and frees her from having to make a morally disapproving judgment.

In addition, Alan Ryan (1988), the brilliant biographer of Russell's "political life," cannot help explaining some of Russell's gaffes as the consequences of old age. According to Ryan, from his late eighties on Russell "was increasingly frail and suffered digestive disorders which prevented him going out very much; he was thus inevitably cut off from much that went on in the outside world" (p. 174). However, I would note that Russell went out enough to get himself arrested and sentenced to a week in a prison hospital. In addition, his main digestive disorder was a difficulty swallowing solid food, so that he had to resort to a liquid but nourishing diet that included his favorite Scotch whisky. It is true that he became increasingly reluctant to travel to London, but the record shows that he was constantly visited by his associates in the antiwar movement, publishers' representatives, journalists (including James Baldwin), and well-wishers.

Furthermore, let us consider the implications of Ryan's (1988) claim that Russell was isolated from the "outside" world at his home in Plas Penrhyn, Northern Wales. There he could easily receive the two national British newspapers, the Times and the Guardian; could hear news broadcasts, commentaries, and discussions on the BBC; and could easily correspond with eminent authorities from around the world who were his personal acquaintances. The issues that most concerned Russell in these years were the arms race, the war in Vietnam, and occasional, widely publicized, international incidents, like the

Cuban missile crisis, the invasion of Czechoslovakia, and the Sino–Indian border dispute. Can Russell's so-called isolation really have been a problem? How many intellectuals of the time really felt that these issues were beyond them simply because they were either not living in a world capital or were unable to travel to the scenes of all the hot spots? The answer, I suspect, is obvious. In his biography Ryan has attempted to blame what he sees as Russell's inconsistencies and shortcomings on isolation and then attribute that isolation to the inevitable consequences of aging. If only Lord Russell had been younger and possessed a better digestion!

Ronald Clark (1976) mimics Moorehead in letting a source's information go unchallenged and thereby legitimating it. The issue once again is Russell's health or the decline thereof. "'Between [1961] and the [War Crimes] Tribunal the body had begun to give up,'" Clark writes, quoting a source supposedly close (and sympathetic) to Russell during these years (p. 626). Clark follows this with a long list of signs of debilitation supplied by the same source. Again, he does nothing to challenge the observation. The time in question is the period in which Russell would have been eighty-nine to ninety-four years old. But 121 pages earlier in the biography Clark quoted Russell's younger son Conrad recalling his father's love of the Welsh countryside and remembering "him, at 95, swinging over the steps to the balcony for the sheer delight of the view of [Mount] Snowden in the afternoon sun" (p. 505). This would hardly seem to be the actions of a rapidly declining recluse, and Russell obviously did not think that his health was failing. Just three pages after he cites the negative comments on Russell's health, Clark quotes from a letter that Russell wrote to the physician Lord Amulree asking to be taken on as an occasional patient (Russell was usually attended by the local GP). "I am now in my ninety-fifth year," he wrote, "and am fortunate to enjoy good health. I am, naturally, anxious to obtain the best possible advice on continuing this situation" (p. 629). The letter and the son's recollections testify to the physical and mental agility of Russell. The real issue here is not the subject's health but the action of a usually immensely sympathetic biographer in letting the prejudicial observation go unchallenged. Surely, if Russell had been forty years younger, Clark would have paid closer attention to the veracity of his source.

One of the controversial actions taken from his Welsh home was Russell's "break" (the word is Moorehead's) with his British publisher, Sir Stanley Unwin. This break is alleged to be the result of the machinations of Ralph Schoenman, Russell's young American assistant who had worked for him and with him since 1960. In the words of Clark (1976), Schoenman possessed "limitless energy, a refreshing inability to worry about what anyone thought of him, and an alarming ignorance of the damage he could cause" (p. 573). Schoenman was not the first younger man whom Russell had befriended who turned out to be hard to handle and eventually wound up being very hostile. D. H. Lawrence, the novelist, and Ludwig Wittgenstein, Russell's student at Cambridge, are both earlier examples of the same phenomenon. Eventually, Russell would sever all ties with Schoenman, but it is clear that he not only appreciated Schoenman's unconventional and irreverent behavior, but that he needed Schoenman to help him manage the antiwar organizations that he had founded. No biographer seems to appreciate the immense challenge that confronted Russell, who had never run anything larger than a small boarding school (with his second wife), when he undertook to head the Bertrand Russell Peace Foundation and the War Crimes Tribunal. Instead, his utilization of Schoenman's talents, which necessarily implied a certain tolerance for his excesses, is usually seen as another sign of his declining powers (see Levin 1970, 274–277, for a contemporaneous manifestation of this view). The implication is that Russell, old and isolated, allowed himself to be manipulated by his aide into doing things contrary to his character and interests.

In any event, one of the unfortunate incidents Schoenman was alleged to have caused was Russell's "break" with his longtime publisher. The break, it turns out, was personal; that is, Unwin continued to publish Russell's books in England even if the two no longer dealt directly with one another. Moorehead (1993, 536–537) manages to turn the break into a "sad account" resembling a soap opera, in which an elderly author, acting strangely, first demands (or his aide demands) a greater advance on a book and then later announces that he would prefer to deal through an agent in the future. One agent made the journey to Wales only to discover, according to Moorehead, that Russell (or possibly Schoenman) was more interested in "power" than in "good literature" and so withdrew, while Sir Stanley is said to have warned Russell not to take on an agent better versed in tax law than in literature.

Unfortunately, most of the pathos is the invention of the biographer. Moorehead (1993) herself admits, almost 200 pages earlier, that the relationship of publisher and author was hardly warm and personal. They only met when Russell had a manuscript to deliver, and then the two men, "addressing each other by their surnames, would drink a glass of sherry together" (p. 343). Moorehead, in fact, hints that the aristocratic Russell viewed Unwin, whose knighthood was not inherited, as little more than a tradesman. Furthermore, the emphasis on "literature" is a red herring. Russell's income, at least from the end of World War I, was primarily based on the royalties from his writing and his speaking engagements. He had no huge estate, and much of what he wrote, by his own admission in, among other places, the sham obituary cited, was little more than hack work. Perhaps he was too hard on himself, but his writing is almost all comprised of popular studies of either political or social-science issues. He was, in fact, a little embarrassed to have won the Nobel Prize for Literature in 1950, but thought he certainly deserved one for his contributions to philosophy. (There is no Nobel prize for philosophy, but the committee was probably moved in part to give him the award in literature for his *History of Western Philosophy* just as it was moved to give Winston Churchill the award in 1953 for his history of World War II.) Russell wrote over sixty-five books, but, except for two volumes of short stories published in the 1950s and possibly the autobiography, few have ever been regarded as literature, although his prose style has been frequently admired.

However, Moorehead (1993) leaves out the most important consequence of the so-called "break." Russell apparently never hired an agent, but Schoenman did insist that Unwin auction off the American rights to Russell's autobiography. Unwin had been prepared to give it to Simon and Schuster, who had published much of Russell's work in the United States. According to Clark, Simon and Schuster offered $30,000 against royalties. Auctioning off literary rights is fairly common today, but it was new to Sir Stanley, who resisted, and after being compelled to do it expressed "the hope that he would never be forced to do such a thing again" (Clark 1976, 619). Auctioning may not have been genteel, but it produced a bid of $200,000 from Atlantic-Little, Brown, who were awarded the rights. The difference between $30,000 and $200,000 in the life of a professional writer is profound, but Russell at the time was not primarily interested in his own creature comforts. Instead, he was searching for a source of income for his political activities; otherwise, he would have left the autobiography in manuscript until after his death.

Yet even Clark (1976) cannot let Russell have his commercial victory. The details, as supplied by Clark, are sketchy, but apparently the original contract was for two volumes. Eventually the project grew to three volumes. Because Little, Brown did not make money on the first two volumes, they declined to publish the third, and Simon and Schuster brought it out, or, as Clark puts it, the "over-selling" of the original proposal "was crippling; when the third volume was available Little, Brown declined and Simon & [sic] Schuster were left to pick up the bits" (p. 619). Since the volume was indeed published, the only thing "crippled" must have been the genteel expectation that all volumes of a work would carry the same imprint. In fact, the hardbound version continued the same design, making all three look like a uniform set. If Russell shared this expectation or regretted the earlier windfall, neither biographer bothers to mention it.

The economic facts would seem to support a narrative about a man of letters forcing his publisher to strike a deal of great financial advantage to himself and to his dedicated causes. Instead, we are treated by Russell's biographies to the spectacle of an old and "out-of-touch" figure who is manipulated into giving up a lifetime friendship (whose existence is doubtful) and outsmarting himself to the extent that he had to change American publishers two-thirds of the way through the project. Russell eventually broke with the mercurial Schoenman, but in a 7,500-word statement describing the reasons for the break, he never mentions the book contract. Perhaps, given the temperament of the biographers, they would have generated the same narratives about a younger subject, but it can certainly be doubted because the only thing that makes the narrative at all creditable is the subtext of a geriatric biographee who is no longer capable of rational behavior.

This is not the only narrative of betrayal and separation in Moorehead's volume. Russell broke with associates throughout his life, but Moorehead (1993) chooses to make a big deal out of his "break" (again, even the term is questionable) with Fenner Brockway. The whole paragraph deserves quotation:

Fenner Brockway, one of Russell's very few remaining friends from the First World War, found himself slowly ousted from Russell's life. This was partly, he said, because Schoenman had no time for him, and made access impossible, but when he did see Russell he found him changed. "When we were younger, we had been friends, we shared a sense of comradeship. All that had gone. There was no real friendship left. On my part, I continued to feel immense respect for him, except that he didn't seem to have any doubts anymore. He became so confident in his own ideas, so determined to express his opinions." (p. 535)

Russell had never really liked Brockway, and had certainly not become sentimental over the years. How exactly, one might wonder, does the last sentence jibe with the phrase "few remaining friends" in the first sentence? Brockway, like Russell, had been a pacifist in the first war, and, like Russell, he had spent time in jail for those convictions. But he had certainly gone on, as a somewhat Trotskyist revolutionary socialist, to lead a far more doctrinaire and less doubting life than Russell. What would seem to motivate this paragraph is again the stereotype of an old man so crotchety that he is even alienating himself from his "few remaining friends." That Moorehead invokes the stereotype in the first sentence only to contradict it in the last simply emphasizes its power.

Of course, Russell was aware during his last years that he was being accused of senility, and he confronts the accusations near the end of the third volume of his autobiography. The refutation is humane, rational, and, to a certain extent, politically astute. The existence of even one of these qualities would seem to rule out genuine senility. It is humane in that he admits that such charges are painful both to his friends and to himself. It is rational in that he simply lists his achievements of the period, especially publications and media interviews, and invites readers to "make up their own minds." And it is politically astute in that he attempts to remove the debate from the medical to the partisan arena by claiming that such accusations are a "method of diminishing my effectiveness" (Russell 1969, 234).

Clearly Russell was quite capable of taking care of himself. But that is cold comfort when one sees the evidence of how the charges of senility continue to be perpetuated by generally sympathetic sources after Russell's death. Obviously, the problem is larger than the partisan opponents of the Vietnam War years. Perhaps one of the elements at play in what critics have referred to as the "fictive" dimension of biography is what Harold Moody (1988) terms "stage theory," the view of human life as a progression of stages to some kind of final acceptance or serenity. As Moody points out, these stages can become sentimental "projections" (p. 27). As he should also point out, they can also become another club to silence a senior with—something unserene and disturbing but perhaps also useful. If his failure to follow a deterministic pattern of "growth" caused Russell to be accused of mental insufficiency despite a public record of competency, then we are forced to develop a new respect for the power of fictive stereotypes.

PART II

THE AGING FEMALE
IN LITERATURE

Work, Contentment, and Identity in Aging Women in Literature

Rosalie Murphy Baum

Among the pleasures of fiction, many readers consciously focus upon, indeed savor, the selection of details in narratives, aware that this selection is dictated both "by principles of internal coherence and by the writer's sense of a just, plausible correspondence to the social, moral, psychological facts of real existence as he understands them" (Alter 1984, 9). In fact, this dual motive is what makes novels and short stories "both artistically satisfying narrative wholes and probing visions of their time and place" (p. 9). The nature of the "probing" is, of course, complex: on the one hand, fictional narratives can create an illusion of reality for readers; on the other, they can investigate the very illusion they create and thereby influence the readers' mental experience of life. Thus, literature can play a significant role in both reflecting and creating a culture's values.

Literature has, for example, been influential in forming current views of aging. It has done so by acting as a mirror to culturally accepted views of aging and to the underlying assumptions of those views. But it has also done so by investigating those views, by testing new concepts of aging, and by inventing different paradigms for meaningful living in the last stages of life. Examining cultural representations of aging women in twentieth-century short stories and novels reveals the cultural imagination that over the years has informed—consciously, but mostly unconsciously—contemporary attitudes toward aging. Such an examination reveals, in the words of Margaret Morganroth Gullette (1993), "what our own culture is serving up for us, and what each of us has consumed or resisted" (p. 46).

Two primary facts emerge from such an examination. First, most of the fiction written in English in this century is silent on the subject of aging; that is, the fiction seldom focuses upon an aging man or woman. Second, the few aging men who are central characters in fiction often find their happiness, even their identities, at risk; their later years are described as ones of decline and deterioration. But the aging women in twentieth-century fiction — primarily in works written by women — frequently live lives of contentment and accomplishment and continue to develop and realize identities in their later years. (I am using the word "identity" in the plural to emphasize that each person's life is a process, a series of stages in which, when the person is self-reflective and lucky, appropriate and satisfying identities evolve.)

Of course, the fact that fiction in English today is seldom the story of an aging man or an aging woman is, in itself, a significant cultural statement. When cultures are silent on a subject, they are actually speaking very loudly. This silence is also profound in the social studies, where students of aging note with embarrassment the "paucity of theory in social gerontology" (Moody 1988, 23). And although this essay is concerned with fiction in English, studies of folk literature in many cultures suggest that the roots of this silence about aging are universal.

For example, even though the fairy tale was originally a serious narrative for adults that expressed "the hopes, fears, and wisdom of grownups, not children," most fairy tales in most cultures are "youth tales," that is, tales "focused on children or adolescents" and reflecting "the psychology of youth" (Chinen 1992, 1). Allan B. Chinen's work with Japanese, Chinese, Egyptian, Russian, Indian, Polynesian, and Native-American fairy tales reveals that only about 15 percent of the tales are not focused upon youth. Ten percent are about the middle aged, and 4 percent about the elderly (p. 5). Thus, even in the earliest stages of literature, research indicates that narratives about the middle aged and the elderly have not been encouraged or valued, no doubt partially because people seldom lived beyond their forties.

The story of the youth fairy tale — narrated *for* adults but *about* youth — is a familiar one in the world today, not unlike that of Cinderella or Snow White: "The young hero and heroine meet, fall in love, defeat horrible enemies, marry, and then live happily ever after." As Chinen (1992) explains, "We hear the tale in childhood, hope it is true in youth, but find out later that the story runs thin. By midlife, it usually runs out" (p. 1). Significantly, fairy tales of the middle aged and elderly (albeit few) are not widely known today, significantly because these tales are not stories that thin or run out; that is, they do not reflect current societal stereotypes and misconceptions about aging. Rather, they are "iconoclastic and represent something of a counterculture" (p. 3) as they focus upon the struggles of life and people's successful efforts to create meaning in the mid and later stages of their lives. Chinen writes, for example, that "middle tales are astonishingly feminist," with "strong, independent women exercising their talents and overcoming tremendous social oppression" (p. 3). The stereotypes and misconceptions that point toward elderly lives of deterioration and decline grow out of the youth fairy tales that are so well-known today; paradigms suggesting some of the rich possibilities of later life remain buried in the few, almost unknown middle and elder tales.

But life expectancy today is creating a very different world from that of the past. In the early 1800s in America, for example, the average man or woman would be dead by age twenty-five (although there were some people who lived into their eighties). Today's estimates predict that people sixty-five and older will make up a fourth of the American population in 2050. It is no surprise then that writers (even though they may not be aware of the earlier iconoclastic tradition) increasingly are questioning the "thin" story of the youth tales; they are not letting the story simply run out. And it is clear that greater longevity increases the need to examine how attitudes toward the frequently ignored aging have been socially constructed and, when necessary, to modify those social constructions.

The significant differences that exist between the portrayal of aging males and aging females in literature is most unexpected given societal beliefs, and demonstrates the degree to which an individual's attitudes are socially constructed. To begin with, it is interesting to realize that the aging figures in literature who are best known are males whose lives are coming apart. Readers of novels immediately think of such protagonists as George Hurstwood in Theodore Dreiser's *Sister Carrie*, Gustav Aschenbach in Thomas Mann's *Death in Venice*, Willy Loman in Arthur Miller's *Death of a Salesman*, Uncle Ike in William Faulkner's *Go Down, Moses*, Dick Diver in F. Scott Fitzgerald's *Tender Is the Night*, and Samuel Beckett's Malone in *Malone Meurt*. (Moving out of this century and away from fiction, of course, everyone thinks of Shakespeare's King Lear.) With such figures in mind, it is not surprising that "passive aging" (Sheehy 1995, 419) or, worse, disastrous aging has become an assumption of the culture. Many of these fictional men are in the last years of their lives, they are in decline, their lives offer little satisfaction. Clearly these men are redundant. There are very few aging male figures in fiction who are living rich, satisfying lives. The Cuban fisherman Santiago in Ernest Hemingway's *The Old Man and the Sea* is a well-known exception. Some readers might also suggest a protagonist like Macon Leary in Anne Tyler's *The Accidental Tourist*.

Two kinds of questions immediately occur, of course. First, is it significant that these works with declining male protagonists are all written by males? Is there a consensus among males that the later years of a person's life are, at best, limited, or at worst, humiliating? Second, do these fictional characters illustrate what the culture expects? Or has what the culture expects been largely informed by such literary characters? Here the argument for the power of cultural texts, in this case literary texts, is especially relevant. Writers like Christopher Lasch (1979) and Lennard J. Davis (1987), for example, insist that "More and more, our impressions of the world derive not from the observations we make both as individuals and as members of a wider community but from elaborate systems of communication, which spew out information"

(Lasch 1979, 133). These "systems" including literary forms like novels and short stories.

But—paradoxically—many of the aging women who are central characters of twentieth-century fiction in English live rich, satisfying lives—in novels and short stories written by women. (A well-known, notable exception among such aging women is the angry, isolated Judith Hearne in *The Lonely Passion of Judith Hearne*, a novel by a male, Brian Moore.) Women writing about women, then, appear to be iconoclastic, to represent something of the counterculture Chinen (1992, 3) found in middle fairy tales. And this is very puzzling, in that societal beliefs, encouraged in many cases by feminist writers, suggest that growing older "afflicts women much more than it does men" (Sontag 1972, 32). Kathleen Woodward (1991) observes that although "aging is represented primarily in negative terms" (p. 17) in Western culture, the fact that it "is represented primarily in terms of the visual, in terms of the surface of the body" (p. 169), has a much greater effect on women than on men. She argues that it is an "incontrovertible fact that in our society women are more disadvantaged in old age in terms of social opportunities and resources than are men. In our culture, the sexual allure of a woman, still taken to be one of a woman's most important 'economic' possessions, is understood to diminish much more rapidly with age than does that of a man" (p. 16).

Given such societal expectations, the number of literary works written by women that focus upon an aging woman engaged in what Gail Sheehy (1995, 419) would call "successful aging" rather than "passive aging" (certainly not disastrous aging) is remarkable. Many of these women are pursuing interesting new identities in their later years. They are involved in self-discovery, self-affirmation, and new commitments. There is no sense of the last stages of life being ones in which women simply reap the rewards of former years, no sense of culmination; rather, these women are very much living in the present and pursuing new goals and self-realization. Many of these women share certain characteristics: Most of them work outside their homes (many of them would be considered professionals), they live carefully structured lives, they live inner-directed lives, and they realize the value of their lives in its last stages, sometimes enjoying a day-by-day sense of personal importance, sometimes persevering to new accomplishments, sometimes pursuing greater self-awareness. There is certainly no sense of decline or disintegration in their lives (unless they are institutionalized). These characteristics among a number of fictional women, of course, suggest that aging in no way deprives life of significant meaning. Thus, when the literature of this century portrays women, it makes a surprising statement, given societal stereotypes and misconceptions about aging. In fact, it is possible that the reason aging male characters are so much better known to readers than aging female characters is that the men fulfill cultural expectations; thus, in Davis's (1987) words, the fiction about aging males offers more "regularizing and normalizing features" and less "opposition to stasis and power" (p. 17–18) than does that about aging women.

But one other characteristic that aging female characters in literature have in common is troubling. The women are often not understood by the people around them, some of whom may be family members who should know them very well, some of whom are strangers; that is, just figures in a crowd. This tension—between an elderly woman who sees herself living a satisfying and meaningful life and a world that sees little value in her life—is important. It suggests that the young and the middle aged not only can be inadvertently cruel to the aging but also do not anticipate the quality of life possible to human beings as they age. The younger fictional characters, who react to the elderly as inconveniences or jokes assume the qualities in aging women that most of the aging men in literature display, even though the female characters lack these qualities.

Such prejudice, of course, simply reflects the negative attitudes toward the elderly that are so much a part of contemporary culture. Studies indicate most Americans believe that the elderly are "set in their ways" and "conservative," "repeat themselves in conversations," and are endlessly nostalgic about "the good old days" (Atchley 1980, 256); that they are "unalert . . . narrow-minded, ineffective, sexually finished old people rolling away in poor health, without proper medical care and without enough money to live on" (Harris 1974, 4). Novak argues that not only does the public often have "a more negative view of later life" than the older people themselves have, but the public also often identify problems in the lives of the elderly that the aging do not recognize or acknowledge. In fact, Novak cites a Harris poll in the 1970s which concluded that "older and younger people report about the same degree of satisfaction" in their lives (Novak 1985, 13).[1] Robert Butler (1982) believes that "age-ism reflects a deep seated uneasiness on the part of the young and middle-aged—a personal revulsion to and distaste for growing old, disease, disability" (p. 185). And certainly this ageism is a significant part of the lives of the aging women (and men) portrayed in literature.

Despite this context of societal misconceptions about aging, however, many aging women in fiction are portrayed as experiencing their later years as simply one more stage in life; they display a deep sense of what Rollo May (1969) calls "intentionality," that is, "movement toward something" (p. 229). Like Betty Friedan, they recognize that this stage of life requires "new answers, new questions, a paradigm shift" (Hammond 1993, 8X). Among them are figures like Katherine Mansfield's Miss Brill and James Joyce's Maria, who live satisfying day-by-day lives; Eudora Welty's Edna Earle Ponder and Dorothy Canfield Fisher's Aunt Mehetabel, who pursue special goals defined late in life; and Alice Walker's Andrea Clement White, May Sarton's Miss Pickthorn, and Eudora Welty's unnamed woman in "The Purple Hat," who experience periods of significant self-discovery.

Miss Brill, in Mansfield's (1961) short story of that name, and Maria, in Joyce's (1976) "Clay," are excellent examples of aging women who are living satisfying lives. Both women are portrayed very sympathetically by their narrators (and it is significant that one story is written by a woman, the other by a man). Miss Brill is clearly of the upper class, while Maria is of the lower. Living in Paris, Miss Brill has found it necessary to teach English to young pupils and to read to an invalid gentleman four afternoons a week in order to support herself. Her sense of importance arises from the order and grace of the careful, genteel life she maintains and from the epiphany she experiences in the story, her realization that each person is an actor or actress with a role to play in the performance of life. Miss Brill would probably be considered "a lady" by most of her readers; her pursuits are those of the privileged, the professionals—teaching and reading.

Maria, on the other hand, works in the kitchen of the Lamplight Laundry in Dublin. She would be considered a working-class woman by most readers since she works in the kitchen of a laundry. Yet her inclinations and values are those of a professional woman. Maria could choose not to work and simply live with the Donnelly family if she wished. Instead, she has chosen autonomy—defined by working in a kitchen, and a Protestant kitchen at that. Maria's identity includes both independence and outstanding work. She thinks to herself that it is better to be independent and to have your own money in your pocket" (Joyce 1976, 102). In addition, she takes great pride in her work: Everything in the kitchen of the Lamplight Laundry is immaculate, the fire is "nice and bright" (p. 99), and the bread is cut into perfectly even slices. Further, Maria is known for her good humor and for being "a veritable peacemaker" (p. 99) when the laundry women quarrel. Thus, she has established a significant leadership role at the laundry.

The lives of both women might seem limited to some today. In fact, it is clear that Mansfield, in particular, wished readers to appreciate Miss Brill's quiet courage in facing her later years. Both women live very structured days that include their work and, apparently, one social outing each week. Both clearly experience delight in many of the details of their lives, with Miss Brill being largely an observer, Maria an effective participant. But the days of the two women are described as ones of quiet, simple joys. Miss Brill cherishes her fox stole. She exults in the nip in the air "like a chill from a glass of iced water before you sip" (Mansfield 1961, 549), the line of sea between the trees behind the band rotunda, the special "flutey" passages of the band music in the park (550). She enjoys observing people in the park, from the little children "swooping and laughing," to the miniature drama between the "tall, stiff, dignified" gentleman in grey and a woman in an "ermine toque" (pp. 550–551). Maria loves her job, her room and plants, and her regular visits with Joe Donnelly and his family, talking about Joe's job and about "old times" (Joyce 1976, 104), drinking wine, and playing games with the children. Linda Loman, in *Death of a Salesman*, may say that her husband, Willy, is "only a little boat looking for a harbor" (Miller [1949] 1976, 76) but Miss Brill and Maria have found their harbors and are quite content.

That some people in the world around them do not understand them is clear from incidents that occur in both stories. The courting couple in the park who speak of Miss Brill's "silly old mug" and describe her fox stole as "a fried whiting" (Mansfield 1961, 553) are, of course, the young who pigeonhole the aging and may even find them repulsive or distasteful. They hurt Miss Brill terribly with their remarks, but their comments are ignorant, not malicious. To them, Miss Brill is an outlandish, eccentric character; she has as much reality to them as a discarded paper cup on the ground. The youngsters who play a trick on Maria as she joins them in their blindfold games on Hallow Eve simply consider her ridiculous: an aging woman still not married, a woman who laughs too much and whose nose almost touches the tip of her chin when she laughs.

But despite the single unpleasant incident in each story (and Maria is not even aware of the trick that has been played on her), what both short stories portray is contented, occasionally joyful women—who survive despite social constructs that would label them eccentric or ridiculous and attempt to define their lives as so limited as to be meaningless. In addition, even though the lives of the two women are very different, both have a sense of importance stemming from the roles they see themselves playing in the life around them.

Two aging women who have devoted themselves to unacknowledged domestic duties for most of their lives but achieve remarkable artistic accomplishments in the later stages of their lives are Edna Earle Ponder of Welty's *The Ponder Heart* and Aunt Mehetabel of Fisher's (1996) "The Bedquilt." As a relic of a genteel, patrician, semi-feudal Southern world, Edna Earle has adopted a number of assigned roles and created the necessary identities for those roles for some fifty years of her life. During her grandfather's lifetime, Miss Earle, a "Southern belle" who is a "spinster," keeps house for her grandfather and retarded uncle and also acts as go-between for her uncle and a community working to accept his behavioral problems. After her grandfather's death, when she is in her late forties or early fifties, Edna Earle is the only Ponder left to uphold the family's honor and position in the town of Clay as she tries to care for her uncle, run the Beulah Hotel, and manage the family's plantation. In her fifties, she also narrates *The Ponder Heart*, her greatest accomplishment. Here, in what she intends to be a defense of her family's good name, she unwittingly reveals her courage, self-sacrifice, and sharp wit, and in so doing, unwittingly and harshly indicts the Southern patrician code and the cult of the Southern belle.

Although Edna Earle always insists that she has an important role to play both in her family and in the town of Clay, she is clearly never appreciated, either for her loyalty or work, by the members of her family (and perhaps by the community). Similarly, Aunt Mehetabel, in "The Bedquilt," has "never for a moment known the pleasure of being important to anyone" (Fisher 1996, 33). She is, in fact, an invisible woman until she is in her late sixties. A spinster, Aunt Mehetabel has lived with her brother's family, the Elwells, all her adult life and been "expected, as a matter of course, to take upon herself the most tedious and uninteresting part of the household labors" (p. 33): washing the men's shirts, ironing, stoning cherries, hulling strawberries. The narrator explains that her brother's family "were not consciously unkind to their aunt, they were even in a vague way fond of her; but she was so insignificant a figure in their lives that she was almost invisible to them. Aunt Mehetabel did not resent this treatment; she took it quite as unconsciously as they gave it" (pp. 33–34).

But Aunt Mehetabel has one skill she has developed over the years, and at the age of sixty-eight she begins working on a quilt, an extraordinary quilt that she intends to enter in a competition at the County Fair. Suddenly, her sister-in-law stops her from doing many of her usual chores. In fact, at one point "the family interest had risen so high that Aunt Mehetabel was given for herself a little round table in the sitting room, for *her*, where she could keep her pieces and use odd minutes for her work" (Fisher 1996, 37). The transformation that this work and the attention she receives has on her life is extraordinary: "The atmosphere of her world was changed. Now things had a meaning. Through the longest task of washing milk-pans, there rose a rainbow of promise" (p. 37–38). It takes Aunt Mehetabel five years, but the extraordinary quilt with the remarkable pattern is finally finished. She receives the First Prize at the County Fair and is at peace. In the closing scene of the story, Aunt Mehetabel sits in an easy chair before the fire in the family room, "on her tired old face the supreme content of an artist who has realized his ideal" (p. 42). It is clear that this accomplishment has given new meaning to the last years of her life.

Aunt Mehetabel is fully conscious of her achievement and basks in self-realization at the end of her story. Edna Earle Ponder, on the other hand, is still engaged in her task to protect her family's name and honor at the end of *The Ponder Heart*. Her accomplishments are many, the dramatic monologue that is the novel being not the least, but the later stages of her life will require that she continue the self-affirmation and family commitment that have given meaning to the last decade of her life.

Three aging women who experience significant periods of self-discovery late in life are Andrea Clement White of Walker's (1971) short story "Fame," Miss Pickthorn of Sarton's (1966) fable *Miss Pickthorn and Mr. Hare*, and the unnamed protagonist of Welty's (1980) "The Purple Hat." The aging Andrea Clement White of Walker's story experiences a significant, if fairly conventional, period of self-discovery and self-assertion late in life. Mary Helen Washington (1982) describes Alice Walker's view of the progress of Black women as having three stages: "suspension [caused by racial and sexual oppression and abuse], assimilation, and emergence" (p. 212). White is an assimilated woman who, late in life, emerges as a Black woman finding meaning in her ethnic roots and traditions. In "Fame," she is seeking meaning in a world in which she is "an institution" (Walker 1971, 55). A very successful author who is in the process of receiving her 111th major award as the story opens and knows she will continue to receive them despite the "liver spots on her cheeks" and receding hair (p. 59), Mrs. White ruminates about her early days as the daughter of a slave in the South and wonders what her life amounts to. She is admired and respected, but the adulation has never been enough, and she is in a state of "chronic dissatisfaction" (p. 56). As she has aged, however, Mrs. White has not begun to rest. She is deeply conscious of "an emptiness, no, an ache, which told her she had not achieved what she had set out to achieve" (p. 55).

During the course of the story, Mrs. White begins to discover a few things: that "in order to *see* anything, and therefore to create . . . one must not be famous" (Walker 1971, 55); that a significant part of herself has been lost in a liberal white world that exults in her being the "first" successful Black writer and thinks "that black people write only about being black and not about being people" (p. 57); and that the strength to get through her days in the present comes from her roots in the past, a past in which her parents were slaves. She realizes that her strength in the world of white adulation comes from her own people. The strength for her to get through the ceremony she is presently participating in comes only from the slave song sung by "a small girl the color of chocolate" (p. 62) who is a part of the ceremony. It is perfectly clear at the end of "Fame" that in the last stages of her life Mrs. White is going through a process of self-discovery that will interrogate both her remarkable achievements and the self she has created through the years. She begins to reassert her racial identity, recognizing that her assimilation into the mainstream of American life has denied her the sustenance of her ethnic identity.

Unlike Mrs. White, Sarton's Miss Pickthorn and the unnamed protagonist of Welty's story experience very unusual periods of self-discovery and self-assertion. Miss Pickthorn is a former Latin teacher who translates Horace in her retirement. She deeply respects "hard work, independence, thrift, courage, and a sense of humor" (Sarton 1966, 80) and, after years of dealing with people, zealously protects her privacy. Called a "Maiden Porcupine" (p. 9) by the villagers, Miss Pickthorn enjoys "very much being old," since one is then "permitted to be eccentric, even rude" (p. 10), and defines "a happy retirement" as one in which the retiree is free "to break every routine; to do the unexpected, at least about small matters; to live outside time" (p. 58). A woman whose contentment flows from autonomy, self-reliance, and order yet eccentricity, Miss Pickthorn is "determined to enjoy life to the hilt" (p. 12) as long as it lasts. When she is eighty, however, after she becomes aware of Mr. Hare, a man whom she exchanges only a few words with on one occasion, she experiences a deep sense of renewal, an awareness of a more romantic, freer, poetic quality in life. Mr. Hare's life inspires in her a new sense of adventure and heroism: with his childlike awareness of the beauty of the world, he helps to deepen her pleasure in the simple details of life. Thus, at the age of eighty, her life is infused with a kind of joy, a "magic," and she knows that "from now on" she will "stay as young as she once was" (p. 92). Hers is an epiphany at the age of eighty.

The death-defying gambler-coquette in Eudora Welty's (1980) fantasy "The Purple Hat" offers a sensual counterpart to the more cerebral yet, finally, poetic Miss Pickthorn in Sarton's fable. This woman, in a "great and ancient and bedraggled purple hat" (p. 223) with plush flowers, appears every day at the Palace of Pleasure in New Orleans to gamble — and meet a young man. She has been coming to the Palace since she was fifty; and she has been coming for thirty years. Of course, a gambling casino is not always the safest of places for a single woman to be, so it is not completely surprising to read that this aging woman has been murdered twice in the last thirty years. But neither death nor the years have stopped her. The fat man declares

Dear God, how the moths must have hungered for that [purple] hat. But she has kept it in full bloom on her head, that monstrosity — purple, too, as if she were beautiful in the bargain. She has not aged, but she keeps her middle-age. The young man, on the other hand must change — I'm sure he's not always the same young man. For thirty years, she's met a young man at the dice table every afternoon, rain or shine, at five o'clock, and gambles till midnight and tells him good-bye. (p. 223)

The fat man tries to explain: Although the aging woman is coquettish and leads the men on, she must be a ghost, and it seems to be the hat the young men fall in love with. But then, "Who are any of us to say what ways people may not find to love? . . . Does it matter how she seeks her desire?" (Welty 1980, 226). A strange story insisting upon life and desire even after death, "The Purple Hat" is a sensuous fantasy with an eighty-year-old protagonist who echoes the eighty-year-old protagonist of May Sarton: I will "stay as young" as I ever once was.

Mrs. White, Miss Pickthorn, Mr. Hare, and Welty's unnamed protagonist are "elderly people who illustrate the idea that in old age it is possible to escape from some of the conventions and become supremely oneself" (Sibley 1972, 135). Mrs. White's epiphany follows a more conventional paradigm, the story of an aging woman who begins to realize her selfhood through a return to her roots. Miss Pickthorn's poetic epiphany is especially remarkable and unexpected since even before she meets Mr. Hare she has enjoyed a retirement of self-affirmation and contentment. Welty's unnamed narrator is a fantastic rendering of a refusal to die. All of the women (and Mr. Hare) are impressive literary renderings of "vital aging" (Hammond 1993, 8X).

The seven women discussed certainly suggest that the last stages of life are ones of many possibilities: contentment at least, occasionally a brilliant new accomplishment, always a continuing search for meaning, identity, and self-realization. Such literary portrayals belie ageism, which "like racism and sexism, is a way of pigeonholing people and not allowing them to be individuals with unique ways of living their lives" (Butler and Lewis 1973, 127). And the substitution of such female literary figures, examples of "successful aging," for the better-known male figures of literature, who exhibit "passive aging"

(Sheehy 1995, 419), can help to influence societal attitudes toward the elderly, help to provide "new answers, new questions, a paradigm shift" (Hammond 1993, 8X).

However, depictions of aging women who have entered or are planning to enter the institutional structures society has formed clearly show how ageism can destroy a person and limit the rich possibilities of an individual's last years. These depictions suggest that society today, acting as a care unit, has not yet clearly defined a role—more accurately, a wide range of possible roles—for the elderly. In today's world, "the fabric of [a technological] society, the center, 'does not hold' the aged" (Erikson, Erikson, and Kivnick 1986, 14), especially when the aging, unlike the seven examples discussed, can no longer care for themselves.

Caro Spencer, in May Sarton's (1973) *As We Are Now*, offers a detailed modern indictment of institutional care for an aging woman. Spencer's retirement home is, quite simply, a "concentration camp for the old" (p. 3). A former teacher, a woman of intellectual passion and great sensitivity, Spencer enters the home in her mid-seventies and quickly feels her mind going, not because she is aging but because she is kept on tranquilizers and has nothing to read and no one to discuss ideas with. She is an example of a woman whose possibilities in her last years are destroyed not by age but by the situation she is in. And her defeat is the more terrible because Spencer is a woman of strength and creativity who consciously wishes to explore old age; she sees herself as an adventurer and old age as "a foreign country with an unknown language to the young" (p. 17). But hers is a situation society does not yet know how to handle: at seventy-six, Spencer has had a heart attack; she cannot manage living in her own home; and her brother, John, is four years older than she with a "much younger" wife with whom Spencer cannot get along. Clearly the kind of retirement home in which she finds herself is not the answer.

Two other fictional women for whom institutionalization is planned but does not occur clarify even further the complex issue of caring for the aging when their health begins to decline. Hetty, in Doris Lessing's (1980) "An Old Woman and Her Cat," is quite willing to move into "a Home run by the Council out in the northern suburbs," even though she has been accustomed to "lively London" and is very much "an urban soul." She is willing because she is aware that her health is deteriorating and she is exhausted from "the extremes of poverty" (p. 434). However, when Hetty discovers that she cannot bring her smelly, deformed, loyal "gypsy" cat—the move is out of the question. She has been willing to make the move—despite the fact that the home is "an institution in which the old were treated like naughty and dimwitted children until they had the good fortune to die," (p. 435)—but she cannot leave the only living creature with whom she has shared love for so many years. She dies painfully and miserably that winter in a derelict building. Hetty is found a couple of weeks after her death by the men in London "who, between the hours of two and five in the morning—when the real citizens are asleep, who should not be disturbed by such unpleasantness as the corpses of the poor—make the rounds of all the empty, rotting houses they know about, to collect the dead, and to warn the living that they ought not to be there at all, inviting them to one of the official Homes or lodgings for the homeless" (p. 44). Her cat is caught weeks later and "put to sleep" at the animal shelter.

Hagar Shipley, in Margaret Laurence's (1966) novel *The Stone Angel*, also resists institutionalization, but for very different reasons. (See my essay "Self-alienation of the Elderly in Margaret Laurence's Fiction" [Baum 1996] for a discussion of three of Laurence's aging women.) Shipley is an outrageous, difficult woman whose life has been an emotional desert. As the novel opens, she is ninety and has been making her son, Marvin, and his wife miserable for seventeen years. Her physical needs and the aging of her son and daughter-in-law, who, for example, can no longer lift her, finally make it necessary that she move to an institution. However, in one aggressive way or another, Shipley has controlled those around her throughout her life, and she is not going to begin cooperating in her last years. Thus, Laurence's aging woman offers a very different view of the kind of problems involved in caring for the elderly, a different case from those that appear in so many (upbeat) studies, like *Vital Involvement in Old Age* (Erikson, Erikson, and Kivnick 1986), or James A. Michener's (1994) novel *Recessional*, in which all of the aging appear pleasant, "sweet," "sensible" (p. 174), and, for the most part, amenable to reason. The Holy Terror in youth and middle age, Laurence makes clear, remains a Holy Terror as she ages.

Still, even though the solution to the situations of Caro Spencer, Hetty, and Hagar Shipley may not be clear, the portrayals of aging women considered here, as well as the many discussed in Barbara Frey Waxman's (1990) *From the Hearth to the Open Road*, indicate a society increasingly concerned with its aging population and eager to understand how the last stages of life can be as rich and full as the earlier stages. The number of narratives examining aging females has become so plentiful, in fact, that Waxman argues for the recognition of a new literary genre, "the *Reifungsroman*, or novel of ripening" (p. 2), "ripening" suggesting vitality and life rather than deterioration. Waxman takes the term "ripening" from "May Sarton's optimistic concept of 'ripening toward death in a fruitful way'" (p. 2). Contemporary *Reifungsromans* will continue the important process of reflecting and probing reality that fictional narratives contribute to a culture. They become, in the words of Edward Said, "events," "a part of the social world, human life, and . . . the historical moments in which they are located and interpreted" (Waxman 1990, 3).

Fictional texts can offer "an alternative ground for theories of aging" that are emerging in the social and physical sciences as they "embrace both the contradictions and the emancipatory possibilities of late life" (Moody 1988, 19). The object of the social and physical scientists is to construct and define theories of gerontology that are enlightening and multidimensional, ultimately setting "the structural conditions for aging as a sociocultural phenomenon" (p. 21). This "multidisciplinary assembly of explanatory schemes" (p. 20) seeks "comprehensive ways of unifying current empirical findings about aging" (p. 23)—essentially a monologic goal even with efforts to remain as flexible and multidimensional as possible. Fiction, on the other hand, offers a dialogic world that resists finalizing or defining, a dialogic world that even resists structure. It begins with "personal experience and free creative imagination"; it is "a genre that is ever questing, ever examining itself and subjecting its established forms to review" (Bakhtin 1981, 39). The reality of fiction is "only one of many possible realities; it is not inevitable, not arbitrary, it bears within itself other possibilities" (p. 37). Thus, fiction's language and logic are crucial "for transforming the theoretical structure of science, including theories of aging" (Moody 1988, 22).

CHAPTER 7

Old Maids and Old Mansions: The Barren Sisters of Hawthorne, Dickens, and Faulkner

Maryhelen C. Harmon

In different times and in different places the never-married woman has pro-voked both individual and societal emotions ranging from extremes of ven-eration—for vestal virgins, the Virgin Mary, and nuns—to the fear and subsequent persecution of witches. The arts, not surprisingly, are rich in rep-resentations of these antithetical responses. The figure of the vengeful older woman, married or not, goes back at least to Homer: the Fury-like murdering and maiming Hecuba in the *Iliad* and Eurycleia in the conclusion of the *Odyssey*, who gloats and laughs over the bodies of Penelope's dead suitors and faithless serving women, are vivid examples. Aeschylus (1970) in the *Eumenides* portrays female deities as repulsive maidens, gray and aged who lust for blood and revenge. The geropsychologist David Gutmann (1987) in his analysis of "The Older Woman as Witch" asserts that "according to . . . society . . . in-creased aggression is not a social asset for older women, but a liability which can make them vulnerable to charges of sorcery" (p. 311). Instances of older women represented in the literature of antiquity provoke affective responses ranging from unbounded admiration for those who challenge the hierarchi-cal male world to pity, ridicule, or scorn for those who must function alone. In particular, and the primary concern in this chapter, is that if "old age is woman's hell," the aging single woman in literature is, even in modern times, conventionally and stereotypically the object of derision or, at best, marginal-izing compassion.

I have chosen several memorable and affecting old, never-married women from the literature of the nineteenth and twentieth centuries who evoke these seemingly contradictory but curiously comingled emotions of compassion and scorn, somewhat like what Aristotle noted as the simultaneous feelings of pity and terror in response to tragedy. These fictional avatars of the legendary abandoned virgins in the folktale of the avenging willies (or villi), much celebrated in ballet and opera, are Hepzibah Pyncheon in Nathaniel Hawthorne's *The House of the Seven Gables*, as well as Edith in his "The White Old Maid," Miss Havisham in Charles Dickens's *Great Expectations*, and Emily Grierson in William Faulkner's "A Rose for Emily."

Each of these women represents the archetypal "spinster," the old woman who remains unmarried and is felt to live a frustrated, loveless, unfulfilled life. The card game "Old Maid" reflects the spinster's definition as half of an unmatched pair. Kernels of unpopped corn are called Old Maids. Betty Friedan's (1993) thesis in *The Fountain of Age* is that society's image of older woman as nags, witches, or worse — is a "chain of denial that had to be broken to release us from that dread of dreary, helpless, sick, lonely age" (p. 54). As she asserts in her Preface, "To break through that image, we must first understand why, how, and by whom it is perpetuated" (p. 30–31). In his study of gerontophobia, Richard Freedman (1978) observes that literature "frequently reveals with unblinking truth the very negative attitudes to the elderly which, if we were honest, most of us would admit we feel" (p. 49). Simone de Beauvoir in *The Coming of Age* reminds us by the thesis of her study that understanding female old age in our contemporary society requires comparison with previous eras and locales, and that a key to comprehending its representation is literature. Another corroborative voice is that of Marco Portales (1989) in *Youth and Age in American Literature*, who agrees that "representative human figures produced by a society's writers . . . offer a particularly revealing view of the people of that culture" (p. xii). Responding to these challenges, I feel that no more fruitful search for society's images of aging could be found than in the fiction of Hawthorne, Dickens, and Faulkner.

Hawthorne (1965) in *Seven Gables* presents the spinster Hepzibah (as well as other female characters) as symbols of his culture's values; specifically, the premium democracy places not on heredity, but on achievement. The reader first meets the gray-haired Hepzibah as she awakens one morning and arises from her bed. Immediately referring to her as an Old Maid, Hawthorne further reveals his authorial bias (thereby cueing reader response) by condescendingly calling Hepzibah a poor lady, not once but twice in his introduction of her. Interestingly, in his original manuscript the author invariably referred to Hepzibah as the Old Maid, but in the course of writing he seemed to become more sympathetic toward her, and so revised his references and quite often substituted either her name or some kinder term.

Hepzibah is indeed worthy of considerable compassion from both her creator and reader; her character having been established in her small circle of acquaintances as an ill-tempered, scowling old maid, she is in fact merely extremely nearsighted, and, as Hawthorne discloses, "Her heart never frowned. It was naturally tender" (Hawthorne 1965, 34). Although born a gentlewoman, the heretofore reclusive "patrician lady is to be transformed into the plebian woman" at the age of sixty by her decision to open a small cent shop in her ancestral home, for, because of financial adversity she "must earn her own food, or starve" (p. 38). She also cares tenderly for her pathetic brother Clifford who loves beauty, yet feels distaste when viewing his sister. Consequently this aging virgin is denied even the satisfaction of being admired, yet she perseveres and accepts stoically the hand that fate has dealt her.

Mary Suzanne Schriber (1987) in *Gender and the Writer's Imagination,* cites the various incompetencies of Hepzibah, but emphasizes that "she is a spinster and is thus a woman displaced from woman's sphere," rendering her, according to societal norms, "a comic figure" (p. 65) as she preens at her morning dressing table, for she cannot possibly appeal to the opposite sex. In an authorial intrusion Hawthorne declares "Our miserable old Hepzibah! It is a heavy annoyance to a writer . . . that so much of the mean and ludicrous should be hopelessly mixed up with the purest pathos which life anywhere supplies to him" (Hawthorne 1965, 40–41). To dramatize his romance's theme of retribution for a "sin of long ago," Hawthorne further complains that he is "compelled to introduce—not a young and lovely woman, nor even the stately remains of beauty, storm-shattered by affliction—but a gaunt, sallow, rusty-jointed maiden" (p. 41).

Yet the private Hepzibah is not without strong passions. Hidden both in her heart and locked in her bedroom is her secret—miniature painting of a young man attired an old-fashioned silken dressing gown, his face capable of gentle and passionate emotion. Hawthorne queries querulously, "Can it have been an early lover of Miss Hepzibah? No; she never had a lover—poor thing, how could she?—nor ever knew, by her own experience, what love technically means" (Hawthorne 1965, 32). The reader discovers that the likeness is that of Clifford, her brother: "Her devotedness toward the original of that miniature [is] . . . the only sustenance for her heart to feed on" (2: 32). Schriber (1987) astutely judges Hawthorne's peevish and sardonic presentation of Hepzibah's secret passion: It "joins Hepzibah's unattractiveness with her failure to win a husband, and it asks the implied audience to pity her, not simply for her personal eccentricity but for her displacement from woman's sphere" (p. 66).

By her selfless and torturing efforts to sustain her "hearth and home," the House of the Seven Gables, Hepzibah evokes the Greek goddess Hestia; their names are strikingly similar. Hestia, while primarily a nurturing fertility figure, is also associated with aging in her role as the archetypal old maid; because a virgin does not belong to any one man, she can belong to everyone. Hestia's name means "hearth," and she never leaves the interior of the home. Hepzibah Pyncheon too has barred herself in her home, only the opening of her shop within its walls signifying the momentous fall of the "barrier between herself and the world," a realization driving her to weep. There is, Hawthorne (1965) writes, "no scene for her, save the seven old gable-peaks, with their moss, and the tuft of weeds in one of the angles" (2: 88). Thematically Hepzibah embodies decayed gentility, sustained only by her delusion of family importance, but lacking any revivifying contact with the outside. By imprisoning herself so long in one place and in the unvarying round of a single chain of ideas, the grim Hepzibah develops into a type of lunatic.

An archetypal analysis of Hepzibah's character suggests all three aspects of the Fates, the daughters of Night. She is patently a virgin; also, in her own way, a nurturer, particularly of her beloved brother Clifford; she is also the crone, whose physical form reflects the ravages of age and the inevitable decay of the body (which Hawthorne repeatedly emphasizes in the narrative). As crone/witch Hepzibah's sexuality remains closeted; as nurturer, she will be replaced by the sunny Phoebe, and thereby neutralized as a life force. Because the over-all theme of the romance is "The Fall of the House of Pyncheon," only by the introduction of a youthful new hierarchy, as well as the physical abandon-ment of the ancestral edifice, can the plot be resolved on a positive note. Hawthorne, unfortunately, exploits the pathetic fallacy in his too impassioned and lyrical description of natural phenomena echoing the renewed fortunes of the old mansion's former inhabitants as the romance is concluded.

A little-known 1835 tale by Hawthorne, included in his 1842 edition of *Twice-Told Tales*, is "The White Old Maid" (Hawthorne 1974). Edgar Allan Poe's (1965) review of this story is enigmatic: He warns, "Even with the thoughtful and analytic, there will be much trouble in penetrating its entire import,"and finds it, "objectionable . . . on the score of its mysticism" (p. 138). Yet in a presentation of the tragic, aging, never-married woman, this brief tale bears a striking resemblance in characterization, plot, and detail to the works of Dickens and Faulkner that we will be considering.

The plot is slender. In a chamber in a spacious mansion two young women (probably sisters) stand over the corpse of a young man who has been the lover of both. Edith, who will become the White Old Maid, accuses the name-less proud and haughty other maiden of killing the young man, apparently because he preferred the gentle Edith. They agree, nevertheless, to meet in the same room many years hence, and if the haughty maiden has endured suffering, she will be forgiven. Years pass, and Edith spends them following funerals in her shroud-like white garment, her white winding sheet. Hawthorne (1974) writes, "She was suffered to pursue her harmless fantasies, unmolested by the world, with whose business or pleasures she had naught to do. She dwelt alone, and never came into the daylight, except to follow funerals" (p. 372). The reunion of the two now-old women takes place in the by-then de-cayed and abandoned mansion, in the very room where the lover's corpse lay. Their disappearance into the house alarms townspeople who send in a senile minister to solve the mystery. He finds the two in the attitude of forgiveness, perhaps with the corpse of their lover still present. The minister will not (or cannot) reveal the secret of what he saw, and the ambiguous tale ends.

Far less admirable in their behavior than Hawthorne's Hepzibah Pyncheon and Edith are two similar literary spinsters, Dickens's Miss Havisham in *Great*

Expectations and Emily Grierson in Faulkner's "A Rose for Emily." Each was courted and then abandoned by her lover; each eccentric is subsequently marginalized by society as long as she stays in the isolation in which she dies.

Dickens's (1963) wealthy old maid lives as a recluse in the decaying mansion Satis House among the ruins of her wedding clothes and banquet remains, frozen in the moment of her betrayal. She exacts her tragically pointless revenge on men by rearing her niece Estella to hate them and to inflict pain on those who would love the beautiful but disdainful young girl. In this grotesque fairy tale, Miss Havisham the wicked fairy godmother/evil stepmother/witch casts her spell on the vulnerable young interloper Pip; Estella is the ice maiden beauty—Snow White, the cold star, as well as a kind of "Sleeping Beauty" in Satis House, the enchanted palace. This curiously named mansion derives its name from the Latin word "enough," suggesting fulfillment of expectations. However, ironically, it is at the loveless Satis House that Pip falls futilely in love with Estella, in a place where little satisfaction can be found. In his study of "Crime and Fantasy in *Great Expectations*," Albert D. Hutter (1990) asserts, "Miss Havisham and Estella are opposite versions of a single woman: the latter a virgin (unobtainable) ideal, the former a debased sexual object. . . . Fairy tales display this split by depicting a disgusting old hag and a beautiful princess" (p. 115). Estella, her former self, is what the narcissistic Miss Havisham sees as she obsessively gazes in her dressing table mirror.

On his many visits, starting when a young boy, Pip is exceedingly observant, but seems surprisingly undeterred by the grotesqueries of life at Satis House, which, of course, although avowedly Gothic, are neither supernatural nor demonic. In *Dickens and Women*, Michael Slater (1983) argues that in novels "the characters and events, however strange, should nevertheless be such as could occur in nature" (p. 280). According to Slater, *Great Expectations* is therefore "ostensibly a novel in the realist tradition" (p. 280). A Miss Havisham, the withered bride, *is* possible (p. 280). As Pip recounts, Miss Havisham was "the strangest lady I have ever seen, or shall ever see." He describes her white hair and tattered, yellowed bridal veil , and commenting, "I began to understand that everything in the room had stopped like the watch and the clock" (Dickens 1963, 69), at twenty minutes to nine, when she was abandoned by her fiancé Arthur Compeyson. No wedding took place, and Pip's sharp eye notes the physical decay that all of the wedding imagery intensifies in this living tomb where Miss Havisham lives in an enforced darkness.

In his study of Dickens's mythology, Bert G. Hornback (1972) observes that what Miss Havisham "is defending herself against is change; the change that follows 'twenty minutes to nine.'" For her, change and time no longer exist. Her stopped life is symbolic of the attachment of the upper classes—the establishment—to the status quo, and demonstrative of the perversity of that attraction" (p. 127). As "an effigy of the dead past" Miss Havisham lives all "barred" and "walled up" in Satis House, and, like the mossy House of the Seven Gables, there too "grass was growing in every crevice" (Dickens 1963,

65). The ghastly room with the long table bearing the remains of the wedding feast appalls Pip; Miss Havisham tells him that this is where she will be laid at her death, foreshadowing its actuality. In a grim parody of the central round hearth of Hestia ritually tended by circling round it, the disabled Miss Havisham forces Pip to walk her round and round the chilled room, with its hearth "more disposed to go out than to burn up" (p. 96).

Pip continues to visit "the dull old house, the yellow light in the darkened room, and the faded spectre in the chair by the dressing-table glass" (Dickens 1963, 140), where time stands still even though Pip ages. His relationship with Miss Havisham intensifies when he mistakenly concludes she is his monetary benefactor, her funds fulfilling his expectations of becoming a gentleman. Pip learns from a friend about the early life of Miss Havisham: that she was reared without a mother; that her father, a wealthy brewer, indulged her to extremes; and that as a rich heiress she was considered a good catch. He is told that twenty-five years ago "a certain man . . . made love to Miss Havisham, . . . a showy man," but not a gentleman. He pursued her, and "she passionately loved him," but was "too haughty and too much in love to be advised by anyone" (pp. 197–198). The intensity of this passion is revealed later to Pip by the abandoned bride: "I'll tell you . . . what real love is. It is blind devotion, unquestioning self-humiliation, utter submission, trust and belief against yourself and against the whole world, giving up your whole heart and soul to the smiter—as I did!" (p. 261). The facts then fall into place for Pip: He knows Miss Havisham received the letter of renunciation at twenty minutes to nine on the wedding day, and he has seen at close hand her reaction to the betrayal. His informative friend adds that, after this shock, she had a bad illness, and on recovery, "never since looked upon the light of day" (p. 198).

When Pip later discovers that Miss Havisham is not his "fairy godmother," he visits her at Satis House and accuses her of unkindness by concealing the deception. She shrieks wrathfully, "Who am I, for God's sake, that I should be kind?" (Dickens 1963, 386). On a later visit, however, Pip's feelings for her soften, and she appeals remorsefully for his forgiveness, weeping and dropping to her knees. Pip responds compassionately to her life in the darkness of perpetual night; he realizes that by "shutting out the light of day, she had shut out infinitely more; . . . that her mind, brooding solitary, had grown diseased" (p. 428). In their final meeting he enters her room and sees her sitting Hestia-like close to the hearth, so close indeed that the fire ignites her papery bridal tatters, and she runs toward him, "shrieking, with a whirl of fire blazing all about her" (p. 431). Thus this blighted and grotesque goddess of the hearth will be destroyed by its consuming fire.

Miss Havisham is laid out on the rotted wedding table, swathed with white cotton burn dressings and covered with a white shroud-like sheet, another example of a white old maid. In his analysis of *Charles Dickens and the Romantic Self*, Lawrence Frank (1984) notes that "her bandages are her chrysalis, a sign that she may once again, if only briefly, be participating in that world of change" (p. 174). And change she does; she considers her wasted life—"What have I done!"—and in her last breath asks for forgiveness (p. 428). Pip returns for his farewell, to forgive her, recounting, "I leaned over her and touched her lips with mine" (p. 433). She lives for a week, and then the furnishings of Satis House are auctioned off. "The house itself," Dickens records, "was to be sold as old building materials, and pulled down" (p. 508).

The upstairs bedchamber in Faulkner's (1977) short story, "A Rose for Emily," chillingly echoes Miss Havisham's rotting bridal chamber. The life of Emily Grierson is seen in retrospect, through the Greek chorus-like collective lens of the townspeople of Jefferson, dryly narrated from the first-person plural point of view. Now that Emily has died, the townspeople hope to uncover the mysteries of her life, reconcile her perversities, and satisfy their curiosity about how she lived. Faulkner's double narrative vision of present-day descriptions and recollected action relates what Jeffersonians remember, bit by bit, as well as what they discover after the funeral. This amassing of evidence becomes the story itself, first published in 1930, of a woman's life that the author saw as "a tragedy." In his 1950 Nobel Prize acceptance speech, Faulkner reiterated his conviction that non-gendered man will prevail because he endures.

The recollected bits and pieces that flesh out Emily's life begin by recounting her perversities as one of the last descendants of the "august names" of post-bellum Jefferson, particularly her refusal to pay taxes. When local officials call on her, the reader is introduced to the aging Emily, "a small, fat woman in black, . . . leaning on an ebony cane with a tarnished gold head" (Faulkner 1977, 121), who adamantly refuses to recant. The people of Jefferson then recall her refusal to account for a bad smell emanating from her house thirty years prior to the tax standoff when Emily stood next to a portrait of her late father.

Mr. Grierson had died two years before the odor incident, and during the interval Emily's strange behavior astounded the townsfolk. It began when they called to offer condolences and the then thirty-year-old Emily told them that her father was not dead; there was no body to be buried. They recalled the tyrannical man who drove away all the young men who would call on his daughter, and they justified her bizarre behavior by rationalizing "that with nothing left, she would have to cling to that which had robbed her, as people will" (Faulkner 1977, 124). Soon, however, a Yankee work crew arrived in Jefferson to build sidewalks, and a foreman named Homer Barron was seen publicly in the company of Miss Emily. The collective recollection of the narrators then mentions the time shortly thereafter when she bought arsenic from the local druggist "for rats." Homer disappeared into Emily's home, and the people remember "that was the last we saw of Homer Barron" (p. 441).

Years passed and her reclusiveness intensified. Her hair turned finally to iron gray, as it was when she died at age seventy-four. Yet the attitude of the townsfolk remained tolerant, even compassionate, as "she passed from generation to generation — dear, inescapable, impervious, tranquil, and perverse" (Faulkner 1977, 442). At her death (the narrative now comes full circle to its opening scene of the funeral for "a fallen monument"), the mourners recall an upstairs room in her home, closed for forty years. After a decent interval, the aptly named Apollonian Jeffersonians force it open to discover a Dionysian bedchamber, "decked and furnished as for a bridal" and within its pervading dust the solution to the mystery of the arsenic purchase, the disappearance of Homer, and the smell (p. 443). There too is the last vestige of Emily Grierson: On the indented pillow next to the grinning corpse, they see "a long strand of iron-gray hair" (p. 444) in a tableau of ultimate covert sexuality, the nuptial nightmare of a permanent wedding night.

Elements of the story by Faulkner join those of Hawthorne and Dickens to point up the remarkable similarity of their characterizations of the never-married aged woman: Hepzibah, Edith, Miss Havisham, and Emily Grierson all failed, one way or another, as positive goddesses of the hearth and home. Furthermore, each of their houses, and particularly their bedrooms (universally a centering sexual locus), suggests a complex and elusive meaning beyond the actual architectural setting and linear progress of the story, often described, not surprisingly, by similar Gothic details. Hepzibah is the spiritual symbol of the House of the Seven Gables and we first encounter her at her shabby toilet and mirror. The sterile Satis House represents the diseased morbidity of Miss Havisham, and she first appears holding perpetual court in her dressing room by her clouded lookingglass. Reunion with the corpse on a bed in "a spacious chamber richly furnished in an antique fashion" in the deserted "old mansion . . . surrounded by neglected grass" reconciles Edith and her haughty rival, if only in death (Hawthorne 1974, 370, 374). Finally, only with Emily's demise "in the house filled with dust and shadows" (Faulkner 1977, 442) are the Jeffersonians able to solve the forty-year-old mystery in a room with a dressing table laid out with the tarnished mirror and brushes of Emily's inconstant lover. All four edifices, despite decay and disuse, resist relentlessly the passage of time and the inevitability of change, just as do their lonely inhabitants, antiquated virgins who grow old ungracefully, incarcerated by their shuttered walls and reflected only in their dark mirrors.

Surprisingly similar details of the physical appearance of the four ladies, as well as their decayed mansions, link them. The withered Miss Havisham is reduced to skin and bone; in life, her fantastic white wedding veil and gown hangs loosely around her; in death, she is enveloped in white cotton. Hepzibah is "a tall figure, clad in black silk, with a long and shrunken waist" (Hawthorne 1965, 32). Edith, the White Old Maid, resembles a shadow enshrouded in her "long, loose robe, of spotless purity" (Hawthorne 1974, 375). The young Emily, "a slender figure in white" when jilted in her thirties is "a slight woman . . . thinner than usual"; when elderly, she becomes "a small, fat woman in black" (Faulkner 1977, 434, 439). Each of the quartet is either gaunt and almost bodiless or grossly obese, wrapped either in crone's black or in virginal white. In their study of the nineteenth-century literary imagination, Sandra M. Gilbert and Susan Gubar (1979) examine "the ambiguities of the Victorian white dress . . . the tension between virginal vulnerability and virginal power," asserting, "It is surely significant that doomed, magical, half-mad or despairing women . . . all wear white," specifically citing Hawthorne's old maid and Dickens's Miss Havisham (p. 617).

Each of the three authors strives to point out the significance of the physical changes of these aged women, how their bodies reflect the ravages of the denial of both reality and the passage of time that is imposed on them. Note the similarity between Miss Havisham and Emily: After her jilting Miss Havisham suffers a serious illness; after the death of her tyrannical father, Emily "was sick for a long time" (Faulkner 1977, 438). All four women are described as suffering some form of mental illness: Hepzibah is a lunatic; the white old maid reveals that a taint of insanity affects her whole life; Miss Havisham admits that Estella considers her mad; Pip observes that the old woman has a damaged and diseased mind; and Miss Emily, motherless like Miss Havisham, has insanity in her family—a crazy great aunt referred to as old lady Wyatt.

From a sociological standpoint, Emily's lover, the Yankee transient day laborer, is emblematic of the radical change in the postbellum South, a rural society that David Gutmann (1977) sees as one "very vulnerable to even glancing contact with modern ways" (p. 320). Barron was socially beneath Emily, just as Compeyson was beneath Miss Havisham. Moreover, Compeyson was a showy man, while Barron was a ready man, who liked to show off.

Both Emily and Miss Havisham also resonate with mythic implications. Emily suggests the crone, the old woman who is the dealer of death, and the black-garbed Fate Atropos who cuts the thread of life that her sister Clotho has spun. When separated from the Fate triad, the crone traditionally assumes satanic form, becoming the malevolent witch (a term Pip uses to describe Miss Havisham). Logically, then, a witch hunt, or suppression of the crone, reflects the denial of death in a patriarchal culture such as Jefferson. Emily, we recall, rearranged reality to her own purposes, and denied the death of both her father and the tax pardoner Colonel Sartoris; she also refused to accept the smell, her tax bills, a postal address, or the role of spinster for forty years, preferring a dead lover to none. Miss Havisham also conflates the three Fates of classical mythology—signifying youth, middle age, and old age, or Virgin/Mother/Crone, or Creator/Preserver/Destroyer—with the Fairy Godmother who visits each child at birth to determine the fate or individual destiny of each person. At one point of his entrapment by Miss Havisham, Pip even refers to her as his fairy godmother.

Last, both Emily and Miss Havisham present portraits of the predatory female of misogynistic literature and lore. Emily fits exactly the profile of the "venomous woman" who uses poison to exert sexual power that Margaret Hallissy (1987,4) analyzes in her study of fear of the female in literature. The toxic spider, particularly the female American black widow variety that eats its mate, weaves a web of entrapment, just as Emily snares her victims in her bedroom. Similarly, Pip's entrapment in the deceitful web of the veiled crone Miss Havisham, as well as by the limitations of his individual fortune, is metaphorically underscored by his being forced to view the room laid for the wedding feast, now "heavily overhung with cobwebs, . . . spiders with blotchy bodies . . . running out" (Dickens 1963, 215). Miss Havisham particularly directs his attention to the decayed wedding cake near the cobwebs.

In *Faulkner and Southern Womanhood*, Diane Roberts (1994) recognizes the resemblance between these two fictional women when she observes that Emily's "obsession with confounding time is a quotation of Miss Havisham . . . whose dusty room with 'no glimpse of daylight' and antique wedding clothes signify her grim attempt at withdrawal from the mutable world and her desiccated sexuality" (p. 159). Furthermore, Roberts declares that "Miss Emily's house like Miss Havisham's is an emblem of her sterile body" (p. 160), that "the empty, gold, claustrophobic house signifies the body of the spinster in a sexual economy where the female body is appropriately 'completed' by a man, then by a fetus" (p. 174). In an observation relevant to all of the fiction under discussion here, Roberts asserts, "The Old Maid and the house that defines her, always have secrets" (p. 174). We have seen evidential instances of these secrets: Hepzibah's furtive passion for her surrogate lover/brother, the mysterious death of the White Old Maid's lover, Miss Havisham's manipulative and warped duplicities, and Emily's terrible clandestine bridal suite.

My earlier differentiation between the four fictional spinsters was based on the admirability of their behavior, with Hepzibah Pyncheon and Edith, the White Old Maid, deserving both respect and affection. Taking a more literary perspective in his provocative comparison of "Faulkner's Miss Emily and Hawthorne's Old Maid," Daniel R. Barnes (1972) presents his well-documented case that "Hawthorne's tale may well have served as a major source for Faulkner's story" (p. 373). He cites particularly the following similarities: Edith, like Emily, pillows her head beside that of her dead lover on a bed, their hair mingling; a lock of the lover's hair serves as a token of faith between the two rival women, bringing them together again after long years to die in the same room where their lover was on his death-bed. Indeed, Hawthorne's ambiguous narrative suggests that, as in Faulkner's story, the corpse may still be there. Like Faulkner's Jeffersonians, townspeople in Hawthorne's (1974) tale speculate on the strange affair, especially "the elders, glad to indulge the narrative propensity of age" (p. 378), as they reminisce about the old house's previous inhabitants and social events, foreshadowing Faulkner's (1977) Jeffersonian old men "talking of Miss Emily as if she had been a contemporary of theirs, believing they had danced with her and courted her perhaps" (p. 443) as they too ponder the enigma of her life. The decaying mansions in both stories are described in similar terms: Faulkner's Grierson home had once been in the best section of town, but now "garages and cotton gins had encroached" (p. 433);

the deserted mansion of "The White Old Maid" is also no longer in the se-
lect center of town, "decaying from year to year" (Hawthorne 1974, 374), its
front steps growing mossy from disuse. Each woman has been tended by a
single, aged, silent, and mysterious black servant: Miss Emily by Tobe, Edith
by Caesar. Finally, in both stories, circumstantial evidence alone indicts the
women for the murders of their lovers.

These four rejected societal misfits—Hepzibah, Edith, Miss Havisham, and
Emily—victims of what Gilbert and Gubar (1979) term "the corrupting power
of romance, . . . a mad clinging to romance" (p. 619), exemplify, each in her own
way, the archetypal Outsider. Unrestricted by the role of wife or mother, each is
defined as males define her, both within the fictional narrative and through the
means by which she is characterized by the male author. Each chooses not to
move freely in the world: Hepzibah cannot even face the public in the cent
shop downstairs in her own home; Edith lives alone and never goes out during the day, except to follow funerals; Miss Havisham lives in seclusion in a
large gloomy house; and Emily dies inside her house that only a manservant
had seen within the last ten years. Thereby each ensures for herself a hermited
claustrophobic existence, feeding on self-hatred and denial. René Girard (1965)
terms this condition a form of "ontological sickness" (p. 97).

Sally Page's (1972) view of Emily Grierson, presented in her study of
Faulkner's women, seems equally pertinent to the other three sterile, idle,
and useless women, who defy time and reality. Each author here discussed
emphasizes "that woman's failure to achieve sexual fulfillment through physical love and motherhood initiates her own decay" (p. 93). Denial of "normal
participation in the life of the community because she represents a traditional aristocracy of a higher social class than the norm" causes each woman
to become a victim "of an exclusive, depersonalizing society" (p. 99), out-
raged at life's betrayal of her expectations.

Earlier in this chapter, I emphasized the comingled ambivalent emotions
of compassion and scorn that these three most ostensibly humane writers reveal
in their dramatizations of aged women. Hawthorne's almost Juvenalian ridicule
of Hepzibah alternates with patronizing pity; his description of the kiss of the
shadowy white old maid that might have been death to the little boy who wished
to embrace her is countered by the minister's tribute to her as a true Christian
woman. Dickens underscores Pip's ultimate maturity that enables him to kiss the
lips of Miss Havisham and forgive her. Describing the murdering and necrophilic
Emily, a figure Minrose C. Gwin (1990) sees as "morally ambiguous" (p.
126), Faulkner (1977) admitted that he pitied Emily and that the tributary
rose of the title was a salute; moreover, he presents the fictional Jeffersonians
as sentimentalizing her, having marginalized and depersonalized her into an
icon and a monument. As Freedman (1978) reminds us, "Literature neither
takes sides nor necessarily promotes what we think of as social good" (p. 50).

This chapter has suggested multiform societal dimensions of the aging single
woman in several literary contexts that can be instructive as each of us re-

sponds to Friedan's (1993) challenge to discover the liberating truth, regardless of "how much of [the image of growing old] is imposed by our society's view" (p. 31). Scrutiny of these particular fictional female characters reveals four barren sisters imprisoned not only in their old mansions, but also within the cultural imperatives of their times, as well as by their own emotional frustrations and griefs. One questions why these three great male canonical writers — Hawthorne, Dickens, and Faulkner — in their portrayals of the aging spinster, were unable to break free from the ideologies of their times. Disappointingly, evidence supports the disturbing realization that these artists were themselves incarcerated, like Michelangelo's bound slaves, by the cultural stereotyping of their societies just as their literary creations were imprisoned both within their emotional limitations and within physical dwellings resembling the disorienting Imaginary Prisons (*Carceri d'Invenzione*) of Piranesi. The loss for literature is that the challenge for liberation from an inexorable chain of denial came too late for these three great writers.

CHAPTER 8

The Aging Artist: The Sad but Instructive Case of Virginia Woolf

Joanne Trautmann Banks

Virginia Woolf, who died in 1941, has lived on through her novels and the frequent retellings of her life to become a cultural icon in our time (Silver 1992). Actresses have portrayed her on the stages of London, Toronto, and New York. Her name is a metaphor in Edward Albee's famous play, *Who's Afraid of Virginia Woolf?* made even more famous by the Mike Nichols film with Elizabeth Taylor and Richard Burton. Bookstores across the country sell her caricatured face on book bags and tee shirts. In the process, she has become a model of the creative, free-spirited woman. She was plagued by mental illness, to be sure, but as many feminists might argue what sensitive woman would not be under her circumstances? In fact, it is nearly de rigueur to cite Virginia Woolf when writing about any women's issues whatsoever. I have myself spent many years working with her ideas and for them (Woolf 1975–1980), and I take for granted that in the art and life of Virginia Woolf there is abundant evidence of her greatness.

Nevertheless, when it comes to the matter of age, particularly old age, I submit that Woolf is no role model. With one or two exceptions, the major characters in her mature novels do not get much past fifty: Mrs. Dalloway, from the novel of the same name, is just over fifty-one; Miss LaTrobe, from *Between the Acts*, is presented as seasoned, but not old; *To the Lighthouse's* Mrs. Ramsay, fifty, dies soon after. Virginia Woolf did not let herself get old either. She was only fifty-nine when she loaded her pockets with rocks and walked into the river near her house (Bell 1971, 224–226).

Why, exactly, Woolf killed herself will always remain something of a mystery, but a number of would-be detectives have been on the case. They have explained her suicide with reference to classical psychology, pointing to the numerous family deaths of her mother, sister, father, and brother—in one ghastly decade of Woolf's youth (Spilka 1980). Alternatively, they have drawn on neurological science, claiming that it was her brain rather than her mind that was dysfunctional (Caramagno 1993). And feminists have been attracted to explanations that stress emotional and sexual abuse (DeSalvo 1989).

No doubt all of these causes contributed to her final act, but I want to suggest a cause more basic even than these. I believe that Virginia Woolf— surely one of the most imaginative thinkers of our century—was, in the end, failed by her imagination. Put another way, Woolf could not reinvent herself as an old woman. As it turns out, there are lessons in her failure for all of us who love literature and life at every stage.

Why did Woolf's imagination lose its fire? I am going to offer several reasons, beginning—in the manner of an archeological dig—on the surface of her life, and proceeding downward, through some references in her novels and in her philosophy of literature to—at the bottom of the dig—a general model of how healthy human beings think.

At the surface level is the question of role models. In fact, one of the assumptions on which the chapters in this volume build is that in the aging process role models have tremendous influence, to bad as well as good effect. Among her family, Woolf had rich opportunities to observe aging and aged women. There were aging men too, of course. Indeed, a valuable essay could be written on her father's aging (on the whole, he did it badly) or her husband's (he did it well). But my root subject here is imagination, and, as Woolf (1975–1980) put the matter in a letter, "Women alone stir my imagination" (4:203).

The women in her mother's family (the Jacksons), her father's (the Stephens),and her inlaws' (the Woolfs) often lived into their seventies, eighties, and even nineties. The trouble is that Woolf had deeply ambivalent feelings about all of them. She cared about them, even learned from them, but finally could not, or would not, break out of her family's restrictive epithets for them. For instance, one family fixture in Woolf's first three decades of life was her father's unmarried and religious sister, Caroline Stephen. Dismissed by her brother Leslie as a misguided spinster and called "Quaker" or "Nun" by the thoroughly agnostic Stephen children, she was often a figure of fun. She shows up, somewhat improved, in *Between the Acts* as the widowed, mystical, but dithery Mrs. Swithin. From Leslie Stephen's first marriage, there was Aunt Anny Ritchie, a daughter of the novelist Thackeray. Woolf thought she was a lark too, and put her into *Night and Day* as the comic Mrs. Hilbery, who is forever writing but never finishing her distinguished father's biography. Later came Leonard Woolf's mother, Marie Woolf, who lived to be ninety-one. Virginia admired her in a way—she was "that spirited old lady" (Woolf 1977–1984, 5: 223)—but always returned to her initial impression of Mrs. Woolf as sentimental, chattering, and, worst of all, boring (3: 194–195). When her elderly mother-in-law was in a nursing home, Woolf cruelly complained that the woman had "the immortality of the vampire" (5: 222) and simply would not die. The remark calls to mind the rhetorical question Woolf had asked a short time earlier about a seventy-eight-year-old friend: "Why drag on . . . so as to accumulate years?" (5:214). In short, Woolf saw the late years for all of these women as amusing, at best, and unnecessary, at worst.

There was, of course, a closer role model for female aging. Like most daughters, Virginia Woolf turned chiefly to her mother to see what might lie ahead. What Woolf saw when she looked at Julia Stephen was a great beauty, for that, in a way, was Julia's family epithet. In fact, everyone who knew Julia talked about her beauty in ways that would seem condescending today. She was painted by pre-Raphaelites and photographed by Julia Margaret Cameron. All this was a source of great pride for Woolf (Rosenman 1986, 5–7). Indeed, so powerful was Julia's image that when, in her forties, she grew thin, worn, and less conventionally attractive (photographs and one drawing by William Rothenstein give clear evidence of the startling transformation), her daughter continued to see her as she had been. She wrote to Rothenstein, who had sent her the drawing: "I admit that I think, perhaps with the partiality of a daughter, that my mother was more beautiful than you show her" (Woolf 1975–1980, 4: 7).

When, in her own forties, Woolf looked into her mirror, she saw an ordinary and unfashionable woman, someone who could never compete with her mother on that level (Hyman 1988, 165–166). In actuality, many people saw Woolf as remarkably like Julia, but their opinions could not change Woolf's self-image. And I think that her looks mattered to her, in spite of her tremendous intellectual gifts and in spite of her avowed Bohemianism and feminism. For instance, after she had her hair curled, she had to control her "bottomless despair when [her beautiful sister] Nessa disapproved" (Woolf 1977–1984, 4: 11). Her body concerned her too. Woolf suffered well into her adult years from what we know today as anorexia nervosa and was sometimes forced by doctors to gain weight. Anorexia is thought to be chiefly a pathological method for imposing control on an unruly world, but in Woolf's case anorexia may also have been connected to her fear of aging. In any event, fat and age are connected for one of her characters, the thirtyish North: "Gross, obese, shapeless, [the elderly couple] looked to him like a parody, a travesty, an excrescence that had overgrown the form within, the fire within" (Woolf 1965, 379; Woodward 1991).

This much we know: Her mother's beauty provided Woolf with an ambiguous role model. But that was trivial compared to the grievous fact that her mother's death at age forty-nine left Woolf with no maternal role model whatever for old age. Thus, the luminous Mrs. Ramsay, who is based on Julia, must die at approximately the same age. Even Mrs. Dalloway, who was presumably not drawn from Julia Stephen, is frozen around fifty, and she too "dies" through the suicide of her double, Septimus Smith. At the end, Julia Stephen had influenza as well as what we would now call a compromised immune system. But in the narrative that every family tells about itself, it was said that Julia died young because she had exhausted herself in caring for others. In other words, she did not die from an illness so much as from life itself. Depending of your view of mental illness, the same might be said of her daughter. At any rate, Virginia Woolf (1977–1984) sometimes felt "elderly" (3: 111) in her forties and "so old, so ugly" (5: 208) in her fifties. Her mother's death at forty-nine had left the aging Woolf adrift in uncharted waters. Less than a year before she drowned herself, she was writing, "So the land recedes from my ship which draws out into the sea of old age" (5: 283).

Woolf normally structured her relationships in a manner that went far deeper than simple role modeling. Here I must explain how she developed a sense of who she was, and also why that sense disintegrated as she aged.

Over the years, Woolf worked out what amounted to a theory of personality. If bits from her letters are added to passages from her novels, what emerges is the awareness that, for Woolf, the self is not like a nugget with hard and fast boundaries, but, rather, like a cloud with multiple forms, changing components, and permeable edges. One implication of her "theory" is that when you met Virginia Woolf on Tuesday, you did not see the woman you had met on Monday. There is nothing so surprising in that; most of us are aware that we change in some important particulars from day to day. But Woolf went a good deal further. The friend who met her on Monday—let us say it was Vita Sackville-West—interacted with a quite different person than, say, Ethel Smyth did on Tuesday. And that was because Sackville-West changed Woolf's ego into a new entity, and Smyth changed it again, and Woolf's sister, Vanessa Bell, might affect it on Wednesday, and so on until "Virginia Woolf" was that person who had orchestrated her friends to produce her. It was not so much what Sackville-West and the others consciously did to Woolf, but what she let them do, which, in turn, was dependent upon how she saw them. It was all entirely subjective and entirely fluid.

It was also quintessentially twentieth-century thinking. Her concept of the self sounds very like the ideas that would come along later under the umbrella of "field theory psychology." Psychologists such as Harry Stack Sullivan (1953) and Kurt Lewin (1935) posited that the self was merely the nexus of external stimuli. In her own circle, the so-called "Bloomsbury Group," there was a well-worked-out philosophy of reciprocal friendship based on the ethics of G. E. Moore (Johnstone 1963, 26–31). But this talk of philosophy cannot disguise the probability that for Woolf the process gradually turned troublesome. I believe that it was harder for her to find and maintain a Virginia in isolation than, in the current terminology, to "perform a self" based on a Virginia-with-Vanessa or a Virginia-with-Ethel (Goffman 1959).

Woolf's letters amply demonstrate her relational self. They begin with her polite view that the first duty of a letter-writer is to address the needs of her correspondent. A letter, Woolf insisted, should be "a reflection of the other person" (1975–1980, 4: 98). She went to great lengths to adapt herself to what she imagined her friends expected. But in opening herself to the penetration of others, she gradually saw that the letter was a two-way mirror. What she was doing when she reflected others was defining herself: "This sheet is a [looking] glass" (4: 155). There were some frightening moments when she could no longer be sure that there ever truly was another person out there. Maybe the world was solipsistic: "Do we then know nobody? — only our own versions of them, which, as likely as not, are emanations from ourselves" (Woolf 1975–1980, 3: 245; Banks 1989).

Nevertheless, she kept coming back to her absolute interdependence, not only in her letters, where the form encouraged it, but also in her novels, where she sometimes took the relational self as a theme. The clearest example is probably *The Waves* (Woolf 1959), which she published when she was forty-nine. At an age when, some ego psychologists would insist, she should have been closing in on a sense of self strong enough to counter the difficulties of aging, Woolf has the would-be writer, Bernard, make this offer of aesthetic love to a friend: "Let me then create you. (You have done as much for me)" (p. 85). Throughout the novel, in fact, the six main characters (plus the seventh, who is dead, but still interactive in a way) are seen in such delicate juxtaposition that most readers, following Woolf's own intention (Woolf 1975–1980, 4: 397), have considered them voices in the head of one magnificently collective self. That some of the voices are male, others female, is comparatively unimportant in the novel, where gender is only one more aspect of the continuously migrating self. (Significantly, youth and age in *The Waves* do not have the interchangeability of male and female.)

Of course, Woolf found literature easier to control than life, particularly as she aged. In the letter about the six characters in *The Waves*, she also wrote, "I'm getting old myself—I shall be fifty next year; and I come to feel more and more how difficult it is to collect oneself into one Virginia" (Woolf 1975–1980, 4: 397). Behind this statement may have been the realization that she was the same age as her mother when she died. More to the point, Woolf was at that age when some friends die and others drift away into their own pressing concerns. Therefore, she was particularly fortunate that in her late forties she met a woman who was to become one of the great friends of her life. This was the composer, feminist, lesbian, and generally rowdy presence, Dame Ethel Smyth. Smyth alternately delighted and enraged her. In her twenties, Woolf had written to a friend, "I only ask for someone to make me vehement, and then I'll marry him!" (1:492). Twenty years later, Smyth made her vehement, and as a consequence revived Woolf's life by focusing it.

Dame Ethel, who would live with great vigor to eighty-six, was already old when she pushed her way into Woolf's life. Woolf seems to be carrying on her youthful mockery of aging people when she writes about Smyth to her nephew: "An old woman of seventy one has fallen in love with me. It is at once hideous and horrid and melancholy-sad. It is like being caught by a giant crab" (Woolf 1975–1980, 4: 171). Nevertheless, it was partly under this old woman's influence that in her fifties Woolf wrote her strong feminist book, *Three Guineas* (1966), as well as its novelistic counterpart, *The Years* (1965). The novel takes its main characters from youth to age. It presents, in Rose, a politically active character who bears a resemblance to Smyth, and, in Eleanor, the single most important, as well as the most positive, old character in Woolf's work. Literary critics in general have said that Woolf reached her artistic peak in her forties with the astonishing fecundity of *Jacob's Room, Mrs. Dalloway, To the Lighthouse, A Room of One's Own*, and *The Waves*. But some feminist critics and literary gerontologists have been attracted to the next decade, and have praised what they see as Woolf's creative and independent fifties (Heilbrun 1983; Woodward 1991; Garton 1994). If Woolf's last ten years were productive, some part of her accomplishments are traceable to Ethel Smyth, in the light of whose fiery, confident ego Woolf recreated her own being, for a time.

But other forces intervened. For one thing, the war came. Her nephew was killed during its Spanish prologue, and his mother Vanessa, with whom Woolf had playfully invented herself all her life, withdrew into profound grief. Vita Sackville-West was busy with newer friends, and Dame Ethyl's indefatigable presence began to pall. Most dangerous of all, the war threatened to diminish the bookselling and publishing businesses, thereby cutting Woolf off from all those mirrors that her readers had held up in front of her. As she writes in her diary, "It struck me that one curious feeling is, that the writing 'I', has vanished. No audience. No echo. That's part of one's death" (1977–1984, 5: 293).

I have been looking at the process whereby Woolf knew that the self was real. Now I want to consider how she knew that the world was real, as well as how that worldview served her badly in the light of a certain theory of successful aging.

In spite of her famous fascination with subjective experience, I would say that Virginia Woolf was equally drawn to the world outside the individual mind. For her, this was the world of objects and facts of a perfectly ordinary, everyday sort. Woolf's mind devoured hard data. I have been told by her younger friends that she frequently asked those she met to describe their days: "Now what woke you up this morning?" she would begin, "Was it the sun streaking over the counterpane? Tell me everything." She charmingly demanded facts from her correspondents too. Ethel Smyth was asked, "Haven't you got a ream of paper which you might just as well fill, sitting over your fire (what sort of fire?) in your room (what sort of room?) alone? For what other purpose than to write letters to me brim full of amusement and excitement were you gifted with a pen like a streak of hounds in full scent? And the more odds and ends you stuff in the better I like it" (Woolf 1975–1980, 4: 151). Her drive to speculate about external reality is analyzed in her philosophical short story, "The Mark on the Wall" (1985), in which the narrator is obsessed about the nature of so simple an object as a small black mark on a white wall a few feet away. The narrator is foiled—the mark turns out to be completely other than what she, wrapped in her subjectivity, supposes—but that is exactly as it should be, for, in Woolf's universe, no one can ever apprehend the world in its totality. The best we can hope for is pieces, and some of us miss even that much.

In Woolf's view, a great many people stumble around blindly on the surface of life, greedily surviving and never aware of the world's mystery. These people assume that when they are dealing with how they look or what they own or whom they know they are dealing with that which is real and lasting. They are wrong, of course. But others, those who are sensitive to life in its immaterial as well as material aspects, are vouchsafed "scraps, orts and fragments" (Woolf 1969, 188) of true reality. So the playwright expresses it in Woolf's last novel, *Between the Acts*. The phrase occurs while the actors flash fragments of mirrors and other reflecting surfaces at the audience. In other words, the same "mirror" that I earlier identified as able to give you a glimpse of yourself and give your friend a glimpse of herself can also give you a scrap, an ort, or a fragment of the reality that exists outside you.

Elsewhere she calls such exquisite experiences "moments of being" (Schulkind 1985). She means those brief flashes of insight that shoot straight through the ordinariness of daily life and, with sharp intensity, reveal the world as it really is and also one's place in it. The certainty is always transitory and impossible to capture with words. Indeed, she admitted that her beliefs could not be substantiated except by personal experience, though it might be added that such views place her in a long line of mystics and philosophers, beginning with Plato.

Her conception of reality is completely consistent with her practice of literature in that her fiction is filled with "moments of being." It could even be said that many of her short stories *are* such moments. Several characters from the novels also have their "visions," as one of them, Lily Briscoe, claims at the end of *To the Lighthouse* (Woolf 1955, 209). True to Woolf's philosophy, the visions are not only present in the middle of commonplace events; they are, in a sense, composed of them.

But how does the novelist convey this meaning to the reader? If you believe that society, and therefore fiction, is ultimately the story of great men and women performing heroic acts, you might write a war novel. If you believe that reality rests on how men and women look and how they behave, you might write a comedy of manners. Since Woolf believed that reality was compounded of glittering shards that somehow make it through the lights and shadows of our daily thinking, she wrote what has been called the "stream of consciousness" novel or the "modernist novel."

Whatever "modernism" means, and it has been much debated and defined, almost everyone agrees that Virginia Woolf practiced it. She also described it very well. In an essay called "Modern Fiction" (Woolf 1953a) she rejects the novels of Arnold Bennett, H.G. Wells, and John Galsworthy because they are materialists. In other words, they believe that the real world can be objectively described simply by accumulating unimportant external details. Woolf thinks that their sort of novel imposes a plot on the world rather than taking the world as it truly is. For Woolf, in contrast, "Life is not a series of gig lamps symmetrically arranged; life is a luminous halo, a semi-transparent membrane surrounding us from the beginning of consciousness to the end." As we go

about our business, she says, "The mind receives a myriad impressions —
trivial, fantastic, evanescent, or engraved with the sharpness of steel. From all
sides they come, an incessant shower of innumerable atoms" (p. 154). Thus,
right before Lily has her vision in *To the Lighthouse*, Woolf (1955) records a
dozen atoms from Lily's consciousness: She hears the squeak of a door hinge,
she remembers a reddish-brown stocking, she thinks this and that about art or
love. Because of the momentum of Woolf's faith and prose, all these atoms
finally collide to give Lily the momentary miracle of reality. For me and many
other readers, it is a stunning moment in the history of literature.

But what has all this literary philosophy to do with aging? Just this: For
someone whose reality comes transiently in disparate pieces, it is extremely
hard to achieve the famous Eriksonian "integrity" — that wholeness of self
and of one's worldview that is necessary to counter the despair of old age. For
all the subtle reevaluations of Erik Erikson's work (Friedan 1993, 122–123), I
remain attached to his concept of integrity as both accurate intellectually
and useful in the everyday world. Erikson does not mean, nor do I, that life
must actually achieve completeness, only that the truly mature person acknowledges and blesses the various elements of his or her own world, and
brings them into perspective.

There is nothing in Woolf's philosophy that inevitably prevents integrity.
In fact, in her fifties, Woolf tried to achieve wholeness in a new way, and I will
be discussing her attempt in the next section of this chapter. But it takes a
great deal of strength to live with a personal narrative of the world in which
there is no linear plot at all, no conventional cause–effect, and a slippery
hold on facts and objects, even as you crave them. I emphatically do not wish
to believe it, but it may be that Woolf's brand of modernism is easier, and
more seductive, for the young. After all, psychologists have sometimes described young people as more hungry for stimulus than the old, and more
interested in excitement than security. And neurologists speak of aging neu-
ron receptors which no longer respond quite so flexibly to neurotransmitters.
It may be that just as aging brain cells are not as agile as younger ones, or
even because they are not, the aging psyche is not as agile in maintaining
unity. At any rate, I do believe that the aging Virginia Woolf found she could
not move as flexibly between inner and outer reality. In Yeats's lines from
another context, she discovered that "Things fall apart; the centre cannot
hold;/Mere anarchy is loosed upon the world" (Yeats 1973, 131).

There is a painting of Woolf by her sister Vanessa Bell that, for me, provides the perfect image for the price Woolf ultimately paid for her modernist
perspective on her self and the world. Woolf is seated by her bookshelf. With
her right hand, she is gesturing toward someone or something, but her face is
completely featureless. In contrast to Woolf, certain people need to achieve
integrity at the end of life by opening up old rigidities. This is true for Tolstoy's
Ivan Ilych, for example, whereas for the old woman in "Tell Me a Riddle" by
Tillie Olsen, a Woolf devotee, the world must be filled in (see Banks 1990).

I am now at the bottom of the archeological dig that has been this investigation of Virginia Woolf. It is a little murky down here. No one can say with certainty how the imagination works, let alone how it goes wrong. But I can see the outline of a very basic mechanism in healthy human beings; that is, the method by which we reinvent ourselves in response to a changing world (and who can deny that our world changes dramatically as we age). For reasons that I will try to make clear, Woolf's adaptation mechanism ran down at the end.

In 1932–1933, about the age of fifty, Woolf had her only major failure as a writer. It was a private failure, but no less traumatic for that. With feminist Ethel Smyth in the foreground, Woolf conceived *The Pargiters* as a history of women and families. It is not, however, the content, but the book's experimental form that interests me here. Woolf planned to alternate chapters of fiction with chapters of fact. That is, she would analyze what she had just narrated, and the book as a whole was to be presented as a new form called the "novel-essay." She wrote several fiction/fact pairs before she abandoned the project, split the novel from the essay, and expanded each separately into *The Years* and *Three Guineas*. But she could not let *The Pargiters* go. For the next several years she suffered terribly while writing the two half-books, each of which, like separated Siamese twins, retained some aspect of the other: The novel contained some fact in the form of research on women, and the tract partook of fiction in the form of its imagined letters to organizations. So great was Woolf's physical and mental instability as she wrote these hybrids that she had "never been so near the precipice to my own feeling since 1913"— that is, the year she attempted suicide (Woolf 1977–1984, 5: 24). My hypothesis is that we can trace some of the elements of her instability in the breakdown of *The Pargiters* and what followed from it.

First, I want to say straight out that, to me, the writing of even a few installments of *The Pargiters* took courage. Woolf was attempting to bring analytical writing as close as possible to imaginative writing. She was setting her passion for facts, as explained in the previous section, alongside her love of the experiencing, visionary mind. She had dealt with this dichotomy all her writing life, but always she had carefully separated the two modes. For instance, the novel *Orlando* was the spur for her first feminist tract, *A Room of One's Own*, which followed the next year. The manuscript of *The Pargiters* shows that, this time, she was bringing the two modes of thinking so close that she was aiming for something like the literary version of a unified field theory of knowledge. If that comparison seems too extravagant, let us say that she was struggling to operate on two completely distinct levels of consciousness with near simultaneity. Even consciousness guru Lawrence LeShan (1976) speaks about the difficulty of shifting from one sort of reality to another. At the very least, Woolf was trying to narrate facts, as opposed to analyzing them. None of this was possible, and, in banging her head against an intellectual wall, I am guessing that she went a little crazy. To the extent that *The Years* and *Three Guineas* continued the struggle, the trouble grew.

More specifically, I think that in trying to switch back and forth between two modes Woolf saw that she could no longer practice with ease one of the most basic processes of life. The eminent systematic theologian Paul Tillich (1961) describes this process as a constant oscillation between making closures on experiences, then opening up to new experiences. That is, human beings live in a continual process. We come to conclusions about life, about little matters such as whether a traffic light is red or green, and about bigger matters such as whether that car coming from the right is going to stop in time. We conclude that a relationship is over, or that miracles happen. We conclude, in short, that the world can be accurately described in such-and-such a way, and we close in around that perception. Then, since we are constantly challenged by new data, we open up again to take them in, draw further conclusions, open for data, close, and so on in a perpetual cycle. The strength of Tillich's model is buttressed by his observation that this same oscillation occurs on every level of our existence, from our cells to our social and spiritual relationships.

In healthy people, oscillation happens smoothly, so that as soon as we close on something, we begin to open again. The movement is so natural that it produces no anxiety. Trouble begins if we drop off at either end of the process. That is, if we remain constantly open and therefore without any structure, the resultant anxiety and lack of self-definition can paralyze us. If, on the other hand, we get stuck in the closed position, we cannot handle any changes in our environment, and, obviously, that is dangerous too.

To clarify this dilemma, picture the self as a medieval castle with servants running in and servants running out (my gratitude goes to Samuel Banks for bringing Tillich to my attention in terms of this castle metaphor). That situation is healthy. But some rulers pull up the drawbridges on their castles and keep their servants inside. They station soldiers on the walls. They peer out through arrow slits and do not go out again. That kind of fear and rigidity is one kind of dis-ease (it used to be called "neurosis"). Other rulers leave their castles without their retinues and roam far afield in search of adventure. They are like the man in Hemingway's (1952) *The Old Man and the Sea*, who says dolefully, "I shouldn't have gone out so far" (p. 121). They cannot get back to the security of the castle, and that is a kind of psychosis.

If I am right about Virginia Woolf's oscillation mechanism breaking down, I wonder which extreme she reached before she drowned herself at fifty-nine. There is some interesting evidence that she was locked inside her castle. She held fixed ideas, for instance, about gender and about suicide. But most of the evidence suggests that she was a sort of knight in shining armor who finally ventured too far afield. She was questing after ultimate reality, and that is where she thought it was. She spoke of her personal grail in boundless metaphors of sky and sea that erased the individual. Here, for instance, is a comment on "the mystical side of this solitude": "It is not oneself but something in the universe that one's left with. It is this that is frightening and exciting in the midst of my profound gloom, depression, boredom, whatever it is: One sees a fin passing far out. . . . But by writing I don't reach anything" (Woolf 1977–1984, 3: 113). Hemingway's old man would have understood her obsession with reaching that always elusive fish.

Virginia Woolf was an extraordinarily intelligent, witty, and imaginative person who had a large part in inventing the contemporary literary mind. Sadly, when it came to reinventing herself for the last phase of life, her imagination faltered. Woolf had no family role models for aging, or, rather, she rejected the role models she did have. Moreover, she needed the interactive presence of creative friends in order to feel real, and, as she aged, some of those friends dropped away. Her philosophy of literature and life—modernism built on moments— hindered the development of Eriksonian integrity. And, underneath it all, she found in her fifties that she could no longer oscillate smoothly between the world as it is and the world as she envisioned it. We may not know a great deal about the machinery of the imagination, but surely when it can no longer open and close, imagination has lost its vital force.

Still, we need not be afraid of Virginia Woolf, no matter what Edward Albee says. I began by saying that I found Woolf's story "instructive," and I hope that readers will already have drawn from it several lessons about imagination, identity, reality, and aging. In my opinion, it does not distract from Woolf's sophisticated accomplishments, nor does it trivialize her tragedies, to make practical use of any part of them. If the case of Virginia Woolf causes us, for example, to sharpen our sense of how family and friends construct us in each stage of life, so much the better. If, to take another example, her "moments of being" image prompts us to respect the strong influence of metaphors on our mindsets, we are only doing what all writers ask of us, which is to take them very seriously. If we can decide whether our integrity requires us to firm up our perception of reality or to loosen it, then we can get started on the task. And if we are more attentive to the workings of the imagination generally, then we are better prepared to meet the great adventure of aging that is even now starting toward us from around the next turn.

PART III

AGING IN
THE COMMUNITY

CHAPTER 9

The Sacred Ghost: The Role of the Elder(ly) in Native American Literature

David Erben

This chapter offers readings of examples of Native American literature with particular attention to Leslie Marmon Silko's *Storyteller* (1981) and *Ceremony* (1971). These examples are connected by a shared theme; each of these works focuses on the elder—grandparents, aunts, or uncles—as role models and storytellers. Elders are valued in these texts by a Native American author— each of these works presents a particular configuration of the elder with exemplary clarity, beauty, and depth of insight. By analyzing these texts, I hope to discover not simply "moments" within the consciousness of these works, but also an attitude toward elders typical of Native American cultures.

One morning during the drought-plagued summer before Tayo—the protagonist in Silko's (1977) *Ceremony*—leaves for the war, he rises before dawn to pray for rain in a canyon where a spring drips into a pool, "flowing . . . drop by drop from the big crack in the side of the cliff" (p. 94). Tayo's visit to the spring south of Laguna to pray for rain indicates the depth of his belief in the "time immemorial stories" recounted by old Grandma, while another elder, Josiah, shows Tayo how those stories apply to his everyday existence. Once, when Josiah and Tayo went to the spring to fill the water barrels, Josiah explained that some things were more important than money: "This sand, this stone, these trees, the vines, all the wildflowers. This earth keeps us going" (pp. 45–46). Thus, Tayo is able to sustain his faith in old Grandma's story despite the years he spent at the Indian school. Maintaining his belief in these narratives had not been easy, given the pressure applied by the teachers "not to believe in that kind of 'nonsense'" (p. 19). The problems that arise for Tayo (and many of the protagonists in this literature) are caused by the confusion resulting from education in conflicting beliefs, since the stories told by Tayo's Anglo science teachers directly contradicts those related by Josiah and old Grandma. *Ceremony* thus depicts the importance of the traditional elder in Native American literature, in which a vital, sacred figure (Grandma) plays a pivotal role, acting as the source for the tradition that leads ultimately to Tayo's healing.

In Native American culture, reverence for the past and knowledge of the culture has been traditionally relayed by elders. The stories handed down from these elders were rooted in a deep sense of kinship responsibility, a responsibility central to the identity and sense of belonging essential to Native Americans. Moreover, these stories testified to the richness, variety, detail, and complexity of Native American cultures. From these ancient stories, the children and grandchildren of the elders gained an understanding of where they came from, who they were, and what was expected of them. The aging Crow Chief Plentycoups spoke to Frank Linderman (1962) in 1930, saying, "Our teachers were willing and thorough. They were our grandfathers, fathers, or uncles. All were quick to praise excellence without speaking a word that might break the spirit of a body who might be less capable than others. Those who failed at any lesson got only more lessons, more care, until he was as far as he could go" (pp. 8–9). Charles Eastman (1971), a Wahpetonwan Dakota, reveals in his autobiography, *Indian Boyhood*, the distinct way in which tradition was transmitted: "Very early, the Indian boy assumed the task of preserving and transmitting the legends of his ancestors and his race. Almost every evening a myth, or a true story of some deed done in the past, was narrated by one of the parents or grandparents, while the boy listened with parted lips and glistening eyes" (p. 43). These excerpts highlight both the rigorous and extensive training required of young people and the rich, vital role of elders as storytellers and educators, demonstrating why in Native American cultures it is "particularly important to focus on the techniques by which individuals construct meaning in their lives" (Cohler 1993, 123). For Native Americans, elders were traditionally dynamic, creative individuals who were part of a larger whole which preceded them.

This chapter attempts to profile depictions of elders in a systematic way. "Society" for traditional Native Americans was law. Catherine Archilde's aging mother in *The Surrounded* (McNickle 1936) describes how after Western colonization, the customs, rituals, and practices of law once passed down to the young by the elders, uniting them into a community, have been lost. Instead of being listened to and treated with respect, old people became subjected to western attitudes, in which, as Kathleen Woodward (1993) explains, "Old age is more often than not . . . associated with loneliness and loss" (p. 82). In the central feast scene in *The Surrounded*, the Indians lament the banning of dances, ceremonies, and practices by American secular and religious authorities; the tone of this discussion implies that, under Anglo rule, "anarchy is loosed upon the world." These traditional stories highlight the desperate need, identified by gerontologist Harry Moody (1993), "to recapture [the] moral dimension of old age, to see what tremendous possibilities . . . are at stake" (p. xxxix).

In *Ceremony*, Silko (1977) uses the novel's opening epigraph to draw the reader into this narrative of a textual and social world out of balance. Bertram Cohler (1993) discusses societal change, explaining that "largely adverse factors that pose problems for maintaining a sense of personal continuity over time suggest that change rather than continuity is the most significant factor in the study of life history and that presently experienced continuity is a consequence of a continually revised life story" (p. 111–112). *Ceremony* invites the reader into direct dialogue with the community of storytelling voices, which includes Tayo's Uncle Josiah, his grandmother, and the old medicine men, Ku'oosh and Betonie. Establishing a community of storyteller and audience is an ancient strategy which finds its best models in oral performance genres. However, before the reader and protagonist can form the community, the reader must enter into the social dimension, which stretches back into the mythological past through the role elders play in the text—and thus into the phenomenological act of creation. In this way elders are not static features of the community, but active, creative forces. The dialogue of the narrating community is initially adversarial rather than mutually supportive, but the conflict subtly diminishes as the protagonist moves through the healing process that balances his or her identity. The self-reflexive introductory mythic epigraph warns us that this conflict involves "the stories" themselves, that these stories are not simply entertainment, but are weapons against illness and death (Silko 1977, 2). Thus, the epigraph explicitly foregrounds the healing function of story and the importance of the role of storyteller.

As the speaker of the epigraph focuses on a conflict involving discourse modes, the stories themselves become active agents, potential antagonists in the drama that the reader is witnessing. Like narrating voices and readers, the stories actively participate in the community, struggling to overcome the Western perspective: "All cultures have evolved a worldview linking past, present, and future, although there are no cultures other than the Western that are so explicitly concerned with a linear time perspective" (Cohler 1993, 110). Early in the narrative, Silko uses Tayo's memories to reiterate the conflict between these two perspectives, one taught to him by his elders, the other by white educators: "He had believed that on certain nights, when the moon rose full and wide at a corner of the sky, a person standing on a high sandstone cliff of the mesa could reach the moon. Distances and days . . . all had a story. They were not barriers. If a person wanted to get to the moon, there was a way; . . . it depended on whether you knew the story of how others before you had gone. He had believed in the stories for a long time, until the teachers at the Indian school had taught him not to believe in that kind of 'nonsense'" (Silko 1977, 19). Thus, the teachers' critical vocabulary has introduced a conception of the stories as nonstories—as "nonsense"—and thus without meaning, function, or applicability in the dimension of real experience.

Tayo's experience with his teachers reminds us how ineffectively language has functioned at the intersection of Anglo and Native American cultures. Two factors that have contributed to this ineffective communication are the almost universal illiteracy in Native Americans among the Euro-American populace and the centuries-long political and social "heterglossia"—the extraliterary dialogue—surrounding the whole issue of traditional discourse modes versus the hegemonic culture's "civilized book learning." This dysfunctionality has had a grave political and social impact. Sometimes taken from their homes by the U.S. military, thus effectively removed from their elders and their stories, earlier generations of Native American children were physically punished for using their own languages at Federal Indian schools. Viewing native languages and discourse modes as "nonsense" allows the hegemony to ignore information and insight offered through that discourse and to exclude it from the official discourse community.

In *Ceremony*, the conflict with the labeling power of language is intimately involved in the struggle with identity. Traditionally, the elder had the power of naming and storytelling. As his story opens, Tayo cannot perceive how the mythic, naming mode represented by his elders might be compatible within the singular dimensions of his "realistic" world as defined by his Indian school teachers. In accepting the teachers' derogatory vocabulary and preconceptions, Tayo, like the eponymous "hero" of James Welch's *The Death of Jim Loney* (1979), has lost the stories, our weapons against illness and death, and thus has severed his connection to his family and people (Silko 1977, 45). Yet the intermittent mythic voice, the voice of the elder, like the single unit of the text without chapter divisions, insists implicitly that character and reader make sense of and unify these two initially antagonistic, culturally discrete expressive modes. Tayo, according to Cohler (1993), experiences a kind of "narrative of affliction" and his "personal adversity represents a challenge to the story of his life, which in turn demands increased narrative clarity" (p. 116).

In his search for "narrative clarity," Tayo finally begins to see patterns rather than entanglement, to follow threads rather than to pull apart the fabric of his experience. A part of this healing, this perception of patterns, is his growing ability to recapture the stories lost under the destructive label of "nonsense," and to unify the two seemingly antagonistic forms of discourse and ways of thinking. In one such integrative moment, Silko allows the mythic voice to "animate" the realistic voice, thereby liberating the mythic voice from its demeaning label of "nonsense." This special moment occurs in a passage in which Tayo begins to subtly interrelate the community of dissonant stories, to unite Grandma's stories and the science teacher's stories within the same textual space. The clue to this integration is the appearance of a hummingbird. Hummingbird has served as a sacred representative in the narratives of North and South America since prehistory. Hummingbird appears at the creation in the sixteenth-century Quiche Mayan *Popol Vuh* (Recinos 1952) and functions as a central character in *Ceremony*'s mythic stories. Although, as this passage reveals, its appearance here is subtle, "almost imperceptible," and unmarked by a capital letter, the hummingbird nevertheless carries a heavy symbolic freight. Everywhere Tayo looked he saw a world made of long ago, immemorial stories. The world was alive, changing and moving, "like the motion of the stars across the sky . . . and it was then he saw a bright green hummingbird shimmering above the dry sandy ground, flying higher and higher until it was only a bright speck. Then it was gone. But it left something with him; as long as the hummingbird had not abandoned the land, somewhere there were still flowers, and they could all go on" (Silko 1977, 95–96). This nurturing vision, lyrical in tone and naturalistic in detail, momentarily unifies the text's divided voices. The ever-present context of mythic voices makes Tayo aware that Hummingbird is significant, and the ordinary hummingbird tells him that nearby lies enough water to produce the flowers that can give birth to a future generation of plant, and thus animal life. Thus, the sacred circle and its chain of "ordinary" life remains. In this moment, Silko creates for Tayo a vision in which the mythic and the ordinary can intersect without antagonism, where his individual and communal pasts, lost as "nonsense," have recovered ultimate meaning.

Silko (1977) maintains the implicit interrelatedness of the mythic and realistic narratives consistently into the novel's denouement. As Tayo's immediate social and psychological worlds achieve balance, the mythic and the ordinary life-giving storm clouds return to the people. The achievement of wholeness functions also at a subtextual level for key characters. Ts'eh, (H)hummingbird, the storm clouds, and the people themselves—like Momaday's grandfather Mammedaty—are all conceptually and stylistically "liberating" characters, for they function meaningfully in both extraordinary and everyday dimensions in both mythic and realistic discourses that mutually create the communities of *Ceremony*.

Steven Weiland (1993) notes that the "process of adding meaning is part of the definition of adulthood and old age" (p. 85). Silko's (1981) autobiographical *Storyteller*, a map of "adding meaning," is comprised of personal reminiscences and narratives, retellings of traditional Laguna stories, photographs, short stories, and fiction. This work lovingly charts the fertile ground of the traditional storyteller, usually a older member of the family or community. *Storyteller* uses written text and photographs to recall and reestablish contexts. The photographs reveal the particular landscape and community from which Silko's Laguna tradition derives, as well as depicting specific individuals—Aunt Susie, Grandma A'mooh, Grandpa Hank, and all the other storytellers who accepted responsibility for "remembering a portion . . . [of] the long story of the people" (p. 7). It is a testimony to the fact that "across the course of life, individuals rely upon others as a source of both meaning and solace in their lives. From the initial experience of the infant, comforted by his mother's very presence, to the older adult maintaining continuity of past and present . . . the psychological significance of relationships is intertwined in the remembered story of a life that answers the question of meaning" (Cohler 1993, 123).

The photographs are also arranged to suggest the circular design of *Story-teller* (Silko 1981), a design characteristic of Native American traditions in which elders are central. The merging of past and present through the figure of the elder is manifest in the book's design, as is the union of personal, historical, and cultural levels of being and experience, and through such harmonies—and their periodic sundering—the ongoing flux of life and the value of old age expresses itself. The opening photograph, for example, presents Robert G. Marmon and Marie Anayah Marmon, Silko's great-grandparents, "holding [her] grandpa Hank" (p. 2). The second picture, three pages later, portrays Aunt Susie, of whom Silko is the "self-acknowledged, self-appointed heir" (Wald 1982, 19), and Leslie Silko herself as a child. These photographs do not merely locate Silko within a genealogical context or even an extended family; they situate her within a continuous generational line of Laguna storytellers as well. The last three photographs in the book bring us full circle. The first of these appears at the end of the book's written text; it depicts the adult Silko. The second shows us Grandpa Hank as a young man, and the third portrays the three generations preceding her, including her father as a boy, Grandpa Hank's brother, and her great-grandfather. Silko's arrangement of photographs at the beginning and end of the book foregrounds the importance of elders, subordinating the individual to the communal and the cultural.

The cyclic design is reflected in the episodic structure of *Storyteller* and the accretive process of teaching inherent in it. Each individual item is composed of a narrative episode that relates to other such episodes. According to Walter J. Ong (1982), storytelling "normally and naturally operated in episodic patterning. . . . Episodic structure was the natural way to talk out a lengthy story line if only because the experience of real life is more like a string of episodes than it is like a Freytag pyramid" (p. 148); and real life, "the long story of the people," is Silko's concern. Moreover, the narration of the story, like all storytelling, involves a teaching process. In this process, the reader or listener learns by accretion. Successive narrative episodes cast long shadows both forward and backward, lending different or complementary shades to those preceding them and offering perspectives from which to consider those that follow. Such perspectives are then often expanded or in some way altered as the new material reflects back on them. This kind of learning process is part of the dynamic of the Native American tradition, an oral tradition in which the role of the elder as storyteller/educator is crucial.

N. Scott Momaday (1979) states, "We are what we imagine. Our very existence consists in our imagination of ourselves. . . . The greatest tragedy that can befall us is to go unimagined" (p. 167). Moreover, as Cohler (1993) notes, "A fundamental issue in studying lives over time concerns the manner in which individuals attribute meaning to their presently experienced past and present and their anticipated future. . . . Although the specific criteria for an acceptable life history vary across cultures (the distinction between history and fiction may be important only in the modern West), the need for a narrative of the course of one's life that 'makes sense' in the terms specified by a particular culture appears to be universal" (p. 111). It is apparent throughout Native American literature that, as Silko (1981) phrases it in *Storyteller*, "What we call 'memory' and what we call 'imagination' are not so easily distinguished" (p. 227). In "The Storyteller's Escape," the old storyteller's greatest fear as she waits for death is that she will go unremembered and unimagined. Much of Native American literature is, in fact, a self-renewing act of imagination/memory designed to keep storytellers as well as stories from so tragic a fate. As Cohler (1993) observes, "Within many traditional cultures, the source of personal integrity is founded within a larger, corporate family group" (p. 110), a group which stretches back into the past through elders. This was certainly true of traditional Native American cultures.

In the title story of Silko's (1981) *Storyteller*, a girl comes of age and an old man begins the tale of a great bear pursuing the lone hunter across the ice. The old man relates the narrative lovingly, nurturing every detail with his life's breath, because this story invests his death with meaning. The story is an expression of sacred natural processes, ancient and unending, of which his death is a part, processes Silko will also treat in *Storyteller* in "The Man to Send Rain Clouds" and the poem "Deer Song." But, most importantly, in the intensely beautiful precision of the old man's recounting, the story becomes the girl's legacy, a powerful vision by which she can unify the disparate aspects of her experience to create herself anew in profoundly significant cultural terms. The girl recalls having asked her grandmother, the old storyteller's wife, about her parents, and her grandmother, the historical voice, recounts how the Gussuck store man traded them bad liquor. The grandmother's narrative and that of the giant bear become linked in the girl's imagination. Once, while listening "to the old man tell the story all night" (p. 26), she senses her grandmother's spirit. "It will take a long time," the old woman tells her, "but the story must be told. There must not be any lies." At first, she thinks that the spirit is referring to the bear story because she "did not know about the other story then" (p. 26). This "other story" is, in reality, the conclusion of her grandmother's story, a conclusion that will make it the girl's story. In light of the inaction of civil and religious authorities and the store man's continued existence, the story of her parent's death has not been properly told. Thus, the story must be completed, and the tale of the giant bear "stalking a lone hunter across the Bering Sea ice" (p. 31), tells her how. "She spends days walking on the river," getting to know the ice as precisely as the old man had described it in his tale, learning "the colors of the ice that would safely hold her" (p. 31) and where the ice was thin. She already knew that the store man desired her, so it was easy for her to lure him out onto the river and to his death. Although it appears that he chases her out onto the ice, it is she who is the bear. The attorney wants her to change her story, to tell the court that "it was an accident," but she refuses, even though to follow his advice would mean freedom (p. 31). Hers is the voice that carries the old stories into the present and locates the present within the cycle of mythic time. Through the story, life derives purpose and meaning and experience becomes comprehensible; also, through her fidelity to the story, the girl recreates herself from the fragments of her own story. Her emergence whole and intact from her experience is, in this respect, like Tayo's emergence in Silko's *Ceremony*, a victory for her people. Given the immediate context in which the title narrative of *Storyteller* is placed, it is, like most stories in this tradition, a ritual. As Cohler (1993) observes, the "life-history construct, like all historical accounts . . . may be understood as a narrative" (p. 112).

Following the title story of the book, there appears a picture of Marie Anayah Marmon — Grandma A'mooh — reading to two of her granddaughters, Silko's sisters. She is reading, apparently, from *Brownie the Bear*, a book, we later learn, that she read many times before, not only to her great-granddaughters but to Silko's uncles and father. Accompanying this photograph is a reminiscence of Grandma A'mooh, whose name Silko (1981) as a child deduced from the woman's continual use of "a 'moo'ooh' the language expression of affection directed at a young child" (p. 34), a love that is evident on the faces of the old woman and the little girls.

The title story is preceded by several other narrative episodes, beginning with Silko's (1981) brief reminiscence and history of Aunt Susie, her father's aunt. Aunt Susie was one of the last remnants of a generation of storytellers who passed down an oral tradition (pp. 4–6). In its rhythms and repetitions, Silko's narration here assumes the quality of a chant, reinforcing not only Aunt Susie's role as culture-bearer but her own as Aunt Susie's cultural heir. Their relationship provides a necessary context within which to consider the girl and the old man in the title story. That relationship is complicated in several ways, but this context, along with the photographs that follow "Storyteller," highlights her role as the storyteller-successor to the old man.

The old man's bear story exerts its hold on the girl's imagination through his intensely precise, chant-like, dramatic telling and retelling of it. Silko (1981) recalls a child's story that Aunt Susie narrated about a little girl who ran away. In her own recounting, Silko uses poetic form with varying line lengths, stresses, and enjambment to provide some of the movements and drama of her aunt's storytelling. She also provides several italicized expository passages to evoke the digressive mode of traditional storytellers and the conversational texture of their speech.

Aunt Susie's sad story is about a little girl who, feeling unloved because she does not get what she wants, decides to drown herself. Attempts by a kindly old man and her mother to save her fail, and the child drowns. The grieving mother returns to Acoma where, standing on a high mesa, she scatters the girl's clothes to the four directions, and they all turned into colorful butterflies (Silko 1981, 15). This is a child's story and whatever truths it may teach, it should evoke the child's capacity for wonder and delight. Aunt Susie succeeded in this respect. She brought the characters to life and captured the mother's tenderness and the prophetic foreboding of the old man "that implied the tragedy to come." "But when Aunt Susie came to the place / where the little girl's clothes turned into butterflies / then her voice would change and I could hear the excitement / and wonder / and the story wasn't sad any longer" (p. 15). The child learns something of pain through such a story, but she learns also of life's perpetuity, that from death itself can emerge beautiful life. She learns of the delicate balance in which all things exist, a balance forever threatened and forever renewed.

But harsh realities, having been delicately anticipated in Aunt Susie's story, dominate the two recollections leading directly into "Storyteller." The first offers a brief history of Silko's great-grandparents, and we learn that Robert G. Marmon married a Pueblo woman and learned how to speak Laguna. After leaving Laguna, marmon was sometimes referred to as "Squaw Man" (p. 16). The second recollection relates the Albuquerque hotel incident in which Marmon's two young sons, because they are Native Americans, are not permitted in the hotel.

"Storyteller" is nourished by the various motifs and concerns of the narratives leading into it, and it recasts them in new ways. It is unsparing in its treatment of the nature and consequences of discrimination, and unqualified in its vision of the capacity of tradition not merely to survive discrimination but to use it as a source of power. However, as the narratives that follow "Storyteller" suggest, the tradition is only as strong—or as fragile—as the memories that carry it and the relationships that sustain it.

Silko's (1981) remembrance of Grandma A'mooh, which follows "Storyteller," is warm and moving, yet painful as well. Grandma A'mooh loves the land, her people, her granddaughters, and the stories that evolve from them; yet, in her later years she is removed from all that sustains her and required to live with her daughter in Albuquerque. The daughter has to work, so much of the time Grandma is alone. "She did not last long," Silko tells us, "without someone to talk to" (p. 35).

"Indian Song: Survival," like the narrative episodes which precede it, explores the nature of survival while considering these ideas from a perspective somewhat different from the other stories. The first-person point of view heightens the intimacy of the sustaining relationship of the individual with the land that the poem explores. The poem moves in a sequence of spare yet sensual images, expressing at once the elemental and regenerative power of this relationship, and Silko's versification, like that of most poetry in Storyteller, is alive with motion and the subtle interplay of sound and silence. The story describes a "desperation journey north," but one not marked by either panic or haste. "Mountain lion," Silko (1981) writes, "shows me the way" (p. 36). He is her guide as he has been for Laguna hunters throughout time, and his presence helps to establish the nature of this journey, a journey to reestablish old ties, ties essential to survival in any meaningful sense. As the journey continues, the "I" becomes more inclusive as the speaker becomes increasingly able to merge with nature around her, alternately metamorphosizing from the wind to the "lean brown deer" who runs on the "edge of the rainbow" (p. 37). The "desperation journey" becomes a quest of self-discovery, of finding one's being in the land. The wholeness of the relationship emerging from the "Indian Song: Survival" enhances our understanding of what the young girl in "Storyteller" accomplishes. Her life has been a desperate journey and her final awakening involves the reestablishment of a vital, intimate connection to the land. The poem also further intensifies the poignancy of Grandma A'mooh's last days by compelling us to learn again the value of what, for her own "good," has been taken from her.

Silko (1981) follows "Indian Song: Survival" with a painfully enigmatic story from Aunt Susie, a Laguna "flood" story in which a little girl and her younger sister return home to their village after a day's play only to find it abandoned except for the old people who are unable to travel" (p. 40). Their mother and the others have gone to the high place to escape the coming flood. If "Indian Song: Survival" concerns the establishment of meaningful relationships, this story depicts the sundering of relationships. The story discovers beauty in the girl's devotion to her sister, as well as pain in the mother's desertion of her children. These elements — devotion and separation — are also central to the story, "Lullaby," which follows.

If, as Momaday (1979) says, the greatest tragedy is to go unimagined, the title of Silko's (1981) "Lullaby" achieves a bitter irony. Having been robbed of her grandchildren, the old Navaho woman Ayah sings a song for them, a song that she remembers having been sung by her mother and grandmother, a beautiful song expressing with delicate economy the worldview in which she was raised. Its closing words doubtlessly provide some consolation by proposing that they have always been together and always will be (p. 51). But we cannot forget that there are no children to hear the song and that, although Ayah's "life has become memories," those memories seem dominated by the loss of children — of her son Jimmie in the war and of the babies to the white doctors. For Silko, as for Native American writers in general, to go unremembered is to go unimagined, and in that sense Ayah's story is tinged with tragedy. Conversely, in her last years, Grandma A'mooh is separated from her grandchildren but she does not go unremembered. Such a fate, however, seems likely to befall Ayah, for her babies have been taken not simply to make them well, but also to make them white.

The "Survival" section, however, does not end on a hopeless note. Ayah's "lullaby" expresses a timeless harmony and peace which are reflected in the photograph of the sandhills east of Laguna which close this section. In this photograph, the land seems whole and eternal, and wherever this is so, the people, their stories, and their traditions will survive.

CHAPTER 10

Aging and the African-American Community: The Case of Ernest J. Gaines

Charles J. Heglar and Annye L. Refoe

As the "baby boomer" generation grows older, more scholars are focusing attention on revising the current image of the aged in America. Most elders are stereotyped as sedentary, set in their ways, and physically or emotionally inactive. Betty Friedan's (1993) *The Fountain of Age* reexamines the desire of the elderly to maintain continuing roles or to create new ones for themselves (i.e., organizational and personal involvement in a range of activities). However, while generally valuable in its presentation of the aged, Friedan's book does not include a detailed study of African-American communities. An excellent starting point for various literary depictions of the aging African American is Marian Gray Secundy's (1992) *Trials, Tribulations, and Celebrations: African-American Perspectives on Health, Illness, Aging, and Loss.*

Harry R. Moody (1988) has pointed out that "the perspective of the humanities can offer an alternative ground for theories of aging to embrace both the contradictions and the emancipatory possibilities of late life" (p. 19). Turning to African-American literature for such "alternatives," one notes a wealth of elderly black characters who demonstrate such "emancipatory possibilities." For instance, the slave narrative often foregrounds grandparents: Both Frederick Douglass (1845) and Harriet Jacobs (1861), among others, give a central place in their autobiographies to their grandmothers. In one of the best Harlem Renaissance novels, *Their Eyes Were Watching God*, Zora Neale Hurston ([1937] 1978) depicts Janey's grandmother as occupying an equally important role. Other figures range from Charles Chesnutt's ([1899] 1969) Uncle Julius, the aged trickster in *The Conjure Woman*, to Arna Bontemps's (1970) Jeff and Jenny Patton in the short story, "A Summer Tragedy." Moreover, in his short stories, Rudolph Fisher (1987) often returns to the image of the elderly in conflict with the younger generation. Finally, the death-bed revelations and dream appearances of the grandfather direct the quest of Ralph Ellison's ([1952] 1990) *Invisible Man*, much as Baby Suggs directs her granddaughter Denver in Toni Morrison's *Beloved*.

Gerontological studies targeting African Americans confirm the accuracy of the literary view that elderly blacks hold honored positions within their families and communities. Unlike white society's stereotypical view of the aged as warehoused in retirement homes, as inflexibly living in the past, or as relics, these studies present the black aged as living within the community (Cazenave 1979), as willing to change with the times (Gillespie 1976), and as integral parts of an intergenerational community (Dilworth-Anderson 1981). However, these active roles of the elderly are not reserved for blacks only. Jacqueline Jackson (1980, 3), an expert on aging and minorities, has discovered that aging among ethnic groups has more similarities than differences, especially when socioeconomic factors are considered. Other researchers calculate that just 5 percent of the elderly from all ethnic groups suffer from Alzheimer's disease, and only 5 to 10 percent are in nursing homes (p. 22).

Traditional Southern African-American communities are composed of groups of blood relations and special friends; such extended families range in age from newborns to centenarians. The black elderly garner respect within these specific, close knit, emotionally bound aggregations. They can give advice whether solicited or not, they can express themselves undiplomatically, and they can speak to adults as if the adults were children. Usually this behavior is tolerated because the prevailing view is that these elders have earned the right to do and say what they please; they have endured humiliation and indignities in order that their children might have better lives. In the words of the poet Stephen Caldwell Wright (1987), "My child will survive if die do I must" (p. 98). They have worked hard or, to paraphrase James Weldon Johnson (1963, 3), they have labored long in the vineyard; they are tired, they are weary, and it is time to rest.

Of the many African-American authors who depict the aged in African-American letters, Ernest J. Gaines is perhaps most noteworthy in making them central characters. For Gaines, the aged do not simply exist, they "survive with dignity," a quality that they pass on to the next generation (Gaudet and Wooton 1990, 66). In the fictional Louisiana parish of Bayonne, which is Gaines' usual setting, technology has destroyed the old way of life based on the manual labor of slavery and sharecropping. The younger generation has moved from the Quarters to urban areas, leaving the old ways and the old people behind. Thus the Quarters form a community headed by the aged; the elderly lead the church and maintain the community's social cohesion. In this setting, a recurring conflict develops between the children of the elderly, who sense a need for change, and the old ways of accepting things, which the older generation through their sacrifices have encouraged their children to supersede. In this conflict, the aged often represent the need to maintain dignity in spite of or even because of the need for change. They force recognition of an obligation to the past as a foundation for the future. The bond between the older and younger generation is so well understood that Gaines often depicts it by having characters decode facial expression and body language. For example, in *A Lesson Before Dying* (Gaines 1993), when Grant Wiggins's Aunt Louise wants him to get out of his car and come to her, he, as first person narrator, observes, "I knew that stand, I knew that look. I knew she was not coming one step farther and that I would have to come to her" (p. 77). However, although Gaines writes of elderly black men and women, he seldom emphasizes both in the same novel. He foregrounds his depiction of the aged black female in two novels: *The Autobiography of Miss Jane Pittman*, published in 1971 and adopted for television in 1974, and his most recent work, *A Lesson Before Dying*, published in 1993. Elderly black male characters dominate *A Gathering of Old Men* (Gaines 1983), performed as a television movie in 1987.

The Autobiography of Miss Jane Pittman (1971), perhaps more than any other example of Gaines's fiction, stresses the age of the central character. The frame for the novel is a teacher's desire to tape and edit the memories of the oldest member of the community. After editing the tapes, he notes that this oral history is both Miss Jane's story and that of her group; frequently, the elderly women and men who care for Miss Jane aid her in remembering or adding significant details. In this way, "Miss Jane's story is all of their stories, and their stories are Miss Jane's" (p. viii). Her memories span one hundred ten years and include slavery, reconstruction, legalized segregation (i.e., "Jim Crow Laws"), and the civil rights movement of the 1960s, all of which require her and the community to change as the larger society changes. Even when Miss Jane tells of her youth as a slave, it is from the reflective position of an elderly woman who can recognize her youthful ignorance and impatience. In fact, a large part of the community's respect for Miss Jane is based on her ability to adjust and survive with dignity.

In novels stressing aged black women, Gaines frequently depicts an elderly aunt or godmother raising a child to adulthood as a device to construct a maternal bond uniting the generations. In Miss Jane's case, she is physically unable to have children, but, through circumstances, she becomes a surrogate mother to the orphaned Ned, who calls her mama. Later, she also bears a maternal relationship to Jimmy, the civil rights leader who is killed at the end of the novel. In *Catherine Carmier, Of Love and Dust* and *A Lesson Before Dying*, Gaines also portrays his young male protagonists as raised by an aunt or godmother. In this way, he stresses the nurturing bond between characters and generations. This bond recalls the description by sociologist E. Franklin Frazier (1948, 114–124) of the black "Granny," whose family crossed generational and blood ties. According to Frazier, the "Granny" was a repository of lore, a midwife, a second mother to the community, and a caretaker of orphans. As the "oldest head," she frequently kept the black family together in both slavery and freedom.

Both Ned and Jimmy, Miss Jane's metaphorical sons, leave the Quarters only to return because they feel an obligation to repay the isolated, rural community by initiating change. While most members of the Quarters fear modification, Miss Jane accepts and abets it, especially when Ned and Jimmy present it as a route to improvement. In fact, the novel closes as she leads most of the residents of the Quarters into town to protest segregation and to support the slain Jimmy. Gaines depicts Miss Jane's adaptability both seriously and humorously. At one hundred and ten years old, she leads the community in changing the old ways, yet she is also stripped of her title, "mother of the church," because of her fondness for the comics and for baseball— especially Jackie Robinson.

While *The Autobiography of Miss Jane Pittman* presents the elderly through the evolving, reflective point of view of a centenarian, Gaines's (1993) latest novel, *A Lesson Before Dying*, depicts the elderly from the first-person perspective of the younger generation in the person of Grant Wiggins. Like Ned and Jimmy, Grant Wiggins is a teacher, but his position is more formalized as the only instructor in the one-room public school for the children living in the Quarters, which is also the black community's church on Sundays. Grant's relationship to his Aunt Louise resembles that of Ned and Jimmy to Miss Jane; his aunt has been a mother to him after his parents moved to California in search of greater opportunity. She has sacrificed to send him to school so that he can teach, the only dignified role available for an educated black during the late 1940s, the time frame of the novel.

Although his aunt and her best friend Emma are churchgoers, Grant refuses to attend because he has lost his faith, not only in religion but also in the possibility of any change, even that achieved through education. The central conflict between the older and younger generations occurs when Emma's godson Jefferson—whom she has also raised as her son—is wrongly convicted in the robbery and murder of a white storekeeper. In pleading for Jefferson's life, his lawyer argues that, given his client's low level of civilization, sentencing him to death would be the same as sending a hog to the electric chair. However, even this degrading rationale does not soften the verdict of the jury of twelve white men.

Both Emma and Louise decide that Jefferson must go to his execution as a "man," that is, with dignity. They also decide that since Grant is a teacher and a man with a sense of dignity, he must teach Jefferson how to die, thus the title. Grant does teach Jefferson, while Jefferson teaches Grant and the whole community. However, one of the most interesting elements of the plot is how these two seventy-year-old women bring about the changes that they desire but do not know how to accomplish themselves; in other words, how they shape and influence the next generation. Both women can demand a lesson in dignity because the whole community, and especially Jefferson and Grant, is indebted to them physically and emotionally. Because of the intimate bond between older and younger generations—"mothers" and "sons"—they can communicate their demands and their insistence through body language and facial expressions. While the crisis of Jefferson's pending execution is a serious matter, this nonverbal language allows Louise and Emma to continue to insist, without the need for excessive speeches that might appear as nagging or selfish demands.

Somewhat like the roles of "good cop/bad cop," Emma and Louise take on the characteristics of tough and tender matrons in persuading Grant to attempt to teach what he considers to be impossible. As he fumbles for an excuse not to become involved, Emma says repeatedly, "You don't have to do it," which his Aunt Louise immediately negates with, "He go'n do it" (p. 13). Despite the seeming contradiction of their words, Grant understands the unequivocal force of their expressions: "I could tell by her face and by my aunt's face that they were not about to give up on what they had in mind" (Gaines 1993, 13). In the end, Grant and Jefferson develop the dignity in which these two old women believe. In the Christ-like death of Jefferson, the old women unite the generations and the community. Perhaps the most important lesson in the book is the one that Grant learns. Prior to his experience with Jefferson, he had lost faith in human dignity; his aunt and Emma serve as catalysts for both his and Jefferson's renewals.

Gaines (1983) continues his lessons in the survival of the elderly with dignity in *A Gathering of Old Men*; however, as the title indicates, the emphasis is now on the elderly black male and rather than emphasizing the preservation of values, Gaines stresses the capacity of the aged for transformation. The old men who gather to protect one of their own have accepted their prior passive behavior by placing it in the category of survival. Despite this acceptance, they have always abhorred their inability to fight back. Now, they have decided to reject that attitude and publicly display what they have always known privately: Though aged, they are men and deserve to be treated with respect and dignity. It is equally important for the white landowners to recognize their humanity and right to be respected as men.

Gaines's images of older, Southern African-American men contrasts sharply with the widely accepted view of them as men who have lost their courage, dignity, and self-respect. More often than not, literary images of older black men conflate the preconceived notion of passivity with the "saintly" behavior of Harriet Beecher Stowe's Uncle Tom to produce a subservient, head-scratching individual undeserving of even the smallest courtesy. The men in this novel refute the stereotype with their steadfast, courageous "rebellion." Gaines develops the old black men through chapter-length interior monologues that capture the history of the relationship between African Americans and whites in rural Louisiana. Their private thoughts juxtapose the rationale for their previous behavior with the reasons for their present defiance, so that the reader ascertains the difference between what was and what will be. Gaines infuses these men with an outward poise reflecting an inner fortitude manifested in their ability to maintain some semblance of self-respect despite society's effort to continue the status quo (i.e., white superiority).

Until this point, white landowners have controlled these now elderly black men. They could not drink alcohol in a public place unless the white landowner sanctioned it; if jailed, the white landowner's permission was necessary for their release; and the old men had always been impotent in their ability to protect their families or to protest the humiliation that they suffered daily. Candy Marshall, the white landowner's niece, is determined to protect Mathu, the black man on the Marshall place who helped to raise her and whom everyone believes murdered a white man. Her determination represents the dependent relationship that exists between blacks and whites in the time frame of the novel. It is Candy who initially calls the men together to protect Mathu from mob injustice, but it is the men who give their stand meaning.

In addition to interior monologues, Gaines (1983) structures this novel as if it were a play viewed through a gauze curtain. The unfolding events are visible but always partially obscured by the influence of the past on the lives and identities of the old men. Gaines uses the unspoken southern custom of calling black men "boy"—no matter what their age—and of treating them as if they were chattel—devoid of humanity—as an implicit backdrop for the novelty of black men standing up to white landowners and assuming their manhood. The use of diminutives and nicknames for old men instead of respectful titles (e.g., Mister or Sir) further stresses white society's patronizing attitude toward these men. (It must be noted, however, that the use of diminutives within the African-American community is not a reflection of disrespect but more a sign of familial affection.) Gaines enhances the poignant and extraordinary nature of the old men's stand by juxtaposing the fear and terror that have been the motivating forces of their lives with the courage needed for these elderly men to join Mathu.

Gaines (1983) centers the novel around the shooting of Beau Boutan in the Marshall Quarters. Initially, Gaines presents the assumed viewpoint of the rural South. Tales of night riders circulate along with rumors that the Boutan crowd will come into the Marshall Quarters to avenge Beau's death. From this perspective, Gaines proceeds to give the reader entree into the psyches of the seventeen old men who gather at Mathu's. Each has a reason to stand up to the Boutans and to the system of oppression that has shaped their lives to this point. For instance, Mathew Lincoln Brown (Mat) comes to Mathu's because his son bled to death when hospital personnel refused to treat him because of his color. Billy Washington joins the group because of the beating that sent his son Jackson to the institution for the insane, and "Uncle Billy" describes his son as a man who now eats like a hog—a man robbed of his dignity. Cyril Robillard (Clatoo) becomes a member of the "rebellion" because Forrest Boutan almost raped his sister, who then spent the rest of her life in jail for protecting herself and died insane. By vividly revealing the emotional and physical hardships of African Americans in rural Louisiana, Gaines simultaneously highlights the enormous step these old men are taking in making a stand. The older women standing with these men represent the tacit understanding of the community that one does what one has to do in order to survive.

The old men admit their fears to themselves; each interior monologue honestly describes the character's actions prior to the critical confrontation when stragglers who support the Boutans arrive to force a dramatic and surprising fight. Robert Louis Stevenson Banks (Chimley) relates the old men's general feeling when he says, "I had knowed about fights, about threats, but not killings. And now I was thinking about what happened after these fights, these threats, how the white folk rode. I was sure Mat was doing the same" (Gaines 1983, 29). The men have no illusions about how they have lived their lives nor about the contempt the white men in the parish have for them or their own contempt for their prior impotence, but their resolution to redeem themselves is equally clear. Mat puts it best when he avows, "I'm too old to go crawling under that bed. I just don't have the strength for it no more" (p. 31). Ironically, he phrases this spiritual rejuvenation in terms of his failing physical strength, an irony that pervades the novel.

Gaines (1983) embodies the repugnance of the white community for black men in Sheriff Mapes, who also represents civil authority. Joseph Seaberry (Rufe) states, "He was big, mean, brutal. But Mapes respected a man. Mathu was a man, and Mapes respected Mathu. But he didn't think much of the rest of us, and he didn't respect us" (p. 84). As the only one of the old men to have consistently displayed his "manhood," Mathu is depicted by Gaines as the descendant of a pure line of Africans. As the only male protagonist without an interior monologue or the need to reclaim his dignity, Mathu's character commingles his internal and external selves and serves as the model for the change the other old men undergo.

A part of Mathu's observable behavior centers around his relationship with Candy Marshall, the white woman who now runs the Marshall Plantation. Traditionally, white men pass the power of running "plantations" from one male member of a generation to a male member of the next generation. However, in the Marshall family, the pivotal generation that should accept the reins of power from Jack Marshall is dead. Candy's mother and father were killed in an accident, and she came to live on the Marshall place when she was five or six. Myrtle Bouchard (Miss Merle), a woman in love with Jack Marshall, establishes the relationship between Candy and Mathu when she says, "Surely, Mathu here in the quarters, and I at the main house had done as much to raise her as had her uncle and aunt" (Gaines 1983, 18). Societal norms dictate that Mathu call Candy "Miss Candy" and to observe a time-honored tradition of distance between classes (i.e., landowner and field worker); however, he does neither. In addition, Mathu treats Candy as if she were his subordinate—his student. Although Mathu has been a father figure to Candy, the relationship between Candy and Mathu is ambiguous: He is both parent to her and someone for whom she is responsible, both Candy's father substitute and Candy's substitute child. The conflict between Candy's respect for Mathu and her desire to protect him and the other older blacks in the Marshall Quarters presents a poignant emotional crisis for Mathu. While Gaines does not fully illustrate this crisis, he clearly shows a change in the relationship between Candy and Mathu as the novel closes. Candy sees herself as a protector, even a surrogate mother to the older people who still live on Marshall land but no longer work in its fields or the owner's house. The old men's stand to protect Mathu is originally her idea; however, once assembled, they reroute her intention and break with her to pursue their own goals. When the sheriff arrives to interrogate Mathu, Candy steps between them to prevent Mapes from striking Mathu as he has some of the other men; however, even at this juncture, Mathu renders Candy's protective gesture superfluous by facing Mapes himself. Rufe describes the scene: "When [Mathu] reached the ground, he bowed to thank her; then he turned to Mapes. He was up in his eighties, head white as it could be but you didn't see no trembling in his face or in his hands" (Gaines 1983, 84).

Mathu maintains his virility throughout the novel despite his age; coincidentally, he is rooted in and connected to a glorious past of rulers who decided their own destiny. His interaction with the other male and female inhabitants of the Marshall Quarters has been distant. He apologizes for his actions near the end of the novel: "I ain't nothing but a mean, bitter old man. No hero. Hating them out there on that river, hating y'all here in the quarters. Put myself above all— . . . Hate them 'cause they won't let me be a citizen, hated y'all 'cause you never tried" (Gaines 1983, 182).

Mathu's different behavior and attitude is mired in his obvious connection to this past. When the seventeen other men act as a conduit to their past, they achieve manhood in the eyes of everyone involved and acceptance from Mathu. This connection to a proud past revitalizes the aged plantation community. Johnny Paul chronicles the African-American past of the parish, and, as he does, he establishes a break with tradition and declares a new day:

Mama and Papa worked too hard in these fields. They mama and papa worked too hard in these same fields. They mama and they papa people worked too hard, too hard to have that tractor just come in the graveyard and destroy all proof that they ever was. I'm the last one left. I had to see that the graves stayed for a little while longer. . . . I did it for every last one back there under them trees. (Gaines 1983, 92).

By establishing a link with the past and breaking with tradition, each old man—Mat, Clatoo, Johnny Paul, Uncle Billy, Chimley, Cherry, Rufe, Rooster, Coot, Dirty Red, Jacob, Yank, Clabber, Gable, Jean Pierre, Dink, and Bink— becomes the equal of Mathu. More important than the respect garnered from the community is the new respect they now have for themselves. They are proud of standing their ground.

Once the old men have established a new level in their relationship to the social order, one last detail must be addressed: Mathu's relationship with Candy. As with all parent–child relationships (although the identity of parent and child is ambiguous), separation is necessary for the formation of a new identity. Gaines (1983) addresses this detail in the last scene of the novel which Lou Dimes, Candy's lover and the only white male who participates in her plan, describes: "She asked Mathu if he wanted her to take him back home. He told her no; he told her Clatoo was there in the truck, and he would go back with Clatoo and the rest of the people" (p. 214). Mathu's decision to ride back to the Marshall Quarters with the other black people indicates his decision to change the relationship he has maintained for over twenty-five years with Candy. It also concretizes Mathu's acceptance of the other blacks whom he has previously held in contempt. Mathu's empowerment can now be shared with the other old men which removes the need for Candy to protect them. Her assumption of the old men's need for protection is implicit in a statement that she makes early in the novel: "I won't let them touch my people" (p. 17). The conclusion of the novel transfers power to the old men themselves, placing them in charge of their own lives.

Through *The Autobiography of Miss Jane Pittman, A Lesson Before Dying,* and *A Gathering of Old Men,* Ernest Gaines presents elderly men and women who not only take control of their destinies but also positively affect the destinies of future generations. They are agents of both preservation and change, vitally connected to their communities. They cast a shadow over their community's young that connects veneration of past generations and present self-respect as prerequisites for surviving with dignity.

CHAPTER 11

Aging and the Continental Community: Good Counsel in the Writings of Two Mature European Princesses, Marguerite de Navarre and Madame Palatine

Christine McCall Probes

Since antiquity, age has been associated with wisdom and a hoary head considered a "crown of glory" (Solomon in Proverbs 16:31, "Gray hair is a crown of glory"). The good counsel and encouragement of the aged is commonly recognized as one of their most valuable contributions. However, today's scientific thinking about age is characterized by dichotomy. Robert Butler (Butler and Gleason 1985), former director of the National Institute on Aging, speaks of aging as a "progressive universal deterioration of . . . physiological systems, mental and physical, behavioral and biomedical," while simultaneously affirming "concurrent psychosocial growth in capacities for strategy, sagacity, prudence, [and] wisdom" (p. 7). Betty Friedan's (1993, ch. 2) review of recent scientific studies, including certain longitudinal ones, leads her to posit "Two Faces of Age" as she demonstrates strengths and new dimensions of age in *The Fountain of Age*.

Friedan (1993) documents the "new professional interest in studying wisdom" (p. 620), which includes the research of Margaret Clark, James Birren, and Erik and Joan Erickson (p. 119–122). Clark's studies reveal a definite link between mental health and "the fruitfulness of a search for meaning in one's life in the later years" (p. 119). According to Clark's findings, "a broader perspective, . . . wisdom, maturity [etc.]" is characteristic of healthy elders (p. 119). Birren and the Ericksons also emphasize wisdom as a task of old age, demonstrating the mature person's concern for and responsibility to the human race. Friedan reminds us that Carl Jung believed "that the older person must devote serious attention to the inner life" (p. 121–122). In the proceedings of the first Presidential Symposium of the Gerontological Society of

America, *Late Life Potential* (Perlmutter 1990), Paul B. Baltes and his colleagues of the Max Planck Institute for Human Development and Education in Berlin report their conclusion that wisdom is "one facet of successful aging" (p. 63). Using a framework "informed by concepts and methods associated with cognitive psychology and with the study of knowledge systems," (p. 66) Baltes and his colleagues advance wisdom as "the prototype of an area of cognitive functioning in which older adults, because of their age, have the opportunity to hold something akin to a world record" (p. 65).

This chapter explores wisdom and attitudes toward aging in the writings of two European princesses: Marguerite de Navarre, sister of François I, and Elisabeth-Charlotte von der Pfalz (Madame Palatine), sister-in-law of Louis XIV. A comprehensive view of aging and French literature would include not only Ronsard's (1950) admonitions of carpe diem to girls whose flower will certainly fade (pp. 260, 419) and Molière's (1962) comic depiction of an old man's obsession in *The School for Wives* (pp. 174–199), but also portraits of dedicated, courageous, and wise elders such as Racine's (1962) Andromaque, who is willing to defend her son to the death; Madame de La Fayette's (1966) Madame de Chartres, who warns her daughter, la Princesse de Clèves, of the dangers of court and persuades her to undertake the useful life; and La Fontaine's (1954) rich farmer, who demonstrates to his children that work is a treasure. Indeed, just as Betty Friedan (1993), despite the American denial of age and "entrapment within the values and perceptions of youth" (p. 30), finds confirmation for a strong face of age both in scientific research and in numerous interviews with people "who had crossed the chasm of age" (p. 18), so French literature provides ample evidence for the two faces of age. This chapter offers a response from the humanities to Harry Moody's (1993) question, "How then do we give positive content to an 'emancipatory' ideal for the last stage of life?" (p. xxvi).

A positive view of aging may be found in all of the literary genres of Early Modern France, but nowhere is it so striking as in the *Heptaméron* of Marguerite de Navarre (1984) and in the *Lettres françaises* of Madame Palatine (Van der Cruysse 1989). While the first work is a collection of prose nouvelles, the second is a private correspondence that was never intended for publication. Notwithstanding the very real difference in genre, the two works share three qualities that lead us to juxtapose them: a high regard for truth; a reflective/dialogic nature; and a common rhetorical figure, the maxim. Marguerite's fictional frame narrative contrasts with the nouvelles, which are accepted by the interlocutors as "true report[s] of . . . recent event[s]" (Duval 1993, 243). Indeed scholars have corroborated many of the historical and biographical facts of the nouvelles (Jourda 1930). In those cases in which fiction is "simply disguised to look like real news" (Duval 1993, 245), scholars propose that the assurance of truth may be considered "une loi du genre" (a rule of the genre) (Cazauran [1976], in Berthiaume 1994, 4). In this chapter, I consider the perspective of Oisille, the oldest and wisest among the storytellers of the

Heptaméron, and the witty yet profound observations of Madame Palatine, which reveal her optimistic view of life and admirable character. In addition, I examine the relevance of an important stylistic feature in each work, the maxim or proverb, which Aristotle (1967) judges "suitable for one who is advanced in years" (2: 21).

The *Heptaméron* is a collection of some seventy stories incorporated into a framework of prologues and *débats* (discussions) by the storytellers. If Parlamente, one of these storytellers, notes Marguerite's intent to "do the same as Bocaccio" (Marguerite 1984, 68), in the next breath she observes the significant difference between the two: All of these stories are to be truthful. As the Prologue explains, five men and five women, all aristocrats attempting to return to France after a *cure* at the spa town of Cauterets, survive various hazards, including a flood, only to find themselves at an abbey where they must remain while a bridge is built. After praising God for delivering them from peril, they attempt to find amusing and virtuous types of entertainment (p. 66). They give the task of organizing their days to Oisille because, as the eldest, she has experienced life, and she serves as a wise widow, she "occupies the mother figure to the women (p. 65–66). Oisille's proposal stems from her experience that the reading of the Holy Scriptures brings spiritual joy, health, and bodily repose (p. 66). Her recommendation includes, along with this reading, worship at mass and devout prayers. After some discussions, the travelers adopt Parlamente's suggestion to add the telling of truthful stories. They agree to organize their day thus: an hour lesson from the Scriptures read and expounded by Oisille (readings are from Romans, I John, and Acts), mass at the abbey, lunch, a period of private pastime, afternoon storytelling in a green meadow, vespers, supper, an evening discussing the day's stories and inventing new ones, a few games, and bedtime. Hircan, Parlamente's husband, proclaims that while everyone is to be on equal footing in the storytelling activity (p. 70), with consequent differences of focus and interpretation, they are all in common agreement on the authority and the usefulness of the Holy Scriptures (p. 67).

In a brilliant recent article that develops the proper understanding of nouvelle as "news," Edwin M. Duval (1993) describes the "assembled friends" as "an evangelical community founded on a spiritual consensus greater than any of their particular disagreements and on mutual bonds stronger than any personal tensions and rivalries" (p. 255). Duval understands by "spiritual consensus," the underlying conviction of the interlocutors that the "'bonne nouvelle' is the absolutely authentic and authoritative Word of God and that 'nouvelles' are, on the contrary, contingent and open to different interpretations" (p. 255). He underscores the "interconnected and complementary" (p. 251) quality of the assembly's two activities, the telling of stories or "news" and the reading of the Gospel or the "Good News." Proof of this connection lies not only in the basic organization of the schedule, in which the biblical quotations from the morning lessons recur in the afternoon stories, but, in the invention of a story that will correspond to the scriptural lesson (Marguerite 1984, 251). The story is a cautionary tale about trust, an "example" of the truth found in numerous passages of Scripture, such as Psalms 118: 8–9. In the introductory pages of the *Heptaméron*, Oisille testifies to the joy she finds in her psalter as she sings various beautiful psalms and hymns (p. 66). Although Duval (1993, 251) points to Oisille's words as the explicit connection between the intent of the afternoon stories and the teaching of the morning lessons, one could as well cite the comments of another storyteller, the young widow Longarine, who calls on Oisille, saying, "The lesson she read us this morning was so beautiful that she cannot fail to tell us a story worthy to complete the glory she won this morning" (Marguerite 1984, 428).

Duval (1993) identifies the "fundamental question" of the *Heptaméron* thus: "How can we live in the world of news, yet still live according to the Word of the Good News?" (p. 254). I propose that a close look at the principles of the stories told by Oisille, as well as at Oisille's maxims sprinkled generously throughout the volume, will shed light on this question. This examination may also alleviate the frustration of many critics who find themselves at an "impasse" and, in the words of Cathleen Bauschatz (1993), appear "baffled in their attempts to find a coherent and unified message in the book" (p. 104). Furthermore, such a perspective may offer support and direction to the person who seeks wisdom and meaning in life, the "task of old age" as recognized by researchers such as Clark, Birren, and the Ericksons. Although in this chapter, I am primarily concerned with the way "aging" helps us to formulate a life response to Francis Schaeffer's (1976) question, "How Should We Then Live?" in reality, learning to live is an age-neutral task.

Oisille's stories and maxims are particularly relevant to the task of living because of her privileged role as the wise widow whom the interlocutors charge with ordering their days (and their stories). Her voice powerfully represents the spiritual consensus of the community of storytellers as well as, some scholars argue, the perspective of the mature author of the *Heptaméron*. Philippe de Lajarte (1993) has written persuasively about the "univocality that profoundly characterizes the narrative discourse of Marguerite's tales" (p. 186). He sees behind the "commotion of multiple narratorial voices . . . a single voice [which] speaks at the heart of this discourse: the author's voice" (p. 186). In another study, *Les devisants de l'Heptaméron*, Regine Reynolds (1977) gives Oisille the privileged status of "porte-parole des idées religieuses de Marguerite," (spokesperson of Marguerite's religious ideas) (p. 15), despite the fact that Parlamente has traditionally been identified with Marguerite and Oisille with Marguerite's mother, Louise de Savoie, or more plausibly, as Paul Chilton—the translator of *The Heptameron*—suggests, with Louise de Daillon, lady-in-waiting to Marguerite (Marguerite 1984, 38).

Oisille's seven stories are nothing if not varied, focusing on a courageous poor mule-driver's wife, Marguerite's brother King François I, a gullible gentleman too devoted to the cult of Saint Francis, a husband who forces his unfaithful wife to drink daily from a cup fashioned from her dead lover's skull, a lecherous Franciscan, a powerful but wicked duke more concerned with furthering the interests of his line than with pure and noble love, and a duchess whose unrequited adulterous love turns to wrath, causing three deaths including her own. Although a story may emphasize a particular virtue, such as chastity or compassion, Oisille's voice of wisdom and experience rings never so clear as when she speaks of truth and trust. Numerous warnings, inscribed within the stories and the maxims, alert the reader to the danger of placing his or her trust in an untruthful person.

In story number seventeen, Oisille praises King François I for his courageous discernment when confronted with evidence of treachery by a count in his service whom he thought brave and honorable. A letter reveals an assassination plot that other intelligence confirms. The king's method of discovering truth is to confront the count alone in the forest, engage him in conversation about a hypothetical assassination plot, have him admire the King's sword and proclaim: "I'd regard him [the assassin] as wicked indeed if he happened to find himself alone with me, without witnesses, and didn't attempt to carry out his plan" (p. 210–211). Although the count declares that such an attempt would be madness, he thinks he has been discovered and immediately resigns. While the King's courage is the focus of the story, trust and a true heart are secondary emphases, reflected in the warnings of a faithful servant, the Seigneur de La Trémouïlle, and the King's own mother Louise de Savoie. Finally, in the discussion following the story, a maxim by Parlamente highlights the secondary theme: "For the praises of all the men in the world cannot satisfy a true heart as much as the knowledge that it alone has of the virtues which God has placed in it" (pp. 212–213).

Story number thirty-two, narrating the suffering of a beautiful but unfaithful wife whose husband has her hair shorn and causes her to drink daily from a goblet made of her dead lover's skull filled in with silver (Marguerite 1984, 331), has been the object of the careful and illuminating scholarship of François Rigolot. In a 1993 study he elucidates a reference to Mary Magdalen made in the discussion following the story when Ennasuite is "moved by the sinner's sincere repentance, . . . [and] is ready to argue in favor of forgiveness" (p. 226). In a later article, Rigolot (1994) maintains that the scene of the unfaithful woman drinking from the lover's skull "could be viewed as a staged perversion of relic worship, a practice much frowned upon in evangelical circles favored by Marguerite" (p. 57). To validate his reading, Rigolot cites biblical texts featuring forgiveness and correspondence between Marguerite and other evangelicals such as Guillaume Briçonnet, as well as art and literature associated with the Magdalen, including a biography of the saint commissioned by Louise de Savoie. Louise's interest in the Magdalen seems to give more weight to an allegorical interpretation since, as Rigolot reminds us, scholarship has traditionally linked Louise with storyteller Oisille (pp. 66–67).

Certainly story thirty-two stresses compassion (the husband forgives his wife and they have "many fine children" after an envoy, witness to the wife's contrition and beauty, arranges to have her portrait painted by the King's artist

Jean de Paris), and allegory and iconography can be helpful in its interpretation, although "the question of allegory remains an open one" (Rigolot 1994,
72). I would, however, draw our attention to the function and meaning of the
maxims surrounding the story. Oisille's wise sayings frame the narrative, providing transition from the previous story and its discussion as well as immediate commentary following this story. The focus of the first set of Oisille's
maxims is death, which she views as "the end of all our woes" and "our joy
and repose" (Marguerite 1984, 330). Two maxims cryptically suggest the subject matter of the story she is about to narrate: "Man's greatest woe . . . is to
desire death and not to be able to have it," and "the greatest punishment that
can be meted out to an evil-doer is not death but continuous torture, torture
severe enough to make him desire death, yet not so severe that it causes death"
(p. 330). Such was the unfaithful lady's daily torture of drinking from her
lover's skull. A second set of maxims completes the frame, underscores the
story's exemplary character, and emphasizes trust as the lesson. Oisille calls
her fellow storytellers and today's reader to place their trust in God, adding
that only His goodness can restrain us from actions like those of the beautiful
unfaithful lady. To her negative maxim, warning against pride and trust in
self, "Women who trust in their own strength and virtue are in great danger of
being tempted" (p. 334), Oisille adds her own knowledge of "many whose
pride has led to their downfall" (p. 334). As she counsels humility, she closes
her commentary with a positive maxim: "That which God guards is guarded
well" (p. 334).

Oisille's story number seventy is her longest and the only one of the collection which breaks the rule that requires that one not tell stories from a written
source (Marguerite 1984, 512). Parlamente encourages Oisille to retell the
thirteenth-century poem, "La Chastelaine de Vergi," claiming that it can be
regarded as new since, originally, it was written in antiquated language (p.
512). While the maxims pronounced by the characters in the story focus on
love — "the fire of love cannot for long be hidden" (p. 519) and "there is no
love so secret that it is not known" (p. 526), as does Oisille's in the commentary "the more one's love is virtuous and noble, the more difficult it is to
break the bond" (p. 532) — the very beautiful but sad story is a triple case of
misplaced trust which results in triple deaths.

Elsewhere in the *Heptaméron* numerous themes are featured in Oisille's
maxims, from the physical, on rest, "an hour before midnight is worth three
after" (Marguerite 1984, 234), to the spiritual, "there can be no perfect pleasure, if the conscience is not at ease" (p. 366). Oisille's voice, privileged because of her advanced age and wisdom, offers lessons on living which are
applicable to both young and old. Her wisdom holds in high esteem justice,
equity, and equality, "One should not judge anyone but oneself" (p. 499)
and, before God, men and women are considered equal; both plant, "and
God alone gives the increase" (p. 505). Her maxims, and indeed those of
other speakers such as Parlamente who warns "the first step man takes trust-

ing in himself alone is a step away from trust in God" (p. 321), complement the stories which are, more often than not, exempla of conduct to be avoided such as treachery, perfidy, misplaced affection, and so forth. Oisille relates the entire narrative venture to trust when she describes the storytellers' purpose of truthtelling (often "evil-telling") as removing "the trust placed in the mere creatures of God . . . that our hope may come to rest upon Him who alone is perfect" (p. 416). Man's word is contrasted to God's word (p. 460), and reading of the latter protects against deception. After one of the many Franciscan stories and a declaration by Parlamente that God's word is the only touchstone of truth and falsehood, Oisille's maxim, complete with epilogue, ties truth and trust together: "Whosoever reads the Scriptures often and with humility will never be deceived by human fabrications and inventions, for whosoever has his mind filled with truth can never be the victim of lies" (p. 400).

Although they wrote in different centuries and different genres, the same foundational concern for truthtelling and a common Reformation heritage unite Marguerite de Navarre with our second princess, Madame Palatine. Daughter of Palatine Elector Karl Ludwig von der Pfalz-Simmern, Elisabeth-Charlotte, or "Liselotte" as she was fondly called, was the granddaughter of Elizabeth Stuart, herself the daughter of England's King James I. Her Calvinistic and Lutheran heritage would stand her in good stead throughout her life, bringing her genuine happiness and tranquillity at the French court, where she was sent to be the wife of Louis XIV's homosexual brother, a marriage characterized by her biographer Dirk Van der Cruysse (1984) as "a sacrifice on the altar of a Franco-Palatine alliance" (p. 347). According to Van der Cruysse's conservative calculations, Madame is the author of at least 60 thousand letters (60% in German and 40% in French). Of this "montagne épistolaire" about 7,500 have survived; 4,000 have been published (Van der Cruysse 1993). Madame corresponded with philosophers such as Leibnitz and with members of the royal families of numerous countries, including King George I of England, her first cousin. An exceptional mirror of a crucial period of European history, Madame's letters are extolled by historians and literary critics alike who recognize their value as an authoritative record from the royal family itself. Thanks to the determination and skill of Van der Cruysse, whose recent edition of the *Lettres françaises* (1989) has received wide acclaim, we have the privilege of discovering firsthand the truth of Sainte-Beuve's (1850) exclamation: "Madame est un utile, un précieux et incomparable témoin de moeurs" (Madame is a useful, precious and incomparable witness to her time) (9: 78).

Over 80 percent of Madame's *Lettres françaises*, prized for their spontaneity, verve, and humour, were written after she had reached the age of fifty. Madame writes in an educated but unaffected prose ("I could say like Monsieur Jourdain [Molière's character in *Le bourgeois gentilhomme*] . . . 'I've written prose without realizing it'" [Van der Cruysse 1989, 269]) and did not

intend the letters for publication ("I would be horrified to see my letters published" [p. 269]). Her sense of humor, as well as her literary awareness, is
revealed in a letter to Queen Sophie Dorothée de Prusse: "Your majesty will
find that I am as stuffed with proverbs as Sancho Panza; I have something of
his figure also" (p. 605).

What are some aspects of Madame's reflections and counsel offered in the
form of concise sayings and expressions of collective wisdom? They range
from the banal, "Better late than never" (Van der Cruysse 1989, 734), to the
profound paraphrases of Solomon's opening words in Ecclesiastes 3, "For
everything there is a season" (p. 390), and of Jesus' words in Matthew 26,
"The spirit is willing, but the flesh is weak" (p. 417). The maxims highlight
more lengthy deliberations on health, age, death, consolation, friendship,
marriage, spirituality, and true happiness. They may identify the letter writer
with her correspondent through shared sentiments and reveal Madame's optimistic outlook and admirable character, confirming Aristotle's (1967) observation: "If then the maxims are good, they show the speaker also to be . . . of
good character" (2: 21). Conversely, Madame's honorable character validates
her counsel, bearing out Quintilian's (1967) comment that the speaker's character "lend[s] weight to [his]. . . words" (8: 3).

Madame speaks often of age, in a realistic, balanced, and wry manner.
While she shared the prevailing view that "youth is a time of joy and pleasures, old age is for seriousness and sadness" (Van der Cruysse 1989, 247,
667), and found even in her thirties that "the years blow in as quickly as the
wind" (p. 82), she refused to wallow in self-pity and burden her correspondents with her chagrins.

Madame recognizes throughout her letters the therapeutic value of laughter and good humor, finding even in the pomp and ceremony surrounding
death something to chuckle over. When her niece, the young princess of
Hanover, dies, Madame writes a letter of consolation to a good friend, encouraging her not to become frightened and reclusive. To give her a laugh,
Madame recounts her own amusement at her attendant's eagerness to wear
Madame's funereal finery which would, according to custom, be passed to
the attendant (Van der Cruysse 1989, 73–74). Madame enjoyed a generally
robust health and, despite her large size, was very active, walking almost daily
and regularly accompanying King Louis XIV to the hunt. When illness did
strike her, she extolled remedies from her Germanic homeland, such as
Westphalian ham and sausage for stomach trouble, rather than the bloodletting and purging prescribed by the French doctors (p. 666). She sagely warns
that often by precautionary measures such as bloodletting one becomes really ill (pp. 237–238), and relates a serious incident when she lost much more
than the intended amount of blood due to her doctor's fainting (p. 727). Anticipating contemporary theories of affirmative aging, Madame establishes
repeatedly the connection between good humor and health, affirming that
"good health is a treasure" (p. 670) and "sadness a real poison" (p. 627). Al-

though she recognizes the benefits of time, reason, distraction, and patience (pp. 271, 626, 60–61), she observes realistically that without some illness and sadness one would never be ready to leave this world (p. 633).

The faithful affection of true friends, whether human or canine (she adored her numerous spaniels) was a great comfort to Madame. She considers true friendship rare and to be cultivated: "Of all this world's pleasures, I value most a good and sincere friendship" (Van der Cruysse 1989, 40). Her reflections on friendship could be phrased sharply, as in the maxim, "A person incapable of friendship and thankfulness isn't worthy to live" (p. 265).

Madame corresponded with Leibnitz, sharing some of his philosophical notions. She believed with him that animals possess intelligence and have immortal souls; she expected to be reunited in the hereafter with not only her relatives and good friends, but also "all my little animals" (Van der Cruysse 1988, 428). Madame refers to her dogs as "the most loveable persons in the world" and recounts a story of a woman who hated dogs when she was young and loved them dearly as she aged. When asked for an explanation, the woman spoke of the faithfulness of dogs, "who love you, wrinkles and all" (Van der Cruysse 1989, 233).

Madame's letters express a horror of serious illnesses and death along with a natural desire to preserve life. She believes this is a God-given attitude and finds that such a view imitates nature since "all animals fear death and destruction" (Van der Cruysse 1989, 478). True comfort came, she believed, through submission to God, a constant theme in her correspondence. Ten years before her death, during a period of severe illness which she describes as "torment," she writes that her only comfort was found by placing herself in the hands of her Savior (p. 474). It is no coincidence that this letter is written on the day of Pentecost when the attention of the Christian Church is traditionally focused on the Holy Spirit as "Comforter" (John 14: 16).

How does the wisdom of our two European princesses converge? What insights can the mature person today gain from the "news" of Oisille and the news-bearing letters of Madame Palatine? Do we have a right to expect literature to help with the "task" of aging or, as Margaret Clark (1966) would say, with a search for meaning in one's life in the later years? Some would say not, such as Harold Bloom (1994) who challenges the claim of "relevance" for literature, electing to assert instead its esthetic value. A review of his *The Western Canon* in *Newsweek* (Gates 1994) quotes Bloom as confining the role of literature to "the proper use of one's solitude" (p. 75). In an interview in the same issue, Bloom announces his unhappiness with what he calls the "school of resentment," scholars who "put the arts, and literature in particular, in the service of social change" (p. 75). However, I would concur with Anne M. Wyatt-Brown (Wyatt-Brown and Rossen 1993) that "exploring the experience of growing old adds insight to our understanding of literature *and life*" (p. 1,emphasis added). Their volume, *Aging and Gender in Literature*, provides "case studies of individual writers whose lives demonstrate how complex the creative experience can be" (p. 4). Moreover, as we examine Marguerite de Navarre and Madame Palatine for relevant insights into the life task of the maturing individual, we have not only the encouragement of preeminent scholars of today such as Wyatt-Brown and her collaborators but the authority of Saint Augustine (1966, 30), who defended the study and use of letters as appropriate to the discovery of truth.

The *Heptaméron* and the *Lettres françaises*, both the fruit of creative maturity, offer positive portraits of aging. Their emphasis on wisdom presents an encouraging perspective from the humanities that supports the conclusions of today's scientists who "suggest that wisdom may become a viable topic for scientific psychological research" (Baltes et al. 1990, 77). As the Berlin scientists develop their criteria and convincingly propose wisdom as a "prototypical goal of positive ontogenetic development and a . . . marker of late-life positive change" (p. 69), they recognize the concept's debt to the Greeks: "Since the birth of ancient Greek philosophy, and carried into modern times, wisdom has been considered as the peak, the capstone of knowledge about the human condition" (p. 74). We remember that Aristotle (1967) judges storytelling and maxims (distilled wisdom) to be appropriate for persons of advanced age. If good, the maxims reveal the speaker to be of good character. Although the Berlin scientists do not specifically mention Aristotle, it is fascinating that one of the criteria under their consideration is the "nature of the 'character' of the person holding wisdom-related knowledge" (Baltes et al. 1990, 68).

The reader of the *Heptaméron* and the *Lettres françaises* may receive a "double" encouragement. Each work serves as an example of late life creativity as well as a model of serious attention to the inner life; the latter, although certainly not age-specific, is often equated with the task of maturity (Friedan 1993, 119–122). Marguerite's masterpiece is the fruit of the last ten years of her life, 1540 to 1549 (Reyff 1982, 24). Simone de Reyff brings a necessary corrective to Marguerite scholarship as she warns not to "travestir la vieille reine en quelque insipide nonnain" (misrepresent the old queen as some dull nun) (p. 12). Reyff's archival research and careful attention to Marguerite's abundant correspondence lead her to accentuate the "triumphant vitality" and "passion" of this last period of Marguerite's life (pp. 11–12). Marguerite's characters entrust the task of ordering their days to the oldest and wisest among them, Oisille, whose nouvelles warn of deceit and call for wisdom. Using the richly allusive metaphor of the mirror, Oisille identifies it with her text, inviting the listener/reader to look into the story and "turn to Him in whose hands your honour lies" (p. 351). Whereas rhetorical ornament is generally eschewed for fear of "falsify[ing] the truth of the account" (p. 69), the maxim is allowed a prominent place. Its association since antiquity with truth and distilled wisdom makes it a device consistent with the vision of Marguerite, while its dialogic quality, as Jean Lafond (1984) reminds us, invites collaboration between writer and reader.

Similarly, the *Lettres françaises* represent, to a great extent, Madame Palatine's creative maturity, since over two-thirds of them were written in her fifties and sixties. Highly therapeutic for this German princess, who was nostalgic for her homeland and dismayed by the vapidity of the French court, the letters receive high praise today from prominent historians who consider them a privileged and authoritative record of early modern Europe (Le Roy Ladurie 1983, 21–41). The maxims of the letters, rich in metaphors and images, reveal a humorous, wise princess who offers good counsel, treasures friendship, and prizes tranquillity, the latter achieved by submission to God's providence and by a discipline which is strikingly reminiscent of Oisille's "prescription that keeps [her] happy and healthy in [her] old age" (66).

CHAPTER 12

Aging and Academe:
Caricature or Character

Helen Popovich and Deborah Noonan

Betty Friedan (1993), in her important work *The Fountain of Age*, examines the Janus-faced aspect of age depicted by contemporary gerontologists. One facet of this dual portrait portrays the mask of physical and mental deterioration traditionally drawn by the medical profession and by society. The other presents the face of freedom, dignity, and wisdom delineated by a new generation of gerontologists (David Gutmann, John Rowe, Harry Moody). While Gutmann (1977, 202–213) argues that in more traditional folk societies, the natural gerontocracies, and in settings in which elders have social leverage to arrange matters in accordance with their own priorities, striking evidence exists of psychosocial development in both aging men and women. He also discusses the emergence of contra-sexual potentials in men and women after they are relieved of parental duties. This allows both sexes to reclaim qualities gendered "masculine" or "feminine" by the culture, suggesting a release of untapped potential as people age. Moreover, Rowe and Robert Kahn (1987,143–144) suggest that many data sets showing average physiologic decline with age also reveal older persons with minimal or no physiologic loss when compared to the average of their younger counterparts. Finally, Moody's (1988) discussion of a "dialectical gerontology" in "Toward a Critical Gerontology" challenges the traditional portrait of age. According to these gerontologists, then, the first face of age turns back to the attitudes and stereotypes of the past; the other gazes forward to a new and hopeful future. Like the rabbit/duck of Gestalt psychology, therefore, each visage of age contains a contingent validity and each interpretation is accurate from a certain perspective. Gestalt psychology often deploys the metaphor of a single image which appears to represent a rabbit when viewed from one perspective, and a duck when viewed from another.

Upon examination, the image of the aging academic in literature often bears a similar dual aspect. On the one hand, the traditional portrait of the academic presents an aged or somehow ageless character who is likely to be a caricature rather than a well-rounded character. On the other hand, some authors reject society's stereotypes while anticipating the insights of contemporary gerontology; they present a positive picture of aging as a time of growth, emancipation, and even the acquisition of wisdom. The following discussion exposes the double visage of the aging academic displayed by fiction.

Traditionally, aging has been viewed as a process of decline, degeneration, and senescence. Although stage theorists such as Erik Erikson (1982, 61) have underscored the spiritual benefits of affirmative aging, arguing that "wisdom, the informed and detached concern with life itself in the face of death itself," is the reward of a fulfilled old age. Such wisdom can only be obtained by the resolution of the conflict between integrity and despair, the developmental task of old age. However, a clinical model based largely on institutionalized elders continues to pervade our consciousness and our fiction. Friedan (1993, 76) insists that many earlier studies of the aged were focused on those living in institutions, and this population would be more likely to show progressive physical and mental decline than those living in their own communities and studied longitudinally. The social construct of debilitating old age persists, and stories about schools and their teachers often combine with stereotypes of the academic to create an unappealing figure. Whether relatively young, like Ichabod Crane in "The Legend of Sleepy Hollow" (Irving, 1964), or old, like Robert Crane in Willa Cather's (1953) *The Professor's House*, Roger Chillingworth in *The Scarlet Letter* (Hawthorne 1962), or Old Spencer in J. D. Salinger's (1951) *The Catcher in the Rye*, or ageless, like the Rev. Edward Casaubon in George Eliot's (1930) *Middlemarch*, the academic is almost always thin, gangly, physically unattractive, sexually unappealing, and often poorly or oddly dressed. These "grotesques" convey, by their very appearance, the notion of the scholar as an object of ridicule or scorn, and such an image is superimposed upon the traditional negative stereotype of the aged. Thus, Ichabod Crane is described as a "scarecrow eloped from a cornfield" and "tall, exceedingly lank with narrow shoulders, long arms and legs . . . with huge ears, large green glassy eyes, and a snipe nose . . . perched upon his spindle neck" (Irving 1964, 23–24). The hapless Robert Crane of *The Professor's House* possesses "hands long and soft-looking, a reddish matted beard, pale eyes and eyebrows" and a "big, startling red mouth" (Cather 1953, 41), while Roger Chillingworth presents "a pale thin scholar-like visage, with eyes dim and bleared by the lamp-light that had served them to pore over many ponderous books" (Hawthorne 1962,46).

The physically unappealing academic is also often portrayed as asexual or sexless, focused on intellectual matters to the exclusion of the body and the material world. This image conflates the stereotype of aging as a deterioration of physical, sexual, and creative powers to construct an academic protagonist who is sexless and (therefore) old, and who is inept, unimaginative, and often laughable. Margaret Morganroth Gullette (1993, 26–30) argues that aging, flagging sexuality, and diminishing creativity became linked early in the twentieth century and permeate such novels as Thomas Mann's *Death in Venice* and F. Scott Fitzgerald's *Tender Is the Night*. She demonstrates how a group of "midlife decline" novels written during the early years of the twentieth century helped forge a link between male creative decline, waning sexual potency, and aging that is accepted even today. Although recent research shows that people can remain sexually active into their nineties if healthy and not deprived of a sexual partner (Friedan 1993, 68), figures like Aschenbach in *Death in Venice* underscore the linkage between aging, decreasing sexuality, ill health, and academic figures. Thus, Ashenbach paints his crumpled face in a hopeless effort to appear young, and Old Spencer in J. D. Salinger's (1951) *Catcher in the Rye* inhabits an apartment with "pills and medicine all over the place" where "everything smelled like Vicks Nose Drops" and wears "a very sad, ratty old bathrobe . . . he was probably born in or something" (p. 11). Everywhere in these two works the decay of age destroys beauty, health, and sexuality.

Moreover, caricatures of elder academics depict them not only as physically repulsive but also as emotionally stunted; monsters of cruelty, pedantry, and egotism who seek power and fulfillment by persecuting others, often their students. This egocentric monster appears again and again in literature: Father Dolan in *A Portrait of the Artist as a Young Man* (Joyce 1964), Serebrykov in *Uncle Vanya* (Chekhov 1912), Mr. Ramsey in *To the Lighthouse* (Woolf 1955), Old Spencer in *The Catcher in the Rye* (Salinger 1951), and Edward Casaubon in *Middlemarch* (Eliot 1930), to mention only a few. Old Spencer, his voice dripping with sarcasm, cruelly embarrasses Holden by reading his failed examination paper aloud; Father Dolan beats young Stephen Dedalus. Cruelty and egocentricity combine with the dominant parody of the aging academic as a buffoon, a bumbling incompetent who cannot function in the material world and who, like the Greek philosopher Thales, is fully capable of falling into a well while looking at the stars. Professor Welch, the aging History department chair in Kingsley Amis' *Lucky Jim* (1953), is ridiculed for his absent-mindedness, his foppery, and his total ineptitude in performing such mundane tasks as driving an automobile. Similarly, the common stereotype presents aging as "second childhood," a creeping loss of physical and mental powers that renders the aged foolish and incompetent and requires their constant care within an institutional setting (Friedan 1993, 50).

Although middle-aged academic protagonists are generally more complex than the preceding caricatures, they often exhibit the same physical and psychological defects as their older counterparts; sometimes they too are little more than mere conglomerations of idiosyncrasies. George, the middle-aged history professor in *Who's Afraid of Virginia Woolf* (Albee 1962), wages a vicious war of words with his wife, Martha, and their guests, Honey and Nick. Similar rancor and futility emanate from Casaubon in *Middlemarch*, a man whose life's work deteriorates into a circular, endless search for more and more data in his Faustian quest for the key to mythology; incapable of entering what Erikson describes as true adulthood, with its accompanying "generativity and productivity," Casaubon is doomed to futility. In *Life Cycle Completed* (1982), Erikson outlines the psychosocial crises accompanying developmental stages, including the conflict between intimacy and isolation in young adulthood and the generativity versus stagnation and self-absorption in mature adulthood.

When viewed through the lens of Erik Erikson's (1982) theory of identity formation, both the caricatures and the more complex characterizations of academics in literature fit the paradigm of the aging process. Erikson argues that individuals establish an identity in late adolescence or early adulthood that must be reshaped in midlife to meet the challenge of positive aging. In addition, each developmental step is grounded in all the previous ones; while at each stage, the developmental maturation (and psychosocial crises) of one of these virtues gives new connotations to all the "lower" and already developed stages as well as to the higher and still developing ones (Erikson 1982, 59). Those who cling to youthful goals long after they seem compelling can fall into despair or become rigid and intellectually immobile, like Casaubon, Father Dolan, or even Old Spencer.

Often, the struggle to refashion identity in the face of midlife or late life crisis forms the heart of the protagonist's struggle and the canvas of what Janice Rossen (1993, 7) calls the university novel. The central figure of Willa Cather's story of academia, *The Professor's House* (1953), must suffer the "little death" of his earlier self, which Gail Sheehy (1995, 145) describes in her own study of aging, before he can rise above depression and despair. Such a task presages successful resolution of the later conflict between integrity and despair that Erikson and other stage theorists mark as the major task of aging (Erikson 1982, 56–57; Sheehy 1995, 168–169). These protagonists can then emerge with the wisdom that is the hallmark of a fulfilled aging, what Friedan (1993) calls integration and Sheehy (1995) describes as integrity. The heroes and heroines of the *Vollendungsroman*, or story of growing older (Rooke 1988), often demonstrate the truth of Jung's (1969) contention that the "upheavals of midlife can lead the sufferer into new paths which are potentially regenerative" (pp. 398–399).

Such characters inhabit fiction in the form of fully developed characters to be admired and emulated. Among the most familiar of these are James Hilton's (1962) Mr. Chips and Frances Gray Patton's (1954) Miss Dove. Models of integrity and dignity, neither Mr. Chips nor Miss Dove becomes ridiculous, pathetic, cruel, or egocentric as he or she grows older. Indeed, like the thousands of successfully aging individuals interviewed by Friedan (1993) in *The*

Fountain of Age or by Sheehy (1995) in *New Passages,* these academics, as they age, become sources of wisdom and of influence in their respective communities. Within the professoriate, both Godfrey St. Peter, the protagonist in Willa Cather's (1953) *The Professor's House,* and William Stoner, the eponymous hero of John Williams's (1988) *Stoner,* are multifaceted characters who share the same dignity and integrity, and who achieve the integration described by Friedan and the wisdom delineated by Erikson. Again, like the elders discussed by Erikson, Gutmann, Friedan, and Sheehy, they are individuals who balance profession and family, autonomy and apathy, integrity and despair, to achieve the integration and wisdom which is the true hallmark of an affirmative old age.

Chips escapes the emotional atrophy of a Casaubon by falling deeply in love with Katherine, a young woman half his age. Although she dies in childbirth two years after their marriage, the deep emotional feeling they shared changes his life and prevents him from sinking into "the dry rot of pedagogy" (Hilton 1962, 36). He balances Eriksonian despair and integrity, developing empathy for the boys he teaches, thereby becoming a better teacher and reaping the rewards of "the sudden love of boys for a man who was kind without being soft" (pp. 37–38). At age seventy, fifteen years after retirement, Chips is still inviting each new class to tea, fulfilling the grand-generative function of linking generations together by passing on nurturance and knowledge (Erikson 1982, 63).

Miss Dove at first appears to fit the caricature of the spinster school teacher. Tall, skinny, and punctilious, she demands order, discipline, and responsibility from her students, but does so out of her genuine concern for them and their futures. As a young teacher, Miss Dove had learned of her father's embezzlement and had shouldered the burden of paying his debt after his death. She integrates this episode into a larger vision of the world and shares that image of order and duty with her students, performing the grand-generative function heralded by Erikson as the procreative goal of the aging.

Neither Mr. Chips nor Miss Dove become ridiculous or inept as they age. Instead, they have reconciled despair with integrity to fashion a wisdom which guides and shelters other, younger human beings. Such dignity, integrity, and wisdom is also displayed within the professoriate by Godfrey St. Peter, the protagonist in Cather's (1953) *The Professor's House,* and William Stoner, the eponymous hero of *Stoner* (Williams 1988). These complex characters experience initial despair as they traverse the passage to old age, but eventually seize its opportunity to integrate earlier versions of the self with the more mature identity which emerges from middle age. The old house where Godfrey St. Peter continues to work embodies the young adult identity as a husband and scholar that he fashioned within its confines. St. Peter's refusal to work in his new house, bought with the rewards of fame and money, can be seen as his initial refusal to construct a more mature identity incorporating the responsibility and recognition—both spiritual and material—that later life brings. His withdrawal from his family, his scrutiny of their flaws, and his loss of interest in his work resonates with the "crisis of meaning" which marks the passage to later life (Sheehy 1995, 148–149). While Gullette (1993) argues that St. Peter never emerges from despondency and stops being productive through "complicated interactions with aging" (p. 27), recent studies on aging suggest other interpretations. Working on a final project in his old study overlooking Lake Michigan, St. Peter finds himself drawn more and more into memories of the young boy he once was. He bypasses his young adult identity to connect to the purity of his childhood and of his rural past. He realizes that this time was "the realest of his life . . . all the years between had been accidental. His career, his wife, his family, were not his life at all, but a chain of events that had happened to him; all these things had nothing to do with the person he was in the beginning" (Cather 1953, 264). A similar primitive purity is described in the writings of Tom Outland—St. Peter's protégé who was killed in the war—whose journal St. Peter is editing. As St. Peter struggles to integrate his aging self with the boy he once was, he also considers and almost welcomes death. Yet when death confronts him, he is saved by his own instinct and by the propitious arrival of the devout family seamstress. His actions, coupled with her appearance, suggest the annihilation of despair, the emergence of new hope, and the rebirth of a new self, grounded in Eriksonian wisdom rather than in delight. This regeneration finds its emblem in the new grandchild St. Peter learns that his daughter is to bear.

Another professorial hero, Stoner, overcomes the hostility of a frigid wife and the actions of a vicious department chair through the love of a young instructor. She mitigates his midlife despair, that "moment in his age when there came to him . . . a question of such overwhelming simplicity that he had no means to face it . . . whether life were worth the living; if it had ever been" (Williams 1988, 179). Stoner's love affair with Katherine Driscoll emerges from this crisis, reaffirming the clinical finding that crucial life transitions may cause depression but can also offer new opportunities to meet "old instinctual and interpersonal needs" (Vaillant 1977, 222). Katherine's love and the discovery of true emotional intimacy enable Stoner to successfully negotiate the midlife passage and to face aging with equanimity. When Katherine is forced to leave, Stoner overcomes despair and is regenerated by his love of teaching, of literature, and of his students. Another academic whose strength is linked to his rural past, Stoner displays the resilience of his farming forbearers: "Though he seldom thought of his early years on the Booneville farm, there was always near his consciousness the blood knowledge of his inheritance, given to him by his forefathers whose lives were obscure and hard and stoical and whose common ethic was to present to an oppressive world faces that were expressionless and hard and bleak" (Williams 1988, 219). His inheritance enables Stoner to live by his principles and maintain his values throughout his life and as he dies. Left alone in the last moments before his death, he thinks of failure and then pushes the idea aside as unimportant. Waiting for an answer, he is conscious of bright sunlight, the laughter of group of students and, finally, he reaches for the book that he had written long ago and "felt a tingling, as if those pages were alive. . . . A sense of his own identity came upon him with a sudden force, and he felt the power of it. He was himself, and he knew what he had been" (pp. 277–278).

Both Stoner and Godfrey St. Peter emerge from despair and find rejuvenation and meaning through nurturing their students and expanding their relationships with them. In doing so, both echo what Gutmann (1977) calls the sex-role crossover of later years; men feel free to reclaim their nurturing qualities and to foreground human relationships while women become more assertive and dominant. Gutmann argues that a benefit of aging is the freedom to reclaim the repressed aspects of the self (p. 312). These aspects of the aging process are manifested by St. Peter, who rediscovers his boyhood and his affiliation with nature by editing the journals of his brilliant and beloved student, Tom Outland. Stoner recovers from the loss of Katherine through his students, finding that the returning World War II veterans, "strange in their maturity . . . intensely serious and contemptuous of triviality" bring to the classroom "the best years of his teaching and . . . in some ways the happiest years of his life" (Williams 1988, 248).

Despite the many-faceted portraits of Stoner and St. Peter, the conventional academic caricature persists and is embodied by other characters in each novel. In *The Professor's House*, Robert Crane is depicted as a work-obsessed, disease-ridden, impractical physicist who allows his wily and greedy brother-in-law to manipulate him. In *Stoner*, Hollis Lomax fulfills the role of the twisted, egocentric "monster of cruelty" who blocks Stoner's aspirations during a twenty-year campaign that culminates in Katherine's termination as instructor. Lomax, a "grotesquely misshapen" hunchback who is crippled emotionally as well as physically, launches the attack after Stoner refuses to pass the student, Charles Walker, who is also physically disabled but also an intellectual fraud. The conjuncture of disability and intellectual deception constructs a metaphor for academic life that is threaded through this and other university novels. The sophistry of the fraudulent scholar becomes a trope which operates in several works, finding embodiment in the pathetic Casaubon, who can never complete the work he endlessly pursues. Concomitantly, the division between mind and body, between the intellectual and physical world, helps to create the stereotypes of academics while also constructing the cultural terrain often mapped by the literature about them. Janice Rossen (1993) cites the "irreconcilable conflicts" at the heart of academic life, clashes erupting from the constant tension between idealism and practicality. The authentic scholar is individualistic, idealistic, and a seeker of truth, pursuing abstract, often absolute principles in matters of infinite complexity. Accomplishment in the material world, even the scholarly world, is marked by the ability to negotiate, to simplify, and to focus on a concrete plan of action in order to succeed. Thus, to be a scholar requires purity of vision; to "get on" in the world requires compromise. This dichotomy and its inherent contradictions lie at the core of many stories about schools and their teachers. Drawn as a caricature, the idealistic, dreaming scholar becomes a buffoon, like Thales falling into the well; impractical, ineffectual and embittered, the professor becomes a malevolent egotist, like Lomax or Casaubon. Conversely, the pragmatic professor, when etched in extreme colors, becomes the scheming scholar embodied by Charles Walker or by the success-seeking, globe-trotting characters in David Lodge's satirical novels of academic life, *Changing Places* (1985) and *Small World* (1984).

More complex, fully drawn characters also become enmeshed in the clash of these irreconcilable opposites. While St. Peter achieves both intellectual and material success, the latter threatens to poison the purity of his intellectual effort much as the material success of Tom Outland's effort threatens to infect the lives of those for whom he cares. Stoner's refusal to compromise his intellectual principles results in his isolation and poverty, and contributes to the loss of the woman he loves. The complex protagonist often tries to reconcile the purity of his vision with the necessity of compromise but fails in the attempt, and that failure often forms the heart of the story.

The conflict between the ideal and the practical is not limited to the academic world; it creates a consistent tension within the lives of most people. The story of the scholar, legitimated to pursue the life of the mind but forced to live in the material world, vividly foregrounds the clash and, as a result, the academic protagonist becomes a prototype for all who seek to resolve these contradictions. Viewed in this light, the conflation of stereotypes about aging and about academia seems more comprehensible; as we age, the need to resolve these oppositions becomes more imperative and more possible. Stage theorists argue that as we age the integrity that engenders wisdom embraces the ability to balance seemingly irreconcilable opposites, the ability, according to Thomas Moore (1992), to "stretch the heart wide enough to embrace contradiction and paradox" (p. 11). Studies show that fulfilled older people have the ability to handle life's conflicts without passivity, blaming, or bitterness through the process of balancing seemingly contradictory positions. This process, what Friedan (1993) calls "integration" and Erikson (1982) calls "wisdom," is what the academic protagonist seeks, but often fails to find. The search, however, is one that every person undertakes in his or her life, and one in which fictional characters can often lead the way.

CHAPTER 13

Aging and the Public Schools: Visits of Charity— The Young Look at the Old

Ralph M. Cline

Life, if thou knowest how to use it, is long enough.
(Seneca the Younger "On the Shortness of Life")

Allan Bloom (1987), in *The Closing of the American Mind*, complains that students who enter the University of Chicago have experienced a "decay of the family" (p. 109). The younger generation seems to be alienated from the older. "Social Security, retirement funds and health insurance for old people," he continues, "free their children from even having to give them financial support, let alone taking them into their own homes to live" (p. 86). Teachers often see the harsh and negative attitudes formed by children toward the old. What Lear says ironically—"Age is unnecessary. On my knees I beg/That you'll vouchsafe me raiment, bed, and food" (*King Lear* 2.4.155–156)—many American students accept at face value. The old are often considered unnecessary burdens.

If the old have been warehoused, and the young's interaction with them has been dramatically reduced, where does young America interact with old America? One answer is in "American Lit," that place where for generations, more or less against their will, young America has interacted with people like Bartleby the Scrivener, Ichabod Crane, and Hester Prynne. In the venerable American Lit. class, American high school juniors "graze" (in Bloom's term) a surprisingly stable pasture of literary selections. The study of American literature in the penultimate year of high school is, as nearly as I can determine, a nearly universal American experience—closer to being universal, perhaps, than any other exposure of American citizens to the humanities. The ubiquitous nature of the American Literature course is demonstrated informally in several ways, in conversations with sales representatives from six publishers of American Literature texts, in conversations with the English Language Arts supervisors from Hillsborough and Pinellas Counties, in subject/level meetings at the National Council of Teachers of English Conventions in Los Angeles (1987) and San Antonio (1986), and in International Baccalaureate Conferences in New York, Miami, and Montezuma, New Mexico (1987–1994). American Lit is offered in virtually every public, private, or parochial high school in the country, and it is usually offered to students who have either not yet or only recently attained the age of sixteen, the earliest voluntary dropout age in most states.

Not only is the American Literature course omnipresent, but selections read in the course are remarkably consistent from text to text. Due to the great influence of four states (New York, California, Florida, and Texas), almost all American Lit textbooks contain pieces by the same list of authors— indeed, often exactly the same selections. These states "adopt" textbooks for the entire state school system (rather than allow each county or each school to adopt its own textbooks); thus, to sell a series of literature texts to one of these states is to make a considerable profit. Before adoption of textbooks, each of the states issues a list of specifications; a publisher who does not meet the specifications may not submit a textbook for consideration. In this way, the major publishers of literature texts tailor their anthologies to rather narrow and specific needs. Then the publishers make these texts available to other states and school districts who thus have a very circumscribed choice. (See Appendix A for a comparison of the tables of contents for the six largest publishers of American literature textbooks.) When the texts do differ, the differences occur in the areas of ancillary materials (e.g., manuals, test booklets, audiovisuals). Several of the selections included in these American Literature texts are concerned with old people and their interaction with young people. I had the opportunity recently to "teach" four of these short stories to five classes of junior American Literature at Countryside High School in Clearwater, Florida: Eudora Welty's "A Visit of Charity" (1968) and "A Worn Path" (1994); Katherine Anne Porter's (1965) "The Jilting of Granny Weatherall"; and Nathaniel Hawthorne's (1994) "Dr. Heidegger's Experiment." These four short stories lend themselves to this study for two reasons: They are skillfully written and culturally important stories about growing and being old, and they appear in virtually every American Literature textbook published in the United States today. They are, in short, "chestnuts," liable to be read by almost every American between sixteen and eighteen years of age.

In "A Visit of Charity" (Welty 1968), a fourteen-year-old Campfire Girl named Marian makes a required visit to an Old Ladies' Home. She does not care which old ladies she visits; "any of them will do," she adds (pp. 515–518). Once inside the Home, Marian, potted plant in hand, proceeds through the

"Ages of Woman," so to speak. She encounters a middle-aged, virtually genderless nurse who ushers her down the hall to "pick out an old lady" (p. 516). The white-clad nurse has close-cropped hair that looks like a "sea-wave" (p. 515) and contrasts sharply with the young, blonde maid Marian, who is dressed in red and white. The nurse notices the plant and calls it by its scientific name, *multiflora Cineraria* (from the Latin for "ashes"). Thus passing middle age, Marian finds herself symbolically out to sea: "Marian felt as if she were walking on the waves" (p. 515) of bulging linoleum. The nurse pushes Marian from the hall into the moist interior of a room and into the presence of its two inmates. The two old women who receive Marian's uncharitable charity are consistently described in animal terms: with "claws" they "pluck" her cap and "snatch" her potted plant; they "bleat" like sheep (p. 516). The two old women are unpleasant in the extreme and in all aspects of their interrelations. They bicker about every topic of conversation breached (the potted plant, the visit, previous visits, their health, especially their ages) until one is reduced to weeping like an infant and the other to begging like a toddler for pennies and nickels. Marian is, of course, no help to the old ladies in their misery. She is there to receive "a minimum of only three points in her score" (p. 515). She runs in tears from the Home and "imperiously" (p. 518) commands the passing bus to stop. After taking a second to retrieve an apple she had hidden in a thornbush before going into the Home (so that she would not have to share it), she jumps aboard the bus to make good her escape from the stages of aging that she has been forced for a moment to confront.

The students were chilled by the story which seemed to us to be an awful and accurate picture of the horror that the old can cause in the young, especially when the old act childishly in the presence of a child. Discussion showed that many of the students were embarrassed that Marian, a character showing frightening callousness, so accurately portrayed their real feelings about interacting with old people. The story seemed to suggest by its very architecture that any sort of positive relationship between the generations was impossible. Marian's world was brittle, cold, bright, and solid while the Home was dank, warm, dark, and fluid. Marian's world was escape and mobility; the Home was dateless eternal imprisonment. Especially telling details to the students were the moistness and the smells that Welty so convincingly evokes. Despite the intellectual recognition that the moistness came from constant cleaning and that the smell was one of disinfectant—present to defeat disease and death—the sensual perceptions of smell and feel had a profound effect upon the students (see Appendix B for some examples of their comments).

We took heart, however, with the next two selections, "A Worn Path" (Welty 1994) and "The Jilting of Granny Weatherall" (Porter 1965), and the readers of this chapter can also take heart that the portrait of aging shown to high school students is one of beauty as well as of terror. Barbara Frey Waxman (1990) would call these two stories *Reifungsroman* or "fictions of ripening," in which the old are shown "to be active, useful citizen[s] at every age" (pp. 1–23).

Moreover, "A Worn Path" (Welty 1994), has a wonderful surprise ending that caused even strangely tonsured young heads to bow briefly!

In "A Worn Path" an old African-American woman named Phoenix Jackson makes a trek on foot—along a path worn largely, one suspects, by her own feet. Phoenix is spectacularly old. Throughout her long walk, she is unable to remember the reason for her trip. She simply relied on her feet to determine her path (Welty 1994, 456–461). Her infirmities make every step torture for both Phoenix and the reader as Welty presents the old woman's obstacles in epic style and proportion. First she encounters a daunting hill— "seems like there is chains about my feet, time I get this far" (p. 456)—but she conquers the hill. Second, she accuses the thorns of "doing your appointed work. Never want to let folks pass" (p. 457). Then comes the "trial" of crossing a log, an endeavor so frightening that Phoenix must close her eyes (p. 457). She then has to "creep and crawl" through barbed wire (p. 457), and be frightened by a scarecrow which her old eyes take to be a foe (p. 458). She falls in a ditch from vertigo and fatigue and must endure the condescension of the young white man who pulls her out and inquires after her health without showing her even a modicum of respect (pp. 458–460). Even after finally arriving at her destination (which is a hospital), the reader and Phoenix are unaware of her purpose for coming. The nurses have to press her relentlessly until she recollects: "It was my memory had left me. There I sat and forgot why I made my long trip" (p. 461).

The old woman, despite her brave good humor in facing her obstacles, despite the disarming poetry of her conversations with a countryside that refuses to make her journey easy, despite her undeniable dignity, is becoming an object of derision both to the reader and to the nurses. She becomes, however, an object of great admiration—even to high school students who are lamentably slow to admire—when we discover the purpose of her trip. Her grandson, with whom she lives, swallowed lye two years ago and lives in constant pain. Phoenix has not made her journey for selfish reasons, to see the town or to see relatives as the white man at the ditch had suggested. She is at the hospital to get medicine for her grandson. She has made the journey for love, as only someone of her dignity could have made the journey. Moreover, as one of the students pointed out, she could not have had such dignity had she not been so old!

Another portrait of dignity with great age is Katherine Anne Porter's (1965) "The Jilting of Granny Weatherall," a story portraying the last hours of a flawed yet quite admirable woman. The story evokes sadness while deftly escaping even the shadow of sentimentality. Admittedly, we high school English teachers have dealt far too much with Porter's cipher at the end of the story, and not enough with the character of the woman at the story's center. Near the close of the story, Granny Weatherall—slightly cryptically—refers to having been twice jilted, even though there is evidence in the text of her having been jilted only once, by a man who left her at the altar. The suggestion here is that God has somehow jilted Granny Weatherall and that she dies, therefore, in dignified self-assertion, without making herself abject before Him. However, Porter's depiction of Granny Weatherall throughout the story employs a number of sophisticated techniques that should be considered. During much of the tale, Granny oscillates between linear time and internal time. In addition, Porter uses stream of consciousness, a technique which we high school teachers love to display in front of our students (and which, perhaps, accounts for the popularity of the story in American Lit books and courses).

More important, however, than all the literary shenanigans is Porter's (1965) unforgettable lesson that Ellen Weatherall was not always a Granny and that a woman's strengths often lie in what she heroically does not do and does not have despite her great human desires. Into Granny's last thoughts swirl the important characters of her life, such as dutiful daughter Cornelia (a Learish echo), young Dr. Harry whom she once spanked and who now just thinks he can take a real physician's liberties, George the jilter whose name has become an involuntary mantra in Granny's last hours after years of repression, and John her husband whom she had admired and cared for and tried to love. Ellen Weatherall dies holding a grudge against God, against George, and against injustice: "For the second time there was no sign. Again no bridegroom and the priest in the house. She could not remember any other sorrow because this grief wiped them all away. Oh, no, there's nothing more cruel than this—I'll never forgive it. She stretched herself with a deep breath and blew out the light" (p. 89).

High school juniors see, therefore, two admirably drawn faces of aging. In "A Visit of Charity" they see the worst imaginable scene. They see the young hopelessly separated from the old—not only unable to offer charity, but also unable to want to offer charity—unable to be anything but appalled at the sights and smells of age and afraid of aging. In "A Worn Path" and "The Jilting of Granny Weatherall," they see simply that people of great age, even unto the very margin of death, are capable of all the traits and gestures so admired in the young. Moreover, the old are capable of these gestures in a graceful iambic that to many young people is a welcome rest from the trochees of their own confused young lives.

Nathaniel Hawthorne would be surprised at his overwhelming popularity with high school English teachers today. If American Lit is our most universal cultural experience, then Nathaniel Hawthorne is our most studied avatar (even if he is studied, from time to time, through the lens of Messrs. Cliff and Monarch). One might convincingly argue that only six or seven people have actually read the other great 1851 novel, *Moby Dick*, but *Moby Dick* is not assigned in American high schools. *The Scarlet Letter*, on the other hand, certainly is. Present in all but one of the textbooks I surveyed (see Appendix A) is another Hawthorne favorite, "Dr. Heidegger's Experiment" (1994). Written when Hawthorne was thirty-three, this story is in many ways atypical of Hawthorne's stories, which may go a long way toward explaining its popularity with English teachers.

The characters seem so completely allegorical in this uncharacteristically short Hawthorne story that readers need not bother sorting out different planes of meaning in the text. Indeed, they are so comic-book-like that they seem to speak almost chorally throughout most of the story, thereby obviating the need even to differentiate between them: "'Give us more of this wondrous water!' cried they. 'We are younger—but we are still too old!'" (p. 200). Indeed, only the Widow Wycherly is singled out for self-damning dialogue. The silliness of the male characters when they become young again is usually merely summarized. The vocabulary is quite simple. In this story–sermon about the excesses of youth, Hawthorne, the master of the synonym and of the near meaning, leans quite heavily upon a few vivid words to denote age: old (twenty-nine times), venerable (five times), white-bearded, withered, old-fashioned, antique, faded, deathlike, dotage, grey, decrepit, and sapless; all within eleven high school pages (i.e., with much white space, several pictures, room for readers' hints for further understanding and vocabulary definitions). But "Dr. Heidegger," at least for us today, lacks the depth and reality of the other stories discussed in this chapter. The physical ugliness of age is hammered on in this story. The Widow Wycherly is not really a woman because she is old; not until she is considerably "youthened" does she feel "almost like a woman again" (p. 201). Hawthorne repeatedly employs phrases like "palsied hands," "ashen visages," "ashen hue," "corpselike," "rheumatic, withered grandsires," "skinny ugliness of a withered grandam." In cartoon contrast, the old folks are pictured as little more than decrepit. Any seeming regret they might exhibit is only the result of their physical inability to pursue the follies of their youth. Of course, the simple message is verified by the old folks' behavior once they have drunk from the Doctor's crystal pitcher containing the water of the Floridian fountain. They instantly array themselves again in the worst habits of their youth and again childishly embroil themselves in a four-way tussle of affection. In the throes of this infantile behavior, they smash the container of Ponce de León's water, thus physically and allegorically ruining by their immature behavior the possibility of health and youth.

The real sadness of the story, as the students and I saw it, is the conception of old age as a punishment for youthful indiscretion rather than as a natural stage of life—and of the maniacal fixation upon the physical ugliness of age. Of course, one could well argue that Heidegger himself represents the dignity of age and, throughout the story, remains in his own way quite attractive. But the students also thought that if this characterization of Heidegger is accurate then the story is in some way an insult to the young, a statement that to be young is to be less human than to be old and that young people, by definition, are unable to harness their energies and are destined to destroy their youth by the possibility of a vigorous old age. To the students, therefore, "Dr. Heidegger's Experiment" was nearly as fatal a picture of aging as was "A Visit of Charity." We felt that the experience was simply too complex to be rendered faithfully by the doctor's experiment with his four shallow friends and that he, himself, was altogether too facile.

What generalizations may we now draw from what we know about the exposure of American high school juniors to aging? First, we know that high school students are indeed exposed to many views of the process of growing old. In addition to the works examined in this study, American high school students of all ability levels read works like *Death of a Salesman*, "Stopping by Woods on a Snowy Evening," "Because I Could Not Stop for Death," "A Fly Buzzed," "The Bear" (always, "The Bear"), and "Death of a Hired Man." (They do not read "Thanatopsis" anymore.) So the situation of growing old is often and richly treated in the literature to which most young Americans are exposed.

Second, we can see that public-school educators have taken the task of preparing students for aging and for existing with the elderly very seriously. They have chosen the works of serious and talented authors, and they present them as well as they can. And they present them each year, year in and year out!

Third, we can see that, rather than some sort of gap between generations, young people's opinions of old people are fairly well spread across the spectrum. The young are not some monolithic establishment united in their hatred of all people older than they. Despite what we may wish to believe, the haircuts that look like a dead squirrel on a rock and the language that clots blood are less attempts to say that they hate us than they are—alas, understandably—attempts to be other than us. Appendix B shows that, in my small but careful sampling, 35 percent of the students questioned had wholly positive comments to make about their elders. These positive comments center upon the elders' great experience and the joy the students find in' hearing about their great experience. These positive comments are often quite charming, and most students ask, in one way or another, "What was life like when they were my age?" Another 19 percent responded ambivalently, probably the most honest of all the students responding. These ambivalent students seemed to honor those old people who communicated the same sort of *joie de vivre* that young people are fabled to possess (but most of the time do not). While 45 percent of the students responded wholly negatively, many of these comments reflected peevishness rather than genuine dislike. They centered, comically and ironically, upon the driving habits of old folks (this from the most accident-prone segment of the American population) and upon their smell (this from some of the most olfactorally egregious beings ever created).

Most telling about the negative responses, however, was the simple and understandable refrain of being afraid (and, thereby, irritated) at not living up to old people's expectations. Again and again, vitriolic responses mentioned how certain the students were that nothing they do and nothing they are could ever please older people: "They think I'm some kind of evil kid that wants to mug them," "They avoid me," "I act as I think they would like me to be," and "I feel like they are watching my every move to make sure that I am acting and behaving correctly." If these young people are representative of their peers, what we see is a set of negative feelings based more upon the students' own feelings of inferiority than upon any characteristic of the people at whom they direct their dislike. Old people are a handy screen for the projection of their fears, especially because the lifestyles of the two groups are more different in many cases than the behaviors and customs of people from entirely different cultures, and because members of both groups are hardly hesitant about expressing these differences orally and publicly.

Fourth, we can see that the public schools, despite the stylish and consistent attacks upon them, address this important social issue in mature and measured ways—at least in high school English classes—and give young citizens the opportunity at least to form balanced and compassionate opinions about those who were high school juniors so long ago.

APPENDIX A

A Comparison of the Tables of Contents of Six American Literature Textbooks

	Author		
Publisher	W. Irving	E. A. Poe	R. W. Emerson
Harcourt Brace Jovanovich	The Legend of Sleepy Hollow	The Fall of the House of Usher The Masque of the Red Death The Raven	from Self-Reliance The Concord Hymn
Holt Rinehart and Winston	Rip van Winkle	The Fall of the House of Usher Masque of the Red Death The Raven	Self-Reliance The Concord Hymn
McDougal-Litell	The Legend of Sleepy Hollow	The Pit and the Pendulum The Raven	Self-Reliance
Prentice-Hall	The Legend of Sleepy Hollow	The Fall of the House of Usher The Raven	Self-Reliance The Concord Hymn
Scott-Foresman	The Legend of Sleepy Hollow	The Cask of Amontillado The Raven	Self-Reliance The Concord Hymn
Macmillan	The Legend of Sleepy Hollow	Fall of the House of Usher The Raven	Self-Reliance The Concord Hymn
	W. Whitman	Mark Twain	W. Faulkner
Harcourt Brace Jovanovich	from Song of Myself Astronomer Patient Spider	from Life on the Mississippi	The Bear

	Author		
Publisher	W. Whitman	Mark Twain	W. Faulkner
Holt Rinehart and Winston	from Song of Myself Astronomer	from *Life on the Mississippi* from *Huckleberry Finn*	Spotted Horses
McDougal-Litell	from Song of Myself Patient Spider Astronomer	from *Huckleberry Finn*	Barn Burning
Prentice-Hall	from Song of Myself Astronomer Patient Spider	from *Life on the Mississippi* The Celebrated Jumping Frog of Calaveras County	The Bear
Scott-Foresman	from Song of Myself Astronomer Patient Spider	from *Life on the Mississippi* The Celebrated Jumping Frog of Calaveras County	The Bear
Macmillan	Astronomer Patient Spider	from *Life on the Mississippi* Jumping Frog of Calaveras County	The Bear

	H. Melville	N. Hawthorne	E. Dickinson
Harcourt Brace Jovanovich	from *Moby-Dick*	Dr. Heidegger's Experiment The Minister's Black Veil	Because I Could Not Stop for Death A Fly Buzzed
Holt Rinehart and Winston	from *Moby-Dick*	Rappaccini's Daughter The Minister's Black Veil	Because I Could Not Stop for Death A Fly Buzzed
McDougal-Litell	Bartleby the Scrivener	Dr. Heidegger's Experiment The Minister's Black Veil	Because I Could Not Stop for Death A Fly Buzzed
Prentice-Hall	from *Moby-Dick*	Dr. Heidegger's Experiment The Minister's Black Veil	Because I Could Not Stop for Death A Fly Buzzed
Scott-Foresman	from *Redburn*	Young Goodman Brown	Because I Could Not Stop for Death A Fly Buzzed
Macmillan	from *Moby-Dick*	The Minister's Black Veil	Because I Could Not Stop for Death A Fly Buzzed

Publisher	Author	
	E. Hemingway	R. Frost
Harcourt Brace Jovanovich	In Another Country	The Road Less Travelled Stopping by Woods on a Snowy Evening Death of a Hired Man Mending Wall
Holt Rinehart and Winston	In Another Country	Mending Wall Death of a Hired Man
McDougal-Litell	Old Man at the Bridge	The Road Less Travelled Stopping by Woods on a Snowy Evening Death of a Hired Man Mending Wall
Prentice-Hall	In Another Country	Mending Wall Death of a Hired Man Stopping by Woods on a Snowy Evening
Scott-Foresman	In Another Country	Stopping by Woods on a Snowy Evening Mending Wall
Macmillan	In Another Country	The Road Less Travelled Stopping by Woods on a Snowy Evening Mending Wall

Note: All anthologies are prepublication 1989 editions provided by the publishers for previewing purposes for this study, except the Macmillan, which is the 1984 edition.

APPENDIX B: AMERICAN LITERATURE STUDENTS' COMMENTS ON AGING

These comments followed a reading of Eudora Welty's "A Visit of Charity" (1968) and "A Worn Path" (1994), Nathaniel Hawthorne's (1994) "Dr. Heidegger's Experiment," and Katherine Anne Porter's (1965) "The Jilting of Granny Weatherall." The students responded to a simple prompt: How do you feel in the presence of old people? Their responses have been categorized and respelled and repunctuated in several cases.

Positive Responses (27 of 77, 35 Percent)

1. I like to hear the stories that they have to tell of how it used to be in the days before there were TVs.
2. Older people are usually more apt to listen to you because so many other people just ignore them.

3. The things that youth can speculate or predict about their future may very well have already been experienced by the elderly.

4. They maintain dignity (most of them) although time has humbled them emotionally and physically.

5. I feel like they have experienced a lot more in life than I have, and I can learn from them. Out of their knowledge, it is my duty to respect them.

6. They are also artifacts of the past which may tell us how people's lives were before we were born.

7. I want to know things about them: Do they still love their spouse after all these years, did they ever experiment with things, did they go to Woodstock, were they hippies, how was life when they were my age?

8. Elderlies are treated like children, and I feel that type of treatment is extremely disrespectful.

9. I have an 88-year-old great-grandmother, and she [is] just as nice and fun and loving as anyone else.

10. Older women especially have the knowledge that could teach younger people how life really works.

11. Older people are so much more mellow, and they like to talk more.

12. I treat them with great respect and am treated the same way in return.

Ambivalent Responses (15 of 77, 19 Percent)

1. I feel three different emotions. One is respect because they have lived this long in this jungle we call America. One is caution because they are old and very fragile. The third is anger because of the way they stereotype young people.

2. I believe there are two types of elderly people: those who let themselves get old and decrepit; and those who hold on to their youth.

3. They give you dirty looks when you're around and they think that all we do is cause trouble. But then there are the few [sic] who enjoy to see [sic] kids have fun.

4. To me old is not a number or age, but a state of mind. A ninty-year-old with a childlike laugh that [sic] still plays bridge or walks every day is young. A twenty-year-old hypochondriac is old.

Negative Responses (35 of 77, 45 Percent)

1. Most elders make me feel like I am from a different world.

2. When I notice that an old person is coming in the front door, my patience begins to drop.

3. I feel like they are watching my every move to make sure that I am behaving and acting correctly.

4. No matter what we do most times it seems as if it is not good enough because it is not how things were done when they were our age.

5. They are always grumpy and they tell stories that I know aren't true. I can't stand them, all except my grandparents.

6. I can't figure out why they smell. They just do.

7. Anywhere I go in public, old people seem to avoid me. They think I'm some kind of evil kid that wants to mug them.

8. Older people talk about the deterioration of values and their example isn't helping their case.

9. They always say how things have changed and how young people are out of control.

10. Not to mention that strange smell they emanate. I hope that doesn't happen to me.

11. They treat me like I will be five years old for the rest of my life.

12. I can talk to elderly people and listen to them — but not as myself. I act as I think they would like me to be.

Part IV

AGING IN THE FINE AND POPULAR ARTS

CHAPTER 14

Aging and Contemporary Art

Linnea S. Dietrich

Many of our attitudes toward aging (like those toward women, sex, sexual preference, race, ethnicity, religious preference, handicapped status, and so on) are based on the visual, on seeing difference. Thus, the visual arts are especially complicitous in the project of talking about aging and identity. Speaking of gerontology's traditional dissociation of ideas, images, and attitudes from the "facts" of aging, gerontologist Thomas Cole (1992b) writes that this separating of facts from images is "an epistemological stance which denies that the experience and cultural representation of human aging help to constitute its reality" (p. xxi). Just as visual representation—art—can contribute to the problem of popularizing negative images of aging people, art can also contribute positive images of aging people which in turn build positive attitudes and achievements. What the eye sees registers not just what something is, but also what is valued, what is considered beautiful or appealing or meaningful to us. Visual representations by definition objectify and signify; form embodies content and asks or demands that we make judgments about it, judgments that again are built into our conscious and unconscious constructions of attitudes and reality.

In art, great age is often a great value. The sculpture of the *Fertility Figure from Willendorf, Austria* is about 40 thousand years old—our great, great (!) grandmother. The mummy of Rameses II, pharaoh of Egypt, is 3,500 years old. Representations of the nude female body, like the aging body, are problematized in current art and art-historical practice: a Greek Aphrodite is considered to be a beautiful object representing a beautiful woman, but Hiram Powers's *Greek Slave* (1846) offends because with it one must pretend not to see her nudity, her nakedness; the cross she wears veils her body, at least according to the pamphlet circulated by the artist when he toured the work around the country making a fortune from people paying to see this "religious" work. The *Portrait of Hélène Fourment in Fur* (by Rubens, circa 1638–1640) is acceptable, although nude, because we know how much Rubens loved this woman, his second wife. Courbet's *Origin of the World* (1966) offends, because while the human anatomy represented here may be beautiful, this headless torso is without agency, and defines Woman as merely a furry vagina. The gaze is powerful because it confers the power of judgment on the viewer and allows us to say this is mine, or this is beautiful, just as we might say this is old and good, or this is old and not so good. Seeing images of aging people depicted as in decline or deteriorating and seeing youthful ideals of beauty both reinforce the message that only a youthful body is good. Betty Friedan (1993) quoting David Gutmann, speculates that the "catastrophic view of the aging process *causes* many of the very symptoms we associate with age" (p. 460) and reinforces stereotypes which not only hurt older people but prevent them from developing more positive self-images.

In the Western tradition, to take just one example of the negative view of aging, Giovanni Bologna's sculpture, the *Rape of the Sabine Women* (1583) depicts a moment when, in the founding of Rome, the men realized that they had no women on whom to found the empire. They further noticed that their neighbors from Sabina had women, so they carried some off. In the sculpture, the young Roman wrests the woman away from her aging Sabine husband. The message is clear: Older men lose the prize to the young men and civilization marches forward.

Other traditions, as in China, privilege age — usually old men. Shen Chou was eighty years old and highly respected when he painted his *Self Portrait* in 1507 and indicated his age on the painting. He was a member of the Taoist school of landscape painting and this school held that nature prolongs life and vitality and that painting landscapes expands one's vital spirit. Shen Chou painted a landscape of an old man sitting under a tree, demonstrating the serenity and power of both nature and painting, since the activity of painting keeps one vital. The painting seems to suggest that being active keeps you active, that being connected to nature keeps you connected to nature and to worthwhile activity, and especially nourishes the spirit which, in turn, invigorates the body. It is almost as if painting what one wants materializes, or realizes, the desired state, the reversal of the stereotype that tells people that they are old and not so good. Art, therefore, although guilty of reinforcing negative stereotypes, can also constitute new, more positive ones, and the artists presented in this chapter are doing just that.

June Blum, in her 1976 portrait *Betty Friedan as the Prophet*, deconstructs the Western notion of the prophet as an older male: one need think only of Old Testament prophets, classical philosophers, church officials, Santa Claus, or university professors. But here, Blum selects a woman in a landscape and a somewhat barren landscape at that, and paints the woman in the landscape holding a book. This is a radical reversal of roles and a powerful image of what happens when one gives disenfranchised people privilege, position, and books, and places them in the field, literally in history, into the picture. They become powerful and the picture is changed. Friedan, whatever else she may be, appears in Blum's painting as the prophet of the new dispensation, with *The Feminine Mystique* in 1963, and, we might add, *The Fountain of Age* thirty years later.

Friedan's productivity, like that of artists in the history of art, is proof of the assumption that keeping active keeps one active, hence the concept of the old-age style (*Alterstil*) in art, literature, or any creative endeavor. In the history of art, the notion of an old-age style is well documented, and one immediately thinks of the late works of Michelangelo, Titian, Rembrandt, Monet, or Cézanne. Julius S. Held (1987), an art historian who wrote in the *Art Journal's* special issue on "Style and the Aging Artist," said that the median age of artists is sixty-seven and that in the nineteenth and twentieth centuries, 76 percent of artists whom he surveyed lived beyond age sixty (p. 133). But generally, discussions of the late style of artists like the ones just mentioned assert that, having gained wisdom and spiritual vigor in their later years, these artists abandoned their weakening bodies and concentrated on abstract or visionary—less physical—forms and themes. I suspect that much in these arguments is compensatory hogwash. While we may hope to attain wisdom and spiritual understanding in later life, perhaps sooner than later, there is no reason to believe that it comes at the cost of the body, as if one can have one or the other, but not both. I would argue that valuing the body, the senses, and the frailties and pleasures of the body is a highly spiritual idea, and one with which contemporary artists are grappling.

In addition to the careers of the well-known artists mentioned, I note in the following section some examples of successful careers by artists less familiar. Sofonisba Anguissola painted her self-portrait around 1620 when she was ninety-some years old. Rachel Ruysch began signing and dating her paintings with her age when she was eighty-three; she lived eighty-six years, from 1664 to 1750. Lorenzo Homar, a contemporary artist from Puerto Rico, painted his self-portrait in 1986, age seventy-three, and depicts himself as wary, his face lined, but with eyes powerful behind the lenses of his glasses. Georgia O'Keeffe appears in a photograph at the age of ninety-seven with her assistant, Juan Hamilton; she died, after an enormously productive life (1887 to 1996), a few months short of her hundredth birthday. Naturally, we could study artists like these, comparing early and late works as if to measure just how much these artists learned in the interval and just how their wisdom "looks" on canvas or in stone; however, at this juncture I would rather explore a more uncharted territory: how contemporary artists have been dealing with aging as a subject and theme in art.

Aging is a relatively recent theme in art, introduced into the fields of art and art history largely, I suspect, through the interventions of feminist art and theory, which asserts the value of personal experience as a valid subject in art. Generally speaking, all art is a form of personal expression. But, in the past, the personal was relegated to the service of the state or church or society at large, or, in the first half of the twentieth century, to art's own self-definition, what has been called Modernism. Recently, because of feminism and what is loosely called Postmodernism or pluralism, art and art history deal with subjects previously avoided or subordinated—subjects like civil rights, postcolonialism, queer theory and homosexual and lesbian practice, sexuality in general, and, of course, aging—treating them sometimes separately, sometimes in combination. Thus, both art historians and artists are confronting the discouraging aspects of aging but also its opportunities, and if one factor binds them together, it is their refusal to abandon the body for the spirit. Surprisingly, in fact, it may not be the body that lets us down in later years (given freedom from disease), but our belief that our body must decline. Our image of ourselves creates our sense of failing powers, or at least contributes to it. Much recent research may help reverse this negativity. A 1994 study by cognitive psychologists Itiel E. Dror and Stephen M. Kosslyn suggests that "although there is slowing with age, individual imagery processes are affected selectively by aging" (p. 90). In certain tasks involving image generation, image maintenance, and image inspection, older people performed as effectively as young subjects. Although their research is ongoing, they conclude thus far that there is "no evidence that the course of aging is simply the inverse of the course of development" (p. 101). Artists may intuitively know this since they work with image identification and transformation in a particularly focused way, and, in turn, present viewers with images we use to decode, identify, and understand ourselves. Contemporary artists sensitive to the issue of aging are affirming both the body and the spirit, or denying the distinction, and insisting on a new social construction of aging which is freeing and empowering and which they are helping to construct in their work. Art historian Joanna Frueh (1994b), who has written extensively on art and aging, asserts that "old(er) women's art making is action and prophecy, the creation of a possible world" (p. 267). Remember the image of Betty Friedan as prophet! What follows is a brief discussion of some artists and their works, artists who are working in their later years and works which demonstrate not only their makers' vitality but which affirm the body, explore sexuality and gender (sometimes playfully) and use the visual as a force for positive image building.

Clyde Connell became a full-time artist in 1960 at the age of fifty-nine. Her work deals with the human struggles of African Americans in her native Louisiana, of southern white women, of human progress in general, and with the redemptive powers of nature. Most of her sculptural work is concentrated on the human figure; she uses tall plank-like wooden forms which recall African sacred statues and which are meant to be sited out of doors. They often have machine and household items attached to the surface to indicate body parts. Her *Non Person* series (1977) depicts mothers and daughters, disengaged from each other and lacking faces. The mothers, women of Connell's own generation, were disengaged from life itself, as Charlotte Moser (1991,43) states in her monograph on the artist. The women were too caught up in the conditioning and social expectations of their time, consequently they experienced repression and separation from the natural, both in terms of nature and spontaneous human behavior. A work from her *Dancer* series (1986) shows the figure breaking out of its box-like container and entering life, activating space, flowing along with an unheard harmony. Connell writes

Nobody stays still. I don't stay still in art, in thinking, in feeling. I don't think people can stay still. They are constantly going on, either forward or backward. People don't want to stay still. They couldn't, just dealing with change and experience. Everything is movement to me. Sound is movement, thinking is movement. Life is a continual process. The way that I feel about art now is just a continuation of where I've been. You leave one time, of course, but you don't leave certain things. It's the idea of adjustment and continuity, that life prevails. (Moser 1991, 71)

Alice Neel (1900 to 1984) painted her *Nude Self-Portrait* in 1980 at the age of eighty. She sits, paint brush in hand, looking at the viewer with an expression of total self-acceptance. She is objective about her body, with its wrinkles and dumpling shape. She is concerned with neither youth nor conventional beauty; she is unconstrained, if alert or tense. "Here I am," she seems to say, "This is the way it is and I accept."

Jacob Lawrence (b.1917) did his *Self-Portrait* in 1977, at age sixty. The painting is full of color and celebrates a career of survival from the Harlem Renaissance, when African-American artists first began to question the received styles of that time and forge their own, to the present, in which stereotypes and archetypes intersect or invert. The small painting, gouache on paper, is dynamically filled with multicolored and rhythmic shapes—relating to his earlier work on Harriet Tubman—and asks whether the stereotypical associations of black people with color and rhythm are in fact archetypal, or chosen to celebrate one's identity and achievement. In this case, the self-portrait was painted on the occasion of Lawrence's acceptance into the National Academy of Design.

Louise Bourgeois (b.1911), in a famous photograph by Robert Mapplethorpe of 1982, grins while holding one of her sculptures, a penis-like object called disarmingly *Fillette* (little girl). Another piece, based on the *Diana of Ephesus* (second century B.C.), shows her as the many-breasted goddess: she wears a costume she made and donned for the photograph. She has both phallus and breasts— by claiming them, by putting them on, not by mere biological accident.

The Diana image appears again in the work of Betsy Damon. In 1977, she did a street performance on Wall Street in New York City entitled *7000 Year Old Woman*. The little bags (breasts) of her costume were filled with pigment and during the performance she removed them one by one, giving some to the audience and dusting some in a labyrinthine pattern on the ground. Thus, according to art writer Lucy Lippard (1983), she "divested herself of the burden of time," creating a "female space in a hostile city," while stripping herself of the burdens of gender roles as well (p. 167). According to Gloria Orenstein (1994), in a chapter of *The Power of Feminist Art* called "Recovering Her Story: Feminist Artists Reclaim the Great Goddess," in making the new labyrinth Damon "reclaimed 7000 years of women's erased herstory from the Neolithic period to the inception of the patriarchal era. Damon, who lived in Turkey as a child (1944–1948) near the ancient Neolithic sites of ancient Anatolia, was directly influenced by the presence of the Goddess there" (p. 185).

Also in 1977, Elizabeth Layton (1909 to 1993), after going through a divorce, supporting five children, experiencing a thirty-five year depression, and suffering the death of an adult child, enrolled in her first art class at the age of sixty-eight. Her graphite drawing, *Indian Pipes: Self-Portrait with Glenn* (1984) depicts both herself and her remembered but long-divorced husband, sitting in front of a fictive Native American village. Layton (1994) said that she had been thinking about the practice of some groups of putting old people outside the village when they grow too old to function. She and Mr. Layton sit outside the village wrapped in Indian blankets, getting snowed on. Layton described the work:

I'm knitting something and he's holding an arrowhead he'd made, so we're not totally useless yet. It is about aging. Our hair is wet from the snow, and we'll eventually die of exposure. But we're not miserable about it; we keep on working. We've still got much to do. . . . I was thinking or reading about the fungus called Indian pipes, which grows on dead organic matter and helps it to break down and decay, therefore contributing to the whole process of life, death, and life. There are Indian pipes on our blankets near the bottom, see? (p. 54)

Margaret Bailey Doogan's *Mass* (1991) shows a woman screaming in prayer, her nude flesh alive with an energy both physical and spiritual (Frueh 1994b, 281). It is a work of near photographic exactitude, yet it is a painting of oil on linen and nearly life-size. The woman stands, arms outstretched, her figure charged with a grandeur made visible by the light on her body.

Rachel Rosenthal's performance piece, *Pangaean Dreams* (1990), "frustrates age and gender expectations" (Frueh 1994a, 71). Rosenthal says in the performance, "I am a gay man in a woman's body. . . . Men don't want me because they sense something funny. Gay men don't want me because they see me as a woman. Women want me, but I don't want them because I want men, but not as a woman" (Frueh 1994b, 278).

Lesbians celebrate love in *Nitrate Kisses*, a sixteen millimeter film of 1992 by Barbara Hammer. The film depicts the life of a lesbian couple in their seventies and "explodes the myth that older women are neither sexy nor sexual" (Frueh 1994a, 70). A still shot from the film shows the two women in bed, embracing, their faces covered by joyous smiles.

Anne Noggle (b.1922) became an artist and art historian in her forties, after serving as a captain in the U.S. Air Force as a pilot and flight instructor. Her photography focuses on aging and seeks to debunk stereotypical notions about aging, ideas that she herself grew up with. Her *Thoroughly Modern Me* (1989) is a very self-aware and honest laugh at herself. And *Stellar by Starlight #1* (1986) shows her reveling in the jacuzzi with two younger men. Says Noggle (1994), "What I see in people's faces is most important. Certainly it is not the wrinkles, but the summing-up of what's happened to us and of our giving up selfconsciousness. By the time you are older, you are what you are." (p. 60).

Sari Dienes (1898 to 1992), in her *Silhouette Self-Portrait* (1977) (spray paint on board), proudly depicts herself with a "cloud-like halo of white hair" (Dienes 1994, 38), her silhouette superimposed as a cut-out profile on a land-scape. She presents herself as literally in the land, growing from it and returning to it. Nature, for her, is transformative and restorative. She describes art as "humanity's expressing, giving form to their understanding of the reality of the moment. . . . Reality is a sphere without circumference, where the center is everywhere" (p. 38). She calls this a Zen definition of reality, but it is very compat-ible with current border theory, which examines people's relations to each other as they strive to position themselves from the margins to the center. Dienes is known as an artist who uses mixed media, collage, assemblages, boxes, and so on, again without hierarchy or privilege of one medium over another. She encapsulates time into shining moments, as in this work; she is leaf, light, face, ephemeral, eternal. As she says, "Millions of years are in the landscape. Experiencing the natural formations as pieces of sculpture changed my whole life" (Dienes 1986, 26). She states further, "Art changes all the time: because reality changes. Nothing is more positive, nothing more constant, nothing more certain than change" (p. 38). When asked if age influences the subject matter in her art or affects the way she experiences life, Dienes responded, "I have this definition that spirit has no age, no sex, no color" (p. 39).

I conclude with a photograph by John Coplans, his *Self-Portrait as a Fertil-ity Goddess* (1985), done when the artist was sixty-five. Coplans's portrait is a brave work: the rounded forms of his penis, testicles, and tummy resemble the rounded shapes of the *Fertility Figure from Willendorf*, the image with which I began this chapter. Although he is an aging man, the artist subordi-nates those categories to the creative activity represented and embodied in both these works.

In this chapter I have merely surveyed the topic of aging and art by using images and the statements of artists and scholars, but I have done so with a purpose. Artists offer us gifts of love and wisdom and tell us who we are. Art history takes us ever backward in time until we can learn the lessons of the present. These include the following insights: We have control over the defi-nitions of our self and others, we can create a "visible difference" that affirms and includes rather than rejects and excludes, we are part of nature and must protect the environment, and being active is its own reward. My main point is that there are many artists aging and working on the theme of aging, so many I could discuss only a few. It therefore must be true that art enhances one's vitality, both making it and seeing it in the right body and spirit.

CHAPTER 15

The Return Home: Affirmations and Transformations of Identity in Horton Foote's *The Trip to Bountiful*

Carol J. Jablonski

Softly and tenderly Jesus is calling
Calling for you and for me.
See, on the portals he's waiting and watching,
Watching for you and for me.
Come Home, Come Home
Ye who are weary Come Home.
(Will Thompson 1914)

I was visiting my father when he had a remarkable dream. His body failing after many years of battling heart disease, Dad dozed off and on. At one point he woke up, obviously agitated. He had been dreaming he was playing basketball, he said. He motioned toward his legs, commenting on how he could not use them anymore. I was struck by the fact that he had been running in his dream, and said so. Yes, he replied, but Ray got around me and got a basket. He seemed disgusted that he had let his best basketball buddy beat him. It was so much like my father. A star athlete in college and later a professional basketball player, he had been a skilled team leader and tenacious problem solver throughout his business career. As I watched him tell the story, I could see him mentally replaying the move, figuring how he could have blocked his buddy's shot. Then it occurred to me, not only had he been dreaming of a time in his life when he had been in peak physical condition, but he had been dreaming of the place where he had grown up and played basketball. The realization was made more poignant by the fact that my seventy-three-year-old father had only recently moved to a town he had never lived in before. His dream had taken him back to his childhood home.

Aging in our culture is a particularly difficult crisis of dislocation, not only because of the numbers of the aged who move to different dwellings, but because of a loss of a culturally sanctioned identity. In retirement, one loses role identity as a worker and, from the perspective of an ageist culture, identity as a "productive" and "contributing" member of society. Physical decline produces an even deeper rupture of identity. The loss of vitality and competence separates one from a past in which one could depend on and enjoy the body, and it disrupts plans and hopes for the future. For Americans, physical decline carries the additional burden of being perceived as a failure to age "successfully." As Thomas R. Cole (1992b) observes in his social history of aging, "American culture has characteristically oscillated between attraction to a 'good' old age (the healthy culmination of proper middle-class living) and repulsion from a 'bad' old age (punishment for immoral, unhealthy behavior)" (p. 237). From this perspective, physical decline is not merely a threat to personal autonomy; it represents moral failure. The aged who face debilitating illnesses in their final years may feel a heightened sense of dislocation because of the way our culture regards aging and the declining body. I certainly sensed this with my father. Instead of marveling (as I did) at the physical prowess he experienced in his dream, he berated himself for not being able to get out of bed.

Is the loss of identity associated with physical deterioration in aging inevitable? Or can it be resisted, moderated, or eliminated with alternative constructions of what it means to grow old? Humanists who study aging acknowledge the tenacity of culturally ingrained attitudes toward aging, yet they also believe in the possibility of changing the cultural conditions under which identities in old age are formed. The cultural components of ageism can be overcome, humanists argue, if physical decline is accepted as part of the human condition and if aging is understood as a context in which human character and relationships develop. As Cole (1992b) puts it, "We are all vulnerable to chronic disease and death. This vulnerability, once accepted, can become the existential ground for compassion, solidarity, and spiritual growth" (p. 238). Rather than representing moral failure, physical decline and the advance of death are seen as an opportunity for personal development (Moody, 1988; Conrad 1992; Friedan 1993; Cole 1992b). A developmental perspective restores to the conceptualization of aging the idea that the aging individual has moral agency. From a developmental perspective, the "way one ages" is not a sign of — or judgment on — one's past choices, but an unfolding process that confronts the individual with moral choices to be made in the here-and-now, in the context of others. Aging thus becomes an occasion for growth for the aged and for those who relate to them.

In a technocratic society that treats aging as a symptom to be denied or cured, literature plays an important role in helping us reimagine the potential for human development in late life. Stories of characters struggling with the needs and vulnerabilities of aging bodies foster awareness of the complex meanings and emotions people associate with aging and the loss of vigorous health. Such narratives also highlight the moral development that can occur, not only among the aged but within the larger community, as elderly friends, neighbors, and relatives experience physical decline. As Robert Coles (1989) demonstrates in *The Call of Stories*, literature provides positive and negative role models for the kind of people that we want (or do not want) to be when we are dying and for the kind of people that we want (or do not want) to be when we relate to people approaching the end of their lives.

Narratives that build conflict and suspense around an aging character's efforts to "return home" are particularly interesting texts for exploring human development in the final stages of life. "Returning home" can be a potent symbol of the processes—and the outcomes—of achieving the "sense of *coherence* and *wholeness*" that Erik Erickson (1982, 65) associates with the "last stage" of life, what he calls *integrity*. Of course, the "return home" may be suggestive of something less comprehensive than Erickson's conception of integrity. Simone de Beauvoir (1974) argues that one's final years of life need not—and often do not—provide closure on the meaning of one's life. From this viewpoint, "returning home" might be interpreted as a symbolic alignment of location and memory that has the potential to illumine one's current or past situation.

In this chapter I examine a film that explores the tasks of identity in late life through the vehicle of a "return-to-home narrative." *The Trip to Bountiful* lends itself to a developmental interpretation of the life process along the lines suggested by Erickson. At the same time, the film underscores the importance of relationships in assisting with the tasks of late-life development. In its portrayal of an elderly woman's efforts to escape the apartment of her son and daughter-in-law and return to her childhood home, *The Trip to Bountiful* challenges culturally inscribed notions of what it means to be old and infirm. An analysis of the film illustrates the power of story and of film to expand viewers' moral sensitivities toward the aged.

Originally staged in 1953 as a Goodyear Television production and later on Broadway starring Lilian Gish, the 1985 screen version of Horton Foote's play won the Academy Award for Best Actress for Geraldine Page, who starred as Mrs. Carrie Watts. The story is set in 1947 in rural Texas. Carrie Watts, a woman in her late seventies, sets out for the home she abandoned over a decade earlier, the home to which she feels she must return before she dies. Her journey is fraught with humor and peril, but, in the end, Carrie succeeds in returning to Bountiful, seemingly wrapping up her life as she does.

A number of scholars have noted the relevance of *The Trip to Bountiful* to aging studies. Marcie Parker (1991), for example, identifies *The Trip to Bountiful* as one of several narratives that embody what she calls the "great escape motif," since the film develops dramatic tensions around Carrie Watt's escape from her son's and daughter-in-law's apartment. To Parker, Carrie's escape and subsequent journey to Bountiful illustrate stages in a "rite of passage" that leads to an acceptance of impending death. A systems theorist, Parker does not comment on the moral questions that are raised by Carrie's treatment at the hands of her daughter-in-law, Jessie Mae, who has her own reasons for preventing Carrie from "escaping." Parker suggests instead that Carrie's unhappiness with Jessie Mae is symptomatic of a process by which some individuals ritually progress toward death.

Harry R. Moody (1993), on the other hand, cites *The Trip to Bountiful* as exemplifying the importance of "life story" in aging (p. xxxiii). According to Moody, Carrie's journey home illustrates the "gift of grace" that comes when one is able to find coherence in one's life. Moody's analysis is drawn from the work of Bertram Cohler. Cohler (1993, 108) stresses the importance of "life story" throughout one's life, particularly in the later years, when the prospect of dying without some sense of "coherence" creates anxiety and low morale. Coherence, whether wrought through the structures of religious belief or a more postmodern configuration of meanings, is facilitated through reminiscence and the creation of one's own life story. According to Moody, because it depicts Carrie telling her life story throughout her adventurous journey, the film strongly invites one to see her return home as lending closure to her life and preparing her to accept her death.

Religious symbolism in the film certainly reinforces such a reading. The title song, the traditional Protestant hymn "Softly and Tenderly," offers the world-weary the comforting promise that Jesus is waiting for them, calling them "home." Carrie appears to be striving for, and reaching, a moment of redemption. The salvation–afterlife theme fits a familiar American cultural pattern, one that appeals even to a secular or postmodern sensibility. A survey published in 1986 suggests that, at that time, 70 percent of Americans believed in an afterlife (Conrad 1992, 77). Those who do not have a specific belief in life after death could recognize the "redemptive" import of the journey home held by believers (like the fictional Carrie), since it is a common theme in literature and popular culture.

The popular appeal of *The Trip to Bountiful* may well be to a cultural preoccupation with "individual achievement of salvation." Carrie's quest, however, is more than an individual effort and individual accomplishment. Focusing exclusively and unreflectively on the protagonist's struggle to achieve "salvation" reinforces the concepts of self as "autonomous" and "perfectible," concepts that, in Cole's (1992b) view, perpetuate ageism. The inclusion of primary and secondary relationships in the analysis of Carrie's journey helps to underscore the notion that we, like the characters in Horton Foote's story, are connected, and that the life course of one individual affects the life development of all individuals. The film's potential to challenge stereotypical beliefs about aging resides not only in Carrie's success in reaching Bountiful but also, and more importantly, in the dramatic creation and resolution of relational tensions among the primary characters.

The secondary characters in the film are equally important. All of the characters furnish the audience with alternatives to the way Jessie Mae and Ludie view Carrie. These alternative perspectives help audience members to move from their own stereotypical gaze toward the elderly to a more accepting and compassionate one as the movie unfolds. The moral contrast between the primary and secondary characters helps to set up a final scene in which Jessie Mae and the values she represents can be judged as morally flawed. Ludie, on the other hand, experiences a moral reawakening. Ludie's redemption, in fact, appears to be part of Carrie's own, and is made possible by her successful journey home.

The opening scenes of *The Trip to Bountiful* establish Ludie as a character who is preoccupied with his failures. Like his mother, he has trouble sleeping. When he wakes up, finding Carrie sitting in the darkness humming one of her hymns, she asks him if he is worried about keeping his job. She knows that Ludie has been ill, and although he is now recovered, he is without the means to buy a house or to rent a larger apartment and is thus considering asking for a raise. We also learn quickly that Jessie Mae and Carrie do not get along. Unlike her husband and mother-in-law who grew up in the country, Jessie Mae has been raised in Houston. Jessie Mae seems more concerned with her social life than with running the household. Carrie fixes and serves Ludie breakfast; then she dusts and vacuums the living room. Jessie Mae, on the other hand, appears in a fine suit and spectator heels as she makes plans to meet a friend for cokes at the drug store. She asks what Carrie has done with a recipe, then berates the older woman for having found it among Jessie Mae's things. Jessie Mae asserts that this is her home and that Carrie must do what she says, and although Ludie tries to smooth things over, he can do little to ameliorate the tensions in the household; the apartment clearly is too small for all of them. The squabble over the recipe only enhances Ludie's sense of failure and strengthens his resolve to ask for a raise.

Jessie Mae and Carrie have one thing in common; both are anxious. Jessie Mae is worried about Carrie's heart condition and fears that she will die. Adding to Jessie Mae's anxiety is her uncertainty over whether or not Carrie will hand over her government check when she receives it, since Carrie's government check enables Jessie Mae to spend more money than she would be able to do on her husband's salary. When Ludie was ill, for example, Carrie's government check pulled the family through. But now that he is employed, Carrie's check has become a bone of contention between the two women. Carrie wants to use her money for a trip to Bountiful, because she is afraid that she will not get there before she dies. In the past she has hidden checks, cashed them at the grocery store, and tried to get to Bountiful on her own; however, now Jessie Mae tells Carrie that she has instructed the grocer not to cash her checks anymore. The conflict over the government check signifies a clash between Jessie Mae's drive toward upward mobility (which Ludie has failed to provide) and Carrie's drive to return home.

In the first scenes of the family, the film does not discourage what literary critic Kathleen Woodward (1986) has described as the stereotypical gaze that "allows one to reject the elderly as a class more easily . . . as unreal, a mere illusion, a grotesque and transitory spectacle, a piece of theatre that will soon be over, covered by the fall of the curtain" (p. 111). *New York Times* reviewer Vincent Canby (1986), clearly sympathizing with Jessie Mae's irritation at Carrie's constant humming and hymn-singing, remarks on how difficult Carrie is to live with. In another review, he describes Carrie's appearance as she escapes from the apartment as grotesque, noting her absurd dress and her hat that looks as through she had been sitting on it for years (Canby 1985). Carrie's encounters with strangers, however, progressively challenge and alter this stereotypical gaze. Carrie is charming (even girlish) with the railway and bus ticketing agents as she tries to tell them "there is a Bountiful." She averts capture because she is clever and daring, and because she is able to win the sympathy and aid of minor characters.

After learning that she could not buy a train ticket to Bountiful, Carrie manages to get to the bus station, where she determines that the bus can take her within a few miles of her destination. Her joy quickly turns to distress, however, when she learns that the ticket agent will not cash her government check. She begins what for many of us would be a humiliating process: counting the change in her purse in hopes that she has enough money to buy a ticket. Until this point in the film, audience members have seen the character of Carrie primarily through her interactions with Jessie Mae and Ludie. Like those characters, we may question Carrie's competence to travel on her own, especially as she struggles to purchase a ticket. If Carrie finds that she has enough money, she will seem capable—or perhaps merely lucky. At this point, the properties of the medium (camera shots and editing) become important in challenging our stereotypical gaze.

Through the camera's eye, we see customers in line growing impatient. We might expect the ticket agent to expedite the sale, or to turn Carrie away. When we see the ticket agent, however, he does not appear hurried. The shot changes to a close-up of Carrie at the window, filling the screen and blocking out the harried passengers behind her. The camera work helps us to see Carrie as the ticket agent does—deserving of courtesy and of the time it takes for her to count her change. The careful editing thus counterbalances the perspective established earlier of Carrie as incompetent or feebleminded. Throughout the scene with the ticket agent, the uncashable government check takes on a different meaning. No longer the stumbling block to her independence or a sign of her incompetence, the uncashable check becomes simply a matter of inconvenience (to Carrie) and of routine or policy (to the ticket agent).

Carrie's interaction with Rebecca, the young war bride with whom she shares the bus ride, further shapes our gaze; we see the things that irritate Jessie Mae about Carrie in a different, more compassionate light. Unlike Jessie Mae, Rebecca does not seem to mind Carrie's hymn singing, politely questioning the older woman, "What is the name of that hymn?" We also see changes in Carrie's behavior as she interacts with Rebecca. Becoming aware of how much the young bride misses her husband, Carrie offers her own formula for coping—Psalm 91, which she immediately starts reciting. Far from being consoled, however, Rebecca begins to cry. This shakes Carrie out of her self-absorption, and they trade stories. Rebecca's tale of family relationships contrasts sharply with Carrie's current and past situation. Rebecca is in love with her husband, and they get along well with one another's parents. Carrie, on the other hand, was not in love with her former husband; her father had kept her from marrying the man she loved. As the bus takes her closer to Bountiful, Carrie tells her young companion about the life she had led there and her current situation. She had buried two babies in Bountiful, one a daughter; moreover, her current existence with her daughter-in-law is difficult. Carrie describes how life will be when she returns to Bountiful: She will work the soil and take care of herself and her land once again. Rebecca appreciates Carrie and shares her meal with her. The reciprocity displayed in the sharing of stories is important since each woman accepts the other as being at different stages in journeys of equal significance.

Carrie's life review does not take her into a past that excludes those who are conversing with her. Encouraging us to see Carrie through Rebecca's eyes, the film reveals Carrie to be an interesting companion who has a rich and complex story in process. Carrie's story is happening in the present, and we, like Rebecca, may be part of it. The film also goads audience members to recognize themselves in Carrie's behavior. When we empathize with Carrie in this scene, we recognize the limits of our own prescriptions for coping through our sharing of the experience of others' lives, and we appreciate the need to let others have a chance to tell their story.

Carrie's struggle to return home reaches a climax in the final scenes of the film. Although she is determined to reach Bountiful before she dies, Carrie has not made peace with her death. Not until she faces the possibility of not getting there, of having come so far and still not seeing her home, does Carrie finally confront and accept the reality of her own death. Once she embraces her mortality, Carrie is able to complete her quest by helping Ludie come to terms with his loss of home.

On reaching the bus station twelve miles from Bountiful, Carrie makes two devastating discoveries. First, the friend with whom she had fantasized starting a new life in Bountiful has been buried that very morning. Second, the sheriff appears to tell her that Ludie and Jessie Mae are on their way to collect her, and that she will not be able to complete the final part of her journey. As Carrie falls onto the shoulder of the Sheriff, beating him and begging him to take her home, all politeness, all charm, all evidences of being a God-fearing Baptist woman fall away. In Ernst Becker's (1973) terms, she experiences in that moment "the destruction of the self through facing up to the anxiety of the terror of existence" (p. 89). On seeing Carrie's despair, the sheriff agrees to take her to Bountiful, where he gently helps her through the discoveries she experiences in the ruins of her old life. The sheriff models a moral choice, one Ludie has not been able to make. The sheriff's efforts to get Carrie to Bountiful raise the question: Why hasn't Ludie done this? Years of attempts to escape by a determined Carrie represent numerous requests to go home that have fallen on deaf ears. What has kept the son from honoring the desperate request of his mother to return to Bountiful before she dies?

After the sheriff leaves Carrie alone for a few minutes, Ludie arrives and Carrie reminisces about her father, asking Ludie if he remembers him at all. Ludie bitterly replies that he remembers the funeral. Ludie had been a young boy then, and all he wanted to do from that point on was to name a child after his grandfather. Ludie's reluctance to bring his mother home to Bountiful begins to make sense: "Bountiful" is a cruel reminder of his failure to have children. After a pause, Ludie acknowledges that he is glad to have returned to Bountiful and the sudden admission suggests that Ludie has reconciled something in himself. He realizes that his separation from home, rather than his failure to have children, may have been the cause of his depression.

The Trip to Bountiful dramatizes the redemption of the mother and, not so incidentally, that of the son. Indeed, Carrie's journey seems to have required Ludie's reconciliation to his situation to fulfill its redemptive purpose. The opening of the film supports this interpretation. The screen is black as a solo female begins singing a capella, "Softly and Tenderly, Jesus is Calling." The musical accompaniment joins the solo voice as an image appears. A long-range shot reveals a young Carrie running across a dazzling field of Texas bluebonnets, chasing a child that we take to be Ludie. Slow motion blurs the scene, achieving an impressionistic quality. As the camera closes in, we see that Carrie is not playing. A close-up, in slow motion, captures her pulling up her long, aproned dress, her face grimacing with effort. As the soloist sings "Come Home," a close up of Ludie appears. With the words "Ye who are weary," the camera again closes in on Ludie as the word "weary" is sung. Finally, as the verse ends, Carrie reaches the boy, picks him up, and twirls around with him in her arms. As the image dissolves, we hear the older Carrie humming the same psalm. She has been dreaming, dreaming of running after Ludie, the same son who, on hearing her, rises to face another anxious day.

The Trip to Bountiful provides a model of moral conduct that links individual and communal integrity in all phases of life to remembering and honoring the value of home. Those who fail to recognize the importance of home are shown to be cut off from a spiritual wellspring and from their own better selves. Certainly the character of Jessie Mae invites such a judgment. Jessie Mae accompanies Ludie to Bountiful, but does not want to even get out of the car. When she comes on the scene, the heel of her shoe is broken and she is looking for water. Jessie Mae's inability to appreciate the value of Bountiful, like her inability to make what was, in that time, considered a "proper home" (with children), has crippled her and has left her thirsting spiritually.

We might not have seen Jessie Mae in such a pejorative light had not the story unfolded as it did in the film. A stereotypical gaze toward the elderly might have privileged an interpretation of Carrie as having fulfilled her life-long quest, with Ludie politely playing out the scene of his mother's departure from life's stage by pandering to her need to extol the virtues of Bountiful. Such a perspective would have vindicated Jessie Mae. Having lost control of Carrie (and her check), Jessie Mae produces a list of conditions that Carrie must concur with in order to return to the apartment. Carrie agrees to stop running and singing, and Jessie Mae is able once again to "rule her roost." According to this point of view, Jessie Mae appears triumphant. However, because the film interpolates viewers besides Jessie Mae—such as the ticket agent, Rebecca, the sheriff, and a reformed Ludie—we are encouraged to come to another, transformative conclusion. Carrie has successfully negotiated the world, brought her life to closure, and guided her son home.

CHAPTER 16

Animated Gerontophobia: Ageism, Sexism, and the Disney Villainess

Merry G. Perry

> Whereas man grows old gradually, woman is suddenly deprived of her femininity; she is still relatively young when she loses the erotic attractiveness and the fertility which, in the view of society and in her own, provide the justification of her existence and her opportunity for happiness. With no future, she still has about one half of her adult life to live. . . . Long before the eventual mutilation [menopause], woman is haunted by the horror of growing old.
>
> (Beauvoir 1974, 640)

In 1957 Simone de Beauvoir echoed the general cultural attitude toward women who reach the third female crisis, menopause. According to Beauvoir, puberty and sexual initiation are the two preceding stages, and all three are "dangerously abrupt." She calls menopause the "dangerous age" because prior to this time "woman is haunted by the horror of growing old." Unfortunately, attitudes in the 1990s concerning aging and menopause are still negative, and society continues to revere youth and deplore aging. In her monumental work, *The Fountain of Age*, Betty Friedan (1993) discusses some of the problems, myths, and stereotypes of aging. This landmark study derived from Friedan's interviews with women who have moved beyond the "feminine mystique — that definition of women solely in terms of their sexual relation to men and their biological role as mothers" (pp. 13–14). Friedan found a surprising number of vibrant, older women who had not experienced the trauma of menopause, thus concluding that aging does not need to be as negative an experience as is commonly believed.

An important aspect of Friedan's (1993) research concerns the presentation of aging by the mass media. Discovering a blackout of images of women or men visibly over sixty-five, engaged in any vital or productive adult activity, she decided to research media images of persons younger than sixty-five. She then discovered that the "Blackout of images of people over forty-nine . . . in and as targets of print advertising, TV commercials, television programs, and movies was in place by the beginning of the 1980s" (p. 43). She concludes that the media presents the consistent message of age as "acceptable only if it passed for or emulated youth" (p. 43). While Friedan could identify almost no positive images of aging in the mass media, she had no problem exposing negative ones. One nationwide study of television conducted by the Gray Panthers "found older people depicted as 'ugly, toothless, sexless, incontinent, senile, confused, and helpless. . . . Old age has been so negatively stereotyped that it has become something to dread and feel threatened by'" (p. 49).

The Fountain of Age has made me aware of the insidious influences of the media upon perception. I have a six-year-old son and, like many other parents in the 1990s, I carefully monitor his television and video viewing so that I can control his exposure to violence, racism, sexism, and other undesirable influences. One day after viewing 101 *Dalmatians* my son asked, "Why are the *old* ladies always so bad?" After my rather ineffectual attempt at explaining about villains, I began to consider my son's use of the term old and its implications for Disney's animated portrayal of the aging female. As I reviewed more and more animated films, I identified quite a few aging female villainesses who exhibited many of the negative stereotypes of aging. Walt Disney studios and the films that it creates are important cultural icons that mimetically reinscript certain societal beliefs. Culture mirrors society and society mirrors culture. While some recent feminist research does interrogate gender and ideology in Disney films,[1] most critical discussions of Disney films have failed to consider the characters as representative of negative cultural stereotypes. My feminist reading of these films will employ what Elaine Showalter (1985b) defines as a "feminist critique," an analysis of the negative stereotypical image of the aging female in Disney's popular animated full-length feature films. Utilizing the ideas of Betty Friedan and Simone de Beauvoir, I will consider our society's discomfort and double standard concerning aging. Then, I will examine the ageism and sexism reflected in the villainesses in six popular Disney films: *Snow White and the Seven Dwarfs, Cinderella, Sleeping Beauty, The Little Mermaid,* 101 *Dalmatians,* and *The Rescuers.*

Gerontologists have suggested many reasons for our discomfort with the idea of aging. Charles Russell (1989) contends that one of the "explanations is that we have a youth-oriented culture." He further suggests "that modern culture changes so fast that the words old and obsolete have become almost synonymous" (p. 2). Many people simply consider the word "old" to be a negative term; whereas others associate it with "worn out, secondhand, fading, unattractive, and worthless" (p. 22). It is still socially unacceptable to ask a person's age, and some people begin to lie about their age soon after they become uncomfortable with the encroaching years. As Kathleen Woodward (1991) observes, "From the moment of birth on (in fact even before), age is a fundamental and endlessly interesting category" (p. 4) Parents know the exact age of their unborn and then newborn child, young children feel quite proud when they finally reach the next birthday and become a "big" boy or girl, teens wait anxiously for the magical age of twenty-one, and adults discuss how many years separate husband and wife. In spite of the notion that it is impolite to ask a person's age, the media frequently identifies people first by their name, then by their age. We learn, whether or not we really care, the age of important world figures, presidents, and all celebrities (pp. 4–5).

I believe that women have been conditioned to be particularly concerned with age and aging. According to Marilyn Block, Janice Davidson, and Jean Grambs (1981), the image of the "older woman as an inactive, unhealthy, asexual, and ineffective person has been perpetuated over the years through the transmission of inaccurate information. The cultural denigration of older woman is taught through fairy tales and children's picture books" (p. 12) and, I might add, movies. As Karen Stoddard (1983) notes, "It is difficult to find masculine counterparts to terms such as crone, witch, and hag, each of which has the ability to call forth strong visual images of maliciousness and degeneracy" (p. 3). Moreover, commonplace and seemingly innocuous examples of sexist and ageist language abound; "Research texts frequently use 'old wives' tales' as a metaphor for ignorance" (Reinharz 1986, 509) similarly, "little woman" and "little old lady" illustrate the pervasive use of "little" as a "hint at socially approved belittling, i.e. the mandate for females to be small and dominatable" (p. 509). As Friedan (1993) discovered, the negative portrayal of aging men and women can be seen in the majority of mass-media forms, especially television and movies. Although Douglas Street (1983) contends that the children's novel has "both in the critical and the popular arena been long maligned" (p. xv), and that this attitude has been translated to children's movies, I think that the cultural effects of the animated masterpieces created by Walt Disney Studios cannot be ignored. Many Disney movies have received both nominations and Academy Awards: In 1991 *Beauty and the Beast* became "notable as the first animated feature to be nominated for the Best Picture Oscar" (*VideoHound's* 1997, 179). There is no doubt that Disney movies reach a large audience and have an impact on our society. As Street (1983) notes, the "name and aura of Walt Disney have so pervaded this film market that the casual moviegoer thinks him synonymous with it" (p. xix).

Snow White and the Seven Dwarfs (1937), Disney's first feature-length animated film which "made more money than any film in 1938 – $8 million, at a time when the average movie ticket cost twenty-three cents, a dime for children" (Thomas 1991, 77), offers the first portrayal of a long line of aging Disney villainesses who would be viewed by millions of children and adults all over the world. Adapted from one of Grimm's fairy tales, *Snow White* narrates the story of an aging woman who will stop at nothing to retain her status as the "fairest of them all." In *The Second Sex*, Simone de Beauvoir (1974) describes a woman not unlike Snow White's stepmother who "puts up a battle. But hair-dye, skin treatments, plastic surgery, will never do more than prolong her dying youth. Perhaps she can at least deceive her mirror. But when the first hints come of that fated and irreversible process which is to destroy the whole edifice built up during puberty, she feels the fatal touch of death itself" (p. 641).

The opening sequence states that Snow White's stepmother is afraid that "some day Snow White's beauty would surpass her own; thus, she dresses the little princess in rags and forces her to work as a Scullery Maid." While obsessed with her own appearance, she daily queries her looking glass: "Magic mirror on the wall, who is the fairest one of all?" Unfortunately for Snow White, one day the mirror informs the queen that Snow White is more beautiful because "rags cannot hide her gentle grace." For the remainder of the movie, the jealous queen tries to regain her beauty title and destroy Snow White. First, she orders the murder of Snow White, but her henchman has mercy and lets the threatened princess escape into the forest. Then, the wicked queen disguises herself as an old peddler selling apples, preparing a poisoned apple not unlike the fatal fruit offered to Eve by the serpent. The ugliness of the queen's disguise mirrors the grotesqueness of her obsession with youth and beauty. Moreover, her inability to accept her own aging and loss of beauty reflects an insecurity that the audience might subconsciously understand. The queen, alone in her castle without a husband or other traditional loving relationships, relying on her black-crow as company, represents the aging beauty queen who cares more for her own attractiveness than for other people. Thus, she is the personification of evil, and her peddler disguise—she would barter anything for eternal youth and beauty—reveals the appearance of her soul. At the end of the movie, the wicked queen is destroyed and Snow White is rescued by her prince. Love, beauty, and *youth* conquer all.

Cinderella (1950) represents another Disney movie containing an aging wicked stepmother who mistreats her stepdaughter. The narrator describes Cinderella's stepmother as "cold, cruel, and bitterly jealous of Cinderella's charm and beauty," a woman who envies Cinderella because her own youth is fading. The stepmother, a tall, thin, woman with a pointy chin and black hair with grey streaks, not unlike a stereotypical wicked witch, is unemotional and her cat, significantly named Lucifer, demonstrates the "same mean qualities of his mistress . . . [those of a] vindictive villain" (Johnston and Thomas 1993, 102). Like Snow White, Cinderella is punished for her youth and beauty by being forced to do all the household chores. Besides illustrating the unattractive stereotype of the cruel stepmother, Cinderella's nemesis shows herself to be a pathetic mother to her natural daughters. Two other aging characters, the fairy godmother and the aging King, act as foils to the wicked stepmother. The kindly white-haired fairy godmother rescues Cinderella and makes it possible for her to attend the ball, while the aging King, a kindly Santa Claus type with white bushy mustache and eyebrows, is depicted as an incurable romantic who wants his son to marry and produce grandchildren. Although some critics might argue that the fairy godmother presents a positive portrayal of an aging female, I suggest that her goodness is connected to her magical powers, so that she serves as an ethereal, rather than a realistic example of how age should assist youth. In contrast, the king is a simple man, a bumbling elderly gentleman who fantasizes about his future role as the kindly grandfather. Finally, with the help of her benevolent fairy godmother, and in spite of her stepmother's attempts to prevent her from attending the ball, Cinderella meets her handsome prince, falls in love, and lives happily ever after.

The character of Maleficent in *Sleeping Beauty* (1959) offers yet another example of the evil, senescent witch. On the day of the christening of Princess Aurora, the court assembles to give the princess gifts, and the evil fairy/witch Maleficent arrives in a magnificent burst of flames to complain that she was not invited. As in the two films already discussed, Biblical associations identify her with evil; in this case, she wears a black cape with a black two-horned cap that emulates Satan, whereas her face resembles Margaret Hamilton's wicked witch in *The Wizard of Oz*. Throughout the movie, references to Maleficent's alignment with the forces of darkness remind the audience of her malignity, establishing her as the stereotypical wicked witch who enjoys evil for its own sake. Even the good fairies note that she "doesn't know anything about love or kindness or the joy of helping others." While the good fairies might represent maternal love and self-sacrifice, Maleficent limns one of the most horrifying portraits of womanhood—the older, childless woman who would curse a baby to death. I believe that even in the enlightened 1990s many people feel that it is more horrific for a female to attempt infanticide than for a male, illustrating the confused notion that due to biology women are inherently more sympathetic to children than are men. First, Maleficent places a curse upon the baby Aurora, so that on her sixteenth birthday she will prick her finger on a spinning wheel and die. While Cinderella has a fairy godmother assisting her, Aurora is aided by a trio of fairy godmothers: Merryweather, Flora, and Fauna. Fortunately, Merryweather's potent powers alter the curse, so that on Aurora's sixteenth birthday she will merely fall asleep until "love's first kiss." In contrast to Maleficent, the trio of kindly, rotund grannies lovingly raise Aurora in the woodcutter's cottage. For sixteen years Maleficent searches for Aurora so that she can destroy her. Maleficent's hatred is never explained, but I believe that, like the stepmothers cited, she is jealous of Aurora's beauty and youth. Sixteen, the age of Aurora's scheduled death, represents the golden age of entrée into womanhood and sexual desirability. For an aging villainess, this magical number represents the peak of female appeal; thus, Maleficent may wish to thwart Aurora from the sexual

desirability and beauty that Maleficent lost long ago. Also, she may be envi-
ous of Aurora's virtue, since Aurora is well-loved and honored whereas
Maleficent is hated and feared by all. Stereotypically, Maleficent's assistants
are the black raven and a horde of beastly guards, while her domain is called
the Forbidden Mountains where she has a fortress worthy of Satan. Once
Maleficent succeeds in putting Aurora to sleep, she sets out to capture Prince
Philip, who has met Aurora in the woods and fallen in love with her. Maleficent
and her beasts entrap Prince Philip and imprison him in their dungeon so
that she can mentally torture him. She reveals her obsession with her own
aging and her desire for youth and love as she scornfully taunts the prince,
telling him that she plans to keep him imprisoned for one hundred years
while Aurora sleeps her ageless slumber. Then Maleficent will free the aging
and decrepit Prince, so that he may wake his beloved "with 'love's first kiss'
and prove that true love conquers all." This vision of the aging Prince kissing
the ever-youthful Aurora gives Maleficent much pleasure, because she fears
her own rapidly fleeing youth and beauty. Although sixteen years have passed,
Maleficent has retained her appearance, possibly through the exercise of the
black arts. After the good fairies help the Prince escape the dungeon, he
battles and kills the dragon/witch Maleficent, so that youth and beauty may—
once again—marry and live happily ever after.

Like *Snow White and the Seven Dwarfs* and *Sleeping Beauty*, *The Little
Mermaid* (1989) continues the formula of Princess and Prince versus Evil
Witch. *The Little Mermaid* recounts the story of Ariel, a beautiful sixteen-
year-old mermaid who falls in love with Prince Eric, a human whom she
rescues from a sinking ship. Ariel's father, King Triton, does not want her to
associate with humans because he thinks that they are all wicked. Desperately in love, Ariel makes a pact with the evil sea-witch Ursula, by which Ariel
will exchange her beautiful voice for human legs. However, Ariel has only
three days to get Prince Eric to kiss her; if she fails, she must return to the sea
and become Ursula's slave. It is interesting to note that *Snow White*, *Sleeping
Beauty*, and *The Little Mermaid* all rely on a male rescuing a female by giving her "love's first kiss." These heroines may be young and beautiful, but
they are essentially powerless without the assistance of a man. This rework-
ing of the Hans Christian Andersen fairy tale about the little mermaid contains one of Disney's most hideous aging female villainesses. The film contrasts
Ariel's delicate auburn-haired beauty with Ursula's disgustingly obese female
form, with the upper body of a Sumo wrestler and the lower body of an octo-
pus. Ursula has wild white hair, large red lips, purplish skin, and a deep masculine voice, and, like Maleficent and Snow White's wicked stepmother, lives
with her devilish pets, in this case, Flotsam and Jetsam, the two moray eels.
Ursula represents the stereotypical power-hungry witch who desires the powers of King Triton. Power represents an important issue for the aging, and
since media images shape one's self-concept, which includes "identity, attitudes and behaviors," the "meaning that the elderly have in our society, par-

ticularly the meaning of being physically unattractive and relatively power-less, is frequently internalized by the elderly themselves" (Reinharz 1986, 504). Perhaps this is true in Ursula's case as well; in order to gain power, Ursula will do whatever it takes. While trying to convince Ariel to trade her voice, Ursula sings and dances in a grotesque parody of a senescent sex symbol, saying, "Don't underestimate the power of body language. She who holds her tongue gets her man." The underlying message is clear: A woman should remain quiet and subservient, using her body and her sexuality to conquer a man. I read this as potentially damning for both men and women. Ursula is suggest-ing that men are gullible and shallow, and that women use their own bodies to lure and trap their vulnerable yet willing victims. I agree with Roberta Trites's (1991) assertion that "Frightening Freudian images proliferate in Ursula's castle, further typifying mature women as predatory" (p. 149). While King Triton and Prince Eric both live in tall phallic-shaped towers, one en-ters Ursula's palace "through the mouth opening of a skeletal animal, and the swimming entrant must traverse the long neck of the animal before pen-etrating the womb-like inner chamber where Ursula resides. In the rear of this inner chamber is a conch shell, its lips spread open to reveal a gaping hole leading to some unknown place. This gynophobic image is a grotesque parody of the female anatomy" (p. 149). Moreover, this film's portrait of Ursula strongly represents what Germaine Greer (1991) terms "anophobia," derived from the "Latin *anus*, meaning 'old woman,'" and defined as "an irrational fear of old women" (p. 4). In order to enchant Prince Eric, Ursula adopts the appearance of a young, lovely girl and almost bewitches him into marrying her. At the climax of the story, Ariel rescues Prince Eric from the mock mar-riage so that he can fight Ursula and destroy her. True (and young) love con-quers all, and the audience assumes that the lovers live happily ever after, or at least until Ariel grows old and unattractive. According to Bob Thomas (1991), "*The Little Mermaid* was a thundering success, selling $84 million worth of tickets in the United States and Canada alone, a record for the first release of an animated feature. Americans bought eight million of the videocassettes" (p. 120). These statistics make Ursula one of Disney's most familiar and horri-fying villainesses.

101 Dalmatians (1961) presents the tale of the kidnapping and subsequent rescue of Pongo and Perdita's fifteen Dalmatian puppies. Cruella De Vil, tall, very unattractive, with a witchlike pointed chin and nose and half black and half white hair, wears a slinky black evening gown, long gloves, a white fur coat and matching handbag, and constantly smokes a cigarette from a long cigarette holder. She presents one of Disney's most well-known female antagonists. (Glenn Close does a magnificent job as Cruella de Vil in Disney's live-action version of *101 Dalmatians* released in 1996.) Cruella's clothing and speech parody the stereotype of the aging, anorexic, film star, somewhat reminiscent of an aged Gloria Swanson; Cruella's face is hideously ugly, and her angular, pointed cheekbones and chin resemble a frightening skull.

Throughout the movie, she is referred to as a "devil woman," and her exits and entrances are sometimes signaled by a flash of lightning. Her name, Cruella De Vil, suggests a "cruel devil," who dwells in a hideout called "Hell Hall." One particularly ugly scene shows Cruella lying in her red-curtained bed sans makeup, with curlers in her hair, speaking on her red phone, decorated with the shape of a devil, as yellow smoke swirls throughout the room. Her coarse speaking voice and deep throaty laugh contribute to the unattractiveness of this devil woman. Even the song that Roger composes supports the idea of Cruella as an aging she-devil: "At first you think Cruella is a devil, but after time has worn away the shock, you come to realize, you've seen her kind of eyes, watching you from underneath a rock, this vampire bat, this inhuman beast, she ought to be locked up and never released, the world was such a wholesome place until, Cruella, Cruella De Vil." This wicked she-devil has the fifteen puppies dognapped and acquires eighty-four more so that she can have them skinned and made into a dog-fur coat, asserting that furs are "my only true love. I live for furs. I worship furs." She tells her thugs, Horace and Jasper, to kill the puppies, and she does not care how. They can "poison them, drown them, bash them in the head." Fortunately, all ninety-nine puppies are rescued by Pongo and Perdita, and Cruella does not acquire her repulsive dog-fur coat. The final chase scenes of the movie present Cruella as a "crazy woman driver"—a particularly sexist comment—whose yellow bulging eyes contribute to the portrayal of her as an "old, mad lady," an ageist and sexist tag. This stereotype of the "crazy woman driver" seems totally ridiculous. Cruella does represent a dangerous and reckless driver, as do Horace and Jasper. However, I cannot understand why men are not called "crazy men drivers" when, on the average, their insurance rates—a reflection of the driving ability and accident rate of the insured—are often considerably higher than those of women. Even simple comments by dalmatian puppies can contain a wealth of ageist and sexist commentary, illustrating the power of ideology to influence perception.

Cruella De Vil would have understood the materialistic greed of Madame Medusa in *The Rescuers* (1979). This greedy hag—a pawn shop owner with flaming red hair, bulging green eyes, and unattractive crooked teeth—wears an ugly halter dress, made even more unattractive by her sagging bosom and shapeless body. It might be difficult to imagine anyone uglier than Cruella, but Medusa, as hideous as her name implies, is ugly enough to turn the audience to stone, and many of the close-ups of her face threaten to do just that. Greedily desiring a large diamond, named rather appropriately the "Devil's Eye," the evil Medusa—aided by Snoops, a chubby ineffectual man who obeys Medusa's orders as best he can—kidnaps an innocent orphan, Penny, from the Morningside Orphanage in New York. Like the stepmothers of Snow White and Cinderella, as well as Maleficent and Ursula, Medusa also owns gruesome pets, in this case two large crocodiles aptly named Nero and Brutus, who emprison and guard Penny on an old riverboat on the Devil's

Bayou. At low tide, Medusa unmercifully sends the small frightened orphan down into a cave to search for the enormous diamond. If Penny will not attempt to retrieve the diamond, then Medusa vows to destroy Penny's teddy bear. Dark waters threaten to drown the young girl if she does not work quickly to satisfy Medusa. This frightening cave scene, reminiscent of Ursula's gynophobic maw of darkness and evil, horrifies young children and completes the characterization of the heartless villainess. However, Penny, assisted by the "Rescuers," Bernard and Miss Bianca, escapes from Madame Medusa and Devil's Bayou and makes her way back to New York. The final shot of Medusa shows her angry reaction to the frustrating loss of the enormous diamond. According to Thomas (1991), Medusa "took her place alongside the Witch of *Snow White*, Maleficent, and Cruella De Vil as a classic Disney villainess. Yet Medusa's menace was diffused by one simple scene. When she leaped onto a chair upon seeing the mice, she became a comic villainess, dangerous but less threatening" (p. 112). Some viewers might consider Medusa less threatening than Disney's other aging villainesses, but she still represents another unattractive portrait of an aging female determined to conquer and abuse a younger person.

These six Disney animated feature-length films each contain at least one aging female character who exhibits stereotypical behaviors traditionally associated with aging. Although "women are only a fraction [albeit a large one] of the Disney villains, with only a few exceptions they are remembered more strongly than the men" (Johnston and Thomas 1993, 25). The stereotype of the "mean old lady" needs to be recognized for what it is—a stereotype—and we need to become aware of the insidious influence of stereotypical portrayals in the movies. By continually depicting aging as negative, the media creates a society that denies and mistrusts all persons who are past their youth.

What age is considered old? Studies have shown that "50% of the men and 57% of the women thought 65–75 was a suitable age to call men 'old.' Over 80% of both men and women thought that women become older earlier than men do—at age 60–65" (Russell 1989, 23). Russell offers two reasons for this discrepancy: First is the biological inevitability of menopause, and the second is our society's different value systems for women and men. "In women, we value youthful beauty; in men, social power" (p. 23). Because social power is usually achieved well past the youthful years, men may seem more attractive "late in life because of their influential positions; but we rarely acknowledge mature beauty in women no matter how great" (p. 23). In a 1975 *Time* cover story entitled "New Outlook fot the Aged", Gerontologist Robert Butler, "who coined the term *ageism*, declares that [because of public prejudice] the process of growing old has 'been made unnecessarily and at times excruciatingly painful, humiliating, debilitating, and isolating through insensitivity, ignorance, and poverty.'" This article continues by suggesting that the "elderly may still be productive contributors to society, if we let them" (quoted in Woodward 1991, 30).

America is currently experiencing an aging explosion. The years following World War II, from 1946 to 1964, produced the Baby Boomers and, considering that the average life expectancy is seventy for men and seventy-eight for women, "we can forecast that by the year 2000, nearly 35 million persons aged 65 and over will make up 13% of the population. By 2030, when most of the Baby Boomers have reached the upper age brackets, 64.5 million Americans age 65 and over will represent 21.2% of the population. In the 40 years between 1990 and 2030, the proportion of the population over 65 will grow 75% — a huge increase" (Russell 1989, 6–7). These statistics illustrate the need for a cultural revolution in our ways of thinking about aging. Movies reflect our culture and reinforce stereotypes. I believe that a study of the aging male in Disney movies might also reveal some interesting ageist attitudes and stereotypes. At any rate, I was surprised to discover that many Disney movies, especially those with a male antagonist, contain few positive female characters. Many of the movies have no mother figure at all, and when the older female is present, she is usually portrayed as either a powerless victim or as a negative stereotype. Lynda Haas (1995) contends that "the typical mother is absent, generously good, powerfully evil, or a silent other, a mirror that confirms the child's identity without interference from others. In this way, mothers are either sentimentalized or disdained; in either case, their identity or their work are simultaneously erased, naturalized, and devalued" (p. 196). This ideological "erasure" of the mother is evident in several animated Disney films: In *The Hunchback of Notre Dame* Quasimodo's mother is killed in the opening scenes; in *The Lion King* Simba's mother is relegated to a minor role; in *Aladdin* both Aladdin and Princess Jasmine are motherless; in *The Jungle Book* Mowgli is an orphan who does have a father figure in the male bear, Baloo, but no mother figure; in *Pinocchio* the title character is motherless; and in *The Rescuers Down Under* the mother appears briefly only twice. In addition, in *Pocahontas* the title character's mother is dead, and in *Bambi* the mother dies early in the film.

However, I do not wish to suggest that I dislike Disney's animated films or believe that they do not contain numerous redeeming qualities. Besides being incredibly entertaining and heightening our appreciation of our natural environment and the many wonderful species that inhabit it, in recent years Disney films have explored some of the nation's most politically significant issues, and exploded some of our most treasured stereotypes. Three of the most recent examples include *Beauty and the Beast*, *Pocahontas*, and *The Hunchback of Notre Dame*. In *Beauty and the Beast* the male antagonist Gaston, a young, good-looking, mindless buffoon, wants to marry Belle, the Beauty, insisting that Belle give up her books and devote herself to waiting on him and their future children. However, Belle has a wonderfully independent spirit and rejects his advances, eventually choosing the unattractive Beast over the handsome buffoon. I applaud Disney's portrayal of an antagonist who is handsome but deplorable, and a heroine who possesses intelligence and is not desperately seeking a handsome Prince to rescue her. Another refreshing movie, *Pocahontas*, interrogates negative attitudes toward Native Americans, presents a view of American colonization very different from that suggested by many history books, and portrays a strong, admirable, Native American heroine. At the end of the movie Pocahontas chooses duty over love and decides to remain with her people, affirming an alternative future from that chosen by the typical Disney heroine and suggesting that not every woman must get married. Finally, *The Hunchback of Notre Dame* questions prejudicial treatment of those who are different, presenting a sympathetic portrait of the physically handicapped—the hunchback Quasimodo—and of persons outside the dominant culture—Esmeralda and the gypsies.

While I applaud Disney's sensitive treatment of certain important issues, I believe that the films I have discussed in this chapter present ageist and sexist views that cannot be ignored. When a small child experiences the curious lack of positive mature female role models in Disney movies, he or she is inevitably influenced by it. We have an obligation to our children to present them with an affirmative view of the aging process and the aged, particularly since we are an aging society and our ranks of aged grow with each passing day. Instead of looking for the illusory fountain of youth, it is "time to look at age on its own terms, and put names on its values and strengths as they are actually experienced, breaking through the definition of age solely as deterioration or decline from youth" (Friedan 1993, 69). We must rethink our attitudes and try to discover Friedan's "Fountain of Age," and a powerful culturally conditioning force like Disney's films should aid us in this endeavor.

ANIMATED FILMS CITED

Beauty and the Beast. Dir. Kirk Wise and Gary Trousdale. Buena Vista, 1991. 84 min. Academy Awards 1991: Best Song ("Beauty and the Beast"), Best Score. Academy Awards Nominations: Best Picture, Best Song ("Belle", "Be Our Guest"), Best Sound. Golden Globe Awards 1992: Best Film—Musical Comedy.

Cinderella. Dir. Wilfred Jackson. Buena Vista, 1950. 76 min. Academy Awards 1950 Nominations: Best Song ("Bibbidy-Bobbidi-Boo"), Best Sound, Best Original Score; Venice Film Festival 1950: Special Jury Prize.

The Hunchback of Notre Dame. Dir. Kirk Wise and Gary Trousdale. Buena Vista, 1996. 86 min.

The Little Mermaid. Dir. Jon Musker and Ron Clements. Buena Vista, 1989. 82 min. Academy Awards 1989: Best Song ("Under the Sea"), Best Original Score; Academy Awards 1989 Nominations: Best Song ("Kiss the Girl"); Golden Globe Awards 1990: Best Song ("Under the Sea"), Best Score.

101 Dalmatians. Dir. Clyde Geronimi, Wolfgang Reitherman, and Hamilton Luske. Buena Vista, 1961. 79 min.

Pocahontas. Dir. Mike Gabriel and Eric Goldberg. Buena Vista, 1995. 90 min. Academy Awards 1995: Best Song ("Colors of the Wind"), Best Score. Golden Globe Awards 1996.

The Rescuers. Dir. Wolfgang Reitherman and John Lounsbery. Buena Vista, 1977. 76 min.

Sleeping Beauty. Dir. Wolfgang Reitherman, Clyde Geronomi, and Eric Larson. Buena Vista, 1959. 75 min.

Snow White and the Seven Dwarfs. Dir. David Hand. Buena Vista, 1937. 83 min.

CHAPTER 17

8½ and Me:
The Thirty-Two-Year Difference

Norman N. Holland

By comparing my two readings of Fellini's 8½, thirty-two years apart, I can ask, "How has aging changed my perception and evaluation?" I now prize a film I once dismissed, but I see the same themes I did. My conclusion is that aging does not change perception and cognition much, but our evaluation of what we perceive may change utterly.

One morning, late in April 1995, my phone rang. It was an old friend, Gerry O'Grady, my former colleague at SUNY Buffalo in media study. As it developed, Gerry's call would take me (at sixty-seven) back thirty-two years. It would allow me to compare the way I saw a film then and the way I see the same film now. It would allow me ultimately to ask, and perhaps to answer, this question: How much have thirty-two years of living really, deep down, changed me?

Gerry had called to urge me to talk at a conference on 8½ he was running at Harvard to celebrate the retirement of another old friend, Vlada Petric. Not only would several other friends be participating, but I would also be able to address Alan Hobson, whose experimental work on dreams I know and admire and whose relentless Freud-bashing I regret and would like to mollify.

The conference sounded like fun and opportunity, but it also presented problems. Whenever I approach a new project these days, I face the question, "How shall I write?" How does one write a reader-response paper about, say, 8½? I do not want to repeat the theoretical things I wrote in the 1970s and 1980s. I also feel that the usual critical essay has become wearisome. Always, the reader-response criticism that I favor demands a fresh approach requiring a different kind of essay for every new topic. As a result, I have been experimenting with novel ways of writing criticism; for example, as fiction. Gerry's telephone call thus left me with a problem. How would I write this reader-response paper, particularly since *8½* has been written about and written about: at least three whole books, two collections of essays, and more articles than I could shake a footnote at?

Reader response starts with free associations, and the first thing that comes to me about *8½* is that I reviewed the film back in 1963, when I was doing film criticism for the *Hudson Review*. Like most critics of the day, I was disconcerted by an autobiographical film, and I was pretty nasty about it (Holland 1963). The review had two parts. The first half was, as one of the standard bibliographies says, "a supercilious retelling of the film's plot" (Price and Price 1978). The second half, however, was one of my earliest excursions into psychoanalytic aesthetics. As Dwight Macdonald (1978) complained, "Mr. Holland groans under a massive load of primitive Freudianism" (p. 215).

Actually, I was not groaning. I was happy. I had been studying psychoanalysis and psychoanalytic criticism for just a few years, and I was quite crazy about it. I was beginning to develop theories that would become, in 1968, a book called *The Dynamics of Literary Response*.

My argument in that book was that a story or a poem or a film, any work of art really, consists at its core of fantasies that would ordinarily create anxiety. But these fantasies are managed by form and meaning toward a feeling of satisfaction. In a work of art, form and meaning act the way defense mechanisms do in a person: They transform unconscious fantasies into ideas acceptable to the conscious ego. The readiest model for all this is a joke: The "point" of a joke and the way it moves aesthetically toward that "point" authorize the nasty sexual and aggressive content of the joke. Form and meaning legitimate fantasy. In effect, my 1968 theory of literary response extended Freud's model of the joke to all art.

This transformation from anxiety-evoking fantasy to satisfying meaning and aesthetic unity all happened inside the work of art itself. In effect, a work of art embodies a psychological process. Then, when you or I take in the work of art, we incorporate this process into our own psychic processes. We tack onto this transformational process whatever personal analogies seem appropriate to us. In a nutshell, a film like *8½* is a dream dreamed for us.

The trouble with *8½*, as I saw it in 1963, was that it was so purely personal: Fellini "uses his fantasies raw to express his own problems as a director" (Holland 1963, 429). It did not contain a meaning that could serve as a transforming defense for Fellini's fantasies. And the adjectives I tacked onto meaning were "universal," "moral," and "intellectual." I spoke of the "gamut of the mind" running from "a universal, abstractable meaning" to deep unconscious fantasies (435–436). A work of art that runs the whole gamut is "better" than one like *8½* that confines itself to one level, the autobiographical fantasies.

All this transforming was, in the manner of 1963, in the film itself. I could argue that the film had to have "moral and intellectual content." And, as implied by that word, "content," all this moral and intellectual stuff was supposed to be contained in the film. As I wrote, "Fellini's last three films seem to me to rank in merit according to the amount of 'meaning' in each. *La Dolce Vita* fairly reeked of 'meaning,' with its Christ-symbols, parallels to Dante, moral indictment of a contemporary life-style, and what not. The *Boccaccio 70* episode had its little fabulated moral. But 8½ has little or no intellectual content" (Holland 1963, 435). Note again the "in" or "content." Meaning is contained in the film. That seemed obvious in 1963.

Today we recognize that that "in" is metaphorical. We are using a container metaphor for the film, and containers are simply one of our commonest metaphorical structures for describing works of art or language and not a very accurate description of the psychological processes involved. Container metaphors are crude, and we can be much more sophisticated today.

And what were Fellini's fantasies in 8½? As I saw them in 1963, he was interested in turning people into mere images and sounds. His fantasies about women were that they were either all-powerful good or all-powerful bad, either a virgin–mother–goddess who would bring utter happiness and fulfillment, or a Saraghina, dangerously, sinfully sexual. Men were impotent creatures of words and thoughts, empty by comparison.

I summed up the pattern by pointing to the two *cardinali* in this film. There is the male *cardinale*, an aging, incoherent clergyman nattering on about guilt and salvation and the church, clearly missing the point so far as Fellini is concerned. The other is Claudia *Cardinale*, a Muse, a virgin goddess who will bring cleanliness and order and sex and frees up Fellini's imagination. But, as it turns out, he is too weak for her to help. He is just another helpless male.

What has happened to all this since 1963? Would I say the same in 1995? Well, one thing I have noticed is that the mind rambles more freely in these latter decades of life. Perhaps it is the climate of the times, perhaps it is just me, but I am easier with just random thoughts. So let me offer you three random thoughts about 8½ in 1995. Just to be properly scholarly and analytical, I will give them three titles:

Federico's Answer to Ingmar

Why Did Fellini Build the Launching Pad?

Why Was Harvey Greenberg So Disappointed in this Movie?

FEDERICO'S ANSWER TO INGMAR

I began to notice similarities among the differences between these two giants of mid-century cinema. Let me start by pointing out just one similarity. The dance of life at the end of 8½ exactly parallels and contrasts with the dance of death, the *Totentanz*, at the end of Bergman's *The Seventh Seal*. This is something that both John Simon and I picked up in our early reviews of 8½ — and his, by the way, was as unfavorable as mine (Simon 1967). That

particular image, Bergman's allegorical characters silhouetted against a brooding sky as death leads them off, became the image for anyone interested in
avant-garde cinema in the 1960s. Contrast that with the statement of Daumier
in 8½, at his first interview with the filmmaker about the script for this film
which he has just read: "Your main problem is, the film lacks ideas, it has it
has no philosophical base. It's merely a series of senseless episodes. . . . It has
none of the merits of the avant-garde film and all the drawbacks." I think it is
hard not to say that Fellini was feeling competitive with this other avant-garde
or intellectual filmmaker so completely different from himself.

In fact, Fellini said in 1965, not that long after making 8½, "The author of
today's films that I admire the most and find most congenial and that I feel as
a brother is Bergman. I have seen only two films, *Wild Strawberries* and *The
Silence*, but they were enough to make me love him as a brother, a milk
brother" (Levine 1965, X13). Without sibling rivalry?

Let us consider the films Bergman and Fellini had achieved in 1960 when
Fellini first outlined his plan for 8½. Bergman had recently released *The
Seventh Seal* (1957), *Wild Strawberries* (1957), *The Magician* (1958), and *The
Virgin Spring* (1959). Bergman was becoming, as I read him, more realistic.

Somewhat after 1959, Fellini began changing from his early neo-realism to
the later more fantastic or "Fellini-esque" style. The relevant pictures would
be *I Vitelloni* (1953), still strongly realistic; *La Strada* (1954), still realistic but
with elements of fable and fantasy; *Il Bidone* (1955), strongly realistic again;
and *Le Notte di Cabiria* (1957), the same year as *The Seventh Seal* and *Wild
Strawberries*, and quite realistic. Then came *La Dolce Vita* (1960), which was
realistic, including realistic treatment of magical and fabulous elements.

In the 1960s, nobody paid much attention to Fellini's episode for *Boccaccio
70* (1962), *The Temptation of Dr. Antonio*, but this little *scherzo* seems to me
quite crucial to his development. The film has a forty-foot Anita Ekberg step-
ping down from a sexy billboard advertising milk to torment a would-be cen-
sor, the puritanical Dr. Antonio, waving his puny umbrella against those
mighty breasts. Clearly here is one of Fellini's major themes presented in a
largely fantastic way: the all-powerful woman or image of woman, contrasted
to the impotence of the moralistic male. Later critics have recognized its
importance. Peter Bondanella, for example, in his massive 1992 study of Fellini,
shows how Fellini's decisive encounter with Jungian psychology led to his
interest in dreams and his keeping of dream notebooks (starting in 1960). His
interest in dreams led in turn to the dreams, surrealism, and metacinema of
this sixty-minute film and ultimately to 8½.

In 8½, Fellini finally decisively breaks with realism, turning instead to fantasy. Indeed, that is what this film is about. He shows us how difficult it was
for him to go off into this new kind of film. He shows us how everybody
around him doubted what he was doing: his producer, his assistants, the press,
the critics, the intellectuals. He shows us his helplessness as he tries to make
a totally new kind of film for him, for anybody really. All this really happened
in real life: Fellini deliberately manipulated the press to make it happen. As

Fellini so often pointed out, however, Guido never succeeds in making his film, but he, Fellini, did.

If you describe some of these films in the manner of *TV Guide*, you can see the similarities between Bergman's works and *8½*. A woman is victimized and shows magical powers (*Virgin Spring* or the wife cum prophetess in *8½*). An aging man tries to understand himself, aided by a magical young woman (Sara in *Wild Strawberries* or Guido in *8½*). The girl (played by Bibi Andersson in *Wild Strawberries*, Claudia Cardinale in *8½*) is magical because she plays several different roles. A man troubled by his age and health has a dream with a coffin in it (*Wild Strawberries* again). *8½* mixes realism, memory, dream, and daydream as Bergman does in his 1957 to 1959 films.

There are also some specific similarities between *8½* and *The Seventh Seal*. I have mentioned the big one: Fellini's dance of life as contrasted to Bergman's dance of death. I would note too that the life figures in *The Seventh Seal*, the juggler and his wife and child, are dancers, although Bergman does not give us a dance of life. Fellini does the opening dream on high-contrast black-and-white film stock, a technique Bergman used, not so much in *The Seventh Seal*, although it does appear there, but very much in *Wild Strawberries*. Also, it is a Scandinavian airlines hostess who announces Guido's visit to the Cardinal who epitomizes male futility and religion. Both *The Seventh Seal* and *8½* have a numerical title. Both are very characteristic of their directors. But, whereas Bergman's sends us to the murky world of the Book of Revelation, Fellini's sends us to his own career as a filmmaker.

In general, Bergman's theme of tormented intellectualizing set against the simple appeal of life runs all through his films. In relation to Bergman the figure of Daumier in *8½* becomes important. Notice how he even looks like Bergman. When Guido wakes up from his opening dream, Daumier is the first person he sees from the film world, and he is the last person Guido sees before the dance of life at the end of the film begins. In that last appearance, sitting in a car with Guido, he is spouting all kinds of intellectual stuff about the importance of keeping silent instead of producing art that has no intellectual point—rather like my 1963 review. And now I remember the opening dream, when Guido is locked in a car and this noxious vapor starts to asphyxiate him. That noxious vapor comes from the passenger side, just like our friend Daumier.

Notice his name, that of an artist who brilliantly combined pictures and words to create cartoons of acid social criticism. In *8½*, Daumier is the spokesman for the Word. He is the intellectual, committed to verbal meaning and social criticism. He beckons, indeed commands, offering exactly the opposite direction from the one Fellini–Guido is finding for himself. His name is French, and France was certainly the center for making intellectual comments on film in those days and perhaps now.

His Frenchness reminds me of the French actor Alain Cuny, who played the saintly intellectual Steiner in *La Dolce Vita*. Steiner says, "We should come to love one another outside of time, beyond time, detached, to live detached." This is exactly the opposite of what Guido–Fellini becomes. Daumier in this film seems to me to echo Steiner: "You are . . . primitive as a gothic steeple," one of Steiner's friends tells him, "You're so high that our voices grow faint in trying to reach up to you." Unexpectedly, Steiner commits suicide, and in 8½ Guido imagines Daumier hanged. Indeed, in the first ending, Guido himself commits suicide under the demands of critics that he be intellectual. Steiner was something of a bourgeois puritan. So is Daumier, who seems so inept with women here. And, of course, the puritan par excellence is Dr. Antonio in the short film that Fellini made just before 8½, a film that the curious "½" of 8½ is supposed to remind us of.

In other words, I see as a crucial thematic figure in 8½ a male who has connections to France or Scandinavia, who is associated with death, who is a bit of a puritan, who is an intellectual, who is committed to the Word, who does not create anything (just talk) who is a little removed from life, and who is "Northern" in Thomas Mann's sense. This Daumier–Steiner–Dr. Antonio figure makes a total contrast to Fellini's utter Southernness, his fondness for noise and mess and sex and looking instead of thinking.

Fellini did not meet Bergman until 1968 when they took a famous night prowl around Rome competing as to who knew the most about death (Baxter, 1993). They did agree to try to collaborate on a film about love, but it never materialized. Fellini claimed in one of his interviews that, until he met Bergman in 1968 he had seen only one Bergman film. Frankly, I find that hard to believe, given that in another interview he said he had seen two, given the stir that Bergman's movies had created since the mid-1950s, and given the similarities I see between 8½ and Bergman's work of the period 1955 to 1960. Of course, there are major differences; for example, the launching pad in 8½.

WHY DID FELLINI BUILD THE LAUNCHING PAD?

One particularly fine study of Fellini up through *Juliet of the Spirits* is Peter Harcourt's (1966) "The Secret Life of Federico Fellini." In this study, he comments on a rather peculiar image that recurs in Fellini's work: "The first image we see in the first film directed by Fellini himself is an image of a structure sticking up out of the sand with a piece of cloth blowing in the wind. In front of this structure . . . sits the White Sheik on his horse in all his phony splendor. But it is really in *Cabiria* that this purely visual absurdity acquires its most consistently surrealist force" (p. 11). He gives several examples from *Cabiria* of random structures in various scenes, "but most absurd of all and most characteristically Fellinian is the strangely functionless structure that exists outside Cabiria's house. How did it come to be there and what purpose does it serve? Questions like that can have no answer on any rational plane, but the presence of this structure dominates a number of scenes in the film; and of course it is related both to the beach structures that we've seen more naturalistically in *The White Sheik* and *I Vitelloni* and that structure to end

all structures that looms over 8½" (p. 11). The launching pad is the quintessential useless structure. Harcourt suggests that the people walking up and
down the structure in 8½ are like the little boys who are constantly clamber-
ing around the poles outside Cabiria's bungalow. He concludes that both sets
of climbers continue a theme in Fellini of purposeless activity, "a kind of
physical meaning to the absurdity of life, . . . movement without direction,
life essentially without a goal" (pp. 11–12).

That makes good sense, but I see another possibility. These useless constructions go up. They point to the sky. They connect to another theme in
Fellini, the theme of altitude. We first see the White Sheik high up on a
swing. We can hardly forget the airborne statue of Christ that opens *La Dolce
Vita*. In the opening dream in 8½ Guido flies high and is pulled down in an
Icarus fantasy of flying and falling. In other words, besides Harcourt's idea
that these constructions symbolize an absurd life without a goal, I think we
are also looking at a good old-fashioned phallic symbol. I think these constructions are gendered, and they are gendered male. They seem to me dis-
tinctly linked to phallic striving, to male aspirations, pretensions, and ideas.
Remember how Steiner was like a gothic steeple.

As many people have pointed out, there is a theme of verticality in Fellini.
Fellini himself spoke before 1963 of "the fear of falling, of being buried. . . .
Each day, each minute, there is a possibility of losing ground. . . of falling
toward the beast" (Herman 1969, 258). When I put that quotation from Fellini
alongside these images of men up high or flying, I hear Fellini complaining:
I have to try to do these futile, even ridiculous male things. I have to try to do
abstraction, philosophy, ideas, religion, this "high" stuff. If I fail, I fall. I will
be engulfed, overwhelmed. I will fall into a monster.

That is, of course, the fantasy of the opening dream of 8½. Guido is trapped
in his car in a huge traffic jam in an underpass. He clambers out of his car
and flies up, apparently escaping out the mouth of the tunnel. Over his head
we see wires like those for a trolley car or an electric train. He continues to
soar, and we hear the sound of the steaming, noxious vapor in the car giving
way to a high, free wind outside. We see sun, clouds, but suddenly, as if it
were attached to those trolley wires, we glimpse a huge scaffolding. Lo and
behold, although we may not recognize it unless we have seen 8½ before,
this is the partially constructed space launching station that is such a crucial
part of Guido's film project.

Fellini cuts quickly away to a man in a cloak riding a horse along the sea-
shore, silhouetted against the sunlight (perhaps another echo of *The Seventh
Seal*). A second man is lying on the beach—we will see both of them later, as
part of Claudia Cardinale's entourage. The second man pulls on a rope attached to Guido's ankle. As he does so, he calls out to the cloaked rider,
"Awocato, lo preso" (literally, "Lawyer, I've got him").

Why a lawyer? In this country we always need a lawyer, but in Italy, the
only answer I can think of is that this refers to some contract that ties him to

making the mysterious film that uses this space launching station we have just seen. In fact, later in the film, this actor will appear as Claudia Cardinale's manager. It is he whose contractual obligations tie Guido's fantasies of Cardinale as a Muse to the low practicalities of actually making a movie.

"Down, come down," calls the lawyer. The grip yanks repeatedly on the rope attached to Guido's ankles, which Guido is frantically trying to untie. Finally he falls into the sea. The lawyer, who not only wears a cloak but has a peculiar insignia on his forehead, pronounces, "Giu, definitivamente" ("Down, definitively down"). And Guido wakes as he falls into the sea, wakes to the doctors and "la cura," the cure, the therapy, if I can use that word.

In short, the opening dream deals with flying and verticality, phallic symbols if you will, and specifically associates them with Guido's film project. He tries to rise, to soar, and the space launching station is the phallic symbol of that wish. But he is pulled down by his contract to make a film, and his phallic failure ends in therapy.

Following out my associations, I notice that 8½ involves various agings: Guido's aging, Guido's father's death, the assistant that Guido–Fellini dismisses as "old man," and Fellini's own aging. The conference I attended also involved aging: Vlada Petric's retirement, Gerry O'Grady as an "old" friend and "old" colleague who Gerry decided to retire a few months after the conference. And "old" me—the me of 1963, the me of now. Surely there is a lot in the situation about male assertion and, as always with aging, the threat of lost sexuality.

Again, following out my associations, I should point out that "construction" has a meaning in psychoanalytic talk. A construction is the analyst's positing an event in childhood to explain something in the patient's adult patterns. One might, for example, posit sexualized baths given by a seductive mother to explain Guido–Fellini's mixed fear and adoration of women.

Like Guido's constructions, these psychoanalytic constructions are expensive. Some people, including Fellini I think, would say such a psychoanalytic construction is useless. It goes nowhere. It wastes time and money. It is like the huge launch pad in this movie, pointless. It is like the male intellectual stuff put forward by Daumier or Ingmar Bergman. Some people would say the best thing you can do is climb down off it, off this male, psychoanalytic construction.

Therapy, however, brings me to the third random thought I had, looking at this film in 1995.

WHY WAS HARVEY GREENBERG SO DISAPPOINTED IN THIS MOVIE?

Harvey Greenberg is an analyst in New York who writes regularly—and excellently—about films from a psychiatric, psychoanalytic point of view. He has a particularly long and disappointed analysis of 8½ in his 1975 book, *The Movies on Your Mind*. Dr. Greenberg concludes that Fellini, as early as *La Dolce Vita*, was using "cinematic creation in itself as a crucial ingredient in the working through, the mastery of conflict, internal and external" (pp. 159, 167). But *8½* did not achieve resolution. He considers and praises *8½* as a film, then goes on to look at the films that followed *8½*. All, he concludes, are failures, "empty displays of exceptional technique that ring increasingly inferior and hollow at base" (p. 167). Perversity and sadism are the panacea for Juliet's ills. *Toby Dammit* (1968) is like a bad dream. *Satyricon* (1969) ends in self-seeking callousness, the acceptance of ultimate blasphemy (p. 163). *Clowns* (1968), *Roma* (1972), and *Amarcord* (1973) are all "genial trivialities" (p. 163), "entertaining, but hardly memorable" (p. 163), "as unsatisfying as the meagre leftovers from a banquet" (p. 164) (pp. 167, 163, 164).

From Dr. Greenberg's (1975) point of view, these later films are not just bad films, they are pathological. They show, he writes,

a heightened sense of unreality or "surreality," a facile disregard for the exigencies of time and space, elements the analyst customarily interprets as signatory of more archaic mental activity, experienced nightly in dreams, but often daily by the emotionally disturbed. The intrusion of such perceptions into the conscious thinking processes of a patient, if sufficiently persistent and global, would raise the spectre of an impending psychosis—or at least would warrant one's sharpened concern. (p. 165)

The psychiatric problem is embodied in *8½* with its "terrible relinquishments and false insights. . . . In psychoanalytic terms, Guido has sustained an overwhelming rupture of his tie to the nurturing maternal image and inevitably to the entire world. . . . The brave reconciliation of the ending, from this perspective, bears the mark of an abortive attempt at restitution" (pp. 154, 167).

Moreover, this problem with women, which is Fellini's as well as Guido's, is never resolved:

It is impossible to look unmoved upon the dance of life that ends *8½*, yet from all we have intuited about Guido, it is obvious that the rapturous harmony of this felicitous conclusion obscures—*must* obscure—his still desperate frame of mind. . . . If the conflicts of *8½* never reached favorable resolution for the film's creator, what then follows [these films that are failures] may well be the bitter fruits of Fellini's crisis in middle life; the disillusion and dissoluteness of the later pictures may betoken his mounting hopelessness and disintegration. (pp. 154, 165)

As for Fellini's later career, "After the spurious joy that concludes *8½*, the great director has given us only the barren declensions of that fearful stillness of the heart" (p. 168).

Consider another psychoanalytic reading, by David Herman (1969), far more jargon-ridden, which sees Guido–Fellini, indeed all of Fellini's works, as sick: "Exposed and vulnerable, he is humiliated by the caprices of a female figure" (p. 257). In defense, he creates a universe whose inhabitants merge to form a single environment. Boundaries between internal and external fade away. Guido–Fellini's fantasies about women are polarized between a de-

vouring, huge woman and the angel, who is, however, innocent and ignorant, and whom Guido–Fellini wishes to eat cannibalistically. He is obsessed
with scoptophilic fantasies in which eye equals breast equals penis. Underneath all the outer romp and playfulness of Fellini's movies, there is despair.
Defensively, Fellini turns to circus and vaudeville people as magical, divine
manipulators. He himself turns toward spiritualism. He uses these idealized
objects and his visions of purity and innocence to project outward and receive back narcissistic supplies. He imagines himself omnipotent, playing all
the parts in his movies (Herman is referring to his directorial style). This is
not exactly the picture of mental health.

We can contrast these two readings, which see 8½ as pathological, with a
recent reading by Harry Trosman (1993), an analyst in Chicago. Dr. Trosman
would agree that Guido's supposed cure is not a cure at all. As he says, "There
is little to suggest the type of working through we generally attribute to someone who has undergone a successful conflict resolution as a result of insight"
(p. 18). But Trosman nevertheless regards 8½ as a masterpiece.

Dr. Trosman (1993) notes, as I do, the way Fellini got past the limits of neo-
realism by including fantasy in his earlier films. Dr. Trosman sees this as
Fellini's establishing subjective reality and "endopsychic perception" as the
basis of his creations. "He has recaptured the imaginative capacities of childhood. . . . To the extent that artistic creation is heavily dependent on the
conflation of reality, memory, dream and fantasy, 8½ is a brilliant depiction
of this interweaving. . . . The creative potential has been generated" (p. 21).
Trosman summarizes, "The achievement of 8½ lies in Fellini's having conceived the task of creativity in terms of giving prominence to intrapsychic
experience" (pp. 25–26).

One would expect three people looking at the same film in essentially the
same very specific way—that is, psychoanalytically—to agree. There is, to be
sure, some agreement among these three psychoanalytic critics, but also considerable disagreement. The disagreements come about because the three
readings are based on value judgments. Greenberg and Herman do not like
the films after 8½, and, although Greenberg admires it, they both disapprove
of 8½ itself. Trosman, however, admires 8½ and likes what follows from it.

Why? Greenberg and Herman concentrate on pathology. Fellini in 8½
demonstrates all kinds of pathology: depression, a crippling work blockage,
narcissistic object relations, "as if" character, Don Juanism, and bad attitudes
toward women. But at the end, they hear Fellini saying, "Who needs therapy?
I can just go on with my neuroses, feeling happy, enjoying numerous women,
and making beautiful movies. Isn't that what old Sigmund wanted us to be
able to do? To love and to work. Well, I am doing just fine, thank you." And
he was. How can any board-certified, card-carrying psychoanalyst accept that?
One needs anxiety, one needs therapy, one needs insight, one needs a successful conflict resolution as a result of insight. 8½ is not the answer a self-
respecting psychiatrist wants to hear.

Dr. Trosman (1993) also feels the supposed therapy has not worked. In fact, he suggested to me that he should entitle his article, "How to Make a Great Movie Without Getting Well." But he greatly admires 8½. Dr. Trosman has written extensively on creativity and he values what Fellini has done with creativity in this film. Fellini is riding Dr. Trosman's favorite hobby horse.

In other words, our three psychoanalytic critics are responding to 8½, not in a vacuum, but in the context of their own personal concerns. Greenberg and Herman see 8½ as unsuccessful, Trosman as successful. They are each responding to needs.

What is true of them is true of me, looking at this film first in 1963, now in 1995. 8½ is not just something "out there" to be talked about in the abstract, to be "thematized" in current jargon. I read the film in terms of my life, just as Fellini or Greenberg or Trosman do. And Fellini knew we would. Listen to him in 1965:

Every person has his own fund of experiences and emotions which he brings to bear on every new experience — whether it is to his view of a film or to a love affair, and it is simply the combination of the film with the reality already existing in each person which creates the final impression of unity. As I was saying, this is the way the spectator participates in the process of creation. This diversity of reaction doesn't mean that the objective reality of the film has been misunderstood. Anyway, there is no objective reality in my films, any more than there is in life. (Fellini 1964, 75; 1965, 85)

What Fellini has stated here, in my world of literary criticism, is the purest kind of reader-response position. The idea is that readers make the experience of a film out of their own psyches, using the materials of the film. You read the film the way you do because you are the kind of person you are and because you come from the culture you come from.

That brings me back to 8½ and me. I am a devout reader-response critic. I would not go so far as to say there is no objective reality, but I would say, for all practical purposes, there is no way to know this film or talk about it except through the frame of some human perception of the film. There is no god's eye view, as I thought in 1963, with me as the god. There is only a limitless variety of human constructions of the film. For all practical purposes, the film does not exist "out there," but only "in here," or more precisely, between out there and in here.

Recognizing this truism puts the critic in a very different position from the "objective," analytical stance that I took in 1963. In 1963, I found things "in" the film. I could claim that themes, meanings, or patterns were there; I simply discovered them. In 1995, I need to bracket my claims about the film with phrases like "I believe," "as I see it," "in my construction," and so on. Such phrases will, I hope, state the psychological process we all use when reading. That is, we construe the film using various shared or personal techniques. We project our construction into the film, seeing it or finding it "there" or "in" the film, to use the familiar container metaphors. I try to convey this process by phrases like, "I hear in this film," "I see as a crucial thematic figure," or "I think we are looking at." One is not speaking so much about the film as such as about one's perception projected into the film.

In general, I think spectators construct the film using the materials of the film. Hence, we should ask each other the following: What do you feel toward this film? And how do you over there feel? What is your fantasy? And your fantasy? And yours? What is your defense? What is your interpretation? That way, we open the film up to a conversation. Each of us constructs the film, partly as everybody else does, partly as some other people do, and partly as nobody else does. Hence, any given statement about the film is simply one speech in a conversation that in principle need never end.

I feel this film is about wanting and being frustrated. Fellini is stifled in his dream, but wakes to doctors who do not give him what he needs. His mistress, his wife, Claudia Cardinale, none of them give him what he needs. At the same time, he is not giving other people what they need. His producer who wants him to cast the film, the actress who wants to know about her part, the writer who wants to know about the script, the journalists who want to know his ideas—to none of them does he give what he or she needs.

In 1995, the world of 8½ seems to me a world in which people do not get what they need. And what is Fellini's answer? The images of satisfaction in 8½ are Guido in an idealized childhood, Guido in the harem scene, Guido at the end in the dance of life. All unreal. All fantasy. The answer Fellini makes to his and Guido's and everyone's needs is to imagine, to fantasize total gratification; in effect, to make movies.

Why, in my response, am I so preoccupied with need? Where am I coming from? As I said, one morning in late April of 1995 the telephone rang. It was my old friend and colleague, Gerry O'Grady. I did not need this. This came at just the wrong time of year for me. I was busy trying to organize the program for the Twelfth International Conference in Literature and Psychology in Freiburg in June. I was trying to shepherd through the proofreading and indexing process our huge annual *IPSA Abstracts and Bibliography in Literature and Psychology*. I was trying to get some lectures ready for psychoanalytic institutes in Russia. I was busy. I was needing. I wanted somebody to take care of me. I did not want to have to give to all these projects and people. I did not want to have to do this chapter. I felt the same kind of suffocating pressure that Guido feels in his opening dream. Those are my feelings and associations, just as if I were in analysis.

I was in analysis in 1963, at the time I wrote that old review, and doing papers like this one was in fact a big issue for me. I was an active, energetic critic, imposing my own powerful New Critical analyses on all kinds of texts, including this movie. What analysis suggested was that it might be good if I were able to relax, to be passive, to lie back, to simply enjoy the work. But that felt very dangerous to me. To be passive would be to be feminized with all the fantasies and stereotypes that that implied to someone who grew up in the 1930s and 1940s. To be active, in control of literary works, that was the male thing.

In effect, I needed to do just what I hear Fellini preaching in this movie, and was I resisting! By contrast, Guido–Fellini, in his final fantasy, accepts himself as he is, accepts the world, life, imperfection; he stops trying to be Bergman or Daumier; he puts aside male strivings; he gives up his directorial position; and he joins the dance.

Isn't that what I needed to do in 1963 and still need to do in 1995, for that matter? To recognize that what you have is what you need. If you need less you worry less about giving papers at fancy conferences, about male rising, male achievement. You can be less preoccupied with ideas, and more with people. You can take time to smell the roses or, in Florida, the jasmine and gardenias. I know all that consciously, but it was and still is hard for me to do. I did end up writing this chapter, just as Fellini did end up making his movie. To be sure, I wrote a reader-response paper rather than the old-fashioned analysis of 1963. I found a way.

What would a reader-response treatment of 8½ be like? What is this chapter like? You do not look for themes, but accept your reading as it is. You listen to your thoughts and feelings as you see the film, and you accept them. That is what the film itself is about: accepting yourself. And that perhaps is the ultimate story of 8½ and me.

It seems to me that Fellini's move at the end of 8½ exactly parallels my own move as a critic. I have changed from the psychoanalytic critic of 1963, discussing themes and fantasies "in" the text, to the reader-response critic of 1995, discussing themes and fantasies in me. I was not able to do this until a half-dozen years after my analysis ended. But I did finally accept the arts as something less to be analyzed than to be experienced.

Again, to quote from Fellini, this time in 1965: "In my films, what is constantly repeated is the attempt to suggest to . . . modern man a road of inner liberation, of trying to accept and love life the way it is without idealizing it, without creating concepts about it, without projecting oneself into idealized images on a moral or ethical plane. To try to give back to man a virginal availability, his innocence as he had it in childhood" (Levine 1965, X13). In other words, just enjoy the movie, enjoy the story, enjoy the poem. How that would liberate my profession from its tired and jargon-ridden critical procedures!

Profession aside, what about me? It seems to me now, in 1995, thirty-two years after my review criticizing this film for its lack of intellectual meaning, that I am finally catching on. I hear Fellini saying to me, "C'mon Norm, that's the whole point. We *don't want* intellectual meaning. This is a film about how great it is just to have images and sounds and experiences, particularly of sexy women. Why do you want themes? Abstractable meanings? Why are you writing these critical articles anyway, going to conferences, all that stuff? Are you trying to be another Dr. Antonio? A Daumier? A Bergman?"

I was such a Bergmaniac in those days. There was no way I could prize 8½ in 1963 as I do in 1995. Now I am as enthusiastic about the film as I was negative in 1963. As for that old review, I have a cartoon tacked up on my office wall that shows a professor addressing a class, and one student in particular, saying, "There are no wrong answers, but if there were, that would be one."

Yet when you come right down to it, how differently do I see 8½? How much have I changed, really? I still see the same themes I saw in 1963. I still see it as a film polarized between male abstraction and female earthiness, between ideas and images, between intellect and emotion. Did the film change me? Did either Fellini or I do what I think the film advocates? I do not notice that Fellini slowed down after making 8½ any more than I slowed down after seeing it.

So why am I doing all this stuff? Why am I pressuring myself this way or letting myself be pressured by others? Am I still carrying on that male striving for achievement that was such an issue for me in 1963, that was my central concern in looking at 8½? I guess so.

I see the film the same way, and I behave the same way, but my values have changed. The polarity is reversed. What was positive is now negative. What I thought was bad I now think is good. What I thought was good ("universal" meanings or striving for academic fame) I now doubt. But I still see the film as rejecting meaning, as identifying the male tendency toward abstract ideas and discursive themes with death, as opting for a feminine perspective defined as full of life and love and sex, passive, nurturing, subservient—and dangerous. In that sense, I think my 8½ thoughts lead me to something about human nature. A theme, if you will. I will not say it is a theme for 8½, though, as I did in 1963. It only focuses my experience of 8½.

We do not change very much as we age. We change about as much as Guido changes in this film. Because we are not going to change very much, we need to accept ourselves as we are. That is the ambiguity of the double ending. To reject yourself is to kill yourself. Accept yourself and others, but that's unreal. At the beginning Guido knows he needs therapy, but he rejects therapy, and it is not clear at the end whether he still needs therapy or not. And there I go again, still asking for things to be "clear." Am I still on that search for triumphant and controlling knowledge? Am I still being Daumier?

You see, there are no cures. We can go to the spa or the psychoanalyst, and we may unblock our writer's block, we may feel better, we may live happier, but we really do not change deep down, at the core, at the center of our identity where we perceive. As I have argued in many books over these thirty-two years, identity means we have a core theme or themes on which we play out endless variations as we live our lives. One way of putting it would be to say that, like a creative writer, we write in the same style over and over, but change the content. In the case of 8½, I see it the same way, as male versus female, intellect versus sensation, but I have changed my values.

Now I feel I need not look for themes in film, nor judge it as film or as therapy, but simply to accept it as it is. I need to accept my experience of the film rather than seek some "right" reading. We need to accept our experiences; we need to accept ourselves—including the fact that we are not going to change very much. We need to accept that we are what we are, and we are going to stay that way. But I am still not quite able to do that.

That is how I experience the film in 1995: It is about accepting the very fact that we cannot quite accept ourselves. I have come to a paradox that fits the paradoxes of fiction and reality Fellini plays with in 8½. We cannot quite accept that we cannot quite accept ourselves as we are. And (as Andrew Gordon has suggested to me) by coming to that conclusion, I have been able to finish this chapter, just as Guido was able to finish his film.

As I see it now, 8½ is neither healthy nor unhealthy in the psychoanalysts' terms. It is just the way we are. We are who we are. Get used to it. At least that is the way I see 8½ now, in 1995. Who knows about 1996?

Notes

INTRODUCTION

1. Deats and Lenker, *Youth Suicide Prevention, The Aching Heart, Gender and Academe*.

2. See Lyell, *Middle Age, Old Age*; Alexander, *Women and Aging*; Martz, *When I Am an Old Woman*; Sennett, *Full Measure*; Bagnell and Soper, *Perceptions of Aging*; Rubin, *Of a Certain Age*; Yahnke and Eastman, *Aging in Literature*; Fowler and McCutcheon, *Songs of Experience*; Sennett and Czarniecki, *Vital Signs*; Kohn, Donley, and Wear, *Literature and Aging*; Thomas, *The Women We Become*; Porter and Porter, *Aging in Literature*; Cole and Winkler, *Oxford Book of Aging*.

3. See Spicker, Woodward, and Van Tassel, *Aging and the Elderly*; Van Tassel, *Aging, Death, and the Completion of Being*; Cole and Gadow, *What Does It Mean*; Birren and Bengston, *Emergent Theories*; Cole, Van Tassel, and Kastenbaum, *Handbook of the Humanities and Aging*; Cole, Achenbaum, Jakobi, and Kastenbaum, *Voices and Visions*; Pearsall, *The Other within Us*; Booth, *Art of Growing Older*.

4. See Woodward, *At Last, the Real Distinguished Thing*; Birren, "Age, Competence, Creativity, and Wisdom"; Wyatt-Brown, "Late Style"; Cohen-Shalev, "Old Age Style"; Rankin, "Emergence of Creativity"; Simonton, "Does Creativity Decline"; Arnheim, "On the Late Style"; Kastenbaum, "The Creative Process"; Wyatt-Brown and Rossen, *Aging and Gender*; Wyatt-Brown, "Creativity as a Defense."

5. See Spicker, Woodward, and Van Tassel, *Aging and the Elderly*; Bagnell and Soper, *Perceptions of Aging*; Woodward and Schwartz, *Memory and Desire*; Woodward, *Aging and its Discontents*; Rooke, "Hagar's Old Age" and "Old Age in Contemporary Fiction"; Waxman, *From the Hearth*; Gullette, *Safe at Last* and "Midlife Heroines"; Pearsall, *The Other within Us*.

CHAPTER 1

1. See Birren, "Age, Competence"; Baltes, Smith, and Staudinger, "Wisdom"; Manheimer, "Wisdom and Method."

CHAPTER 6

1. See Eisdorfer and Altrocchi, "A Comparison of Attitudes"; Tom Hickey, et al., "Children's Perceptions."

CHAPTER 16

1. See Bell, "Somatexts at the Disney Shop"; Henke, Umble, and Smith, "Construction of the Female Self"; Hoerrner, "Sex Roles in Disney Films"; O'Brien, "The Happiest Films on Earth"; *Women's Studies in Communication* 19 (2) (Summer 1996) for an entire issue devoted to Disney and gender.

Bibliography

Achenbaum, W. Andrew. 1989. Introduction to *Perceptions of Aging in Literature*, ed. Prisca von Dorotka Bagnell and Patricia Spencer Soper. New York: Greenwood Press.

Adelman, Janet. 1992. *Suffocating Mothers: Fantasies of Maternal Origin in Shakespeare, "Hamlet" to "The Tempest."* New York: Routledge.

Aeschylus. 1970. *The Eumenides*. Ed. Hugh Lloyd-Jones. Reprint. London: Prentice-Hall.

Agich, George J. 1993. *Autonomy and Long-Term Care*. New York: Oxford University Press.

Albee, Edward. 1962. *Who's Afraid of Virginia Woolf?* New York: Atheneum.

Alexander, Jo, ed. 1986. *Women and Aging: An Anthology by Women*. Corvallis, Oregon: Calyx Books.

Alter, Robert. 1984. *Motives for Fiction*. Cambridge: Harvard University Press.

Amis, Kingsley. 1953. *Lucky Jim*. New York: Viking Press.

Angiollilo, Melanie, and Charles F. Longino, Jr. 1996. The Dualistic Nature of Popular Images of Aging. *Journal of Aging and Identity* 1:117–124.

Apter, Terri E. 1995. *Secret Paths: Women in the New Midlife*. New York: Norton.

Aristotle. 1967. *Rhetoric*. 2. 21. Cambridge: Harvard University Press.

———. [1926] 1975. *The "Art" of Rhetoric*. Trans. John Henry Freese and ed. G. P. Goold. Reprint, Cambridge: Harvard University Press.

———. [1926] 1982. *Nichomachean Ethics*. Trans. H. Rackham and ed. G. P. Goold. Reprint, Cambridge: Harvard University Press.

Arnheim, Rudolph. 1990. On the Late Style. In *Late Life Potential*, ed. Marion Perlmutter. Washington, D.C.: Gerontological Society of America.

Asp, Carolyn. 1986. "The Clamor of Eros": Freud, Aging, and *King Lear*. In *Memory and Desire: Aging—Literature—Psychoanalysis*, ed. Kathleen Woodward and Murray M. Schwartz. Bloomington: Indiana University Press.

Atchley, Robert. 1980. *The Social Forces in Later Life*. 3d ed. Belmont, Calif.: Wadsworth.

Augustine. 1966. *De doctrina christiana*. In *The Fathers of the Church*. Washington, D.C.: Catholic University of America.

Bagnell, Prisca von Dorotka, and Patricia Spencer Soper, eds. 1989. *Perceptions of Aging in Literature: A Cross-Cultural Study*. Westport, Conn.: Greenwood Press.

Baker, Carlos. 1952. *Hemingway: The Writer as Artist*. Princeton: Princeton University Press.

Bakhtin, M. M. 1981. *The Dialogic Imagination*. Trans. Caryl Emerson and Michael Holquist. Austin: University of Texas Press.

Baltes, Paul B., Jacqui Smith, Ursula M. Staudinger, and Doris Sowarka, eds. 1990. Wisdom: One Facet of Successful Aging. In *Late Life Potential*, ed. Marion Perlmutter. Washington, D.C.: Gerontological Society of America.

Banks, Joanne Trautmann. 1989. Introduction to *Congenial Spirits: The Selected Letters of Virginia Woolf*. San Diego: Harcourt.

————. 1990. Death Labors. *Literature and Medicine* 9:162–171.

Barnes, Daniel R. 1972. Faulkner's Miss Emily and Hawthorne's Old Maid. *Studies in Short Fiction* 9:373–377.

Baum, Rosalie Murphy. 1996. Self-Alienation of the Elderly in Margaret Laurence's Fiction. In *New Perspectives on Margaret Laurence*, ed. Greta M. K. McCormick Coger. Westport, Conn.: Greenwood Press.

Bauschatz, Cathleen M. 1993. "Voyla, mes dames . . .": Inscribed Women Listeners and Readers in the *Heptameron*. In *Critical Tales*, ed. John D. Lyons and Mary McKinley. Philadelphia: University of Pennsylvania Press.

Baxter, John. 1993. *Fellini*. New York: St. Martin's Press.

Becker, Ernst. 1973. *The Denial of Death*. New York: Free Press.

Bell, Elizabeth. 1995. Somatexts at the Disney Shop: Constructing the Pentimentos of Women's Animated Bodies. In *From Mouse to Mermaid: The Politics of Film, Gender, and Culture*, ed. Elizabeth Bell, Lynda Haas, and Laura Sells. Bloomington: Indiana University Press.

Bell, Quentin. 1971. *Virginia Woolf*. Vol. 2. London: Hogarth.

Benson, Jackson J. 1969. *Hemingway: The Writer's Art of Self-Defense*. Minneapolis: University of Minnesota Press.

————, ed. 1990. *New Critical Approaches to the Short Stories of Hemingway*. Durham: Duke University Press.

Bentley, Eric. 1957. *Bernard Shaw: A Reconsideration*. New York: New Directions.

Berthiaume, André. 1994. Rhétorique et vérité chez Marguerite de Navarre. *Dalhousie French Studies* 26:3–9.

Bertolini, John. 1991. *The Playwrighting Self of Bernard Shaw*. Carbondale: Southern Illinois University Press.

Besant, Annie. [1889] 1961. Industry under Socialism. In *Fabian Essays in Socialism*, ed. George Bernard Shaw. Reprint, New York: Doubleday.

Besdine, R. W., R. D. Dicks, and J. W. Rowe. 1990. Delirium in the Elderly. In *Principles of Geriatric Neurology*, ed. R. Katzman and J. W. Rowe. Philadelphia: F. A. Davis.

Bevington, David, ed. 1997. *The Complete Works of William Shakespeare*. Updated 4th ed. New York: Addison Wesley Longman.

Birren, James E. 1985. Age, Competence, Creativity, and Wisdom. In *Productive Aging. Enhancing Vitality in Later Life*, ed. Robert N. Butler and Herbert P. Gleason. New York: Springer.

Birren, James E., and Vern L. Bengston, eds. 1988. *Emergent Theories of Aging*. New York: Springer.

Block, Marilyn R., Janice L. Davidson, and Jean D. Grambs. 1981. *Women over Forty: Visions and Realities*. New York: Springer.

Bloom, Allan. 1987. *The Closing of the American Mind: How Higher Education Has Failed Democracy and Impoverished the Souls of Today's Students*. New York: Simon and Schuster.

Bloom, Harold. 1994. *The Western Canon*. New York: Harcourt, Brace.

Bondanella, P. 1992. *The Cinema of Federico Fellini*. Princeton: Princeton University Press.

Bontemps, Arna. 1970. A Summer Tragedy. In *From the Root: Short Stories by Black Americans*, ed. Charles L. James. New York: Dodd, Mead.

Booth, Wayne, ed. 1992. *The Art of Growing Older: Writers on Living and Aging*. New York: Poseidon.

Butler, Robert. 1982. Age-Ism: Another Form of Bigotry. In *Readings in Aging and Death*, ed. S. Zarit. New York: Harper and Row.

Butler, Robert, and Myrna I. Lewis. 1973. *Aging and Mental Health*. St. Louis: C. V. Mosby.

Butler, Robert, and Herbert P. Gleason, eds. 1985. *Productive Aging*. New York: Springer.

Campbell, O. J. 1948. The Salvation of Lear. *ELH* 15: 93–109.

Canby, Vincent. 1985. Film: Geraldine Page in "A Trip to Bountiful." *New York Times*. 20 December, C-10.

———. 1986. Geraldine Page: Out of Marengo, Ill., and Bound for Glory. *New York. Times*, 6 April, 2–19.

Caramagno, Thomas C. 1993. Suicide and the Illusion of Closure: Aging, Depression, and the Decision to Die. In *Aging and Gender in Literature*, ed. Anne M. Wyatt-Brown and Janice Rossen. Charlottesville: University Press of Virginia.

Cather, Willa. 1953. *The Professor's House*. New York: Knopf.

Cazauran, Nicole. 1976. *L'Heptaméron de Marguerite de Navarre*. Paris: Société d'édition d'enseignement supérieur.

Cazenave, Noel A. 1979. Family Violence and Aging Blacks: Theoretical Perspectives and Research Possibilities. *Journal of Minority Aging* 4:99–108.

Chekhov, Anton P. 1912. *Plays, by Anton Tchekoff*. Trans. Marian Fell. New York: Charles Scribner's Sons.

Chesnutt, Charles W. [1899] 1969. *The Conjure Woman*. Reprint, Ann Arbor: University of Michigan Press.

Chew, S. C. 1948. This Strange Eventful History. In *Joseph Quincy Adams Memorial Studies*, ed. J. G. McManaway, G. E. Dawson, and E. E. Willoughby. Washington, D.C.: Folger Shakespeare Library.

Chinen, Allan B. 1992. *Once upon a Midlife*. New York: Tarcher/Perigee.

Chodorow, Nancy. 1978. *The Reproduction of Mothering: Psychoanalysis and the Sociology of Gender*. Berkeley and Los Angeles: University of California Press.

Clark, Margaret. 1966. The Anthropology of Aging. Paper presented to the American Anthropological Association Conference, Denver.

Clark, Ronald. 1976. *The Life of Bertrand Russell*. New York: Alfred A. Knopf.

Coffman, G. R. 1934. Old Age from Horace to Chaucer: Some Literary Affinities and Adventures of an Idea. *Speculum: A Journal of Mediaeval Studies* 9:249–277.

Coggin, B. W. 1982. Studies in Shakespeare's Treatment of Old Age. Ph.D. diss., University of Texas, Austin.

Cohen-Shalev, Amir. 1989. Old Age Style: Developmental Changes in Creative Produc-
     tion from a Life-Span Perspective. *Journal of Aging Studies* 3 (Spring): 21–37.
Cohler, Bertram J. 1993. Aging, Morale, and Meaning: The Nexus of Narrative. In
     Voices and Visions of Aging: Toward a Critical Gerontology, ed. Thomas R.
     Cole, W. Andrew Achenbaum, Patricia L. Jakobi, and Robert Kastenbaum.
     New York: Springer.
Cole, Thomas R. 1992a. The Humanities and Aging: An Overview. In *Handbook of
     the Humanities and Aging*, ed. Thomas R. Cole, David D. Van Tassell, and
     Robert Kastenbaum. New York: Springer.
———. 1992b. *The Journey of Life: A Cultural History of Aging in America*. Cam-
     bridge: Cambridge University Press.
Cole, Thomas R., W. Andrew Achenbaum, Patricia L. Jakobi, and Robert Kasten-
     baum, eds. 1993. *Voices and Visions of Aging: Toward a Critical Gerontology*.
     New York: Springer.
Cole, Thomas R., and Sally A. Gadow, eds. 1986. *What Does It Mean to Grow Old?:
     Reflections from the Humanities*. Durham: Duke University Press.
Cole, Thomas R., David D. Van Tassell, and Robert Kastenbaum. 1992. *Handbook of
     the Humanities and Aging*. New York: Springer.
Cole, Thomas R., and Mary G. Winkler, eds. 1994. *The Oxford Book of Aging*. Ox-
     ford: Oxford University Press.
Coles, Robert. 1989. *The Call of Stories: Teaching and the Moral Imagination*. Bos-
     ton: Houghton Mifflin.
Conrad, Christoph. 1992. Old Age in the Modern and Postmodern Western World.
     In *Handbook of the Humanities and Aging*, ed. Thomas R. Cole, David D.
     Van Tassel, and Robert Kastenbaum. New York: Springer.
Covey, H. C. 1989. Old Age Portrayed by the Ages-of-Life Models from the Middle
     Ages to the 16th Century. *The Gerontologist* 29:692–698.
Cox, E. H. 1942. Shakespeare and Some Conventions of Old Age. *Studies in Philol-
     ogy* 39:36–46.
Cumming, Elaine, and William E. Henry. 1961. *Growing Old: The Process of Disen-
     gagement*. New York: Basic Books.
Davis, Lennard J. 1987. *Resisting Novels: Ideology and Fiction*. New York: Methuen.
Deats, Sara Munson, and Lagretta Tallent Lenker, eds. 1989. *Youth Suicide Preven-
     tion: Lessons from Literature*. New York: Plenum.
———. 1991. *The Aching Heart: Family Violence in Life and Literature*. New York:
     Plenum.
———. 1994. *Gender and Academe: Feminist Pedagogy and Politics*. Lanham, Md.:
     Rowman and Littlefield.
de Beauvoir, Simone. 1972. *The Coming of Age*. Trans. Patrick O'Brian. New York: Putnam.
———. 1974. From Maturity to Old Age. In *The Second Sex*, trans. and ed. H. M.
     Parshley. New York: Vintage.
Derrida, Jacques. 1976. *Of Grammatology*. Trans. Gayatri Chakravorty Spivak. Balti-
     more: Johns Hopkins University Press.
DeSalvo, Louise. 1989. *Virginia Woolf: The Impact of Childhood Sexual Abuse on
     Her Life and Work*. Boston: Beacon.
Dickens, Charles. 1963. *Great Expectations*. New York: New American Library.
Dienes, Sara. 1986. *Elders of the Tribe*. New York: Bernice Steinbaum Gallery.
———. 1994. Interview by Robert Berlind, May 4, 1990. *Art Journal* 53:38–39.

Dietrich, Richard F. 1989. *British Drama 1890–1950*. Boston: Twayne.
Dilworth-Anderson, Peggye. 1981. Family Closeness between Aged Blacks and Their Adult Children. *Journal of Minority Aging* 6:56–66.
Dinnerstein, Dorothy. 1976. *The Mermaid and the Minotaur: Sexual Arrangements and Human Malaise*. New York: Harper and Row.
Donow, Herbert S. 1992. "To Everything There is a Season": Some Shakespearean Models of Normal and Anomalous Aging. *The Gerontologist* 32:733–738.
———. 1994. The Two Faces of Age and the Resolution of Generational Conflict. *The Gerontologist* 34:73–78.
Douglass, Frederick. 1845. *Narrative of the Life of Frederick Douglass, an American Slave; Written by Himself*. Boston: American Anti-Slavery Society.
Draper, J. W. 1940. The Old Age of King Lear. *Journal of English and Germanic Philology* 39:527–540.
———. 1946. Shakespeare's Attitude towards Old Age. *Journal of Gerontology* 1:118–126.
Dror, Itiel E., and Stephen M. Kosslyn. 1994. Mental Imagery and Aging. *Psychology and Aging* 9:90–102.
Duval, Edwin M. 1993. "Et puis, quelles nouvelles?": The Project of Marguerite's Unfinished Decameron. In *Critical Tales*, ed. John D. Lyons and Mary McKinley. Philadelphia: University of Pennsylvania Press.
Eagleton, T. 1983. *Literary Theory: An Introduction*. Oxford: Basil Blackwell.
Eastman, Charles. 1971. *Indian Boyhood*. New York: Dover.
Eisdorfer, Carl, and J. Altrocchi. 1961. A Comparison of Attitudes toward Old Age and Mental Illness. *Journal of Gerontology* 16:940–943.
Eliot, George. 1930. *Middlemarch*. London: Dent.
Eliot, T. S. 1926. *Criterion* 4:389.
Ellison, Ralph. [1952] 1990. *Invisible Man*. Reprint, New York: Vintage Books.
Erikson, Erik H. 1979. Reflections on Dr. Borg's Life Cycle. In *Aging, Death, and the Completion of Being*, ed. David D. Van Tassel. Philadelphia: University of Pennsylvania Press.
———. 1982. *The Life Cycle Completed: A Review*. New York: Norton.
Erikson, Erik H., Joan M. Erikson, and Helen Q. Kivnick. 1986. *Vital Involvement in Old Age*. New York: W. W. Norton.
Fahey, Charles J., and Martha Holstein. 1993. Toward a Philosophy of the Third Age. In *Voices and Visions of Aging: Toward a Critical Gerontology*, ed. Thomas R. Cole, W. Andrew Achenbaum, Patricia L. Jakobi, and Robert Kastenbaum. New York: Springer.
Fallis, Richard C. 1989. "Grow Old Along with Me": Images of Older People in British and American Literature. In *Perceptions of Aging in Literature: A Cross-Cultural Study*, ed. Prisca von Dorotka Bagnell and Patricia Spencer Soper. Westport, Conn.: Greenwood Press.
Faulkner, William. 1977. *Collected Stories of William Faulkner*. New York: Vintage.
Fellini, Federico. 1964. Interview by G. Bachmann. *Sight and Sound* 33:82–87.
Fellini, Federico. 1965. Interview by G. Bachmann. *Cinéma* 99:71–89.
Fisher, Dorothy Canfield. 1996. The Bedquilt. In *The Bedquilt and Other Stories*. Columbia: University of Missouri Press.
Fisher, Rudolph. 1987. *The City of Refuge: The Collcted Stories of Rudolph Fisher*. Ed. John McCluskey, Jr. Columbia: University of Missouri Press.
Fogan, L. 1989. The Neurology in Shakespeare. *Archives of Neurology* 46:922–924.

Fowler, Margaret, and Priscilla McCutcheon, eds. 1991. *Songs of Experience: An Anthology of Literature on Growing Old*. New York: Ballantine Books.

Frank, Lawrence. 1984. *Charles Dickens and the Romantic Self*. Lincoln: University of Nebraska Press.

Frazier, E. Franklin. 1948. *The Negro Family in the United States*. Rev. and abridged ed. Chicago: University of Chicago Press.

Freedman, Richard. 1978. Sufficiently Decayed: Gerontophobia in English Literature. In *Aging and the Elderly: Humanistic Perspectives in Gerontology*, ed. Stuart F. Spicker, Kathleen M. Woodward, and David D. Van Tassel. Atlantic Highlands, N.J.: Humanities Press.

Friedan, Betty. 1993. *The Fountain of Age*. New York: Simon & Schuster.

Frueh, Joanna, 1994a. The Erotic Social Security. *Art Journal* 53:66–72.

————. 1994b. Visible Difference: Women Artists and Aging. In *New Feminist Criticism*, ed. Joanna Frueh, Cassandra L. Langer, and Arlene Raven. New York: Icon.

Gabriel, Joseph. 1961. The Logic of Confusion in Hemingway's "A Clean, Well-Lighted Place." *College English* 22:539–547.

Gaines, Ernest J. 1971. *The Autobiography of Miss Jane Pittman*. New York: Bantam.

————. 1983. *A Gathering of Old Men*. New York: Vintage.

————. 1993. *A Lesson before Dying*. New York: Vintage.

Garton, Ann. 1994. Letter to Joanne Trautman Banks. 12 October.

Gates, David. 1994. It's Naughty! Haughty! It's Anti-Multi-Culti. *Newsweek*, 10 October, 73–75.

Gaudet, Marcia, and Carl Wooton, eds. 1990. *Porch Talk: Conversations on the Writer's Craft*. Baton Rouge: Louisiana State University Press.

Gilbert, C. 1967. When Did a Man in the Renaissance Grow Old? *Studies in the Renaissance* 14:7–32.

Gilbert, Sandra M., and Susan Gubar. 1979. *The Madwoman in the Attic*. New Haven: Yale University Press.

Gillespie, Bonnie J. 1976. Black Grandparents: Childhood Socialization. *Journal of Afro-American Issues* 4:432–441.

Gilligan, Carol. 1993. *In a Different Voice: Psychological Theory and Women's Development*. Cambridge: Harvard University Press.

Girard, René. 1965. *Deceit, Desire, and the Novel: Self and Other in Literary Studies*. Trans. Yvonne Freccero. Baltimore: Johns Hopkins University Press.

Goffman, Erving. 1959. *The Presentation of Self in Everyday Life*. New York: Doubleday Anchor.

Gold, D. T., and Schmader, K. 1993. An Introduction to Aging. In *Psychiatry*, ed. P. J. Wilner. Vol. 2. Philadelphia: J. B. Lippincott.

Greenberg, H. 1975. 8½ — The Declensions of Silence. In *The Movies on your Mind: Film Classics on the Couch from Fellini to Frankenstein*. New York: Dutton.

Greer, Germaine. 1991. *The Change: Women, Aging, and Menopause*. New York: Fawcett Columbine.

Gullette, Margaret Morganroth. 1988. *Safe at Last in the Middle Years: The Invention of the Midlife Progress Novel: Saul Bellow, Margaret Drabble, Anne Tyler, and John Updike*. Berkeley and Los Angeles: University of California Press.

————. 1993. Creativity, Aging, Gender: A Study of Their Intersections, 1910–1935. In *Aging and Gender in Literature: Studies in Creativity*, ed. Anne M. Wyatt-Brown and Janice Rossen. Charlottesville: University Press of Virginia.

———. 1996. Midlife Heroines, "Older and Freer." *The Kenyon Review* 18:10–29.

Gutmann, David. 1977. The Cross-Cultural Perspective: Notes toward a Comparative Psychology of Aging. In *Handbook of the Psychology of Aging*, ed. James E. Birren and K. Warner Shaie. New York: Van Nostrand Reinhold.

———. 1987. *Reclaimed Powers: Toward a New Psychology of Men and Women in Later Life*. New York: Basic Books.

Gwin, Minrose C. 1990. *The Feminine and Faulkner: Reading (Beyond) Sexual Difference*. Knoxville: University of Tennessee Press.

Haas, Lynda. 1995. "Eighty-Six the Mother": Murder, Matricide, and Good Mothers. In *From Mouse to Mermaid: The Politics of Film, Gender, and Culture*, ed. Elizabeth Bell, Lynda Haas, and Laura Sells. Bloomington: Indiana University Press.

Hall, Stanley. [1922] 1972. *Senescence: The Last Half of Life*. Reprint, New York: Arno.

Hallissy, Margaret. 1987. *Venomous Woman: Fear of the Female in Literature*. Westport, Conn.: Greenwood Press.

Hammond, Margo. 1993. Betty Friedan Now. *St. Petersburg Times*, 28 September, 8X–9X.

Harcourt, P. 1966. The Secret Life of Federico Fellini. *Film Quarterly* 19:4–19.

Harris, Louis. 1974. Myth. *American Association of Retired Persons Bulletin* 15: 3–4.

Hawthorne, Nathaniel. 1962. *The Scarlet Letter*. New York: Norton.

———. 1965. *The House of the Seven Gables*. Ed. William Charvat, Roy Harvey Pearce, and Claude Simpson. Columbus: Ohio State University Press.

———. 1974. *Twice-Told Tales*. Ed. William Charvat, Roy Harvey Pearce, and Claude Simpson. Columbus: Ohio State University Press.

———. Dr. Heidegger's Experiment. In *Literature and Language: American Literature*. Evanston, Illinois: McDougal-Litell.

Heilbrun, Carolyn G. 1983. Virginia Woolf in Her Fifties. In *Virginia Woolf: A Feminist Slant*, ed. Jane Marcus. Lincoln: Nebraska University Press.

Held, Julius S. 1987. Commentary on Style and the Aging Artist. *Art Journal*: 127–133.

Hemingway, Ernest. 1926. *The Sun Also Rises*. New York: Charles Scribner's Sons.

———. 1929. *A Farewell to Arms*. New York: Charles Scribner's Sons.

———. 1952. *The Old Man and the Sea*. New York: Charles Scribner's Sons.

———. [1938] 1966. A Clean, Well-Lighted Place. In *The Short Stories of Ernest Hemingway*. Reprint, New York: Charles Scribner's Sons.

———, ed. 1942. *Men at War: The Best War Stories of All Times*. New York: Crown.

Hendricks, Jon, and Cynthia A. Leedham. 1989. Making Sense: Interpreting Historical and Cross-Cultural Literature on Aging. In *Perceptions of Aging in Literature*, ed. Prisca von Dorotka Bagnell and Patricia Spencer Soper. Westport, Conn.: Greenwood Press.

Henke, Jill Birnie, Diane Zimmerman Umble, and Nancy J. Smith. 1996. Construction of the Female Self: Feminist Readings of the Disney Heroine. *Women's Studies in Communication* 19:229–250.

Herman, D. 1969. Federico Fellini. *American Imago* 26:251–268.

Hickey, Tom. 1968. Children's Perceptions of the Elderly. *Journal of Genetic Psychology* 112:227–235.

Hilton, James. 1962. *Good-bye Mr. Chips*. New York: Little.

Hoerrner, Keisha. 1996. Sex Roles in Disney Films. *Women's Studies in Communication* 19:213–228.

Hoffman, Steven K. 1990. Nada and the Clean, Well-Lighted Place: The Unity of
    Hemingway's Short Fiction. In *New Critical Approaches to the Short Stories
    of Hemingway*, ed. Jackson J. Benson. Durham: Duke University Press.
Holland, N. N. 1963. Fellini's 8½; Holland's "11". *Hudson Review* 16:429–436.
———. 1968. *The Dynamics of Literary Response*. New York: Oxford University Press.
Holroyd, Michael. 1991. *Bernard Shaw: The Lure of Fantasy 1918–1950*. New York:
    Random House.
Holstein, M. 1994. Taking Next Steps: Gerontological Education, Research, and the
    Literary Imagination. *The Gerontologist* 34:822–827.
Hornback, Bert G. 1972. *"Noah's Arkitecture": A Study of Dickens' Mythology*. Ath-
    ens: Ohio University Press.
Hurston, Zora Neale. [1937] 1978. *Their Eyes Were Watching God*. Reprint, Urbana:
    University of Illinois Press.
Hutter, Albert D. 1990. Crime and Fantasy in *Great Expectations*. In *Critical Essays
    on Charles Dickens's "Great Expectations,"* ed. Michael Cotsell. Boston: G.
    K. Hall.
Hyman, Virginia R. 1988. *To the Lighthouse and Beyond*. New York: Lang.
Irving, Washington. 1964. The Legend of Sleepy Hollow. In *Selected Writings of
    Washington Irving*, ed. Saxe Commins. New York: Viking.
Isocrates. [1929] 1968a. On the Peace. In *Isocrates*. Trans. George Norlin. Vol. 2.
    Loeb Classical Library. Cambridge: Harvard University Press.
———. [1929] 1968b. Panathenaicus. In *Isocrates*. Trans. George Norlin. Vol. 2. Loeb
    Classical Library. Cambridge: Harvard University Press.
Jackson, Jacquelyne Johnson. 1980. *Minorities and Aging*. Belmont, Calif.: Wadsworth.
Jacobs, Harriet. 1861. *Incidents in the Life of a Slave Girl; Written by Herself*. ed.
    Lydia Marie Child. Boston: Author.
Johnson, James Weldon. 1963. Go Down Death (A Funeral Sermon). In *American
    Negro Poetry*, ed. Arna Bontemps. New York: Hill and Wang.
Johnston, Ollie, and Frank Thomas. 1993. *The Disney Villain*. New York: Hyperion.
Johnstone, John Keith. 1963. *The Bloomsbury Group*. New York: Noonday-Farrar.
Jourda, Pierre. 1930. *Marguerite d'Angoulême, duchesse d'Alençon, reine de Navarre*.
    Paris: Champion.
Joyce, James. 1964. *A Portrait of the Artist as a Young Man*. New York: Viking.
———. 1976. Clay. In *Dubliners*. New York: Penguin.
Jung, Carl Gustav. 1969. *The Stages of Life*. Vol. 8. of *Collected Works by C. G. Jung*.
    Trans. R. F. C. Hull. Princeton: Princeton University Press.
Kahn, Coppelia. 1986. The Absent Mother in *King Lear*. In *Rewriting the Renais-
    sance: The Discourse of Sexual Difference in Early Modern Europe*, ed. Mar-
    garet W. Ferguson and Nancy J. Vickers. Chicago: University of Chicago Press.
Kastenbaum. Robert. 1992. The Creative Process: A Life-Span Approach. In *Hand-
    book of the Humanities and Aging*, ed. by Thomas R. Cole, David D. Van
    Tassell, and Robert Kastenbaum. New York: Springer.
Kerrigan, William. 1986. Life's Iamb: The Scansion of Late Creativity in the Culture
    of the Renaissance. In *Memory and Desire: Aging—Literature—Psychoanaly-
    sis*, ed. Kathleen Woodward and Murray M. Schwartz. Bloomington: Indiana
    University Press.
Kohn, Martin, Carol Donley, and Delese Wear. 1992. *Literature and Aging: An An-
    thology*. Kent, Ohio: Kent State University Press.

La Fayette, Madame de. 1966. *La princesse de Clèves*. Paris: Garnier-Flammarion.
Lafond, Jean. 1984. *Les formes brèves de la prose et le discours discontinu (XVI–XVII siècles)*. Paris: Vrin.
La Fontaine, Jean de. 1954. "Le Labour et ses enfants, Fables, Livre V, IX." In *Oeuvres complètes*. Vol 1. Ed. René Groos. Paris: Gallimard. 1:123.
Lajarte, Philippe de. 1993. The Voice of the Narrators in Marguerite de Navarre's Tales. In *Critical Tales*, ed. John D. Lyons and Mary McKinley. Philadelpia: University of Pennsylvania Press.
Lasch, Christopher. 1979. *The Culture of Narcissism*. New York: Norton.
Laurence, Margaret. 1966. *The Stone Angel*. Toronto: McClelland and Stewart.
Layton, Elizabeth. 1994. Interview by Robert Soppelsa and Don Lambert, June 1991. *Art Journal* 50 :53–55.
Lenker, Lagretta T. and Larry Polivka. 1996. Project Rationale and History. *Journal of Aging and Identity* 1:3–6.
Le Roy Ladurie, Emmanuel. 1983. Auprès du roi, la cour. *Annales: Economies, sociétés, civilisations* 38:21–41.
LeShan, Lawrence. 1976. *Alternate Realities*. New York: Ballantine.
Lessing, Doris. 1980. An Old Woman and Her Cat. In *Stories*. New York: Vintage.
Levin, Bernard. 1970. *The Pendulum Years: Britain and the Sixties*. London: Jonathan Cape.
Levin, Jack, and William C. Levin. 1980. *Ageism*. Belmont, Calif.: Wadsworth.
Levine, Irving R. 1965. Fellini Reveals—and Conceals—Fellini. *New York Times* 31 October, X13.
Lewin, Kurt. 1935. Environmental Dimensions. In *A Dynamic Theory of Personality*, trans. Donald K. Adams and Karl E. Zener. New York: McGraw.
Linderman, Frank. 1962. *Plenty Coups*. Lincoln: University of Nebraska Press.
Lipowski, Z. J. 1989. Delirium in the Elderly Patient. *New England Journal of Medicine* 320:578–581.
Lippard, Lucy R. 1983. *Overlay*. New York: Pantheon Books.
Lodge, David. 1984. *Small World*. New York: Macmillan.
———. 1985. *Changing Places: A Tale of Two Campuses*. New York: Penguin.
Lyell, Ruth Granetz. 1980. *Middle Age, Old Age: Short Stories, Poems, Plays, and Essays on Aging*. New York: Harcourt Brace Jovanovich.
Macdonald, Dwight. 1978. Afterward in *The Two Hundred Days of "8½,"* Trans. C. L. Markmann. New York: Garland.
Mack, Maynard. 1965. *King Lear in Our Time*. Berkeley and Los Angeles: University of California Press.
Maddox, George L. 1987. Aging Differently. *Gerontologist* 27:557–564.
———. 1991. Aging with a Difference. *Generations* 15:7–10.
Maddox, George L., and James Wiley. 1976. Scope, Concepts and Methods in the Study of Aging. In *Handbook of Aging and the Social Sciences*, ed. Robert H. Binstock and Ethel Shanas. New York: Van Nostrand Reinhold.
Manheimer, Ronald J. 1992. Wisdom and Method: Philosophical Contributions to Gerontology. In *Handbook of the Humanities and Aging*, ed. Thomas R. Cole, David D. Van Tassell, and Robert Kastenbaum. New York: Springer.
Mansfield, Katherine. 1961. Miss Brill. *The Short Stories of Katherine Mansfield*. New York: Knopf.
Marguerite de Navarre. 1984. *The Heptameron*. Trans. Paul A. Chilton. New York: Penguin.

Martz, Sandra, ed. 1987. *When I Am an Old Woman I Shall Wear Purple: An Anthology of Short Stories and Poetry*. Manhattan Beach, Calif.: Papier-Mache.

May, Rollo. 1969. *Love and Will*. New York: Dell.

McCollough, Laurence B. 1994. Arrested Aging: The Power to Make Us Aged and Old. In *Voices and Visions of Aging*, ed. Thomas Cole, W. Andrew Achenbaum, Patricia L. Jakobi, and Robert Kastenbaum. New York: Springer.

McLerran, Jennifer, and Patrick McKee. 1991. *Old Age in Myth and Symbol: A Cultural Dictionary*. Westport, Conn.: Greenwood Press.

McNickle, D'Arcy. 1936. *The Surrounded*. New York: Dodd, Mead.

Meisel, Martin. 1984. *Shaw and the Nineteenth Century Theater*. New York: Limelight Editions.

Michener, James A. 1994. *Recessional*. New York: Fawcett Crest.

Miles, L. W. 1940. Shakespeare's Old Men. *English Literary History* 7:286–299.

Miller, Arther. [1949.]. Reprinted 1976. *Death of a Salesman*. New York: Penguin.

Miller, Jean Baker. 1976. *Toward a New Psychology of Women*. Boston: Beacon.

Molière (Jean Baptiste Poquelin). 1962. *L'école des femmes*. In *Oeuvres complètes*. ed. Gustave Cohen. Vol. 2. Paris: Sevil 2:174–199.

Momaday, N. Scott. 1979. The Man Made of Words. In *The Remembered Earth: An Anthology of Contemporary Native American Literature*, ed. Geary Hobson. Albuquerque: Red Earth Press.

Moody, Harry R. 1988. Toward a Critical Gerontology: The Contribution of the Humanities to Theories of Aging. In *Emergent Theories of Aging*, ed. James E. Birren and Vern L. Bengston. New York: Springer.

———. 1992. *Ethics in an Aging Society*. Baltimore: Johns Hopkins University Press.

———. 1993. Overview: What Is Critical Gerontology and Why Is It Important? In *Voices and Visions of Aging: Toward a Critical Gerontology*, ed. Thomas R. Cole, W. Andrew Achenbaum, Patricia L. Jakobi, and Robert Kastenbaum. New York: Springer.

Moore, Thomas. 1992. *Care of the Soul*. New York: HarperCollins.

Moorehead, Caroline. 1993. *Bertrand Russell: A Life*. New York: Viking.

Morgan, Margery M. 1972. *The Shavian Playground: An Exploration of the Art of George Bernard Shaw*. London: Methuen.

Morrison, Toni. 1987. *Beloved: A Novel*. New York: Knopf.

Moser, Charlotte. 1991. *Clyde Connell*. Austin: University of Texas Press.

New Outlook for the Aged. 1975. *Time*, 2 June, 44–46.

Noggle, Anne. 1994. Interview by Anne Wilkes Tucker, 11 March, 1993. *Art Journal* 53:58–60.

Norris, C. 1982. *Deconstruction: Theory and Practice*. London: Methuen.

Novak, Mark. 1985. *Successful Aging: The Myths, Realities and Future of Aging in Canada*. New York: Penguin.

O'Brien, Pamela Colby. 1996. The Happiest Films on Earth: A Textual and Contextual Analysis of Walt Disney's *Cinderella* and *The Little Mermaid*. *Women's Studies in Communication* 19:155–187.

Older—But Coming on Strong. 1988. *Time*, 22 February, 76–78.

Ong, Walter J. 1982. *Orality and Literacy: The Technologizing of the Word*. New York: Metheun.

Orenstein, Gloria Feman. 1994. Recovering Her Story: Feminist Artists Reclaim the Great Goddess. In *The Power of Feminist Art*, ed. Norma Broude and Mary D. Garrard. New York: Harry N. Abrams.

Page, Sally R. 1972. *Faulkner's Women: Characterization and Meaning.* DeLand, Fla.: Everett Edwards.

Parker, Marcie. 1991. The Great Escape: The Meaning of the Great Escape Theme in the Humanities and Gerontology. *Educational Gerontology* 17:55–61.

Patton, Frances Gray. 1954. *Good Morning, Miss Dove.* New York: Dodd, Mead.

Pearsall, Marilyn. 1997. *The Other within Us: Feminist Explorations of Women and Aging.* Boulder, Colo.: Westview Press.

Perlmutter, Marion. 1988. Cognitive Potential Throughout Life. In *Emergent Theories of Aging,* ed. James E. Birren and Vern L. Bengston. New York: Springer.

———, ed. 1990. *Late Life Potential.* Washington, D.C.: Gerontological Society of America.

Pifer, Alan. 1986. The Public Policy Response. In *Our Aging Society: Paradox and Promise,* ed. Alan Pifer and Lydia Bronte. New York: W. W. Norton.

Poe, Edgar Allan. 1965. Hawthorne's *Twice-Told Tales.* In *Literary Criticism of Edgar Allan Poe,* ed. Robert L. Hough. Lincoln: University of Nebraska Press.

Portales, Marco. 1989. *Youth and Age in American Literature.* New York: Peter Lang.

Porter, Katherine Anne. 1965. The Jilting of Granny Weatherall. In *The Collected Stories of Katherine Anne Porter.* New York: Harcourt, Brace & World.

Porter, Laurel. 1984. King Lear and the Crisis of Retirement. In *Aging in Literature,* ed. Laurel Porter and Laurence M. Porter. Troy, Mich.: International Book Publishers.

Porter, Laurel, and Laurence M. Porter. 1984. *Aging in Literature.* Troy, Mich.: International Book Publishers.

Price, B. A., and Price, T. 1978. *Federico Fellini: An Annotated International Bibliography.* Metuchen, N.J.: Scarecrow Press.

Quadagno, Jill S. 1982. *Aging in Early Industrial Society: Work, Family, and Social Policy in Nineteenth-Century England.* New York: Academic Press.

Quintilian. 1976. *Institutio oratoria.* Vol. 3. Trans. H. E. Butler. Cambridge: Harvard University Press.

Racine, Jean. 1962. Andromaque. In *Oeuvres complètes,* ed. Gustave Cohen. Paris: Sevil. 2:103–122.

Rankin, Sally H. 1989. The Emergence of Creativity in Later Life. In *Transitions in a Woman's Life: Major Life Events in Developmental Context,* ed. Ramona T. Mercer, Elizabeth G. Nichols, and Glen Caspers Doyle. New York: Springer.

Recinos, Adrian. 1952. *Popol Vuh.* Mexico: Fondo de Cultura Economica.

Reinharz, Shulamit. 1986. Friends or Foes: Gerontological and Feminist Theory. *Women's Studies International Forum* 9:503–514.

Reyff, Simone de, éd. 1982. *Heptaméron.* Paris: Flammarion.

Reynolds, Regine. 1977. *Les devisants de l'Heptaméron: dix personnages en quête d'audience.* Washington, D.C.: University Press of America.

Rigolot, François. 1993. The *Heptameron* and the 'Magdalen Controversy': Dialogue and Humanist Hermeneutics. In *Critical Tales,* ed. John D. Lyons and Mary B. McKinley. Philadelphia: University of Pennsylvania Press.

———. 1994. Magdalen's Skull: Allegory and Iconography in *Heptaméron. Renaissance Quarterly* 47:57–73.

Roberts, Diane. 1994. *Faulkner and Southern Womanhood.* Athens: University of Georgia Press.

Ronsard, Pierre. 1950. "Mignonne, allons voir si la rose." and "Quanol vous serez bien vieille." In *Oeuvres complètes,* ed. Gustave Cohen. Paris: Gallimard. 1: 419, 260.

Rooke, Constance. 1988. Hagar's Old Age: *The Stone Angel* as Vollendungsroman. In *Crossing the River: Essays in Honor of Margaret Laurence*, ed. Kristjana Gunnars. Winnipeg: Truestone.

———. 1992. Old Age in Contemporary Fiction: A New Paradigm of Hope. In *Handbook of the Humanities and Aging*, ed. Thomas R. Cole, David D. Van Tassell, and Robert Kastenbaum. New York: Springer.

Rosenman, Ellen Bayuk. 1986. *The Invisible Presence: Virginia Woolf and the Mother–Daughter Relationship*. Baton Rouge: Louisiana State University Press.

Rossen, Janice. 1993. *The University in Modern Fiction: When Power Is Academic*. New York: St. Martin's Press.

Rovit, Earl. 1963. *Ernest Hemingway*. New York: Twayne.

Rowe, John W. and Robert L. Kahn. 1987. Human Aging: Usual and Successful. *Science* 237:143–149.

Rubin, Rhea Joyce. 1990. *Of a Certain Age: A Guide to Contemporary Fiction Featuring Older Adults*. Santa Barbara, Calif.: ABC-CLIO.

Russell, Bertrand. 1950. *Unpopular Essays*. New York: Simon and Schuster.

———. 1969. *The Autobiography of Bertrand Russell: 1944–1969*. New York: Simon and Schuster.

Russell, Charles H. 1989. *Good News about Aging*. New York: John Wiley.

Ryan, Alan. 1988. *Bertrand Russell: A Political Life*. New York: Hill and Wang.

Sainte-Beuve, Charles Augustin. 1850. *Causeries du lundi*. Paris: Garnier.

Salachas, G. 1963. *Federico Fellini*. Paris: Éditions Seghers.

———. 1969. *Federico Fellini*, Trans. Rosalie Siegel. New York: Crown.

Salinger, J. D. 1951. *The Catcher in the Rye*. Boston: Little, Brown.

Sarton, May. 1966. *Miss Pickthorn and Mr. Hare: A Fable*. New York: W. W. Norton.

———. May. 1973. *As We Are Now*. New York: W. W. Norton.

Schaeffer, Francis A. 1976. *How Should We Then Live?* Old Tappan, N.J.: Revell.

Schriber, Mary Suzanne. 1987. *Gender and the Writer's Imagination from Cooper to Wharton*. Lexington: University of Kentucky Press.

Schulkind, Jeanne. 1985. Introduction to *Moments of Being* by Virginia Woolf. 2d ed. San Diego: Harvest-Harcourt.

Scott, Nathan. 1974. Ernest Hemingway: A Critical Essay. In *Ernest Hemingway: Five Decades of Criticism*, ed. Linda Wagner-Martin. East Lansing: Michigan State University Press.

Secundy, Marian Gray, ed. 1992. *Trials, Tribulations, and Celebrations: African-American Perspectives on Health, Illness, Aging, and Loss*. Yarmouth, Mass.: Intercultural Press.

Seefelt, Carol. 1977. Using Pictures to Explore Children's Attitudes toward the Elderly. *The Gerontologist* 17:506–512.

Sennett, Dorothy, ed. 1988. *Full Measure: Modern Short Stories on Aging*. St. Paul, Minn.: Graywolf.

Sennett, Dorothy, and Anne Czarniecki, eds. 1991. *Vital Signs: International Stories on Aging*. St. Paul, Minn.: Graywolf.

Sewell, Arthur, ed. 1951. Tragedy and the Kingdom of Ends. In *Character and Society in Shakespeare*. Oxford: Clarendon Press.

Shaw, George Bernard. [1890] 1986. The Quintessence of Ibsenism. In *Major Critical Essays*. ed. Michael Holroyd. New York: Viking Penguin Books.

————. [1921] 1970a. *Back to Methuselah.* In *The Bodley Head Bernard Shaw: Collected Plays with their Prefaces,* ed. Dan Laurence. 7 vols. London: Max Reinhardt.

————. [1901] 1970b. *Caesar and Cleopatra.* In *The Bodley Head Bernard Shaw: Collected Plays with their Prefaces,* ed. Dan Laurence. 7 vols. London: Max Reinhardt.

————. [1919] 1970c. *Heartbreak House.* In *The Bodley Head Bernard Shaw: Collected Plays with their Prefaces,* ed. Dan Laurence. 7 vols. London: Max Reinhardt.

————. [1903] 1970d. *Man and Superman.* In *The Bodley Head Bernard Shaw: Collected Plays with their Prefaces,* ed. Dan Laurence. 7 vols. London: Max Reinhardt.

————, ed. [1889] 1961. *Fabian Essays in Socialism.* Reprint, New York: Doubleday.

Sheehy, Gail. 1995. *New Passages: Mapping Your Life across Time.* New York: Random House.

Shengold, Leonard. 1989. *Soul Murder: The Effects of Childhood Abuse and Deprivation.* New Haven: Yale University Press.

Shneidman, Edwin. 1989. The Suicidal Psycho-Logics of Moby-Dick. In *Youth Suicide Prevention: Lessons from Literature,* ed. Sara Munson Deats and Lagretta Tallent Lenker. New York: Plenum.

Showalter, Elaine. 1985a. Representing Ophelia: Women, Madness, and the Responsibilities of Feminist Criticism. In *Shakespeare and the Question of Theory,* ed. Patricia Parker and Geoffrey Hartman. New York: Methuen.

————. 1985b. Toward a Feminist Poetics. In *The New Feminist Criticism: Essays on Women, Literature, and Theory,* ed. Elaine Showalter. New York: Pantheon.

Sibley, Agnes. 1972. *May Sarton.* Boston: Twayne.

Silko, Leslie Marmon. 1977. *Ceremony.* New York: Viking.

————. 1981. *Storyteller.* New York: Seaver Books.

Silver, Brenda R. 1992. What's Woolf Got to Do with It? or, The Perils of Popularity. *Modern Fiction Studies* 38:20–60.

Simon, John. 1967. Fellini's 8½¢ Fancy. In *Private Screenings.* New York: Macmillan.

Simonton, Dean Keith. 1990. Does Creativity Decline in the Later Years? Definition, Data, and Theory. In *Late Life Potential,* ed. Marion Perlmutter. Washington, D.C.: Gerontological Society of America.

Sims, R. E. 1943. The Green Old Age of Falstaff. *Bulletin of the History of Medicine* 13:144–157.

Slater, Michael. 1983. *Dickens and Women.* Stanford, Calif.: Stanford University Press.

Smith, H. 1976. Bare Ruined Choirs: Shakespearean Variations on the Theme of Old Age. *Huntington Library Quarterly* 39:233–249.

Smith, S. 1978. Death, Dying, and the Elderly in Seventeenth-Century England. In *Aging and the Elderly: Humanistic Perspectives in Gerontology,* ed. Stuart F. Spicker, Kathleen M. Woodward, and David D. Van Tassel. Atlantic Highlands, N.J.: Humanities Press.

Snyder, Susan. 1982. *King Lear* and the Psychology of Dying. *Shakespeare Quarterly.* 33:449–460.

Sontag, Susan. 1972. The Double Standard of Aging. In *No Longer Young: The Older Woman in America.* ed. Pauline B. Bart. Ann Arbor: University of Michigan–Wayne State University Press.

Spicker, Stuart F., Kathleen M. Woodward, and David D. Van Tassel, eds. 1978. *Aging and the Elderly: Humanistic Perspectives in Gerontology.* Atlantic Highlands, N.J.: Humanities Press.

Spilka, Mark. 1980. *Virginia Woolf's Quarrel with Grieving.* Lincoln: Nebraska University Press.

Spivak, Gayatri Chakravorty. 1976. Translator's Preface in *Of Grammatology* by Jacques Derrida. Baltimore: Johns Hopkins University Press.

Stampfer, J. 1960. The Catharsis of *King Lear. Shakespeare Survey* 13:1–10.

Stoddard, Karen M. 1983. *Saints and Shrews: Women and Aging in American Popular Film.* Westport, Conn.: Greenwood Press.

Street, Douglas, ed. 1983. *Children's Novels and the Movies.* New York: Frederick Ungar.

Sullivan, Harry Stack. 1953. Definitions. In *The Interpersonal Theory of Psychiatry.* New York: Norton.

Thomas, Ann G. 1997. *The Women We Become: Myths, Folktales, and Stories about Growing Older.* Rocklin, Calif.: Prima.

Thomas, Bob. 1991. *Disney's Art of Animation: From Mickey Mouse to Beauty and the Beast.* New York: Hyperion, 1991.

Thompson, Will L. 1914. *Softly and Tenderly.* Orange, N.J.: Edison Sound Recording.

Tillich, Paul. 1961. The Meaning of Health. *Perspectives in Biology and Medicine* 5:92–100.

Trites, Roberta. 1991. Disney's Sub/Version of Andersen's "The Little Mermaid." *Journal of Popular Film and Television* 18:145–152.

Trosman, Harry. 1993. *8½* and the Disinhibition of Creativity. Manuscript, Dept. of Psychiatry, University of Chicago.

Vaillant, George. 1977. *Adaptation to Life.* Boston: Little, Brown.

Van der Cruysse, Dirk. 1984. La culture religieuse de Versailles. In *La pensée religieuse dans la littérature et la civilisation du XVIIe siècle en France,* ed. Manfred Tietz and Volker Kapp. Tübingen: Biblio 17.

———. 1988. *Madame Palatine, princesse européenne.* Paris: Fayard.

———. 1989. *Lettres françaises.* Paris: Fayard.

———. 1993. Le miroir brisé: les correspondances allemandes et françaises de Madame Palatine. Lecture at Western Society for French History, Missoula, Montana, October.

Van Tassel, David D., ed. 1979. *Aging, Death, and the Completion of Being.* Philadelphia: University of Pennsylvania Press.

VideoHound's Golden Movie Retriever. 1997. Detroit: Visible.

Wald, Priscilla. 1982. Review of Leslie Marmon Silko's *Storyteller. SAIL,* 15–20.

Walker, Alice. 1971. Fame. In *You Can't Keep a Good Woman Down.* New York: Harcourt Brace Jovanovich.

Washington, Mary Helen. 1982. Teaching *Black-Eyed Susans:* An Approach to the Study of Black Women Writers. In *All of the Women Are White, All the Blacks Are Men, But Some of Us Are Brave,* ed. Gloria T. Hull, Patricia Bell Scott, and Barbara Smith. New York: Feminist Press.

Waxman, Barbara Frey. 1990. *From the Hearth to the Open Road: A Feminist Study of Aging in Contemporary Literature.* Westport, Conn.: Greenwood Press.

Weiland, Steven. 1993. Criticism between Literature and Gerontology. In *Voices and Visions of Aging,* ed. Thomas R. Cole, W. Andrew Achenbaum, Patricia L. Jakobi, and Robert Kastenbaum. New York: Springer.

Weintraub, Stanley. 1971. *Journey to Heartbreak: The Crucible Years of Bernard Shaw 1914–1918*. New York: Weybright and Talley.

Welch, James. 1979. *The Death of Jim Loney*. New York: Harper and Row.

Welty, Eudora. 1954. *The Ponder Heart*. New York: Harcourt Brace.

———. 1968. A Visit of Charity. In *The United States in Literature*. Glenview, Ill.: Scott, Foresman.

———. 1980. The Purple Hat. In *The Collected Stories of Eudora Welty*. New York: Harcourt Brace Jovanovich.

———. 1994. A Worn Path. In *Literature and Language: American Literature*. Evanston, Ill.: McDougal-Littell.

Williams, John. 1988. *Stoner*. Fayetteville: Arkansas University Press.

Woodward, Kathleen. 1980. *At Last, the Real Distinguished Thing: The Late Poems of Eliot, Pound, Stevens, and Williams*. Columbus: Ohio State University Press.

———. 1986. The Mirror Stage of Old Age. In *Memory and Desire: Aging—Literature—Psychoanalysis*, ed. Kathleen Woodward and Murray M. Schwartz. Bloomington: Indiana University Press.

———. 1991. The Look and the Gaze: Narcissism, Aggression, and Aging in Virginia Woolf's *The Years*. In *Aging and Its Discontents: Freud and Other Fictions*. Bloomington: Indiana University Press.

———. 1991. Introduction. . . Aging, Difference, and Subjectivity. *Aging and Its Discontents: Freud and Other Fictions*. Bloomington: Indiana University Press.

———. 1993. Late Theory, Late Style: Loss and Renewal in Freud and Barthes. In *Aging and Gender in Literature: Studies in Creativity*, ed. Anne Wyatt-Brown and Janice Rossen. Charlottesville: University Press of Virginia.

Woodward, Kathleen, and Murray M. Schwartz eds. 1986. *Memory and Desire: Aging—Literature—Psychoanalysis*. Bloomington: Indiana University Press.

Woolf, Virginia. 1953a. Modern Fiction. In *The Common Reader: First Series*, ed. Andrew McNeillie. San Diego: Harvest-Harcourt.

———. 1953b. *Mrs. Dalloway*. San Diego: Harvest-Harcourt.

———. 1955. *To the Lighthouse*. San Diego: Harvest-Harcourt.

———. 1956. *Orlando*. San Diego: Harvest-Harcourt.

———. 1957. *A Room of One's Own*. San Diego: Harvest-Harcourt.

———. 1959. *The Waves*. New York: Harvest-Harcourt.

———. 1965. *The Years*. New York: Harvest-Harcourt.

———. 1966. *Three Guineas*. New York: Harbinger-Harcourt.

———. 1969. *Between the Acts*. New York: Harvest-Harcourt.

———. 1975–80. *The Letters of Virginia Woolf*. Ed. Nigel Nicolson and Joanne Trautmann [Banks]. 6 vols. New York: Harcourt.

———. 1977. *The Pargiters*. Ed. Mitchell A. Leaska. New York: New York Public Library.

———. 1977–1984. *The Diary of Virginia Woolf*. Ed. Anne Olivier Bell. 5 vols. London: Hogarth.

———. 1985. The Mark on the Wall. In *The Complete Shorter Fiction of Virginia Woolf*, ed. Susan Dick. San Diego: Harcourt.

Wright, Stephen Caldwell. 1987. And So Many Others. In *Making Symphony*. Baltimore: MAWA Press.

Wyatt-Brown, Anne M. 1988. Late Style in the Novels of Barbara Pym and Penelope Mortimer. *Gerontologist* 28:835–839.

————. 1992. Literary Gerontology Comes of Age. In *Handbook of the Humanities and Aging*, ed. Thomas R. Cole, David D. Van Tassel, and Robert Kastenbaum. New York: Springer.

Wyatt-Brown, Anne M., and Janice Rossen, eds. 1993. *Aging and Gender in Literature: Studies in Creativity*. Charlottesville: University Press of Virginia.

————. 1995. Creativity as a Defense against Death: Maintaining One's Professional Identity. *Journal of Aging Studies* 9:349–354.

Yahnke, Robert E., and Richard M. Eastman. 1990. *Aging in Literature: A Reader's Guide*. Chicago: American Library Association.

Yeats, William Butler. 1973. The Second Coming. In *The Norton Anthology of Modern Poetry*, ed. Richard Ellman and Robert O'Clair. New York: Norton.

Young, Philip. 1966. *Ernest Hemingway: A Reconsideration*. New York: Harcourt, Brace & World.

Index

Achenbaum, W. Andrew, 49
Adelman, Janet, 28–29
Aeschylus, 103; *The Eumenides*, 103
Agich, George J., 6
Albee, Edward, 115, 125; *Who's Afraid of Virginia Woolf?*, 115, 163–164
Alter, Robert, 89
Alterstil, 185
Alzheimer's disease, 39, 140
Amis, Kingsley, 163; *Lucky Jim*, 163
Amulree, Lord, 82
Andersen, Hans Christian, 206
Andersson, Bibi, 217
Angiollilo, Melanie, 7
Anguissola, Sofonisba, 185
Aphrodite, 183
Apter, Terri E., 5, 24, 29; *Secret Paths*, 5
Aristophanes, 51
Aristotle, 62, 104, 151, 156, 158; *Nichomachean Ethics*, 62; *Rhetoric*, 62
Arnold, Matthew, 1
Asp, Carolyn, 29, 33–34
Atchley, Robert, 93
Atlantic-Little, Brown, 84
Augustine, Saint, 158

Baby Boomers, 210
Baker, Carlos, 64–65
Baldwin, James, 81
Baltes, Paul B., 7–8, 62, 150, 158
Banks, Samuel, 124
Barnes, Daniel R., 112; "Faulkner's Miss Emily and Hawthorne's Old Maid," 112
Bauschatz, Cathleen M., 152
Baxter, John, 218
Becker, Ernst, 197
Bell, Quentin, 115
Bennett, Arnold, 121
Benson, Jackson J., 65
Bentham, Jeremy, 77
Bentley, Eric, 51
Bergman, Ingmar, 2, 215–218, 220, 225
Bertolini, John, 51
Bertrand Russell Peace Foundation, 83
Besant, Annie, 48
Beulah Hotel, 95
Bevington, David, 25
Bildungsroman, 68
Birren, James E., 6–10, 149, 152
Block, Marilyn R., 203

Bloom, Allan, 169; *The Closing of the American Mind*, 169
Bloom, Harold, 157; *The Western Canon*, 157
Bloomsbury Group, 118
Blum, June, 184–185; *Betty Friedan as the Prophet*, 184–185
Bocaccio, Giovanni, 151
Bologna, Giovanni, 184; *Rape of the Sabine Women*, 184
Bondanella, Peter, 216
Booth, Charles, 47
Bourgeois, Louise, 187
Briconnet, Guillaume, 153
Brockway, Fenner, 84–85
Butler, Robert N., 93, 209
Butler, Samuel, 48

Cameron, Julia Margaret, 117
Campbell, O. J., 29
Chamberlain, Joseph, 47
Chekhov, Anton P., 2, 17
Chilton, Paul, 152
Chinen, Allan B., 90, 92
Chodorow, Nancy, 6
Chou, Shen, 184; *Self Portrait*, 184
Clark, Margaret, 6–8, 149, 152, 157
Clark, Ronald, 78–79, 82, 84
Close, Glenn, 207
Coggin, B. W., 34
Cohler, Bertram J., 194
Cole, Thomas R., 8, 55, 183, 192, 194
Coles, Robert, 193; *The Call of Stories*, 193
Connell, Clyde, 186–187; *Dancer*, 187; *Non Person*, 186–187
Conrad, Christoph, 192, 194
Coplans, John, 189; *Self-Portrait as a Fertility Goddess*, 189
Countryside High School, 170
Courbet, 184; *Origin of the World*, 184
Cuny, Alain, 217

Damon, Betsy, 187–188; *7000 Year Old Woman*, 187–188
Dante, 215
Darwin, Charles, 50
Davidson, Janice L., 203

Davis, Lennard J., 91–92
de Beauvoir, Simone, 6, 19, 63, 104, 193, 201–202, 204; *The Coming of Age*, 6, 104; *The Second Sex*, 204
Derrida, Jacques, 10
Dickens, Charles, 48, 106–114
Dienes, Sara, 189; *Silhouette Self-Portrait*, 189
Dinnerstein, Dorothy, 6
Don Juan, 47, 222
Donow, Herbert S., 34
Doogan, Margaret Bailey, 188; *Mass*, 188
Douglass, Frederick, 139
Dreiser, Theodore, 91; *Sister Carrie* 91
Dror, Itiel E., 186
Duke University (GET) Clinic, 14, 34–40, 44–45
Duval, Edwin M., 151–152

Eastman, Charles, 130; *Indian Boyhood*, 130
Eliot, George, 162–163; *Middlemarch*, 162–163
Eliot, T. S., 51, 55
Ellison, Ralph, 140; *Invisible Man*, 140
Erikson, Erik H., 2, 6–8, 14, 19, 24, 32, 122, 149, 152, 162, 164–166, 168, 193; *Life Cycle Completed*, 164
Erikson, Joan M., 6–8, 149, 152

Fabians, 48
Fahey, Charles J., 6, 8
Fallis, Richard C., 30
Fates, 111
Faulkner, William, 15–16, 91, 103–114; "A Rose for Emily," 16, 104, 107, 109–113
Fertility Figure from Willendorf, Austria, 183, 189
Fisher, Dorothy Canfield, 15, 93, 95–96; "The Bedquilt," 95–96
Fisher, Rudolph, 140
Fitzgerald, F. Scott, 91, 163; *Tender is the Night*, 91, 163
Francis, Saint, 152
Frank, Lawrence, 108–109; *Charles Dickens and the Romantic Self*, 108–109

Frazier, E. Franklin, 141
Freedman, Richard, 104, 113
Freytag pyramid, 134
Freud, Amelia, 9
Freud, Sigmund, 2, 12, 33, 207, 213–214, 222
Friedan, Betty, 3–6, 8, 11, 13, 19, 23–25, 29, 32, 53, 55–56, 58, 77, 81, 93, 104, 114, 122, 139, 149–150, 158, 161–165, 168, 184–186, 192, 201–203, 211; *The Feminine Mystique*, 185; *The Fountain of Age*, 11, 23, 77, 104, 139, 149, 161, 164–165, 185, 201–202, 211
Frueh, Joanna, 186, 188

Gabriel, Joseph, 65
Galsworthy, John, 121
Garden of Eden, 52
George I, King of England, 155
Gestalt psychology, 161–162
Gilbert, Sandra M., 111, 113
Gilligan, Carol, 6
Girard, René, 113
Gish, Lillian, 193
Goddess, 188
Grambs, Jean D., 203
Greenberg, Harvey, 215, 220–223; *The Movies on Your Mind*, 220–221
Greer, Germaine, 207
Grimm Brothers, 204
Gubar, Susan, 111, 113
Gullette, Margaret Morganroth, 2, 89, 163, 166
Gutmann, David, 4, 5, 8, 23–24, 28–29, 31, 81, 103, 111, 161, 165, 167, 184
Gwin, Minrose C., 113

Haas, Lynda, 210
Hall, Stanley, 51
Hallissy, Margaret, 111
Hamilton, Juan, 185
Hamilton, Margaret, 205
Hammer, Barbara, 188; *Nitrate Kisses*, 188
Hammond, Margo, 93
Harcourt, Peter, 218–219; "The Secret Life of Federico Fellini," 218–219
Harlem Renaissance, 139, 187

Hawthorne, Nathaniel, 15–18, 162, 170, 173; "Dr. Heidegger's Experiment," 18, 170, 173–174; *The House of the Seven Gables*, 15, 104–106, 110; *The Scarlet Letter*, 17, 162, 173; *Twice-Told Tales*, 106; "The White Old Maid," 15–16, 104, 106, 110–113
Held, Julius S., 185; "Style and the Aging Artist," 185
"Hemingway Code," 61
Hemingway, Ernest, 91, 124–125; "A Clean Well-Lighted Place," 14, 61–63, 76; *A Farewell to Arms*, 14, 62, 65, 68–70; *Men at War*, 61; *The Old Man and the Sea*, 14, 61–62, 70–76, 91, 124–125; *The Sun Also Rises*, 14, 62, 65–68
Hendricks, Jon, 54, 56
Herman, David, 219, 221–223
Hestia, 105, 108
Hilton, James, 17, 164–165; *Good-bye Mr. Chips*, 17, 164–165
Hitler, Adolf, 78
Hobson, Alan, 213
Hoffman, Steven K., 64
Holroyd, Michael, 56
Holstein, Martha, 6, 8, 35
Homar, Lorenzo, 185
Homer, 103; *Iliad*, 103; *Odyssey*, 103
Horace, 15, 97
Hornback, Bert G., 107
Hurston, Zora Neale, 139; *Their Eyes Were Watching God*, 139
Hurwick, Cecelia, 6, 8
Hutter, Albert D., 107; "Crime and Fantasy in *Great Expectations*," 107

Icarus, 219
Irving, Washington, 162; "The Legend of Sleepy Hollow," 162
Isocrates, 62

Jackson, Jacquelyne Johnson, 140
Jacobs, Harriet, 139
James I, King of England, 155
Jim Crow Laws, 141
Johnson, James Weldon, 140
Joie de vivre, 175

Joyce, James, 15, 17, 93–95, 163; "Clay," 93–95; *A Portrait of the Artist as a Young Man*, 17, 163
Jung, Carl, 24, 149, 164

Kahn, Coppelia, 28
Kipling, Rudyard, 2
Kosslyn, Stephen M., 186
Kubler-Ross, Elizabeth, 29

Lacan, Jacques, 12
La Fayette, Madame de, 150
Lafond, Jean, 158
La Fontaine, Jean de, 150
Lajarte, Philippe de, 152
Lamplight Laundry, 94
Lasch, Christopher, 91–92
Laurence, Margaret, 100; *The Stone Angel*, 100
Laurentius, Andrea, 44
Lawrence, D. H., 82
Lawrence, Jacob, 187; *Self-Portrait*, 187
Layton, Elizabeth, 188; *Indian Pipes: Self-Portrait with Glenn*, 188
Leedham, Cynthia, 54, 56
Leibnitz, Gottfried Wilhelm von, 155, 157
LeShan, Lawrence, 123
Lessing, Doris, 99; "An Old Woman and Her Cat," 99–100
Lewin, Kurt, 118
Linderman, Frank, 130
Lippard, Lucy R., 187
Lodge, David, 168; *Changing Places*, 168; *Small World*, 168
Longino, Charles F., Jr., 7
Louis XIV of France, King, 150, 155–156

Macdonald, Dwight, 214
Mack, Maynard, 29
Madame Palatine (Elisabeth-Charlotte von der Pfalz), 17, 149–151, 155–159; *Lettres françaises*, 17, 150, 155–159
Maddox, George L., 3, 9–10, 32, 34
Magdalen, Mary, 153
Manheimer, Ronald J., 7; "Wisdom and Method," 7

Mann, Thomas, 91, 163, 218; *Death in Venice*, 91, 163
Mansfield, Katherine, 15, 93–95; "Miss Brill," 15, 93–95
Mapplethorpe, Robert, 187
Marguerite de Navarre (Princess of Navarre), 12, 17, 149–155, 158; *Heptaméron*, 17, 150–155, 158
May, Rollo, 93
McCollough, Laurence B., 57
McKee, Patrick, 57
McLerran, Jennifer, 57
McNickle, D'Arcy, 130; *The Surrounded*, 130
Meisel, Martin, 51–52
"A Metabiological Pentateuch," 50
Michelangelo, 114
Michener, James A., 100; *Recessional*, 100
Mill, John Stuart, 78
Miller, Arthur, 91, 94; *Death of a Salesman*, 91, 94, 175
Miller, Jean Baker, 6
Milton, John, 78
Modernism, 186
Molière (Jean Baptiste Poquelin), 150, 155; *The School for Wives (L'école des femmes)*, 150; *Le bourgeois gentilhomme*, 155
Momaday, N. Scott, 134, 138
Moody, Harry R., 3, 6–8, 10, 20, 48–49, 56, 58, 85, 90, 100–101, 131, 139, 150, 161, 194; "Toward a Critical Gerontology," 161
Moore, G. E., 118
Moore, Thomas, 168
Moorehead, Caroline, 80, 82–84
Morgan, Margery M., 51, 54
Morrison, Toni, 140; *Beloved*, 140
Moser, Charlette, 187
Muse, 215

National Council of Teachers of English, 170
National Institute on Aging, 149
Neel, Alice, 187; *Nude Self-Portrait*, 187
Neugarten, Bernice, 3

Nichols, Mike, 115
Nietzsche, Friedric, 51
Nobel Prize for Literature, 83, 109
Noggle, Anne, 188–189; *Stellar by
    Starlight #1*, 189; *Thoroughly Modern
    Me*, 189
Novak, Mark, 93

O'Grady, Gerry, 213, 220, 224
O'Keeffe, Georgia, 185
Old Age Pensions Act, 48
"Older — But Coming on Strong," 3
Olsen, Tillie, 122; "Tell Me a Riddle," 122
Ong, Walter J., 134
Orenstein, Gloria Feman, 188; "Recov-
    ering Her Story," 188
Orwell, George, 2

Page, Geraldine, 193
Page, Sally R., 113
Parker, Marcie, 193–194
Patton, Frances Gray, 17, 164; *Good
    Morning, Miss Dove*, 17–18, 164–165
Petric, Vlada, 213, 220
Phronesis, 14, 61–76
Pifer, Alan, 79–80
Plato, 121
Plentycoups, Crow Chief, 130
Ponce de León, Juan, 174
Portales, Marco, 104; *Youth and Age in
    American Literature*, 104
Porter, Katherine Anne, 18, 170–173;
    "The Jilting of Granny Weatherall,"
    18, 170–173
Porter, Laurel, 26, 34
Postmodernism, 186
The Power of Feminist Art, 188
Powers, Hiram, 183; *Greek Slave*, 183
Presidential Symposium of the
    Gerontological Society of America,
    149–150
de Prusse, Queen Sophie Dorothée, 156

Quadagno, Jill S., 47–48, 54
Quintilian, 156

Racine, Jean, 150; *Andromaque*, 150

Ramses II, 183
Recinos, Adrian, 132-133; *Popol Vuh*, 132
Reifungsroman, 5, 12, 72, 100, 171
Reyff, Simone de, 158
Reynolds, Regine, 152; *Les devisants de
    l'Heptaméron*, 152
Rigolot, François, 153–154
Roberts, Diane, 112; *Faulkner and
    Southern Womanhood*, 112
Robinson, Jackie, 142
Ronsard, Pierre, 150
Rooke, Constance, 164
Rosenman, Ellen Bayuk, 117
Rosenthal, Rachel, 188; *Pangaean
    Dreams*, 188
Rossen, Janice, 164, 167
Rothenstein, William, 117
Rovit, Earl, 65, 67–68
Rubens, Peter Paul, 184; *Portrait of
    Helene Fourment in Fur*, 184
Russell, Bertrand, 12–13, 15, 77–85; *A
    History of Western Philosophy*, 81, 83;
    "A Poor Man's Worship," 81
Russell, Charles H., 202
Russell, Conrad, 82
Ruysch, Rachel, 185
Ryan, Alan, 81

Sackville-West, Vita, 118, 120
Said, Edward, 49
Sainte-Beuve, Charles Augustin, 155
Salinger, J. D., 17, 162–163; *The Catcher
    in the Rye*, 17, 162–163
Saraghina, 215
Sarton, May, 15, 93, 96–100; *As We Are
    Now*, 99; *Miss Pickthorn and Mr.
    Hare*, 96–98
Savoie, Louise de, 152–153
Schaeffer, Francis A., 152
Schoenman, Ralph, 82–85
Schriber, Mary Suzanne, 105; *Gender
    and the Writer's Imagination*, 105
Scott, Nathan, 64
Secundy, Marian Gray, 139; *Trials,
    Tribulations, and Celebrations*, 139
Seneca the Younger, 169; "On the
    Shortness of Life," 169

Sewell, Arthur, 29; "Tragedy and the Kingdom of Ends," 29

Shakespeare, William, 2, 13; *King Lear*, 13–14, 169; *The Merchant of Venice*, 44; *The Tempest*, 13–14

Shaw, George Bernard, 13–14; *Back to Methesulah*, 14; *Caesar and Cleopatra*, 14, 50; *Fabian Essays in Socialism*, 48; *Heartbreak House*, 14, 50; *Man and Superman*, 55

Sheehy, Gail, 5–6, 24, 29, 91–92, 98–99, 164–166; *New Passages*, 5, 165

Shengold, Leonard, 2

Shneidman, Edwin, 2

Showalter, Elaine, 2, 12, 202

Silko, Leslie Marmon, 16, 129–138; *Ceremony*, 129–133, 136; *Storyteller*, 129, 133–138; "Deer Song," 135; "Indian Song: Survival," 137–138; "Lullaby," 138; "The Man to Send Rain Clouds," 135; "Storyteller," 136–138; "The Storyteller's Escape," 135

Simon, John, 215

Sino–Indian border dispute 82

Slater, Michael, 107; *Dickens and Women*, 107

Smith, Jacqui, 7

Smyth, Dame Ethel, 118–120, 123

Snyder, Susan, 29

Socrates, 9, 27

Solomon, 149, 156

Sowarka, Doris, 7

Spivak, Gayatri Chakravorty, 10

Stampfer, J., 29; "The Catharsis of *King Lear*," 29

Staudinger, Ursula M., 7

Stead, Herbert, 47

Stoddard, Karen M., 203

Stowe, Harriet Beecher, 143

Street, Douglas, 203

Sullivan, Harry Stack, 118

Swanson, Gloria, 207

Thackeray, William Makepeace, 116

Thales, 163, 168

"Thanatopsis," 175

Thomas, Bob, 207

Thompson, Will L., 191; *Softly and Tenderly*, 191, 194, 198

Tillich, Paul, 124

Tolstoy, Ivan Ilych, 122

Totentanz, 215

Travellers' Clubs, 57

Trites, Roberta, 207

Trosman, Harry, 222–223

Tubman, Harriet, 187

Tyler, Anne, 91; *The Accidental Tourist*, 91

Unwin, Sir Stanley, 82–84

Van der Cruysse, Dirk, 150, 155–157; *Lettres francaises*, 150, 155–159

Victoria, Queen of England, 78

Victorians, 48–49

VideoHound's, 203

Vietnam War, 78, 80–81, 85

Virgin of Cobre, 73

Virgin Mary, 103

Volledungsroman, 164

Von der Pfalz-Simmern, Palatine Elector Karl Ludwig, 155

Wahpetonwan Dakota, 130

Walker, Alice, 15, 93, 96–97; "Fame," 96–97

War Crimes Tribunal, 80–83

Washington, Mary Helen, 96

Waxman, Barbara Frey, 5, 49, 100, 171; *From the Hearth to the Open Road*, 100

Webb, Sidney, 47

Weiland, Steven, 133

Weintraub, Stanley, 51

Welch, James, 132; *The Death of Jim Loney*, 132

Wells, H. G., 80, 121

Weltanschauung, 63

Welty, Eudora, 15, 18, 93, 95–96, 98, 170–172, 178; *The Ponder Heart*, 95–96; "The Purple Hat," 15, 93, 96, 98; "A Visit of Charity," 18, 170–171, 173–174, 178; "A Worn Path," 18, 170–73, 178

Wiley, James, 9–10

Williams, John, 18, 165–167; *Stoner*, 18, 165–168

Wittgenstein, Ludwig, 82

The Wizard of Oz, 205

Woodward, Kathleen, 9–10, 92, 130, 195–196, 203, 209

Woolf, Virginia, 12, 16, 17, 115–125, 163; *Between the Acts*, 115–116, 121; *Mrs. Dalloway*, 115, 117, 120; *Jacob's Room*, 120; *To the Lighthouse*, 17, 115, 120–122, 163; "The Mark on the Wall," 120; "Modern Fiction," 121–22; *Night and Day*, 116; *Orlando*, 123; *The Pargiters*, 123; *A Room of One's Own*, 120, 123; *Three Guineas*, 119–120, 123; *The Waves*, 119–120; *The Years*, 117, 120, 123

Woolf's Family: Aunt Anny Ritchie, 116; Caroline Stephen, 116; Julia Stephen, 117–118; Leonard Woolf, 116; Leslie Stephen, 116; Marie Woolf, 116; Vanessa Stephen Bell, 120

World War I, 78, 80, 83, 85

World War II, 77, 83, 167, 210

Wright, Stephen Caldwell, 140

Wyatt-Brown, Anne M., 12, 49, 157–158; *Aging and Gender in Literature*, 157–58; "Literary Gerontology Comes of Age," 12

Yeats, William Butler, 122,

Young, Philip, 68, 71, 76

Zen reality, 189

About the Editors and Contributors

Joanne Trautmann Banks is an Adjunct Professor of Medicine and the Humanities at Pennsylvania State University.

Rosalie Murphy Baum is an Associate Professor of English at the University of South Florida.

Ralph M. Cline is the Coordinator of the International Baccalaureate Program at Palm Harbor University High School.

Kirk Combe is an Associate Professor of English at Denison University.

Sara Munson Deats is Chair and Distinguished Professor of English at the University of South Florida.

Linnea S. Dietrich is Professor of Art History at Miami University of Ohio.

David Erben is Assistant Professor of English at the University of Toledo.

Maryhelen C. Harmon is an Associate Professor of English at the University of South Florida.

Charles J. Heglar is an Assistant Professor of English at the University of South Florida.

Norman N. Holland is a Professor of English at the University of Florida.

Carol J. Jablonski is an Associate Professor of Communication at the University of South Florida.

Lagretta Tallent Lenker is the Director at the Center for Lifelong Learning at the University of South Florida.

Deborah Noonan is a doctoral student in English at the University of South Florida.

Merry G. Perry is a doctoral student in English at the University of South Florida.

Helen Popovich is Director of the Office of Development and a Professor of English at Ferris State University.

Christine McCall Probes is the Acting Chair and Associate Professor of French at the University of South Florida.

Annye L. Refoe is an Instructor at the University of Central Florida.

William T. Ross is Professor of English at the University of South Florida.

Kenneth Schmader is a physician at the Center for the Study of Aging and Human Development and the Division of Geriatrics at Duke University Medical Center.

Phillip Sipiora is an Associate Professor of English at the University of South Florida.

CPSIA information can be obtained
at www.ICGtesting.com
Printed in the USA
LVHW090052030519
615442LV00028B/19/P

9 780275 964795